THE IRISH MILITIA, 1793–1802

The Irish Militia, 1793–1802
Ireland's Forgotten Army

IVAN F. NELSON

FOUR COURTS PRESS

Set in 10.5 on 13.5 point Ehrhardt for
FOUR COURTS PRESS LTD
7 Malpas Street, Dublin 8, Ireland
e-mail: info@four-courts-press.ie
http://www.four-courts-press.ie
and in North America by
FOUR COURTS PRESS
c/o ISBS, 920 N.E. 58th Avenue, Suite 300, Portland, OR 97213.

© Ivan F. Nelson 2007

ISBN 978-1-84682-037-3

A catalogue record for this title
is available from the British Library.

All rights reserved. No part of this publication may be reproduced,
stored in or introduced into a retrieval system, or transmitted, in any
form or by any means (electronic, mechanical, photocopying, recording
or otherwise), without the prior written permission of both the
copyright owner and the publisher of this book.

Printed in England
by MPG Books, Bodmin, Cornwall.

Contents

LIST OF ILLUSTRATIONS	7
LIST OF ABBREVIATIONS	9
PREFACE	11
1 Introduction	13
2 The formation of a militia	28
3 The institution	54
4 Officers	89
5 The militiamen	122
6 'But our militia brave our country will save'	153
7 Rebellion	175
8 A period of change, 1798–1802	217
9 Conclusion	248
BIBLIOGRAPHY	259
INDEX	265

Illustrations

TABLES

1	Regimental establishments of the Irish militia, 1793	46
2	Property qualifications of militia officers	48
3	Militia riots 1793	58
4	Longford Battalion. Location distances, 1796–7	80
5	Accommodation for the Royal Downshire Militia, Newry to Youghal	85
6	Proportion of Catholics to Protestants in the Irish militia	124
7	Ages and heights of militiamen, 1802	127
8	Royal Downshire Regiment, punishment by flogging, 1793–6	134
9	A comparison of rates of pay 1795 and 1799	143
10	Rewards for capturing illegal stills	145
11	Travel allowances for escort duty	145
12	Troop movements, December 1796	163
13	Battalion staff, Light Brigade, 27 March 1799	167
14	Militia sentences for subversion in 1797	172
15	1798 rebellion, militia involvement	214
16	French invasion force, August 1798	218
17	General Lake's dispositions at the battle of Castlebar	220
18	Claims against the militia after the rebellion	228
19	Claims against the Armagh Regiment	229
20	Desertion figures, regiments with eight companies, 1794–8	232
21	Officer volunteers to the Line, 1800	239
22	Regimental quotas and numbers of volunteers	240
23	Volunteers at 19 February 1800	240
24	Militia, fencible, and regular army strengths, 1793–1802	248

MAPS

1	Ireland in 1798	181
2	Counties Wicklow and Wexford showing principal military actions	185
3	Plans of insurgent and government forces, 30 May 1798	191
4	Tubberneering, 4 June 1798	196
5	New Ross town in 1798	198

6 Arklow town plan in 1798 205
7 Ballynahinch in 1798 206
8 Vinegar Hill, 21 June 1798, Army plan 209

PLATES

1 Colonel William Blacker's crossbelt badge 119
2 Duffry Gate, Enniscorthy 189
3 New Ross from Three Bullet Gate 201
4 The Tholsel or Main Guard, New Ross 203

Abbreviations

The following abbreviations have been used in this work:

Bn.	Battalion
Brig.-Gen.	Brigadier-General
Capt.	Captain
CJI	Journals of the House of Commons of Ireland (vols 15–18, 1800)
Col.	Colonel
Cornwallis Corresp.	*Correspondence of Charles, first Marquis Cornwallis*, ed. Charles Ross (3 vols, London, 1859)
Cpl.	Corporal
Ens.	Ensign
Gen.	General
Houlding, *Fit for service*	J.A. Houlding, *Fit for service: the training of the British army, 1715–1795* (Oxford, 1981).
HMC	Historical Manuscripts Commission
IHS	*Irish Historical Studies*
KP	Kilmainham Papers
Lt.	Lieutenant
Lt.-Col.	Lieutenant-Colonel
Lt.-Gen.	Lieutenant-General
Maj.	Major
Maj.-Gen.	Major-General
McAnally, *Irish Militia*	Sir Henry McAnally, *The Irish militia, 1793–1816* (Dublin, 1949)
Musgrave, *Memoirs*	Sir Richard Musgrave, *Memoirs of the different rebellions in Ireland* (4th edn., Fort Wayne, 1995)
NA	National Archives, Kew. Formerly the Public Record Office
NAI	National Archives of Ireland
NAS	National Archives of Scotland
NCO	Non-commissioned officer
NLI	National Library of Ireland
PRONI	Public Record office of Northern Ireland
Regt.	Regiment
RHMS	Royal Hibernian Military School
RP	Rebellion Papers
Sgt.	Sergeant

Preface

In 1993, I went back to Queen's University in Belfast as a mature student to read for a degree in modern history – the subject I should have studied when I left school. This was an enlightening and invigorating experience. My interests were widespread, but the history I found most intriguing was the eighteenth century, in particular the 1790s and the 1798 rebellion. I have always had a fascination with the eighteenth century in Ireland, the longest period of 'peace' in modern Irish history, the period that saw so many advances in the development of the country after the dreadful depredations of the late seventeenth century. There was the erection of one of the first purpose-built parliament houses in Europe, the first canals in the British Isles, the building of literally dozens of country houses, the spread of the common law to the remotest parts of the kingdom, and a more efficient administration of the country. I found that in modern Irish historiography the century is now studied from the point of view of the Irish people, not as an addendum to the history of the larger island, and events leading to the 1798 rebellion and the rebellion itself from the point of view of the insurgents and the United Irishmen. It was here that I became intrigued by the Irish militia, and became very aware that this was an Irish force composed of Irish people, and that although there were very many Irish people involved in the administration and government of the country, the men of the Irish militia seem to have belonged to an army that has been forgotten.

I soon found out that that there was very little original research on the Irish militia, some articles, and one book, but that there was much vilification of the force, some of it contemporary, but much of it a repetition of what others had said without any original research. Indeed, most of what I read about the Irish militia was a repetition of the opinion of others, and the militia was regarded as a purely Irish institution run by Irish politicians and generals who had little control over it, and little interest in its behaviour. Nothing could be further from the truth. The Irish militia was a part of the British army, and although it was composed of Irishmen (and others), as such worthy of study in its own right, it must not be forgotten that it was a part of this larger institution, which provided its commanders. I have a firm belief that nothing in Irish history is exactly as it is depicted, or as its reputation appears so I explored further and eventually 'The Irish militia, 1793–1802' became the subject of my doctoral dissertation.

Only one history of the force has been written. This is *The Irish militia, 1793–1816* by Sir Henry McAnally, a retired civil servant and amateur historian who published his work in 1949, based on researches carried out in the 1930s. McAnally's book has stood the test of time well but I felt that the time had come for a new history that would deal in particular with the areas in which McAnally was weak, for example, training, discipline, loyalty and the fighting in the 1798 rebellion. Like McAnally, however, I have approached the subject from a military point of view, this was an Irish army, composed of Irishmen and deserving of study on these grounds alone. It was the force primarily responsible for the defeat of the 1798 rebellion in which Irishman opposed Irishman, and I have attempted to show why the discipline and loyalty of the militia held together when so many thought it would not. In consequence this is not a political history but one about soldiers, how they lived, trained, what motivated them, and how they performed in action when called upon to do so.

The Irish militia was embodied full-time from 1793 to 1816 with two short breaks in 1802 and 1814. I have chosen to deal with the first part of its existence, from the foundation in 1793 to the short-lived peace in 1802–3 following the Treaty of Amiens.

For permission to consult and quote from documents in their care I would like to thank the directors of the National Archives of Ireland, and the National Library of Ireland in Dublin, the Keeper of the National Archives in Kew (formerly the Public Record Office), the National Archives of Scotland in Edinburgh, the Deputy Keeper of the Records of Northern Ireland in Belfast, and Laurence Blair Oliphant for permission to quote from the Dalguise Muniments in the National Archives of Scotland. I owe a great debt of gratitude to the help of the late Professor Peter Jupp of Queen's University, Belfast, and Professor Ian Beckett of the University of Northampton. There is a saying that if you ever need something done well, ask a busy man to do it, so above all, my gratitude goes unreservedly to Professor David Hayton of Queen's University who read the chapters in preparation, and who offered much good advice and help. I must not forget my old friend, the late Kevin Byrne of Malahide who introduced me to parts of Dublin not normally seen by visitors. I must also thank my son-in-law, Seamus Linden for his computing expertise and priceless help, Jane Adamson for the maps, Sally McAller, Donald and Andrew Borer, Dr Conor Brosnan of Dingle, Co. Kerry, Elizabeth Hunter, and finally my daughters Helen and Oonagh for their patience, wit, and understanding.

My daughters' great-grandfather once commanded the 3rd (Militia) Battalion, Royal Dublin Fusiliers, originally the Kildare Battalion of Militia, and I think their motto appropriate –

SPECTAMUR AGENDO

CHAPTER ONE

Introduction

The French Revolutionary Wars lasted from 1793 to their temporary halt with the Treaty of Amiens in 1802. By the latter days of the eighteenth century, the British government had to raise men to garrison the empire as well as additional men to fight in specific campaigns. Garrisons had to be provided in Great Britain and Ireland, the Channel Islands, Canada, Australia, Gibraltar, the West Indies and India. This required an army 'establishment' of 49,790 men.[1] However, just before the outbreak of the French Revolutionary Wars the army had a total of 36,557 men, a shortfall of 13,233.[2] Of this figure some 11,094 were stationed in Ireland. In 1793 the government raised an army to fight the French in Holland, and as a result, Ireland was rapidly denuded of regular soldiers. But the government still had a duty to defend Ireland from external attack, and to protect the loyal citizens of Ireland from civil unrest. The answer to this conundrum was to revert to the traditional citizens' army, a militia, and a Militia Act that became law in 1793 did this.

It was not the first militia in Ireland, of course. There is a record of a militia in Waterford in 1584, consisting of 300 shot, and 200 billmen.[3] The foundation of a countrywide militia dates from 1661 when the duke of Ormonde raised a Protestant militia with a strength of approximately 15,000 men.[4] This militia had seen a considerable amount of action by the end of the Williamite wars. Between 1661 and 1715 the militia had been raised by use of the royal prerogative, but in the latter year, the first militia act was passed by the Irish parliament.

This statute created a Protestant force, both cavalry and infantry, organized into troops of horse of 50 men, and infantry companies 100 strong.[5] The men were to be paid from the county cess at the rate of 6d. per day for infantrymen, and 12d. per day for cavalrymen. However, the men provided

---

1 'Establishment' in this case is the maximum number of soldiers allowed by the government in a unit, or a command or a garrison. 2 Ron McGuigan, *The British army: 1 February 1793*, www.napoleon-series org/military/cbritarmy 1793.htm. 17 October 2005. 3 Sir Henry McAnally, 'Notes for a history of the Irish militia before 1793' (NLI, MS 5785). These are notes for a book he had hoped to write, but he died before it was written. His widow presented them to the Military History Society of Ireland in 1952. 4 Thomas Bartlett and Keith Jeffery (eds), *A military history of Ireland* (Cambridge, 1996). 5 McAnally, 'Notes'.

13

their own clothing, arms, and rations. In practice a city paid for a city militia, and in the country the nobility and gentry paid for the county militia companies. This statute was continued in 1719, and thereafter at least twelve times to 1765 when it was extended for ten years to 1775.[6] During this period the militia was 'arrayed' or 'called out' in 1719, 1739, 1745, 1756, and 1760. The first three of these arrays were in response to threats of Jacobite uprisings, and the latter two in response to threatened or actual invasion by the French. The militia continued in being until 1765, when it gradually fell into decay. The reasons for this are not clear, but Sir Henry McAnally, a historian of the Irish militia, believed it was because there was a failure to appoint 'commissioners of array' when incumbents died, retired, or left the country. If there were no commissioners, then the militia could not be called out, or ballots arranged for replacement militiamen.[7]

The 1778 Militia Act was an attempt to re-establish the force. It was based loosely on the 1757 Militia Act in England, and it established a Protestant force, infantry only, but still based on independent companies. This act was never implemented, and in effect there was no militia from 1776 to 1793. However, this was the period of the 'Volunteers', who came into existence after 1776 to provide soldiers to defend Ireland during the American revolutionary war. The Volunteers were not under parliamentary control, and the political ambitions of their leaders, supported by the rank-and-file, made them an object of suspicion to the government, so that when a new militia was raised in 1793, the Volunteers were suppressed. Volunteering was not by any means a new phenomenon in Ireland. In 1760 when Thurot landed at Carrickfergus at the head of a small French invading force, the men of counties Antrim, Down, and Armagh were arrayed in Belfast to oppose him. The total force comprised 5,352 men, of whom 2,226 were from the militia. If these figures are correct, then there were 3,125 volunteers willing to face the French.[8]

The government had no militia in 1778, a factor that forced it to accept the Volunteers, but had the act of that year been implemented, the Volunteers could have been incorporated into the militia, and so brought under proper military discipline. Failure to do this is difficult to understand. McAnally believed that Lord Westmorland's opposition to a militia in 1790 was because it transferred power from the (English) army to the country gentlemen of Ireland or, by extension, from the lord lieutenant to the Irish parliament. This could have been a long-standing fear, and could well have been true.[9] A guiding principle of the Westminster government in Ireland was that all the important offices of state should be held by Englishmen (or Scotsmen). Throughout

---

6 Ibid.   7 Ibid.   8 McAnally, 'Notes'.   9 Sir Henry McAnally, *The Irish militia, 1793–1816* (Dublin, 1949), p. 8.

the eighteenth century all the lords lieutenant were English, the chief secretaries before Castlereagh were English, and English appointees held the principal bishoprics. The 'independence' of the Irish parliament in 1782 undermined this policy, making it more difficult for the lord lieutenant to control those matters of policy and religion that were his remit. There was a constant if understated tussle between the Irish parliament and the lord lieutenant. The former wanted more independence and greater gifts of patronage, whereas the latter had to retain Westminster control over relations between the two countries, particularly in matters of trade and religion. For the lord lieutenant to do this successfully required skilfully applied patronage which can be summed up as ensuring the 'right man was in the right job' The difficulty for the lord lieutenant in creating an Irish militia lay in the inevitable granting to the Irish parliament of yet more control over Irish affairs. The senior officers of the militia were bound to be members of the Irish upper classes, many of whom would be members of parliament. Furthermore it would have been a dangerous step because it involved arming the populace, even if it were restricted to Protestants only. However, by 1793 the previous history of a militia in Ireland had shown it to be a very inadequate force. The preamble to the 1793 act admitted as much, 'the militia laws now in force in this kingdom have been found incapable of effecting the purposes of their institution'.[10] This represented a complete break with the past and a new force was created.

The force created in 1793 comprised thirty-eight regiments of infantry, one for each county or county borough in Ireland. It has been a subject of controversy ever since. There are several reasons for this. The general and other officers who commanded the militia were unhappy with its discipline and behaviour. These officers were mostly English, and as regular officers, disliked the 'amateur' ethos of the force for which they were responsible. Their comments should not be taken out of context however, similar comments were made about the English and the Scots militia. The effect of this criticism has been to create the perception that the Irish militia stood alone in isolation, and to reduce in importance the fact that it was a part and parcel of the British army. There were those who disparaged the force for political reasons, a list that stretches from the United Irishmen and Defenders to the present day. It reputedly did not perform well, it was ill disciplined, it was easily defeated in action, Roman Catholics were forced to serve in the ranks, the officers were Protestant, the riots on its formation were the worst seen in the Irish countryside in the second half of the eighteenth century, and it eventually became a 'nursery' for recruitment to the regular army. Indeed, the militia was so distrusted by the Protestant gentry that it was replaced by the Yeomanry as the chief defender of the country.

10 33 Geo. III, c. 22.

These perceptions have been repeated over and over again, yet very few people have examined the militia in detail, gone to extant records, where it may well be that the actuality is very different. None of these views of the militia can be properly evaluated unless the institution itself is understood, its strengths and weaknesses examined, and compared with the remainder of the British army of which it was a part. Historians have written about aspects of the militia, but there has only been one history of the force, written by an amateur historian, Sir Henry McAnally, in his spare time in the 1930s and published in 1949, when the author was seventy-nine.[11] McAnally admitted that the Irish militia was not perhaps an important force, but made the valid point that it was entitled to be judged fairly as much as any other institution of the past. It has to be said that any force that between 1793 and 1802 represented almost two thirds of the army available to the commander-in-chief in Ireland at the most, and more than one third of such an army at the very least should not be ignored.

This should not be entirely unexpected. For example, there has been almost no study of the fencible regiments (infantry regiments raised during the French Revolutionary and Napoleonic wars and liable for service within Great Britain and Ireland only) that served in Ireland in the 1790s, especially the Scottish, for which much material exists. Indeed there has been little study of the regular army in Ireland in this period, but this fact is disguised because the regulars were part and parcel of a larger organization, and much research carried out by the army automatically included the Irish establishment. Indeed, the importance of Ireland, especially Phoenix Park, in the development of training in the British army has been recognized and given due prominence by J.A. Houlding.[12] For the last century and more, the attention of historians has been focused on the insurgents in the conflict of the 1790s. The Irish-Ireland movements of the 1890s encouraged this perhaps, as well as the centenary of the 1798 rebellion itself, and, of course the establishment of the Irish Free State in 1922. Yet it must be remembered that the Irish militia was an almost entirely Irish force. It may be thought of as a Catholic force with Protestant officers, and whether this is true or not (something to be considered later), almost all were certainly Irishmen. Returns from the regiments never gave the religious affiliations of the men, but they did give the national, and this conclusion is easy to reach.

Contemporary information on the militia is to be found in the Rebellion Papers in the Irish National Archives, but these are collections of miscellaneous papers without a continuous theme. The most valuable information is to be found in the Kilmainham Papers in the National Library in Dublin,

---

[11] McAnally, *Irish Militia*. [12] J.A. Houlding, *Fit for service: the training of the British army, 1715–1795* (Oxford, 1981).

and in the Home Office Papers in the National Archives at Kew, because they run chronologically, and can be linked directly as necessary with other relevant letters and documents. There are also surviving regimental books in all of these institutions and in the Public Record Office of Northern Ireland in Belfast. In addition, there is much information in the files of public figures of the time, many of whom were colonels of militia regiments, such as Lord Downshire (Downshire Regiment), Lord Abercorn (Tyrone Regiment), or Lord Clements (Donegal Regiment). The militia also features prominently in the letters of Lord Cornwallis, the lord lieutenant from 1798 to 1801, Lord Camden, Thomas Pelham and General Abercromby, and in the diaries of Sir John Moore (of Corunna fame).

The militia, when embodied, was treated as a part of the standing army of the kingdom, included in its day-to-day administration. This is what makes the Kilmainham Papers so important, as they contain orders for the army, letters to and from the commander-in-chief, admonishments, promotions and supercessions, courts martial, and all the minutiae of military administration which yields so much information. Much has been lost, however, and the survival of the Kilmainham Papers was something of a miracle, for records of decisions on policy, as well as reports on individual units were transferred to the Public Record Office of Ireland, and were destroyed during the Irish civil war in 1922.[13]

The National Archives at Kew contain much that belonged to the Irish army. Particularly valuable are the pay lists and muster rolls (the WO/13 series). All regiments submitted a return to their headquarters twice a year, on 31 March and 30 September, showing their strength on these dates. This was a detailed return showing all the officers and men by name, those absent on leave, without leave, deserters, men on detached duty and to where they were detached. It took some time to prepare, not being submitted to the Castle until up to two or three months after the due date. Because of the time lapse between completion and submission to the Castle, with the vagaries of eighteenth-century record keeping, the returns can be inaccurate – figures or information from outside the relevant period can be included. A good example is to be found in the return of the North Cork Regiment for 31 March 1798, which includes an annotation against the names of all the officers and men killed at Oulart Hill and Enniscorthy, on 27 and 29 May 1798, well outside the period of the return.[14] At first, these returns were on one large sheet of parchment, but from 30 September 1798 the return was produced in book form, which gave the division of officers and men into companies, and allows the relationships within various regiments to be studied

13 Sir Henry McAnally, 'The Kilmainham Papers' in *Journal of the Society for Army Historical Research*, 16 (1937).   14 Pay lists and muster rolls, North Cork Militia (NA, WO/13/2706).

in greater detail. For example, we know that on the evening of 17 December 1801, when Captain John Giffard of the City of Dublin Regiment attended a dinner party – of which much more later – one of his fellow guests was Lieutenant Noble, the officer of the guard. From the pay lists and muster rolls, we can ascertain that Giffard commanded the Grenadiers, the senior company, and that Noble was one of his officers.[15] These papers are almost as important as the Kilmainham Papers.

The other invaluable series in the National Archives is the Home Office Papers (the HO/100 series). The lord lieutenant corresponded with the cabinet on most matters through the home secretary. For much of the period the lord lieutenant was Lord Cornwallis, who was also commander-in-chief, and the home secretary was the duke of Portland. These papers provide evidence of what was happening in the country, as well as the ideas and plans of the Irish administration, and of the British government in London. They give an insight into the Irish papers that were destroyed in 1922, in that they contain letters from the Irish administration, and copy replies. For example, almost the only information available on the Defender troubles and militia riots in 1793 is to be found in newspaper reports, and in the letters from the lord lieutenant to the home secretary, which are in this series.

Regimental records are of varying utility, many are collections of administrative and operational orders. These are useful but tell little about the regiment and its men. The exception to this is H.A. Richey's *A short history of the Royal Longford Militia, 1793–1893* which is informative and analytical.[16] The Armagh Regiment has probably the best surviving records, divided between the National Archives at Kew, and the excellent deposit in the Public Record Office of Northern Ireland, made by the Royal Irish Fusiliers. In many cases, they are copies of orders and instructions, but in some cases, regimental letter books have survived, and these help to give a flavour of the individual units. There is useful and interesting information on the Downshire, Tyrone, Longford, Westmeath, Kerry, and City of Dublin Regiments, among others.

Sir Henry McAnally used many of these sources when writing his book, which was both a social and a military history. This in itself was unusual, because in the 1920s and '30s, military history tended to concentrate on individual unit histories and very little had been done on the army and society, not to mention army families, on which McAnally has a chapter. His interest in the militia undoubtedly stemmed from the fact that he was the great-grandson of David McAnally, who was surgeon of the Armagh Regiment from 1793 to his death from typhus in 1818. McAnally had been a civil ser-

---

15 Pay lists and muster rolls, City of Dublin Militia (ibid., WO/13/2815).   16 H.A. Richey, *A short history of the Royal Longford Militia, 1793–1893* (Dublin, 1894).

vant, and was secretary to the Royal Commission on Militia and Volunteers in 1 9 0 3, which, in fact, led to the abolition of the militia, and the creation of the Special Reserve in its place. As befitted a retired civil servant, McAnally was meticulous in his interpretation of the rules and regulations contained in acts of parliament, and his analysis of the numbers of the government forces engaged at the battle of Castlebar in 1798, for example, remains definitive.[17]

McAnally was well aware that the militia had left a somewhat mixed historical legacy. The strictures of Lord Cornwallis on the militia obviously rankled with him, and in a sense he was broadly sympathetic to the institution, maintaining that it was not at all as it was painted. His book covers the whole period from 1793 to the standing down of the regiments in 1816. He identified a number of themes, dealt with each in turn, including recruitment and the creation of the militia, and outlined the problems of a force designed to serve part-time, which had to serve on a permanent basis. He considered the militia riots in the spring and early summer of 1793 to be a short-term phenomenon, nowhere near as bad as the riots on the establishment of the English militia, with which he compared them. He did not consider the riots in the context of the degree of violence prevalent in the countryside in the 1790s. Similarly, he examined the workings of the ballot in great detail and explained it well, but did not devote much attention to the reasons why it was abandoned or downgraded.

McAnally dealt effectively with the French expeditions to Bantry in 1796 and Connacht in 1798. He emphasized that the bulk of the fighting that occurred was borne by the militia and not the fencibles or the regulars. In this context, he made several pertinent points about the quality of the generals who were, after all, responsible for whatever the Irish militia turned out to be. This does not mean that he made excuses for what he recognized as poor performance. However, McAnally believed that Cornwallis had an 'alternative agenda' (the union), and therefore disparaged the militia because he wanted to show how the country had been saved by 'British' effort, not by the Irish militia. There is some evidence for this: for instance, Cornwallis intimated to Pitt that Abercromby's famous order of 26 February 1798 in which he described the army in Ireland as being 'in a state of licentiousness which must render it formidable to every one but the enemy', as being directed at the militia alone, which it was not.[18]

The biggest weakness in McAnally's book is his treatment of the 1798 rebellion. He did not consider the individual actions, remarking, 'The fog of war rests on the whole rather confused medley of heterogeneous clashes; and

17 Sir Henry McAnally, 'The government forces engaged at Castlebar in 1798' in *IHS*, 4:16 (1945), 316–31. 18 *Cornwallis Corresp.*, ii, 415.

will perhaps always do so.'[19] Instead, he dealt with a series of themes, such as the amount of marching done by the regiments, employment of yeomanry and militia, discipline, with a short consideration of how the militia acquitted itself. He did not deal with the difficult question of why the militia remained loyal in 1798, when so many thought it would not. This whole chapter does not work very well as it is too general, but it may reflect McAnally's use of sources; after all, he spent only ten days reading the Kilmainham Papers, and did not have access to all the sources now available.

While McAnally wrote the only history of the formation and performance of the militia, others have written about various aspects. Principal among these is Professor Thomas Bartlett. One of his articles on 'Indiscipline and disaffection in the armed forces in Ireland in the 1 7 9 0s' is very useful in 'setting the scene' by describing the negligence and laxity of the Irish Army, which was exacerbated by the rapid increase in troops after the declaration of war with France in 1793.[20] In it he made the valid point that officially sanctioned violence was only a step from the 'freelance type', citing the activities of General Richard Whyte who let his dragoons loose on the populace of Belfast in 1793, and General Lord Carhampton in Connacht in 1795 when he acted against Defenders with scant regard for the law. This is important because the militia was in the forefront of the defence of the country. Bartlett credited the militia with defeating the rebellion but makes the point that the defence of Ireland shifted from the regulars to the militia, and finally to the yeomanry: 'After the 1798 rebellion the Irish militia was progressively downgraded; soon it was little more than a recruiting sergeant or crimp for the line regiments.'[21] He claimed that from 1800, 3,000 militiamen were passing into the line regiments every year, which rendered the militia ineffective because the proportion of recruits to trained men was too high, and that the yeomanry therefore assumed its role as the counter-invasion and counter-insurgency army. This disparaging comment – there was a five year gap between the first and second 'volunteering', and two years between the third and fourth – is possibly confusing the roles of yeomanry and militia. They were very different: the yeomanry was composed of very small units, received very little training, served full-time only in an emergency, was unevenly distributed around the country, and certainly could not take the militia's place in the line of battle as it was not their role. What Bartlett may have meant is that the yeomanry, which became increasingly Protestant, was welcomed by those with property as the 'police force', whereas the militia became very much more the army to counter invasion, a threat which gradually receded after 1805 (the year of the second 'volunteering' to the line).

---

19 McAnally, *Irish Militia*, p. 124.   20 Thomas Bartlett, 'Indiscipline and disaffection in the armed forces in Ireland in the 1790s', in P.J. Corish (ed.), *Radicals, rebels and establishments* (Belfast, 1985), pp 115–34.   21 Ibid., p. 130.

Bartlett's other article 'An end to moral economy, the Irish militia disturbances of 1793', argued that the riots on the formation of the militia in 1793 led to the end of the 'moral economy', 'that balance, that tacit understanding, between governor and governed, which had characterized previous disturbances in Ireland'.[22] He argued that violence in Ireland had not been particularly bad until the militia riots, which had an incidence of death five times the number of deaths from rioting in the previous thirty years. This increased intensity of violence, he attributed to the lack of understanding of what the militia ballot was about, the fear of families being left destitute, and a dislike of compulsion. The significance of the violence was a more difficult question to answer, but Bartlett argued that the paternal relationship between landlord and tenant, one Protestant, the other Catholic, in most cases was strong and it was this 'moral economy' that broke down. The French revolution played a part, as did the publication of Paine's famous book, *Rights of man*, also the timing of the Catholic Relief Act of 1793 was unfortunate, since it was followed immediately by the Militia Act, which was seen as an attempt to deprive Catholics of their 'victory', while at the same time Protestants saw that the British government considered them as just another species of Irishman. Bartlett claimed that the answer to these problems was the tacit abandonment of the ballot as a means of raising men, and a downgrading of the (Catholic) militia to the advantage of the (Protestant) yeomanry.

This article is a considerable achievement, but it is equally possible to argue that the increased level and intensity of violence predated and postdated the embodiment of the militia, and that the militia was only another grievance to be utilized by the disaffected. Furthermore, the proclamation dates of all the militia regiments are known, as are the dates on which the regiments were embodied.[23] If these two dates are compared with the record of violence in the county, a different picture emerges. The militia was raised as a part-time force. It was called out for full-time service as soon as the regiments were embodied. To maintain a full-time army a constant flow of new recruits was needed. A ballot held once a year could not provide men in the numbers required, and it may well be that the downgrading of the ballot had more to do with the speed, efficiency and cost of raising men than the rioting, especially as the ballot was never officially abandoned.

Professor J.E. Cookson is a third writer who has considered the role of the militia.[24] Unlike McAnally and Bartlett, he used a mixture of primary and sec-

---

[22] Thomas Bartlett, 'An end to moral economy; the Irish militia disturbances of 1793' in *Past and Present*, 99 (May 1983), 41–64. [23] The proclamation date was the day on which the Castle ordered a county to form its militia, the embodiment date was the day on which the county announced it had obeyed. [24] J.E. Cookson, *The British armed nation, 1793–1815* (Oxford, 1997), pp 153–81.

ondary sources. Cookson claimed that the militia was always distrusted because of the lower competence of its officers and the strong Catholic element in its ranks. He saw the concept of the defence of Ireland being reliant on a Catholic soldiery as anathema to the Protestant upper classes. In his view the militia could be divided into predominantly Catholic or Protestant units, with the former always 'overlooked' or watched over by the latter, or by regulars. 'The ascendancy', he said, 'never was reconciled to Catholic participation in home defence, not even after the union strengthened the British hand in Irish affairs.'[25] Cookson's authority for his claims that the militia was divided into Catholic and Protestant units was taken from the statistics of Edward Wakefield. Much of Wakefield's work, however, was based on hearsay evidence.[26]

The concept of 'Protestant' and 'Catholic' units is one requiring further examination. The authorities in Dublin would do absolutely nothing that would exacerbate religious tensions among the men; they ensured that all soldiers had freedom to worship and the opportunity to do so. It is also difficult to imagine the Irish War Office, with its ramshackle organization, having the ability to segregate militia regiments (for that is what Cookson maintained). Such a division of units would be no secret, it would have created a 'them and us' situation that would have led to affrays between units, and there are few accounts of any such thing happening between militia regiments. Furthermore, Wakefield does not provide any information on some of the units that Cookson claims to be Catholic, and vice versa. Indeed, evidence points towards more Protestants being in the militia than their proportions in the counties, something that will be considered later. Cookson also argued that the defence of Ireland passed from the militia to the yeomanry, but the same comment that was made earlier can be repeated, that the yeomanry became a 'police force' very acceptable to the ascendancy because of its localism and its Protestant religion. It was inappropriate to extend this role to that of an army.

All these works reveal gaps in their understanding of the Irish militia; McAnally dealt badly with the insurrection; Bartlett's theory about the ballot at least needs further examination, and the whole question of religion, not just the interpretations of Cookson, has to be considered. In addition, there is the question of the purpose of the militia. Clarification of whether it was to be a counter-insurgency army or a counter-invasion army was not properly addressed until 1799, and this uncertainty constitutes an enduring theme throughout this book.

It must not be forgotten either, that there was another militia force in the sister kingdom of Great Britain. This was the English Militia, established by

---

25 Ibid., p. 197. 26 Edward Wakefield, *An account of Ireland, statistical and political*, 2 vols (London, 1812).

act of parliament in 1757. (There was no Scots militia until 1797.) The Westminster act was copied almost verbatim by the Irish parliament in 1793, with the result that all the faults of the original were repeated in the copy thirty-four years later, with riots on its establishment, the need for explanatory acts, the problems with the ballot, poor discipline among the men, and poor quality of officers.[27]

The discipline of the English militia reflected the army of the times as it did in Ireland. The English militiamen were turbulent soldiers who were no better disciplined than any other British soldier in the late 1790s. If anything, the English militia was possibly less disciplined than the Irish. There was nothing in Ireland to compare with the Oxford Militia's seizure of meat in Seaford, Sussex, for which five militiamen were executed, or the participation of militiamen in sixteen food riots in 1795.[28] Like the Irish militia, the English militia had difficulties in recruiting officers. The higher ranks were difficult to fill, and the influence of the county hierarchy was used to the full to obtain (or block) commissions. The lower officer ranks were even harder to fill and were 'frankly a disgrace'.[29] It is quite possible to argue that both the English and Irish militia in the period 1793–1802 were similar in discipline and administration to the regular army and that much of the criticism of both forces came from commanders who were attempting to raise standards.

In studying the Irish militia in the first period of its existence, from 1793 to 1802, many areas require discussion and analysis. This book examines the institution thematically, starting with the decision to introduce a militia, whether or not it was to be Protestant, and the problems inherent in the Militia Act itself. The importance of the concept of Catholic soldiers being involved in the defence of Ireland for the first time in over a century cannot be minimized, especially as so many among the landed classes were deeply suspicious of the loyalty of Catholics. Furthermore links between the United Irishmen and Defenders cannot be ignored, nor can the violence of the Irish countryside from which they came.

To this must be added the effect of the Militia Act and the ballot on the raising of militiamen. It is possible to be precise about the process of raising the regiments and to link this to the riots caused by the ballot. This allows a degree of accuracy about the causes of the riots themselves, as well as their locations and ferocity. The mechanics of the ballot itself have been well analysed by McAnally, but the question of the abandonment of the ballot is a complicated one. There is no question that it was unpopular, and there is no question that it was downgraded in importance. But was it abandoned,

27 I.F.W. Beckett, *The amateur military tradition* (Manchester, 1991), pp 62–88. 28 Ibid., p. 72. 29 J.R. Western, *The English militia in the eighteenth century* (London, 1965), p. 314.

and did the riots cause this abandonment, which, after all, is the contention of Professor Bartlett? The ballot was discontinued in some counties, others had no reports of rioting, and it was not abandoned in counties that did ballot, such as Meath. It may be suggested instead that the ballot was discontinued for economic reasons and because it may have been an inefficient means of raising men, being very slow and hampered by the large number of people who could claim or purchase exemption.

In no case did the militia riots prevent a regiment being raised, or 'embodied'. This important fact would be easy to ignore, but raising a regiment included much more than finding officers and men; it also covered arrangements for pay, acquiring equipment and clothing, and quartering. It also included the first effects of military service on the new soldiers, and the consequent problem of desertion. It is possible to compare the length of time needed to train a regular battalion from initial embodiment to being ready for service, with the time needed for a militia battalion because we know what the new militiaman had to learn when he joined, and we know when the first inspections of militia units took place. In many cases, these were impossibly short periods. This would perhaps be understandable if the militia were to have been a part-time force as initially intended but, as the full-time force that it quickly became, it was to all intents and purposes on the same basis as the regulars, and it has been judged by contemporary critics on this basis.

The training of the men can be divided into individual and collective. Individual training was what the private man had to learn to do, such as foot and arms drill, and collective was the exercise of this in group formations. An important part of training was the availability of time to do it. It is here that we start to come up against the perennial problem of the purpose intended for the militia: a defensive army (against invasion) required one type of training, and counter-insurgency another. This was a problem for which there was no solution until Cornwallis devised the plan for a movable and a stationary force in 1799, but it meant that the men were not properly trained for either role, even within the eighteenth-century meaning of these terms, and again this had a detrimental effect on discipline and behaviour. There was no reason why regiments should not have been able to perform both roles (provided the army had enough manpower, which it did not before 1799). A plan was needed which would allow regiments to spend time in one force, followed by a tour of duty in the other. An important addendum to the subject of training the men was the question of the barrack accommodation provided for them. If the late eighteenth-century army were as inefficient as has been depicted, then it would be expected that barracks would be badly run, and in many cases this was true. A barrackmaster appointment was regarded as a sinecure and was given to, or purchased by, civilians, who could act as contractors to their own barracks and wanted to do as little work as possible. More than once, regiments had to rent accommodation in the local town for their men as the barracks were so bad.

Much of the criticism of the Irish militia made by contemporaries is of its officers and men; the officers because of their poor quality, and the men because of their ill discipline. The two problems were linked, since the officers were ultimately responsible for the discipline of the men, and the Castle for the efficiency of the regiment; but it must be remembered that the officers were not appointed by the Castle but by the colonel of the regiment. This meant that the high command had little control over the appointment of officers, whereas they had considerable control over the appointment of officers for the regulars, and could ensure that regular officers were of a quality acceptable to themselves, a point that will be considered later. This in itself would create a divide between the regular and the militia officer. Furthermore, if a colonel did not fill vacancies quickly the regiment suffered, and the military commanders could do nothing to help them, a situation which must have been very frustrating for them. Much criticism of the militia stems from this inability of the regular officer commanding militia units to control effectively all aspects of the troops under his authority. This is a complicated point. In almost all cases regular officers were not Irish. The regulations did not allow militia officers to be appointed to the staff so commanders did not have an officer who could advise and guide them in the command of militia units. The exception to this was the appointment of Major Joseph Hardy of the Antrim Regiment as garrison commander in Co. Wicklow, an appointment that was an undoubted success as we shall see.

Other areas of officer competence need to be examined, in particular the whole question of perceptions of duty. Unlike regular officers, militia officers often had territorial, civic or parliamentary responsibilities. These could not be ignored: in theory parliamentary attendance was compulsory (even if easy to avoid provided permission was requested), and estate management was the source of their wealth. Officers needed regular periods of leave which, of course, conflicted with military duty, and commanders seem to have been unsympathetic. Regular officers seem to have been unaware of, or to ignore, the fact that militia officers had not surrendered their civic rights and responsibilities when commissioned, as they themselves had done. But leave was a problem for the whole army. Although the Castle laid down rules in 1796, many officers ignored them or went on leave without permission. Eventually officers were dismissed for absence without leave. Two of the worst offenders were Lieutenant-Colonel Samuel Ahmuty of the Longford Battalion and Lieutenant Jephson of the Armagh Regiment.

The questions raised by the religion of the officers and men have already been mentioned, but the allied question of the loyalty of the men is an important topic for discussion, one that is very difficult to analyse more than two hundred years later. One of the great questions arising from the history of the Irish militia in the 1790s is why the Catholic soldiers remained loyal when many in the country, both military and civil, thought they would not. There are obvious incentives to loyalty, such as pay, promotion, pensions, education for children, good food and accommodation. The ratio of non-commissioned officers to privates is also important, as is the background of the men who joined the militia, especially as there is a suggestion that these tended to be 'mechanics' and townsmen, rather than landowners or occupiers. Of course such factors do not answer the more difficult subjective reasons for loyalty. The Irish militia regiments were very clannish, and why this should be is a matter for speculation.[30] No doubt county loyalties played a part, as did provincial regionalism; so too would regimental pride, the security afforded by the army, both practical and psychological, and, perhaps the strongest reason of all, the influence of friends. Furthermore, the effects of strong leadership displayed by their officers should not be forgotten.

Finally, there is the question of the performance of the militia from 1793 to 1802. This can be divided into different phases, and each will be examined in turn: first the formation period up to 1795, when the militia was settling down and learning to do its job; then in 1795-6, when the United Irishmen and Defenders, realizing that the militiamen were essentially from the same background as themselves, attempted to subvert the militia in order to make the militia the 'United army', an attempt that failed, but not before the militia had been 'purged' in 1797; finally 1798 saw the short command of General Abercromby, the rebellion, and the French incursion into Connacht in the autumn. Despite suffering some notable defeats, especially at Oulart Hill and Castlebar, the militia enjoyed many successes, and were primarily responsible for the defeat of the rebellion and of the French at Ballinamuck in September 1798. In the aftermath, however, the behaviour of the regiments was called to account, with claims for compensation, and courts martial of those who had failed in their duty. The orders to militia regiments to settle claims made against them marks the start of change in the perception of the force. This change was imperceptible at first, but gathered force with the employment of two regiments in the Channel Islands, and with volunteering to the line in 1800. The issues raised are illustrated in the affair of Lord Downshire which may well have been in part a political episode arising from Downshire's opposition to the Union bill, but also represented a clash between the regular army and the concept of a constitutional militia, after which the militia was to be treated on the same basis as the regulars whilst serving full-time. Reform continued with the Cornwallis's plan for the defence of Ireland, which involved all his forces, regular, fenci-

30 McAnally, *Irish Militia*, p. 122.

ble, militia, and yeomanry, as well as the organization of a corps of pioneers and a weeding out of unfit men by the medical board.

If the militia incurred criticism in our period, who was responsible? The blame for whatever the militia regiments did wrong has been placed on the shoulders of the colonels. This would have suited the generals, including Cornwallis, but responsibility for the behaviour and the performance of the militia lay fairly and squarely on the shoulders of the commanders. Their quality needs to be examined, as do some of their actions, and it can be argued that, in keeping with the poor quality of the army at the beginning of the French wars, the quality, or ability, of the generals was poor as well.

There is still very much to learn about the militia: what it was, how it operated, and how it performed in action; so much in fact that it is not intended to discuss other considerations such as its relationships with other crown forces, the political ramifications of how it should be deployed, how its colonels influenced parliamentary proceedings, or the decisions taken in Dublin Castle, except where relevant to the narrative. This is very much a military history of the militia, not a social or political one. Before relationships with the yeomanry, parliament, the land-owning classes and the government of the country can be discussed and examined, the militia itself, as an institution, must be understood, and that is the aim.

CHAPTER TWO

The formation of a militia

The militia of Ireland, to be raised by ballot, and officered by landowners, was frequently described throughout the 1790s as 'constitutional.' What this meant was that as inheritors of the medieval concept of 'knight service', landowners had a duty to their sovereign to offer their services as officers in an army raised for national defence, and to provide soldiers from their tenantry, selected by ballot. This gave the officers and balloted men an intimate association with the people of their county in a way foreign to the regular army. Service was for a limited period, followed by replacement of men whose term of service had expired by more men selected by compulsion from the county.

The counties and towns of Ireland were by no means necessarily peaceful as many of them had organized societies such as the United Irishmen, and in the countryside, a secret society known as the Defenders. The outbreak of war with revolutionary France in 1793 can be seen as a 'catalyst' because it gave to the United Irishmen the very real possibility of a French invasion which the militant wing of the movement believed necessary, and it offered to the Defenders the probability that they would have more grounds for disturbance in the countryside, and thus a greater appeal to disaffection.[1] There was considerable violence on the formation of the militia occasioned by the Defenders, but there was a background of violence in the countryside before the passing of the act, which in fact gave more impetus to this violence, and it continued after the militia was embodied, although the act ceased to be a cause. The activities of the United Irishmen and the Defenders, combined with a foreign war, gave problems to an administration attempting to govern, and an army attempting to meet the demands of the war against France as well as the security problems in the Irish countryside. The government saw the solution lying in the restitution of the militia, and a suppression of the Volunteers.

---

[1] The United Irishmen were founded in 1791 in Belfast and Dublin with the aims of a reform of parliament, and religious toleration. They were proscribed in 1794 and became a secret revolutionary movement. The Defenders were a rural secret society, anti-Protestant, which committed many depredations in the countryside, particularly in the eastern counties of Ireland and the border counties of Ulster with Leinster and Connacht.

GOVERNMENT AND THE ARMY

The much vaunted 'independence' of the Irish parliament after 1782 was not entirely a sham. It no longer had to send 'heads of bills' to London for approval; it could act independently in the majority of its work. The Irish parliament functioned exactly as Westminster in its rules, its procedures, its administration of the country, its relations with the judiciary, and church, with one major difference. The Irish parliament had no prime minister, or cabinet. The lord lieutenant, who was not in any way responsible to the electorate in Ireland even though he dealt with political matters, filled the role of prime minister. It can be argued that his 'cabinet' consisted of the lord chancellor (the earl of Clare), the speaker of the house of commons (John Foster), and the chief commissioner of the treasury (John Beresford), together with others such as the chief secretary or the primate as required, although this was by no means a 'cabinet' in the Westminster meaning of the term. The lord lieutenant 'managed' all the public business of the Irish Parliament. This does not mean that the parliament lacked power to act for the benefit of the country; rather it meant that the lord lieutenant tried to ensure that the wishes of the Westminster parliament were followed in constitutional and foreign policy matters. This was a task growing ever more difficult since the Irish parliament was given more independence in 1782. Parliament, at this stage of its development, in both Ireland and Britain, may have represented land rather than people, but nevertheless a study of the debates, acts of parliament, financial records which account for all the revenue raised in the country, and the reports on management of government institutions and select committees show that by the 1790s, it is possible to argue that Ireland was administered probably as well as any country in Europe.[2]

That small minority of affairs managed by the lord lieutenant in the interests of the two kingdoms officially, but more often in the interests of the larger, Great Britain, included constitutional matters and trade relations. The former included, among other things, policy towards Roman Catholics, religion generally, and the army. In this period the great political questions were the possible removal of the last of the penal laws against Roman Catholics, and the reform of parliament. The lord lieutenant was expected to follow an agreed line with the cabinet at Westminster on these issues. He worked to the home secretary, who acted as his link to the rest of the government, although he did have direct access to the prime minister, if necessary. However, working through the home secretary gave the latter great power,

---

2 *CJI*. Evidence for this is to be found in the appendices which account for all the revenue raised in the country, the management of government institutions, and reports of select committees.

if as happened, the prime minister was not very interested in Irish affairs. During this period, the prime minister was William Pitt, and the home secretary from 1792 to 1801 was the duke of Portland. Pitt was only intermittently interested in Irish affairs, the exception being in 1795 when the then lord lieutenant, Earl Fitzwilliam, exceeded his brief, and from 1798 when he became convinced that a union was the only answer to the problem of Ireland. Portland was a Whig, and had entered into a coalition with Pitt's government in 1792. He did not abandon all his Whig prejudices, and he had been a lord lieutenant of Ireland. This gave him a knowledge of the country which he was not averse to using, and he did not hesitate to promote his own views, or advance the interests of his friends and relations in Ireland, irrespective of what the lord lieutenant advised, or to use his influence with the king as he thought fit.

The lord lieutenant represented the king in Ireland, and, therefore, the Irish commander-in-chief was subordinate to him. Ireland had its own military 'establishment,' independent of the commander-in-chief in Great Britain. This establishment was 12,000 men, increased to 15,000 men in 1769. The actual army units in Ireland were part and parcel of the British Army, but paid for by the Irish Exchequer, and were totally controlled by the Irish commander-in-chief while stationed in Ireland. The headquarters of the army in Ireland was at the Royal Hospital, Kilmainham, in Dublin, where there was an Irish Board of Ordnance, and Royal Irish Artillery. Regiments were posted to and from the Irish establishment by the War Office in London (colloquially known as 'Horse Guards' from the location of their offices), but once in Ireland, Horse Guards had no control over them. This sounds like a recipe for disaster, but was not by any means so. London and Dublin each kept the other informed of what they were doing.[3] By the 1790s Ireland followed London's lead in all matters of training, but had a considerable influence on the subject as Phoenix Park was the largest military training ground in Europe, and much of the experimenting with army training was carried out there. The training in Phoenix Park 1788-9, resulted in 1792 in the drawing up of the *Rules and regulations for the formations, field exercise, and movements of HM forces*, which governed British infantry drill right up to the Crimean War. These regulations were based on the work of Colonel David Dundas, quartermaster-general in Ireland, 1778-89, and adjutant general 1789-93.[4] In historical terms, too, Ireland was by no means a military backwater, for 'in-pensioners' of the Royal Hospital at Kilmainham predated those of the Royal Hospital at Chelsea and, in the education of the sons and daughters of soldiers, provision was made for the Irish establishment at the Hibernian Military Institute[5] some

---

3 See Houlding, *Fit for service*, pp 4 5ff, for further discussion.   4 Ibid., pp 242ff.   5 Later

forty years before the foundation of the Duke of York's Military Asylum at Chelsea.[6]

The purpose of the army in Ireland was to provide internal security, and to oppose any attempt at invasion. Because Ireland had been 'quiet' for most of the century, the regular army was kept in a reduced state, regiments only being made up to full established strength on posting out of the country. This policy raised enormous problems of training and discipline – a regiment drafted for overseas would have its numbers made up by reinforcements taken at random from others in Ireland, and these men would know nothing of the receiving regiment, and vice versa. If drafted to the West Indies, frequently the destination would be kept secret to prevent desertion and mutiny. Five companies of the 105th and 113th Foot mutinied at Cork in September 1795 on drafting to the West Indies, and the Irish militia put down the mutiny.[7] Regiments could be removed from Ireland and not replaced. In 1745 the forces in Ireland had been reduced to four battalions of foot, and six regiments of cavalry[8] and even in December 1796 regular infantry in Ireland amounted to only 582 men, and 2,711 cavalry.

At this point it would be pertinent to consider the state of the army in the late eighteenth century. The militia became part of this establishment in 1793 and its mustering, training, deployment and behaviour in action should not be seen in Irish isolation, it was a part of a much wider organization whose standards would be reflected to a greater or lesser extent in the Irish militia. Ultimately the standards of the army reflected the degree of interest that the government had in defence of the realm. This was inconsistent, soldiers were seen as a drain on national finances that much of the time brought no return on the investment and as a result neglect was the persistent and prevalent theme. In 1793 William Pitt was prime minister. He was a man with a mercurial temperament, 'His active, enterprising, "improving" spirit led him constantly to seek ways to carry the offensive to the enemy. He could not abide being condemned to a wretched defensive.'[9] Pitt was first lord of the treasury and believed that economic warfare would cripple France when combined with coalitions of her enemies financed by Britain. This led him to plans for multiple operations against the west coast of France, in the Mediterranean, and in the West Indies. There were three problems with this strategy. First, the French defeated all the coalitions on the battlefield, second, it was a piecemeal approach to continental warfare when a full blooded effort was required, and third, good as Pitt's plans were on paper they did

---

the Royal Hibernian Military School, 1764–1924. 6 Now the Duke of York's Royal Military School at Dover. Theoretically, the RHMS was amalgamated with it in 1924. 7 Cooke to Pelham, 7 Sept. 1795 (PRONI, T/755/2/182). 8 Houlding, *Fit for service*, p. 48, n. 98. 9 Michael Duffy, *The younger Pitt* (London, 2000).

not appreciate the reality that Britain did not have forces strong enough to be divided into several theatres of war and as a result the lives of valuable men were squandered to no avail. For example, Pitt's expeditions to Holland in 1793 and in 1799 were a disaster, as was the expedition to the Vendée in 1795 with consequent loss of men and equipment. None of the forces, British and allied, were strong enough in themselves to defeat the French and they were poorly led. Success in the West Indies was peripheral and had to be balanced against the fearsome loss of men to disease. It can be argued that it was not until the government stopped dividing the forces it had available, and concentrated on one major campaign against the French in Europe after 1808 that things began to change. The effect of these strings of defeats that followed on from the American Revolutionary war did nothing to raise morale, or to make the army more efficient. In fact the regular army had a generation of junior and middle rank officers who had never known success.

Sir Henry Bunbury, who had been aide-de-camp to General Abercromby in Holland in 1799, and quartermaster general in the Mediterranean 1805-10, made some pungent comments on the condition of the army and the conduct of operations. He presents a soldier's view of Pitt's policies:

> Men of the present generation can hardly form an idea of what the military forces of England really were ... [O]ur army was lax in its discipline, entirely without system, and very weak in numbers. Each colonel of a regiment managed it according to his own notions or neglected it altogether. There was no conformity of drill or movement; professional pride was rare; professional knowledge still more so. Never was a kingdom less prepared for a stern and arduous conflict.[10]

Bunbury cites evidence of the problems; in 1793 two regiments were left behind in England as unfit to face the enemy.[11] He was critical of the dispersal of the troops, especially of the campaigns in the West Indies and he commented on the administration of the army in Holland in 1793, comments which applied equally to Ireland and Great Britain:

> Every department of the staff was more or less deficient particularly the commissariat and medical branches.[12] The regimental officers in those days, were as well as their men, hard drinkers, and the latter under a loose discipline were much addicted to marauding, and to acts of licentious violence which made them detested by the people of the country.[13]

---

10 Lt.-Gen. Sir Henry Bunbury, *Narratives of some passages in the great war with France, 1799 to 1810* (London, 1854) p. viii. 11 Ibid., p. xi. 12 Neither existed in Ireland until 1797 and 1798 respectively. 13 Bunbury, *Narrative*, p. xviii.

Bunbury confirms that the nature of warfare in Ireland demoralized both officers and men and 'injured' their discipline. He did not elaborate but was obviously referring to the dispersal of troops in small detachments, 'free quarters' and the measure of violence troops were allowed to use against the civil population, together with the intense dislike that soldiers had for counter insurgency operations. He was also scathing about Pitt's war policy:

> Whenever our ministers found that they had a large body of troops at their disposal they showed symptoms of *wanting to do something* [sic]; but they never were prepared beforehand and they seldom looked at the main objects of the contest in which they were engaged.[14]

This was the other side of Pitt's war policy as it appeared to the soldier on the ground. Bunbury was really making two important points; that the senior officers of the army tolerated a 'loose' behaviour (looting, theft, drunkenness, and molestation of innocent men and women); and that Pitt's war policy in effect did not face up to the unpleasant fact that to defeat the French the British army would have to confront them on the European mainland, something which eventually happened.

This was the army, however, in which the Irish militia was expected to form a part. There is a military 'truism' that the discipline and morale of the private soldier starts at the very top, and if the quality of leadership shown by the generals and other commanders is poor, then it will be reflected at the bottom, in the private soldier. In the 1790s however steadfast troops might be in action, their behaviour in the pursuit or retreat left a great deal to be desired. It is in this context that the Irish militia has to be judged. This is not to excuse 'licentiousness' in any way but shows that such behaviour was a part of the malaise of inefficiency that affected the army before 1802. To some extent the successes of the Peninsular war and Waterloo have thrown a glow forward which conceals much inefficiency and incompetence. This too, made the Irish militia appear singular when in fact it was part of the whole.

Army policy seems to have been decided on an ad hoc basis. Expeditionary forces were put together with no thought for replacement. It was an inefficient system, damaging to training, leadership, and morale, and wasteful of men, a finite resource. In 1799, Cornwallis wrote of a proposed recruitment of militiamen to the line as 'that force will be the last British army that you can hope to raise this war',[15] and again, 'I mourn over the British Infantry, once the pride of my heart and the terror of our enemies, and now by various causes reduced to a state which I am ashamed to men-

---

14 Ibid., p. 72.   15 Cornwallis to Henry Dundas, 14 Nov. 1799 (NAS, GD/51/1/331/21).

tion.[16] Cornwallis was lord lieutenant and commander-in-chief in Ireland. His staff, when he assumed command in 1798, had been augmented, but in 1793 the staff ratio was designed to cope with 15,000 men. In January 1794 two lieutenant-generals, and four major-generals assisted the commander-in-chief.[17] There was little delegation of responsibility, the commander-in-chief and the adjutant general at the Royal Hospital handled the functions of training, administration, and commissariat matters. There was an Ordnance Board, and a Barrack Board, but the latter was a civilian sinecure. The commander-in-chief also dealt with such matters as all officers' commissions, approved resignations, half pay, promotions and transfers, with and without purchase, together with the sale and purchase of staff appointments. This latter practice existed in Ireland until Cornwallis took the first steps to abolish it in 1798. In that year, Major Sirr, who arrested Lord Edward Fitzgerald, purchased the appointment of town major of Dublin for £2,500, on the understanding that on sale, the maximum he would receive was £2,000, the appointment reducing by £500 on each sale. Other staff officers received compensation of ten shillings per day.[18]

However adequate the system may have been before 1793, it gradually broke down thereafter under the weight of the problems faced by the Royal Hospital. Reform was piecemeal. In 1794, for example, there was such a shortage of artillerymen in Ireland – they had gone to fight the French, and no one had thought of replacements – that the militia was ordered to garrison the Cork forts, where there was 'no artillerist' at all. This was successful, and the militia was ordered to provide men for artillery training prior to issuing each unit with two curricle guns.[19] Then in 1797 it happened again, and 21 sergeants, 17 corporals, and 283 private men had to report for artillery training at Dublin, Blaris Huts (Co. Antrim), Charlemont (Co. Armagh), Cove (Co. Cork), Athenry (Co. Galway), Limerick, Clonmel (Co. Tipperary), and Mallow (Co. Cork).[20] It was not until October 1796 that Ireland was at last divided into five military districts: eastern, southern, western, northern, and centre.[21] In December 1797 General Abercromby, the then commander-in-chief, wrote to Eastern District in England asking for advice on the establishment of an army commissariat, as one did not exist in Ireland, where there were 40,000 troops.[22] He had a volunteer to run it in Lieutenant-Colonel Charles Handfield, who was appointed on 2 January 1798, on a salary

---

[16] Ibid., 16 May 1800 (ibid., GD/5 1/1/33 1/27). [17] Establishment of general officers in Ireland, 22 Jan. 1794 (NLI, KP/1 0 0 2/2/1 3 5). [18] Taylor to Wickham, 10 Nov. 1798 (NA, HO/1 0 0/7 4/1 8 1). [19] Cunninghame to Douglas, 24 Feb. 1794 (NLI, KP/1 0 1 2/2 7 8). A 'curricle gun' was a light gun mounted on a two wheeled carriage, which was attached to a 'limber', which carried the powder and shot. The whole was drawn by two horses. [20] General order, 18 Feb. 1797 (NA, WO/68/402/204, Cavan Regt. letter book). [21] General order, 26 Oct. 1796 (NLI, M/3474/125). [22] Abercromby to [—], 11 Dec. 1797 (PRONI, T3048/A/6).

of £6 a day, with £3 a day staff pay.[23] In August 1797 the Army Medical Board in Ireland was made permanent,[24] and in December 1798, an order from Horse Guards required all general officers to report before 1 March and 1 September in each year on the state of each regiment under their command; on the field exercise, economy, and good order, and to have a personal knowledge of the merits and capacity of every officer. Cornwallis directed that this order should apply to Ireland.[25] In November 1800 the duties of the various branches of an army headquarters were made explicit. This is the origin of what is known in the modern army as 'G', 'A', and 'Q', and is the foundation of delegated control of operations, training, and administration. 'G' is the general staff responsible for training and operations, 'A' is the adjutant general's department dealing with administration and personnel matters, and 'Q' the quartermaster-general's department dealing with supplies, and the commissariat. It was not expressed quite so precisely in 1800, and they also had a military secretary, a barrackmaster-general, a commissary-general, ordnance and a medical board, and a comptroller of army accounts.[26] This was a major step forward, with lasting consequences. In 1801, the militia was detailed to form a Corps of Pioneers – men trained in simple engineering tasks, such as building earthworks, hutments, and so on.[27] At this time too, the militia regiments, augmented in men twice in 1795, and 1800, were allowed a second major, not in command of a company.[28]

These are but some of the examples of an army becoming more sophisticated, better administered and organized, in order to carry out its duties in an increasingly complex and difficult situation. However, little or none of it was proactive; it was a response to pressures placed upon it, pressures originating in the disturbed state of the country, possible and actual invasion by the French, changes in the economy, and, in 1800, a change in the method of government which removed the independence of the Irish commander-in-chief. It must also be said, however, that the commanders of the army were very resistant to outside advice, be it from any quarter, including the office of the lord lieutenant. In September 1797, Thomas Pelham, Camden's very able chief secretary, who had also been an officer in the Sussex militia for over twenty years, complained that he found constant opposition to every plan he proposed 'for introducing discipline and system in the formation and conduct of the Army'. He determined never to interfere, but he had suggested brigading the light infantry companies of the militia, and also to brigade the army. He also suggested that the very small units of the militia

---

23 Camden to Portland, 2 Jan. 1798 (NA, HO/100/73/12). 24 General order, 5 Aug. 1797 (NLI, KP/1 0 0 4/4/1 7 2). 25 General order, 5 Dec. 1798 (NA, WO/6 8/402/4 2 4, Cavan Regt. letter book). 26 General order, 24 Nov. 1800 (NLI, KP/330/3 5). 27 General order, 9 May 1801 (ibid., KP/330/38). 28 General order, 24 Mar. 1801 (NAI, 999/308/3).

should be stationed in the forts, and kept there (that is, in Cork). Then, when he returned to duty from his illness in the spring, he found that the light infantry companies had been formed into four battalions with regiments of the line, and the army brigaded.[29]

The army was not as separate from the populace at large as it had been twenty or more years earlier. Because Roman Catholics and Dissenters were not allowed to bear arms, recruiting for the army had almost dried up in Ireland. In 1724, 'out of 294 privates in the Inniskillings, 101 were Irish. In 1726, the regiment was down to 81 Irishmen.'[30] Clearly this policy could not continue. As Britain's wars grew more complex, the demand for men became more voracious, and Ireland had a huge manpower pool: by 1800 Ireland's population was as great as today, just over five million.[31] There was no change in official attitudes until the American war in 1775, when George III authorized the recruitment of 2,000 Irishmen for service in America.[32] In 1776, 16 of the 44 battalions in America originated on the Irish Establishment, and were full of both Catholic and Protestant soldiers.[33] From this period on, and in particular after the passing of the Catholic Relief Acts of 1782 and 1793, all shades of Irishmen were recruited. Nonetheless, progress was slow. In November 1796, Thomas Pelham the chief secretary, wrote to the duke of York about the numbers of Irishmen serving in the army and the navy. The number of men raised for the (regular) army between 1793 and 1796 was 23,138, out of a total of 38,365. Furthermore, he was able to classify these men as predominantly 'mechanics' and inhabitants of towns, rather than countrymen:

> Peasants could seldom be persuaded under any circumstances to quit their families and place of nativity. I know that rather than quit a farm, or even a cabin, the tenant would give a sum no Englishman under similar circumstances could afford, which was one cause of the ... poverty ... of the lower order of people.[34]

(And, it might be added, a further cause of the riots when the militia ballot was introduced.)

Two important points need to be emphasized at this juncture. First, in the 1790s senior army officers in Ireland – most of whom were not Irish – would have joined the army twenty and thirty years before Catholics could legally be recruited. They had their prejudices, and naturally had to make a

---

29 Memorandum, Thomas Pelham to Lord Camden, 14 Nov. 1797 (PRONI, Sheffield MSS., T/3465/84).   30 Terence Denman, 'Hibernia officina militum: Irish recruitment to the British regular army, 1660-1815' in *Irish Sword*, 20:80 (1996), 148-66.   31 Cormac O'Grada, *Ireland: a new economic history, 1780-1939* (Oxford, 1994), p. 69.   32 Denman, 'Hibernia officina militum', p. 159.   33 Ibid., p. 161.   34 Thomas Pelham to the duke of York, 14 Nov. 1796, printed in J.T. Gilbert (ed.), *Documents relating to Ireland, 1795-1804* (Dublin, 1893), p. 99.

mental adjustment to the idea of Catholics and Dissenters being 'loyal', which not all could or would do. Second, the regular army contained by the 1790s a substantial number of Catholics and Dissenters, and in the creation of the Irish militia, open to all religions, there were inevitably regiments which would be – and indeed were – exclusively Catholic. It was one thing to recruit Catholics to fight the wars of empire in America, Canada, or India; a different matter when the defence of one of the two kingdoms, for the first time in over one hundred years, lay in the hands of an Irish army which had substantial numbers of Catholic soldiers in it. Moreover, the issue of the morality of the American war had been very divisive in Great Britain and Ireland, and the war had ended in defeat. It is the nature of people to minimize the effect of an unsuccessful war, and it is arguable that the performance of Irish Catholic soldiers in America had not received the prominence it deserved.

For the most part, the officers of the regular army came from the same social class as members of the Irish parliament, the landed gentry, and if they did not, they aspired to it. Indeed, a career in the army was the chosen profession of many younger sons of Irish country gentlemen, of which Arthur Wesley (later Wellesley), from Trim, Co. Meath, is the supreme example.[35] This gentry class was almost an oligarchy. There was a small middle class, some Protestant and some Catholic, mostly to be found in the north of Ireland, and in the large towns. Throughout Ireland, the lower classes were predominantly Catholic. They were the recruiting ground for private soldiers, and it is no wonder that they were regarded with great suspicion by Protestant landowners so that so that rumours about their loyalty, steadfastness, and discipline found an all too receptive audience. It can be argued that this attitude did not change until after the re-formation of the militia in 1803.

SOCIETY AND THE ARMY

In 1822 Edward Handcock, retiring as deputy muster-master general in Ireland (the official responsible for army estimates and the payment of troops), a position he had held from 1772, noted among some 'Miscellaneous (not irrelevant) observations',[36]

> The necessity of a strong military force to maintain the power, and preserve the due authority of government, is fully proved in every page of Ireland's turbulent history. In the weakness of the army grew the hopes of rebellion, and (not to go further back than to the com-

---

[35] He became duke of Wellington. [36] 'A collection of military states, compiled by Mr Handcock, deputy muster-master general', 1772–1822 (NAI, 999/308/3).

mencement of his present Majesty's reign), the following observations will elucidate the truth, that in the spirit and troublesome disposition of the native Irish there is no other safety, no other means of curbing and repressing their insurrectionary activity, but by a numerous standing army.

Handcock reveals in this quotation his alienation from ordinary Irish people, and, at the same time, implicitly his belief in a Protestant regular army. He went on to outline the activities of the Catholic 'Whiteboys' in Limerick, Cork, and Tipperary in 1 7 6 2, the predominantly Presbyterian 'Oakboys' in counties Armagh, Tyrone, Londonderry, and Fermanagh in 1763 and 'Steelboys' in 1771–3. In 1778, when the sovereign (mayor) of Belfast requested military assistance, all that could be sent to him was half a troop of dismounted horse, and half a company of invalids, and, by that year the Volunteers amounted to 30,000 men, over whom the government had no control. Handcock discussed the necessity of British troops rather than Irish, and believed that the 1798 rebellion was put down by the former (which, as we shall see, it was not). He did not discuss agitation and disturbances of the 1790s, and attributed all these endemic disturbances to the nature of the Irish, rather than to any social or economic cause. Nonetheless, an underlying theme in all of this violence was land and tithes, exacerbated by religion.

The Williamite settlement of 1691–1704 had imposed and confirmed by conquest an upper class of landowners who held estates all over Ireland. This class was almost uniformly Anglican, the Irish parliament was an overwhelmingly Anglican one, and the Anglican Church of Ireland the established church.[37] The penal laws against Catholics and Dissenters were enacted mainly in the first part of the century, and irrespective of whether or not they were ever enforced fully, Roman Catholics and Dissenters were effectively disenfranchised until 1780, and land ownership was made difficult for Catholics. No matter how good a landowner might be (and many were – Lord Chancellor Clare, and Speaker Foster, for example), there was an underlying resentment at the loss of land in the Williamite wars, and ongoing friction in the landlord–tenant relationship. The eighteenth century encouraged the growth of middlemen whose aim was to let land for the maximum profit which resulted in the widespread subdivision of estates by grants, sub-grants, leases for nine hundred and ninety nine years, or for lives, or leases for thirty years or less. A lease for lives, usually three, would only be available to Protestants because as such a lease created a freehold and a right to vote.[38]

---

[37] In the late eighteenth century 'Protestants' were exclusively Anglican, 'Dissenters' were Presbyterians, Methodists and other sects now regarded as 'Protestant'. [38] J.C.W. Wyllie, *Irish land law* (3rd edn, Dublin, 1997), p. 25.

For those who could not afford to lease land, or only lease for very short periods, acreages became smaller, dependence on the potato increased, and with the gradual removal of the technicalities of ejectment for non payment of rent throughout the eighteenth century, the threat of eviction increased with no remedy for the tenant.[39] Together with such insecure licences as 'agistment' – a licence to graze animals – and 'conacre' – a licence to till land, grow and harvest crops – in a country being farmed at the beginning of the agricultural revolution, with a population of over five million, the pressure for land was steadily increasing albeit in some areas more than others. Ireland may have been well governed in the administrative sense, but this whole area of landholding was divisive, inefficient, badly organized, and unjust. It was the prime cause of discontent, along with the vexed subject of tithes, and contrasts unfavourably with Great Britain, where there was a class of yeoman farmers who had security of tenure, and also, as it happened, who shared the same religion as the landowners.

The Church of Ireland was the established or state church, and as such all landlords and tenants had to pay the parson a tithe of one tenth of the value of their produce annually. Naturally this caused great discontent, because Catholics had to pay priests' fees also, which in itself could be a source of friction. It must be remembered that tithes were frequently the right of lay organizations, for 'the tithes of religious foundations suppressed at the Reformation, passed partly into that of lay proprietors, and partly formed the corpus of collegiate or educational foundations.'[40] These foundations needed their tithes in order to be able to function, and, what is more, had the power to enforce collection.

The two most problematic organizations in the 1790s were the Defenders, and the United Irishmen. The organization which became known eventually as the 'Defenders,' originated in Co. Armagh in the early 1780s[41] as a result of continuing religious tensions in that county, in areas where Roman Catholics and Protestants were fairly evenly balanced in terms of numbers, and there was competition for work between weavers of both religions. The Defenders have left little in writing, much about them remains a mystery, and much of what is known comes from government sources, which must have an element of speculation in them. Originally, according to Hereward Senior,[42] the Protestants formed gangs, or 'fleets', to raid Roman Catholic dwellings searching for arms – which Catholics and Dissenters were prohibited from owning. A band, led by a dissenting minister, was formed at this time (1783), to protect Catholics. This band eventually became the 'Defend-

---

39 Ibid., p. 26. 40 Ibid., p. 410. 41 Edward Cooke to Thomas Pelham, 21 Sept. 1795 (PRONI, T/755/2/201). 42 Hereward Senior, *Orangeism in Ireland and Britain, 1795–1836* (London, 1966), p. 8.

ers', all Catholic, anti-Protestant, and, according to Thomas Bartlett, 'they sought to regulate tithes and they refused to deal with tithe proctors, or tithe farmers. They complained bitterly about the price of conacre land, and the level of labourers' wages, and they criticized the high level of priest's fees ... It was anti-Protestant, anti-English, and anti-settler, in a way that earlier movements were not.'[43]

By asserting the right of Catholics to bear arms, Defenders not only contravened the law, but also guaranteed continuing Protestant resistance to them under the aegis of 'Peep o' Day boys' (sometimes called 'Break o' Day boys'). Kevin Whelan, however, makes the valid point that 'Arms, not the franchize, constituted the fundamental badge of citizenship in a pre-democratic state, and the bearing of arms was, therefore, a pivotal political issue. If Catholics asserted their right to bear arms publicly, they asserted their right to full participation in the political nation.'[44] Senior also says that magistrates in many cases failed to take action against these gangs – as they had earlier failed in the case of Whiteboys, Oakboys, and Steelboys – because the magistracy was designed to deal with the occasional breach of the peace, but could not cope with the periodic but continuous organized violence.[45] This meant that the army in Ireland spent much of its time on police duties, trying to counter nightly raids and atrocities committed by both sides. According to Senior,[46] the Defenders formed themselves into 'lodges' on Masonic lines, a pattern followed later by Orange societies in 1795 and after, and spread outside the county of Armagh. 'Defenderism proved to be ... remarkably adept at fusing local grievances with an anti-Protestant, anti-English, and anti-state ideology, and this plasticity explains its spread, and acceptance, beyond the borders of Armagh.'[47] First, Defenderism spread into the surrounding counties of Cavan, Monaghan, Tyrone, and Down, and then into Roscommon, Leitrim, Louth, Dublin, Meath, and Wicklow. Where Catholics were in a majority, their activities were directed to disarming Protestants, but in other counties, their activities were directed against landlords, magistrates, and clergy.[48] Protestant organizations soon appeared in reaction that in 1795 became Boyne Clubs, or Orange Boys. Thus violence was endemic in south Ulster the midlands and west of Ireland long before the formation of the militia in 1793, which some historians have argued was a provocation for further trouble.

Before 1789 the cause of reform had been carried on by the Volunteers, but by the 1790s they had been in decline for some time. The ideas of the French revolution found fertile ground in Ireland, and led to the foundation

[43] Thomas Bartlett, 'Select documents xxxviii: Defenders and Defenderism in 1795', in *IHS*, 24:95 (May 1985), 373-94. [44] Kevin Whelan, *The tree of liberty* (Cork, 1996), p. 40. However, the people of Ireland were 'subjects' of the king, not citizens. [45] Hereward Senior, *Orangeism*, p. 9. [46] Ibid., p. 12. [47] Thomas Bartlett, 'Defenders and Defenderism in 1795', p. 375. [48] Senior, *Orangeism*, p. 13.

of the United Irishmen in Belfast in 1791. At first this was an 'enlightenment' phenomenon – an organization dedicated to the elimination of sectarianism, emancipation of Catholics, and a reform of parliament.[49] The organization was typical of eighteenth-century 'enlightenment' societies, being essentially middle class and discursive. It was not illegal, and not very secret, but it did have members determined to achieve its aims by violence if necessary. The American and French revolutions had apparently shown that violence could achieve results, and much of the rhetoric of the United Irishmen was inspired by these two events; it was as if political change could only be achieved by violence, and violence became a political culture.[50] There was, therefore, a growing belief that the only way the United Irishmen could achieve their aims was by armed insurrection, aided by a French invasion.[51] It came to be felt that the Irish parliament, because of its monolithic composition and entrenched views, could only be reformed by revolution.

The United Irishmen – seen in hindsight – sometimes appear to have been the most inept, and irresponsible conspirators in Irish history. The government knew all that went on through a system of 'spies and informers,' although of course the society was neither secret nor illegal before 1794. However, any government would always be interested in an organization promoting Catholic relief, a reform of parliament, and having as its members supporters of the Whig interest, then in opposition. This opposition was regarded by many as being only one step away from treason, because of the contemporary dislike and fear of 'party.' But if the Ponsonbys, Henry Grattan, and John Philpott Curran were sympathetic to the aims of the United Irishmen, they were not, so far as is known, members of the society. The society could really be divided into two; those who would promote its aims by peaceful means, and who resigned or drifted away when the society moved towards violence – men such as William Drennan,[52] and those who came to believe that the connection with England had to be broken, and the only way to do this was by revolution assisted by France: Wolfe Tone, Henry Joy McCracken, the Sheares brothers, James Napper Tandy, and Hamilton Rowan, all United Irishmen, to name but a few.

By the end of 1792 these diverse elements of political life in Ireland were fusing. The Castle faced the problem of Defenderism in the Irish countryside – as soon as they were suppressed in one place, they arose in another; it faced the problem of the United Irishmen, who had able propagandists (such as Tone), and the support of a newspaper, the *Northern Star* in Belfast;

---

[49] See Westmorland to Dundas, 21 Jan. 1794 (NA, HO/100/51/55), for a summary of the aims of the United Irishmen, contrasted with Defenderism. [50] Jim Smyth, *The men of no property* (London, 1992), pp 33-45. [51] Nancy Curtin, *The United Irishmen* (Oxford, 1994), pp 145-73. [52] William Drennan to Martha McTier, 25 June 1794, printed in Jean Agnew (ed.), *The Drennan–McTier Letters, 1794–1801*, 2 vols (Dublin, 1999), ii, 66ff.

it faced the possibility of a revival of the Volunteer movement which it feared because of its independence from government control; and it had to face a Catholic Relief bill promoted by Westminster against the wishes of a conservative Irish parliament. The army, under strength, was involved in counter-insurgency operations, and in guarding possible targets, mostly the houses of the gentry. Then on 1 February 1793 war was declared with revolutionary France.

THE PROBLEM OF DEFENCE

Government now had two problems, not only internal disaffection but possible French invasion, and there was in Ireland an organization that actively wanted such French involvement. To this was added the immediate demand by ministers in London for soldiers to fight the French. In 1793 the Irish establishment had some 9,000 regular army 'effectives' out of its total of 15,000 men. Some 4,000 were permitted to be absent, and many units were at 'skeleton' strength. The government in London was extremely unlikely to allow a large regular army to remain in Ireland, but the Castle had to face problems of internal and external defence, and avoid the possibility of popular clamour for a restoration of the Volunteers. As Bartlett says, 'If only to avoid a Volunteer revival, they simply had to attend to the defence of Ireland. At the same time the problem for the military authorities was that a *possible* [sic] French invasion of Ireland, required the *certain* [sic] presence of a large force of troops there.'[53] These problems could lead to only one conclusion – that the state would have to cease discussing the need for a reserve army, and whether or not armed Catholics should be in it, but to go ahead actually to form one, since the Relief Act of 1793 had removed almost all restrictions, save sitting in parliament (and certain senior positions in the armed services, judiciary and government), such a reserve army would have to include Catholics. The answer was to raise a militia, and on 4 March 1793 the Militia bill was introduced into the Irish house of commons. It went through all its stages swiftly, and became law on 26 March.[54] Thus the defence of Ireland was, for the first time, to be entrusted to its own people, Protestant and Catholic, although the latter were in the eyes of many, uncertain and untried.

---

53 Thomas Bartlett, 'Counter insurgency and rebellion, Ireland 1793–1803', in Bartlett and Jeffery (eds), *A military history of Ireland*, p. 249.   54 *CJI*, vol. 15.

THE MILITIA BILL

The sponsor of the Militia bill was Lord Hillsborough, heir to the marquess of Downshire, who had one of the largest estates in Ireland. Hillsborough himself was something of an enigma. Despite his great wealth he failed to become lord lieutenant, and to obtain the next 'step' in the peerage – a dukedom. He can be described as an 'innovator', he worked hard to get the militia established, and although General Robert Cunningham told him he was 'the father of all the militia in the country',[55] like many people who work tirelessly to get something 'off the ground', once he had done so, he lost interest in it. He became colonel of the Royal Downshire Regiment and his subsequent neglect of his regiment must have counted against him when he ran foul of Lord Cornwallis, the lord lieutenant later in the decade. However, with regard to the militia there was no question but that it would include Roman Catholics; there was to be absolutely no reason 'why in respect of arms, they are to be distinguished from the rest of His Majesty's subjects.'[56] Hillsborough, in the debates on the bill, had to contend with three things: first, to counter the assertion that the creation of a militia would give the Castle more opportunities for patronage in the appointment of officers, and, connected with this, whether or not the lieutenant-colonels commandant of each regiment should be the governors of the counties. There was considerable opposition in the Irish parliament at this time to any increase in the powers of patronage of the lord lieutenant, and considerable jealousy of the powers that he had, for parliament wanted control over patronage to be its own privilege; second, the numbers of men to be raised for each county regiment; and third, provision for the families of balloted men. Hillsborough did not exercise the same degree of care in dealing with each of these questions.

On the first point, Hillsborough assured the House that the bill was a copy of the English act of 1757. The appointment of officers was to be for the country's safety and not a matter of patronage or party. Lieutenant-colonels commandant were to be appointed by the lord lieutenant; they might or might not be county governors; and the lieutenant-colonels commandant were to appoint the officers.[57] In the same debate, General Robert Cunninghame, shortly to become commander-in-chief, observed that forming and embodying a militia would take at least three months, and that there should be no postponement of the passage of the bill, as had been proposed by Henry Grattan, who had risen to say that he was not an enemy of the bill, but that it was being passed by acclamation, not deliberation. 'He wished to confine it to constitutional

---

[55] Gen. Robert Cunninghame to Lord Downshire, 2 Dec. 1793 (PRONI, D/607/C/17). [56] Dundas to Westmorland, 7 Jan. 1793 (NA, HO/100/43/128). [57] *Faulkner's Journal*, 9 Mar. 1793.

principles, there was but one ground upon which it could be necessary – the apprehension of a descent from France, in that case it would be wise to conciliate the nation to it but nothing could tend to make it so completely unpopular as precipitating it through the House.'[58]

In the second matter, at the committee stage of the bill on 8 March 1793, the question of the size of the militia was discussed, as well as the value of the property qualifications of the lieutenant-colonels commandant. In the case of the latter, it was felt that the figure in the English act was too low, so it was raised from £1,000 to £2,000, with that of a lieutenant-colonel going up to £1,600. Hillsborough then outlined his thinking on the numbers of men to be raised, which he based on either the number of acres or the number of hearths in each county.[59] He apportioned 5½ men for every 3,000 acres, or 21 men for every 1,000 hearths. Hillsborough did not say how he arrived at these figures. McAnally thought that it was a prior decision made in order to raise an aggregate of some 16,000 men, and that is probably correct.[60] What Hillsborough found, however, was that, 'notwithstanding the inequality of proportions as to acres and hearths in each county individually, yet, when the whole numbers of men on each calculation were added, the difference between both was not one hundred, that on the calculation of acres was 15,655, and that on the number of hearths, 15,560.'[61]

Consideration of these two points was short, and the implications imperfectly thought through, and in that sense Grattan was right. Vesting the power of appointment of officers in the lieutenant-colonel commandant, and not in the lord lieutenant or the governor of the county (as in England), certainly removed an opportunity for Castle patronage, but, in its stead created one for the commandant. There was nothing to stop him appointing family members, as Lord O'Neill did when he appointed his two sons as ensigns in the Antrim Regiment, and promptly asked for six months' leave for both of them for the benefit of their education at Cambridge University, on full pay when the regiment was embodied, of course.[62] This request was approved. In fact almost every colonel commandant appointed family members to a commission. It also gave the militia colonels more power vis-à-vis the lord lieutenant as many of them were county governors, and others were peers, or members of the house of commons. This power made them hard to manage in an army which was at the disposal of the Castle, for a regular army officer, even colonels of regiments, obeyed the commander-in-chief – and this situation was unfamiliar and unwelcome. Officer competence, and officer absence, became two major problems with the Irish militia throughout

---

58 Ibid., 9 Mar. 1793.   59 Ibid., 12 Mar. 1793.   60 McAnally, *Irish Militia*, p. 24.   61 *Faulkner's Journal*, 12 Mar. 1793.   62 Memorial of Lord O'Neill, 4 Nov. 1793 (NLI, KP/1189/10).

this story, and the powers of the commander-in-chief were limited especially if a commandant did not do his duty and promptly replace officers who had resigned, died, or been dismissed. It is ironic that in this respect Hillsborough himself would become one of the worst offenders, and his regiment, the Royal Downshire, would suffer much from his subsequent neglect.

The numbers of men to be raised by each county may have been equitable in respect to acres or hearths, but this did not make military sense, as each county unit would be of a different strength. In the regular army all infantry regiments were composed of ten companies and had the same 'establishment' of officers and men. In the Irish militia this was not so, with an obvious resulting disadvantage as some regiments would be of no use in certain situations because they were too small (for example, the Drogheda Battalion with only three companies and less than two hundred men was the smallest), or some too large (the biggest being the Royal Downshire with 12 companies). On the march, or in cantonments, a regiment the size of the Royal Downshire would create enormous problems for the barrackmasters. As will be seen, in 1799-1800 the Drogheda was amalgamated with the Louth, and the Downshire divided into two battalions.

Finally, in the debate in the house of lords on 22 March,[63] the third problem was raised but not resolved. The earl of Portarlington, soon to be the lieutenant-colonel commandant of the Queen's County Regiment, claimed that there was no provision in the bill for the families of balloted men. He said that it would be impossible for their families to exist unless something was done for them. Lord Enniskillen, himself soon to be the lieutenant-colonel commandant of the Fermanagh Battalion, agreed and remarked that the 'Militia would be circumstanced in this respect as was His Majesty's army.'[64] This was an unsatisfactory answer. Nothing was done, and not surprisingly when the bill was enacted a few days later, there was an outbreak of violence against it.

THE MILITIA ACT[65]

Before discussing the effect of the Act, and considering what had been created, it would be well to describe the Irish militia on its foundation. The act created a force of 38 regiments of different sizes, one or more for each county or county borough in Ireland. Some counties were divided (the North and the South Mayo, North and South Cork), and the county boroughs that decided to take part were the city of Limerick, city of Cork, city of Dublin, and city of Drogheda. Regiments were divided into groups by size of population as follows:

63 *Faulkner's Journal*, 27 Mar. 1793. 64 Ibid. 65 33 Geo. III, c. 22.

Companies	Strength	Regiments
12	770	Royal Downshire
10	560	Tipperary, Wexford, Galway, Donegal, Londonderry and Tyrone
8	488	Cork City, Cork North and South, Kerry, Waterford, Monaghan, Antrim, Meath
8	420	Limerick County, Dublin City, Kilkenny, King's County, Roscommon, Armagh
7	350	North and South Mayo
6	280	Dublin County, Longford
6	356	Queen's County, Wicklow, Clare, Louth, Fermanagh
6	350	Leitrim, Sligo, Cavan, Westmeath
6	305	Limerick City
5	280	Kildare
5	244	Carlow
3	183	Drogheda

Table 1: Regimental establishments of the Irish militia, 1793

Units of seven companies and more were called 'regiments', and units of six companies and less were known as 'battalions.' This nomenclature will be used henceforth. The act should be looked at from three perspectives. First, raising the officers and men; second, the ballot; and third, conditions of service for officers and men.

In order to put the act into force, the governors of the counties were empowered to call out the militia once a year for twenty-eight days' training. They had to appoint deputy governors throughout the county to conduct the ballot, and other militia business, and the names of the deputy governors had to be submitted to the lord lieutenant within fourteen days (presumably fourteen days from appointment, but on this point the wording of the act is unclear). Deputy governors had to be property owners within the county to the value of at least £200 a year. This property qualification had to be certified before a clerk of the peace, and names had to be published in the *Dublin Gazette*.

Lord Hillsborough was governor of Co. Down, and a record exists of his efforts in March and April 1793 to appoint deputy governors in his own county. He offered a commission to the Hon. Robert Stewart (the future Lord Castlereagh), son of his great rival, Lord Londonderry, but Stewart declined as he had already accepted a commission as lieutenant-colonel of the Londonderry Regiment. He did, however, agree to become a deputy governor.[66] Others who accepted included Robert Johnston Smyth of St John's Point,[67] Thomas Waring of Newry, J. Isaac of Holywood (although he pointed out that he was eighty years old), Thomas Knox Gordon of Loyalty Lodge, Sir Richard Johnston of Gilford, the Revd Cornelius Lascelles of Killough, the earl of Clanbrassil (who had property in Co. Down, but lived in Dundalk, Co. Louth), Robert Ross Rowan of Mulloghmore, Cromwell Price of Hollymount (who became an officer in the Regiment), John Moore of Mourne Park, W. Rainey of Greenville, James Waddell of Islandderry, and Patrick Savage of Portaferry. Those who refused included Arthur Johnston of Rademon (Crossgar), Savage Hall of Narrow Water (who was commissioned into the Armagh Regiment), Nicholas and Francis Price of Saintfield, Henry Savage of Rocksavage, and John Kennedy of Cultra, who refused out of loyalty to the old Volunteers and complained, 'In truth, the want of promulgation to our new laws, renders it difficult for people in my humble sphere of life to know what is law, and what not, or to judge of the beneficial tendency of the same. I cannot but think that a motion, if made in the Houses of Parliament, for the better promulgation of our laws, would prove materially useful to the Kingdom.'[68] Hillsborough had obviously approached Kennedy either before the act became law, or so soon after it that poor Kennedy knew nothing about it. Others who refused included John Waring of Bede Hall, Gawn Hamilton of Killyleagh, Charles Inez of Dromatine, and Thomas Douglas of Grace Hall. This list is probably incomplete, but it does cover most of Co. Down, and also shows that Hillsborough approached those whom he considered best for the job irrespective of their political leanings. Wybrants Oliphant in Co. Donegal when refusing the invitation to be a deputy governor in that county made a prescient comment. He foresaw difficulties in putting the militia act into operation because governors and deputy governors might not always be available, that the clerk of the peace was becoming little more than a recruiting sergeant, and that the laws respecting deputy governors were so strict as to possibly be penal. He objected to the clause in the act levying a penalty for men deficient, 'an arbitrary act of police rather than a free and voluntary union of good citizens, which a militia ought to be composed of,' he said.[69]

The lieutenant-colonel commandant appointed officers, and they, too, had to have a property qualification, sworn before a clerk of the peace, before names could be published in the *Dublin Gazette*. These property qualifications were as follows:

[66] Stewart to Hillsborough, n.d. (PRONI, D/607/B/386). [67] All of these acceptances and refusals are to be found in the Downshire Papers (PRONI, D/607/B/387 ff). [68] Kennedy to Hillsborough, 17 Apr. 1793 (ibid., D/607/B/399). [69] Wybrants Oliphant to Lord Clements, — Apr. 1793 (NLI, Clements Papers PC 633).

Lieutenant-Colonel commandant	£2,000, or heir to £3,000
Lieutenant-Colonel	£1,600, or heir to £1,800
Major	£300, or heir to £600
Captain	£200, or heir to £400
Lieutenant	£50, or personal estate alone, £500, or son of a person of £100 a year, or personal estate of £1,000
Ensign	£20, or personal estate alone, £250, or son of a person of £50 a year, or personal estate of £300

Table 2: Property qualifications of militia officers

Lieutenants and ensigns were expected to be younger men, who may not have inherited, so a 'subaltern', the generic term for both ranks, could be possessed of no property at all, provided he was an heir. Almost certainly this provision was abused, but evidence of such abuse is difficult to find, because deserving NCOs were promoted from the ranks in both the militia and the regular army. Officers appointed to the positions of adjutant, quartermaster, paymaster, surgeon and surgeon's mate did not require a property qualification in order to be commissioned either.

At least two property certificates survive. Both are in respect of the City of Limerick Battalion, and both are signed by Edward Parkes, clerk of the peace. The first is in respect of Charles Vereker, and is dated 16 May 1793. He was appointed lieutenant-colonel by his relative, John Prendergast Smyth, the lieutenant-colonel commandant (and later Lord Gort). Vereker commanded his battalion against the French at Collooney in 1798. The second is dated a few days earlier, on 11 May 1793, and is in respect of 'Hugh Gough Yr' of Woodsdown 'in the Liberties of the City of Limerick', who certified that, 'I am possessed for my own use of a personal estate in this Kingdom of the value of two hundred pounds and upwards'.[70] Hugh Gough soon transferred to the regular army, and, as a major, commanded the 2nd Battalion 87th Foot (later the Royal Irish Fusiliers), at the battle of Barrossa in Spain in 1811 when they captured a French Eagle. He was one of the most famous generals of the early Victorian era in India, and retired a field marshal, and a viscount, probably the most famous soldier to come from the Irish militia.[71]

Deputy governors were responsible for raising the men, through the ballot, or by substitution, or by volunteers (although volunteers were not specif-

[70] Records of the Limerick Artillery Militia (NA, WO/6 8/5 9). [71] Brig. A.E.C. Bredin, *A history of the Irish soldier* (Belfast, 1987), pp 244, 307–10.

ically mentioned in the act), but the ballot was the nub of a constitutional militia. Each year, before 24 October, and giving fourteen days notice, the governor and deputy governors of counties had to arrange an 'annual meeting.' For this meeting parish constables were obliged to make a return of all men dwelling in their respective parishes between the ages of 18 and 45, showing rank, profession, and occupation. These returns had to be with the governor and deputy governors seven days before the meeting, who then made a list of those eligible to be balloted, which was fixed to the door of the parish church. At the meeting the names of those eligible were written on slips of paper, rolled up, and put into a box by the clerk. Then the names of men, to the number in that parish or division or sub-division required by the regiment, would be drawn by the constable in front of the governor and deputy governors. Another meeting was held some fourteen days later, when the balloted men had to appear and take the oath. Everything was to be done in as public a manner as possible. Dates of meetings were published in the press, and the draw was available for all to see.

However, although militiamen were raised by ballot, there were ways to avoid service, or even the ballot itself. First there was a category of exempted persons: peers, commissioned officers of other forces, non-commissioned officers, privates, or commissioned officers who had served four years in the militia, members of the university (of Dublin), clergymen or licensed teachers of any congregation, constables or peace officers, articled clerks or apprentices, seamen, employees of HM Ordnance, any poor man not able to pay Hearth money, who had more than three children born in wedlock, persons with infirmities, or under 5 feet 4 inches in height. Second, a balloted man could pay a fine of £10 and be exempted from service, but at the end of four years would be liable for service again. A balloted man could produce a substitute to serve in his place for four years, and, of course, men could volunteer for service, in which case it might not be necessary to hold a ballot. There was no mention of volunteers in the act, but a very substantial part of the militia was composed of them. The Kerry Regiment, for example, was raised in one day entirely from volunteers.[72] The ballot and its effects will be discussed in the next chapter.

The third aspect of the act was the terms and conditions of service for officers and men. As mentioned, regiments were to have three 'field officers' (lieutenant-colonel commandant, lieutenant-colonel, and major); battalions were to have two field officers (a lieutenant-colonel and a major); and battalions with less than five companies were to have one field officer only (a major). Field officers were also company commanders (captains). There was

[72] Memorial of the earl of Glandore to Lord Camden, n.d., but after July 1795 (NA, WO/68/411/72, Kerry Militia order book).

the 'colonel's company', the 'major's company', and so on. Each company had three officers: a captain, a lieutenant, and an ensign. Battalions had either a 'grenadier' or a 'light' company, and regiments had both. These two specialist companies had two lieutenants, instead of one, and an ensign. The utility of grenadiers in warfare had died out by this time, but the grenadier company was the 'senior' one, and a coveted command. The custom was to select the tallest men in the regiment for this company.

The light company was an innovation of the Seven Years' War in America. Its soldiers were taught to operate in small groups, and to use initiative; they acted as scouts and skirmishers. The grenadier company was on the 'right of the line' (of battle), and the light company on the left of the line. Hence both companies were known as 'flank' companies. The number of men in each company was to be not less than 50, or more than 100. In 1793 it was just less than 60. There were to be three sergeants and three corporals for every 20 men, and two drummers in each company. This ratio of sergeants to men was not always achieved.

If we look at an example of an eight-company regiment, such as the North Cork, stationed at Carrick-on-Shannon, Co. Roscommon, on 30 September 1795, we would expect them to have eight company commanders – three field officers and five captains, and indeed they did: Lieutenant-Colonel Commandant Lord Kingsborough, Lieutenant-Colonel Lord Kingsale, and Major Richard Foote, Captains Edward Heard, James Lombard, the Hon. William de Courcy, William Snowe, and William Johnston. With eight companies, including a grenadier and a light, they should have had ten lieutenants, and six ensigns. In fact there were nine lieutenants and a captain-lieutenant (an old rank, retained in the militia, effectively the senior lieutenant), and there were also six ensigns. The captain-lieutenant was Edward Hoare, who was also adjutant; the lieutenants were Charles Venters, also quartermaster, John O'Hea, Daniel Williams, also surgeon, Michael Bourke, Thomas Paye, Nicholas Cole Bowen, Thomas Davenport, Thomas Daunt, and John Roe; and the ensigns were Charles Barry, Thomas Holmes Justice, also surgeon's mate, John Ware, Thomas McGrath, and Robert Atkins. (We will meet many of these names again in 1798.) The regiment had 432 private men, and on the ratio of three sergeants and three corporals to every 20 men, we would expect to find some 64 of each rank, but in fact, there are 32 sergeants, and 29 corporals. The ratio laid down in the act was never achieved, but the ratio of sergeants and corporals combined to private men at 1:7 was within the parameters of the British Army at the time.[73] Bearing in mind that some sergeants were always employed on administrative tasks, such as clerks, quartermaster-sergeants, and so on, this was more realistic.

73 Muster rolls and pay lists, North Cork Militia (ibid., WO/13/2706).

Each regiment or battalion had an adjutant (the commanding officer's principal staff officer), a quartermaster, surgeon, surgeon's mate, paymaster, and a chaplain. The latter was often given permanent permission by the commandant to be absent, and the spiritual needs of the men were taken care of by 'officiating' chaplains, who were usually local clergy, Protestant and Catholic, and who were paid from the chaplain's army pay. The paymaster could be a clerk, but was almost always an officer. The act gave the rates of pay for sergeants, corporals, and drummers, as well as the 'staff' pay of the adjutant. All non-commissioned officers and men, after 16 years' service, were eligible to be placed on the pension list of Kilmainham or Chelsea Hospitals. In fact the first pensioner from the Irish militia to go to Kilmainham was one Simon Grogan, late of the Tipperary Regiment and the 28th Foot, who was placed on pension on 28 September 1793, and between 1793 and April 1802, 466 men from the Irish militia were granted pensions at Kilmainham.[74]

The regiments or battalions were to be embodied once a year for twenty-eight days, during which time the men were to be subject to the Mutiny Act (but not to 'life and limb'). Provision was made for the militia to be permanently embodied (that is, to serve full time), by command of the lord lieutenant, but it was expressly forbidden to leave Ireland. Finally the Act dealt with bounties for enlistment (one guinea, known as the 'marching guinea'), on embodiment (one guinea), and for prolongation of service beyond four years (one guinea, but when the first period of service ended in 1797, the inducement was much more.)

The act also dealt with a number of administrative matters, but it had a number of major flaws, quite apart from its indecisiveness on whether the militia was to be a full-time or a part-time force, or even to have a full time 'permanent' cadre. Indeed, as will be seen in the next chapter, part-time service, and not serving outside the home county, was used in good faith as a recruiting incentive, yet both turned out to be completely erroneous. The most glaring flaw, however, was the fact that the act did not specifically mention that privates were to be paid, other than a reference in paragraph ninety-four that they were to receive the same pay as regulars if embodied. The reason for this was perfectly understandable in government and regular army circles, because pay was dealt with in the annual 'pay and money' bill, as in Great Britain. In addition, whether full-time, or part-time, there was absolutely no provision for the payment of a family allowance for married men, or for the quartering of families, or provision for the families of balloted men. These were the doubts raised by Lord Portarlington in the house of lords on 22 March 1793 that had gone unanswered.[75] The effect was explosive.

74 Admissions to the Royal Hospital, Kilmainham (ibid., WO/118/36). 75 *Faulkner's Journal*, 23 Mar. 1793.

The act allowed 'dual commissions.' The adjutant, quartermaster, paymaster, surgeon, and surgeon's mate, were also company officers, which meant that in many instances they were no good in either role. One of the officers of the North Cork Regiment killed at Oulart Hill in 1798 was Lieutenant Daniel Williams, the regimental surgeon, but acting as an infantry officer. In so far as surgeons and mates were concerned, dual commissions were abolished in October 1798.[76]

Section six of the act concerned action to be taken if the lieutenant-colonel commandant was out of the kingdom (of Ireland), and it became necessary to appoint or promote officers. The act stated that the power was to devolve to the lieutenant-colonel, of the regiment or battalion, 'or next commanding officer for the time being'. This was confusing: was it to be the lieutenant-colonel, who could be anywhere in Ireland, or the officer actually in command of the unit? It caused a tremendous row in 1798 in the Royal Downshire Regiment between Lieutenant-Colonel Lord Annesley, and Major George Matthews. The latter was in command of the regiment at Loughrea. Annesley was at home at Mount Panther,[77] and Downshire was in England. Matthews promoted an officer to command of the Grenadier Company, which Annesley had promised to another, and Annesley objected under this section of the act.[78] This matter will be discussed later in another context, but there was no resolution to the question. In 1800, however, Lord Granard, colonel commandant of the Longford Battalion, did ask the Castle for a ruling on this very subject, and received an uncompromising reply from the military secretary, Lieutenant-Colonel E.B. Littlehales: 'I am enjoined to state, that it is not the practice in my branch of the King's service that the colonel of a regiment shall be allowed during his absence, in any degree, to interfere with the interior discipline, oeconomy [sic], and command of his Corps.'[79] The 'commanding officer', therefore, was the one actually in command of the regiment.

The act was a slavish copy of the English act of 35 years before. There is no record that Hillsborough sought any advice on the operation of this act, which, it was well known, had caused serious rioting and many deaths when enacted. The Irish act was 'slavish' because it repeated the errors of the earlier act: it did not properly define the period of service, or pay and allowances, or where the militia was to serve. These matters were to cause a great deal of confusion in the coming months in the minds of all concerned, governors and governed. There were some differences, however. The com-

---

[76] Castlereagh to Clements, 10 Oct. 1798 (NA, WO/6 8/2 2 1/5 8, back of book). [77] Between Clough and Dundrum, Co. Down. [78] Matthews to Downshire, 1 June 1798 (PRONI, D/607/F/1 9 1ff). [79] Littlehales to Granard, 9 June 1800 (NLI, M3 4 7 5/3 3, Royal Longford Militia letter book).

plete Irish militia was to be raised in a short period, while the English militia had been raised intermittently between 1759 and 1779; the Irish act was to raise a permanent force, whereas the English act had an initial life-span of five years. Furthermore the Irish act enjoyed the approbation of the Irish landed gentry who were expected to form the officer corps, whereas in England the 1757 act had been unpopular, the gentry had not wished to serve, nor had the ordinary people. But at least Ireland had another army, and the strains of land tenure, of religion, politics, and military necessity, had fused. The effects will be discussed in the next chapter.

CHAPTER THREE

The institution

There was much confusion when the Militia bill became law on 26 March 1793.[1] The commanding officers of the new regiments had to organize places of muster. In many cases they were governors of counties, who had to organize deputy governors in order to apply the act and hold the ballot. They had to appoint field officers, officers for the companies, an agent (every regiment had an agent who issued pay, and acted on the regiments behalf with the commander-in-chief's office on administrative and financial matters), hire a tailor to make uniforms, a chandler to make equipment; find an adjutant; appoint a quartermaster; together with many other things including dealing with solicitations for commissions and advancement. Ireland being an intensely hierarchical society, there was naturally competition to have the best turned out and the smartest regiment. The prefix 'royal' was much sought after, as was the patronage of members of the royal family. In April 1793 Viscount Headfort and Sir Laurence Parsons applied for their regiments, the Meath and the King's County, to be made 'royal'. Parsons did not succeed, but Headfort obviously did, as hereafter his regiment was known as the 'Royal Meath'.[2] In the same month, the Hon. William Conyngham applied for the Donegals to be the 'Prince of Wales's', which was granted.[3] In May Colonel Longfield asked for the honour of becoming a royal regiment for the City of Cork, as did Lord Muskerry for the County of Limerick.[4] These do not seem to have been successful, but Lord Granard was successful in getting the Prince of Wales to agree to his name being added to the Longfords.[5] Lord Abercorn said he was going to ask the king to make the Tyrone's a 'royal' regiment on 15 April 1793, and on 17 April 1793, announced that the king had agreed. The gap between request and approval is suspiciously short, but the regiment was known as the 'Royal Tyrone' ever after.[6] Obviously, having a member of the peerage as a colonel helped in this matter of patronage. Although the city regiments of Dublin, Cork, and Limerick

---

1 *CJI*, xv (1792–94).   2 Westmorland to Dundas, 12 Apr. 1793 (NA, HO/100/39/282).   3 Ibid., 26 Apr. 1793 (ibid., HO/100/39/317).   4 Ibid., 6 May 1793 (ibid., HO/100/39/343).   5 Westmorland to Dundas, 15 May 1793 (ibid., HO/100/39/381).   6 Lord Abercorn to Thomas Knox, 15 and 17 Apr. 1793 (PRONI, D/623/A/77/47, Abercorn papers).

were known as 'Royal', the only truly royal regiments in the Irish militia were the Meath, and the Downshire, but in the latter case the distinction predated the 1793 Act. Regiments formed bands, received colours, and forever asked for distinctions in their uniforms, which were usually refused.

The act could not be effective until the government had ordered the different regiments to 'form up', or 'embody'. The first group – the Dublin City, Dublin County, Kilkenny, King's County, Meath, Westmeath, Carlow, Leitrim, Longford, Louth, and Drogheda, were ordered to embody by proclamation on 20 April 1793,[7] and all the others followed in a series of proclamations made thereafter up to 13 June, the last regiment being the Kildare.[8] These proclamations were the legal authority for the governors of the counties to call the meetings, to hold the ballot, to enlist men, arrange a depot, and for funds to be released to cover the costs. When the regiments had reached a quota of men, the commanding officers informed the Castle that the regiment was embodied, which meant that this 'forming up' or 'embodiment' date triggered an announcement from the commander-in-chief proclaiming the regiment to be 'embodied', and so could be paid, receive arms, and so on. The quota for the Irish militia is not known, but in the English militia it was three-fifths of establishment, and it may well have been the same in Ireland.[9] It was in this period between the proclamation to embody, and the date of compliance, that there were the disturbances now known as the 'militia riots'. Because the proclamations ordering the county regiments to embody were issued on different dates, riots, where they occurred, coincided with this balloting period between April and July 1793.

THE MILITIA RIOTS

The point has already been made that there were disturbances in rural Ireland before the passing of the Militia Act, and that the imposition of this act created yet another event which could be used to foment trouble in the countryside. Historians have accepted the disturbances in March, April, May and June 1793, as the reason why the ballot was abandoned in much of the country later, and this exhibits how unpopular the concept of a compulsory militia was throughout Ireland.

In the period before the Militia bill, the government was most concerned about the violence in the countryside, the activities of the Catholic Committee

---

7 *Freeman's Journal*, 20 Apr. 1793. 8 Ibid., 13 June 1793. 9 Militia Act 1757.

in promoting Catholic relief, the activities of the United Irishmen, and the Defenders. They were very concerned about the reports of arms smuggling, and, at this stage, linked the violence of the Defenders with the aims of the Catholic Committee. Indeed, in November 1792 William Pitt wrote to Lord Westmorland, the lord lieutenant, expressing his concern that arms might reach Ireland, and that any check on the aims of the Catholic Convention may lead to violence or 'signal for a general rising'. Pitt went on, 'My opinion is invariable as to the necessity of vigorously resisting force or menace, but the more I think on the subject, the more I regret that firmness against violence is not accompanied by symptoms of a disposition to conciliate, and by holding out at least the possibility of future concessions in return for a perserverance in peaceable and loyal conduct.'[10] His quotation explains much of the thinking behind the Catholic Relief bill of 1792, but violence in the countryside did not decrease, although it ceased to be linked to the activities of the Catholic Committee in the eyes of the government, and instead was regarded as the work of the Defenders.

There was a report on 1 January 1793 of Defenders in Louth, breaking into forty Protestant houses in a fortnight, and carrying off arms, twice attacking the Primate's house, Rokeby Hall (built by Archbishop Robinson at Dunleer, Co. Louth), being repulsed at McClintock's also in Louth, after a fire of thirty rounds. They got a stand of arms (a musket and a bayonet) at Thomas Foster's (the son of Speaker Foster), and seized a further 120 arms in December 1792.[11] On 24 January 1793 there was a report that the Revd Young, a magistrate, supported by forty gentlemen, and twenty soldiers, had approached near 500 Defenders near Bailieborough, Co. Cavan. The Defenders had fired on them, wounding two of the soldiers. Fire was returned, eighteen men were killed, and twenty more found dead of their wounds in ditches later, while thirty-five were arrested and imprisoned.[12] These two incidents show that a degree of violence had crept into Irish disturbances that had not been there before, occurring some time before the militia was proposed. More examples could be provided of violent incidents that antedated the formation of the militia, but the militia act itself provided an impetus to even more trouble. From the viewpoint of the Castle questions about the utility of a militia as a fighting force, and of the efficiency of the ballot as a means of raising men, loomed as large, if not larger, than the issue of political reaction to the Militia Act and the disturbances it provoked. The government in London was extremely unlikely to allow the 11,094 soldiers in Ireland in 1793 to remain, and indeed the number did decline to less that 2,000 by 1797.[13]

10 Pitt to Westmorland, 10 Nov. 1792 (NA, HO/100/38/375). 11 *Faulkner's Journal*, 1 Jan. 1793. 12 Ibid., 24 Jan. 1793. 13 K.P. Ferguson, 'The army in Ireland from the Restoration

There was some disturbance on the passing of the act. On 21 March 1793 Charles Drake Dillon described to his father, Baron Dillon, how a mob came to his house at Lismullen, Co. Meath. He had to give up two guns and three pistols, windows and sashes were broken, his wife Charlotte was terrified, therefore they had removed to 13 Sackville Street, Dublin. He said the 'militia business' was responsible.[14]

However, the militia riots occurred during the period of the embodiment of the regiments, that is, between the proclamation and the date of compliance[15]. This meant that the disturbances happened at different times in different counties. Some regiments took longer than others to raise, but this had as much to do with size of the county, terrain, population, and the enthusiasm of the deputy governors, as with the occurrence of riots. The sources of evidence for the militia riots are not extensive. They are to be found in newspaper reports, and in the letters of the lord lieutenant to the home secretary in London.[16] All repeated information from each other, which often differed in content, date, and participants, even if it was the same event that was being described. In considering the disturbances, only those where something happened have been counted. There were many reports of mobs, and their intentions, but so often these remained just rumour, one of symptoms of the poor communications of the late eighteenth century. 'The pusillanimity and fear of people here is beyond description, and the alarms and reports they spread are incredible,' said John Straton of Rathkeale, concerning an affair at Bruff, Co. Limerick, in July 1793.[17]

The counties worst affected by the militia riots stretch in a broad band across the middle of Ireland from Mayo in the north west to Carlow in the south east, with only one place above, and one place below this band. It is easiest to consider the riots by counties rather than by provinces because of the different dates of the proclamations or orders to embody. The 'epicentre' of trouble was Co. Roscommon, which was probably the most disaffected county of all. The extent of the riots is summarized in Table 3.

This table shows that the worst month for violence was May 1793, which is hardly surprising as the majority of counties had been ordered to embody their militias in the previous month. The total numbers of those killed in the riots will never be known accurately but it must have been well over one hundred. The riots were worst in the counties which had previously been troubled by Defender violence with the exceptions of Down and Kerry.

---

to the Act of Union' (PhD, TCD, 1980).   **14** Charles Drake Dillon to Baron Dillon, [c. 21 Mar.1793] (NA, HO/100/46). Unbound.   **15** For a further comprehensive analysis of the militia riots and the ballot see Ivan F. Nelson, 'The first chapter of 1798?Restoring a military perspective to the Irish militia riots of 1793' in *IHS*, 33:132 (2003), 369-86.   **16** The NA HO/100 series.   **17** John Straton to the Hon. Revd P. Jocelyn, Stradbally (Queen's County), 21 July 1793 (PRONI, MIC/147/9).

County Regiment	Order to embody	Compliance	Date/s of rioting
North and South Mayo	8 May	6 Sept.	7 July
Sligo	25 Apr.	6 July	17 May
			18 May
			21 May
			30 May
			n.d.
Roscommon	25 Apr.	10 Aug.	9 May
			15 May
			21 May
			23 May
			25 May
Fermanagh	3 May	6 July	30 May
Cavan	25 Apr.	n.d.	19 June
Longford	20 Apr.	6 June	n.d.
Westmeath	20 Apr.	6 July	1 June
Meath	20 Apr.	22 June	17 May
			28 May
			30 May
			n.d.
Louth	20 Apr.	7 June	n.d.
Dublin	20 Apr.	20 June	n.d.
Queen's County	20 Apr.	n.d.	n.d.
Carlow	20 Apr.	17 June	18 June
Kilkenny	n.d.	10 Aug.	3 June
Kerry	25 Apr.	6 July	29 May
			19 June
			n.d.
Down	29 Apr.	31 Aug.	n.d.

Table 3: Militia riots, 1793

18 *Faulkner's Journal*, 12 July 1793 19 *Freeman's Journal*, 17 May 1793. 20 *Faulkner's Journal*, 30 June 1793. 21 Extract of disturbances in Leitrim, Mayo, Roscommon, and Sligo (NA, HO/100/44/7). 22 *Faulkner's Journal*, 30 May 1793. 23 *Freeman's Journal*, 25 May 1793. 24 Extract of disturbances in Leitrim, Mayo, Roscommon, and Sligo (NA, HO/100/44/7). 25 *Freeman's Journal*, 25 May 1793. 26 Capt. John Grey to Col. Cradock, 27 May 1793 (NA, HO/100/44/80). 27 *Freeman's Journal*, 25 May 1793. 28 Ibid. 29 Ibid., 30 May 1798. 30 Ibid., 19 June 1793. 31 Westmorland to Dundas, n.d. (NA, HO/100/44/115). 32 *Faulkner's*

Details

Erris. Riot, 46 rioters and 6 soldiers killed.[18]
Priest threatened over making lists.[19]
Ballyfarnan. 8 local houses attacked[20]
16 prisoners liberated.[21]
Riots against militia.[22]
Skreen. Clergy attacked.[23]
Carrick-on-Shannon. 7 killed by dragoons while trying to liberate prisoners.[24]
Mr Tenison's house ransacked.[25]
41st Foot attacked near Manorhamilton.[26]
Castlerea. Mob seize 70 stand of arms.[27]
Lackey and Turrough. Sir Edward Crofton and 12 cavalrymen attacked. 7 rioters killed.[28]
Enniskillen. Riot, 7 killed, 100 prisoners.[29]
Ballymenagh. Mob demanded, and got, militia list that they destroyed.[30]
Granard. Lord Granard rescued from mob during ballot.[31]
Athlone. Offices of Thomas Harrison set on fire.[32]
Kilbrew. Defenders confronted Mr Hamilton Gorges.[33]
Subdivision meeting broken up.[34]
Athboy market. Riot, Defenders lost 10 killed, 20 wounded.[35]
Kells. Murder of Mr Daly.[36]
Rioting. (No details).[37]
Rathdown. Constable assaulted.[38]
Maryborough. Constable and son burnt to death.[39]
High Sheriff attacked. 7 killed.
Castlecomer. Murder of Mrs Wilson of Mooneenro and her son.[40]
Dingle. Riot.[41]
Dingle. Riot. 12 killed.[42]
Tralee. Riot, 14 killed.[43]
Castlereagh. Riot at ballot.[44]

Journal, 5 June 1793. 33 *Freeman's Journal*, 18 May 1793. 34 Unknown location. Extract of disturbances in Leitrim, Mayo, Roscommon, and Sligo (NA, HO/100/44/7). 35 *Faulkner's Journal*, 30 May 1793. 36 Westmorland to Dundas, n.d. (NA, HO/100/44/115). 37 *Freeman's Journal*, 17 May 1793. 38 Ibid., 11 May 1793. 39 Ibid., 14 May 1793. 40 'Sketch of the history of the old Kilkenny Regiment of Militia,' *Kilkenny Moderator*, 1859 (NLI, J355942). These articles produced much correspondence from survivors and their children. 41 Westmorland to Dundas, n.d. (NA, HO/100/44/115). 42 *Faulkner's Journal*, 19 June 1793. 43 Edward Cooke to 'My dear sir', 27 June 1793 (NA, HO/100/44/183). 44 *Freeman's Journal*, 2 July 1793.

Opposition to the militia in the former was almost certainly due to the strength of the United Irish movement in the county that opposed a militia. Kerry is a different matter. There is no obvious reason, but several can be surmised. There was a strong linen weaving industry in Kerry at that time, and the loss of manpower to the army would be likely to be resisted since weaving was a cottage industry. The second reason is that the riots may have had more to do with tithes and rents than with the formation of a militia.[45] A report in *Faulkner's Journal* said:

> Tralee, June 18 – The accounts we have received from indubitable authority relative to the riots in Dingle continue every day more and more alarming. On Sunday last the insurgents carried their violence to a pitch of daring licentiousness hitherto unexampled in this county. A vast multitude of these frantic wretches assembled in the town of Dingle, and immediately proceeded to the house of Captain Causzer, the windows of which they almost totally demolished, and injured the furniture. They afterwards attacked the houses of some other inhabitants, and burned all the tithe-notes and papers they could get. Fortunately no murder was committed, as many of the gentlemen of the town had prudently taken refuge along with Captain Causzer on board the *Mason* revenue cruiser, then in harbour.[46]

There are two further accounts of trouble which have been ascribed to the militia riots, but belong to the post embodiment period – for just as there were outbreaks of violence before the Militia Act became law, so they continued after the militia had formed up. The first of these was reported on 11 July 1793 in Wexford. (The Wexford Regiment had been completed on 20 June, some three weeks earlier.) A mob assembled to liberate two prisoners in Wexford Gaol, captured Lieutenant Buckley of the 5 6th Regiment, and was stopped by a party of that regiment commanded by Major Charles Valloton. He tried to reason with the mob, but was attacked, and mortally wounded. His soldiers fired and killed nine.[47] A further report adds that the mob wanted a reduction of tithes, and tillage at 6*d*. an acre.[48] This incident had nothing to do with the array of the militia. The second account was of two incidents in Co. Limerick. The first was at Bruff, and as the County of Limerick Militia were involved, it was hardly an incident that had anything to do with raising the regiment. Between twenty and thirty people were killed, and the County of Limerick Regiment, 'have lately behaved well and spirit-

---

45 I am grateful to Dr Conor Brosnan of Dingle, Co. Kerry, for this information 46 *Faulkner's Journal*, 22 June 1793. 47 Westmorland to Dundas, 13 July 1793 (NA, HO/100/44/283). 48 Ibid., 12 July 1793 (ibid., HO 100/44/230).

edly being as anxious as possible to bayonet, shoot, kill, or murder the Defenders in any way we like.'[49] There is another account on 24 July 1793 of a detachment of the County of Limerick being attacked by a mob of fifteen hundred at Loughmore on their way from Rathkeale to Limerick, escorting prisoners who escaped, but, again, this was not violence directed against the Militia Act.

In no case did the disturbances prevent the formation of the county militia regiments. The inadequacies of the Militia Act must be seen as the prime reason for causing problems, particularly in the matter of pay. The government recognized this quickly, and started a belated campaign to put matters right, placing the proper facts before the people. The first action of importance was Foster's Family bill, introduced into the house of commons by the Speaker (hence its name), at the end of May 1793, becoming law the following month.[50] This act was to provide for the families of balloted men only, the sum of 2s. per week for wives, and 1s. per week for each child born in wedlock. A condition was that the family did not follow the regiment, and the maximum amount payable was four shillings per week. The money to pay for this was to be raised by parish cess. There are two important points to be made about this provision. First, there was no provision for parents who were totally dependent on a son who had been balloted, and second the cost was to be borne by the parish cess again until 1795, when it was transferred to the county cess. Rates of cess, or 'rates,' were a charge on landowners, and this should be borne in mind when considering the decline of the ballot.

The second action the government took was to publish a proclamation in the newspapers countering allegations against the militia.[51] The proclamation had nine points, first, that the militia was not to serve outside Ireland; second, that service was for four years, in peacetime for 28 days only; third, service was to be within the county; during the 28 days service pay would be one shilling per day, and the men would be clothed; fifth, if the men were 'drawn out' in time of war, each man would receive a guinea bounty, full pay, clothing, and allowances of the army, and last, no person not paying hearth money, who had three children born in wedlock, could be compelled to serve, or find a substitute; men maimed or wounded on active service would be entitled to go to the Royal Hospital at Kilmainham; any married militiaman could set up as a tradesman anywhere in Ireland; and finally, no religious distinctions were made by the act, with free exercise of religion allowed. This was an important announcement, even though the regiments were 'drawn out' for full time service on completing embodiment, and served,

---

[49] John Straton, Rathkeale, to the Hon. Revd P. Jocelyn, 21 July 1793 (PRONI, MIC/1 49/9.)
[50] 33 Geo. III, c.2 8. [51] *Freeman's Journal*, 18 May 1793, is an example which advertised the first six points only, the *Belfast Newsletter*, 4–7 June 1793 published all nine.

with two short breaks, until 1816. The proclamation, also, deleted 'born in wedlock' from the last sub paragraph

This proclamation was necessary to counter the claims of both the United Irishmen and the Defenders, who had used the Militia Act as yet another grievance. Significantly the counties worst affected by Defenderism in the 1790-3 period were those worst affected by the militia riots. Furthermore, although there is no evidence in 1793 of collusion between the Defenders and United Irishmen, there is one important area in which their interests coincided. This was the steady withdrawal of the regular army from Ireland to fight the French. The response of the Defenders can be summed up by the case of Edward Brown, a shopkeeper in Mayo, who was forced to take an oath by Defenders on 28 May 1793, to be true to the Roman Catholic faith, pay no quit rent, tithes, taxes, or rent for three months as the army was leaving the kingdom, the French would be invited to invade, and they would all get estates.[52] From the United Irish point of view, if the regular army was being withdrawn, then it would be beneficial not to have a militia for this would weaken the government, and create an opportunity for its removal with French assistance. Denis Browne, the MP for Mayo, believed the riots were not caused by the Militia Act, but arose from the new political doctrines, 'which have pervaded the lower classes,' that this came from the publication of Paine's *Rights of man*, and seditious newspapers, and through shopkeepers visiting Dublin, who there, imbibed the ideas of the United Irishmen. He thought French agents might have been involved, and that the insurrection spread from Sligo into his county, Mayo.[53]

There were other reasons for the militia riots. Thomas Pelham, writing to the duke of York on the subject of Irishmen in the army and navy, had remarked on the difficulty of getting people who had any kind of interest in land to leave it.[54] Other commentators had noted this reluctance, so the effect of the Militia Act can be easily imagined. Related to this is a letter published in *Freeman's Journal* on 11 October 1793, from one 'Militius', who pointed out that the ballot was perceived as unfair because it subjected the poor man to equal burden with the rich, something like 'oppression', and 'partiality,' and

> for what can be less like equal justice for all, than the exemption of the wealthy old bachelor, a rich beneficed clergyman, a judge ... from all chance of contributing to the support of the militia – either by service, or the expense of a substitute; yet forcing the distressed artizan to the alternative of either quitting his family for militia service, or

---

[52] Westmorland to Dundas, n.d. (NA, HO/100/44/115.) [53] Ibid. [54] Pelham to the duke of York, 14 Nov. 1796, in J.T. Gilbert, *Documents relating to Ireland, 1795-1804* (Dublin, 1893), p. 100.

devoting a month's earning to supply a substitute, from that family's support – or depriving feeble old age of the dutiful attentions and productive industry of an only son, on whom the lot of service may fall.[55]

It is possible to argue that the militia riots were a part of the ongoing disturbances of the early 1790s, and that the militia act was another cause for grievance. They have certainly been cited as a root cause for the abandonment of the ballot. Yet 17 out of Ireland's 32 counties had no reported trouble at all, the ballot was not immediately abandoned; nor, indeed, is there any evidence of a conscious decision on the part of government to stop using it. This suggests that there may well have been other causes for the downgrading of the ballot.

THE BALLOT

Finding primary evidence of the actual conducting of the ballot in Ireland is difficult. It was held almost all over Ireland in 1793, but was not as newsworthy as riot and mayhem. We have already seen that it was conducted even where regiments were filled with volunteers, as in the Kerry Regiment, or where Sir Edward Crofton announced that he was going to raise his company in the Roscommon by volunteers, yet ten days later we find him balloting parishes in the county. The reason was that in order to raise a regiment of volunteer substitutes, there had to be a substitution, which meant that the ballot had to be held, so that the volunteers could replace those balloted. It was a clumsy procedure, and the next stage was to abandon the ballot, and raise men by beat of drum. But the Militia Act was designed to raise a part-time force, and its inadequacies only came to light with experience. There are three quite well documented accounts of the ballot being held for Down, Meath, and the City of Dublin, while there is also information on the conduct of the ballot in Donegal. Fortuitously, these four places provide a set of different and complementary case studies: a populous county, a county supposedly disaffected, one that is partly mountainous, and a large city.

Down was balloted throughout the period 1793–1802, and thereafter. This was not an easy thing to do, and often required diplomacy on the part of the deputy governors. In 1793, Nicholas Price of Saintfield, a deputy governor, reported to Lord Downshire that there were problems with recruiting.[56] He said that balloted men greatly feared being taken out of the country, despite attempts at persuading them otherwise. They did not want to serve in a

---

[55] *Freeman's Journal*, 11 Oct. 1793.   [56] Nicholas Price to Lord Downshire, n.d. (PRONI, D/607/C/22).

standing army, and, of course, there were problems with 'scoundrels,' who 'traduce every plan of government.'[57] In July 1795, Lieutenant-Colonel Lord Annesley, writing from Loughlinstown, where the regiment was quartered, reported that he had quieted opposition to the ballot by guaranteeing not to take family men, lest their families might become a charge on the parishes.[58] He requested that the insurers or the deputy governors did not send family men as this would have hurt his reputation by forcing him to betray his word. The insurers had made money, and could afford to get good men.

In November 1797 Thomas Lane, Lord Downshire's agent for the Hillsborough estates, wrote:

> The whole county is drawn ... The last round commences at Newry on the 20th, Rathfriland 21st, Down 22nd, Ballynahinch 23rd, Hillsborough 24th, Newtownards 26th, Castlereagh 27th, which concludes the business ... 121 recruits went off to the regiment together and I heard Major Matthews say there never was a finer set of fellows ever joined. Lieutenant Reed is now down for more and I attest them every day, *strapping dogs* [sic] in general.'[59]

The regiment took also volunteers as well as pressed men. In early 1798 it was reported that 'Sergeant Mahood has marched from hence (Hillsborough), for Loughrea, with 18 recruits. Most fine lads, and those not so are drawn men who could not be rejected.'[60]

It is in the advertisements of insurers against being drawn in the ballot, that much can be learned about how it functioned. This is particularly true in the case of both the Meath, and the City of Dublin Regiments. Insurers appear to have specialized in counties or regiments rather than act on a national scale. The Meath insurer was Brett Smith of 38 Mary Street, Dublin, and the City of Dublin insurer was Vincent Dowling of 13 Suffolk Street, and 2 Abbey Street, Dublin. There does not appear to have been any co-operation or collusion between them, at least in public.

Brett Smith, along with a Mr McLean of Trim, and a Mr Holland of West Street, Drogheda, offered insurance against being drawn in the ballot for the militia to gentlemen for 11s. 4d., farmers and those in similar occupations for 6s. 6d., and for livery servants and poor men, 2s. 2d.[61] Smith also issued a handbill advertising his activities, which showed that he had many

---

57 Ibid. 58 Annesley to Downshire, 11 July 1795 (PRONI, D/607/B/114A). 59 Lane to Downshire, 6 Nov. 1797 (ibid., D/607/B/375). 60 George Stephenson, Hillsborough, to Lord Downshire, 4 Feb. 1798 (ibid., D/607/F/43). 61 Fingal Papers, Royal Meath Militia (NLI, MS/8029). This deposit contains what appears to be original ballot slips for John Patican, Jordestown, labourer; Thos. Byrne, Templekernan, miller; Thos. Keegan, Macetown, labourer; and James Smith, Glan, labourer.

problems in providing substitutes.[62] In it he said that at the first ballot at Dunshaughlin he had to provide 13 substitutes for drawn men, insured by him. He brought 15 men from Drogheda, and the deputy governors approved 10 of them who were immediately attested. However, at the regiment, six were turned down – because they would not give one of the guineas of their bounty to pay for 'necessaries' ('necessaries' were shirts, shoes, stockings, gaiters, forage cap, knapsack, stock (which went around the neck), black ball (for blackening), and brushes, normally paid for by 'stoppages' of pay). Smith sent three more who were turned away because they were not Meathmen, but they were accepted at the next meeting at Dunshaughlin.

On 20 July (year not shown, but probable 1793), Smith attended Dunshaughlin with 17 more men, but the meeting was postponed, so he took 15 of them to Trim to allow the deputy governors to choose six in lieu of those who would not give a guinea for 'necessaries'. Eight men were accepted if Smith could give security, and provide others as three of the first group had 'run' or deserted. Smith protested that once attested the soldier became the responsibility of the regiment, and that the demand of a guinea for 'necessaries' was illegal. It is obvious that there was fraud here, the people at the regiment who demanded a guinea for necessaries had no right to it, and some substitutes were making a dangerous living by joining different regiments, collecting the bounty, and then deserting. Certainly, this practice took place in the English Militia, and there is no reason why it should not have happened in the Irish militia because of the gap between attestation and being called forward for service.[63]

Lord Fingal, head of the Catholic branch of the Plunkett family, was a captain in the Meath Militia in 1793 (he resigned in 1797 when he was the lieutenant-colonel.) He was a sympathetic officer as this promissory note reveals.[64] 'Ten days after this date, I promise to pay the Rt. Hon. Earl Fingal or order Five pounds thirteen shillings and ninepence Sterl. to provide a substitute to serve for me in the Royal Meath Militia. Signed by Thomas Lawley (his mark), 15 Aug 1795.' On the back in Fingal's hand is 'Received in part a pig valued at £2.10.6d. Fingal.' This shows that the ballot was used in Co. Meath after 1793, and without violence – probably because it was easy to avoid if one's name was drawn.

As it can be seen in Vincent Dowling's notices in the Dublin papers, and also in the reports in these papers describing the balloting for the militia in the different wards of Dublin city, that the clearest picture can be obtained of how the ballot worked, and the abuses and difficulties which were experienced.[65] Dublin was balloted in May and June, 1793, and Dowling offered

---

62 Fingal Papers, Royal Meath Militia (NLI, MS 8209). 63 Western, *English Militia*, p. 274.
64 Fingal papers, Royal Meath Militia (NLI, MS 8029). 65 City of Dublin Regiment:

his services at the 'Militia Exemption Office' on 21 and 25 May 1793, for a premium of 'three half crowns' (7s. 6d.).[66] For the ballot on 12 June, he still offered insurance at three half crowns, and stated that he had lodged the premium money received with the bank of Messrs Beresford, Woodmason, and Needham, to be used to pay fines, or provide substitutes. Dowling also offered a prize of twenty guineas to each of the persons last drawn for each district of the city. (Quite possibly he had competition, or a disappointing number of clients.)[67] On 12 July he disclaimed all further risk as the regiment was embodied, and he said he had attended four ballots, though contracted for one only. (There must be some sophistry here, as it took six ballots to cover the city.)[68] On 31 August 1793 Dowling claimed that he had attended all six ballots, over 1,000 names had been drawn, and still the regiment was not complete because of the legal exemptions claimed by those drawn, together with the impossibility of finding others who had also been drawn, but who had simply disappeared, emphasizing that the governors would continue to ballot until the regiment was full.[69] (The establishment of the City of Dublin Militia was 4 2 0.) Dowling had stood his premium, but offered another at four shillings until the regiment was complete.[70] On 30 November 1793, Dowling published some interesting information, which allows us to gauge the effectiveness of the ballot. He cancelled all outstanding policies, saying that he had the risk of 450 names out of the 2,000 drawn, but that the regiment was still one third short of its strength, and a new ballot was to be held. He was issuing new policies at half a guinea each for a four-year exemption, or four shillings for the next ballot only. Thus, while 2,000 people had been balloted only 280 had actually been enlisted in the regiment. This was not an efficient, or satisfactory, way to raise men. By 1 December 1793, 170 men were needed to complete the regiment, but it would be necessary to ballot five or six hundred names to get them. The report recommended Dowling's insurance for a 'trivial' premium.[71] The strength of the regiment, however, on 31 March 1794, was 291 rank-and-file, a shortfall of 129.[72] The newspapers carrying Dowling's advertisements gave details of the six ballots held in the city, and some details of those drawn to serve. These included nine pawnbrokers in one parish, while in another, one judge, three barristers, and nine attorneys. On the list were two members of parliament, several private gentlemen, one surgeon, two apothecaries, and two more pawnbrokers.[73] It should not be assumed, however, that Dublin was typical of the country.

Proclamation – 20 Apr 1793, embodied – 6 July 1793, establishment – 420 men, quota for 'embodiment' probably 336. 66 *Freeman's Journal*, 21 and 25 May 1793. 67 Ibid., 11 June 1793. 68 Ibid., 12 July 1793. 69 Ibid., 31 Aug. 1793. 70 Ibid. 71 Ibid., 1 Dec. 1793. 72 Pay Lists and Muster Rolls, City of Dublin Militia (NA, WO/1 3/2 8 1). 73 *Freeman's Journal*, 15 and 18 June 1793.

In 1802, before the disbandment of the militia on the peace of Amiens, William Wickham, under-secretary of state at the Home Department, wrote to Lord Clements, colonel commandant of the Donegal Regiment, what appears to be a circular letter to all the colonels saying that the government would like to have a 'general' system for both the English and Irish militias.[74] He also said that the lord lieutenant had doubts about balloting in Ireland, as it did not produce an effective army, and was neither prudent nor safe. Colonels were asked for an opinion. Clements obviously asked his deputy governors, and three interesting replies survive. John Boyd of Ballymacool said that vestries were badly attended, deputy governors did not turn up, the collection of cess by parishes was nearly impossible because of the number of them – 35 in the see of Raphoe, and more in the see of Derry – in addition the cess was seen as a tax that people did not want to pay, even though the lord lieutenant might want to use the ballot to keep the two kingdoms similar.[75] Andrew Knox said the ballot was difficult in Ireland, that the deputy governors would not do their job, and that the exclusion of the Yeomanry made the manpower pool small.[76] Richard Maxwell (who had been the lieutenant-colonel), said the ballot or parochial assessment was no use, and fruitless in remote mountainous situations. The only method was for the government to issue money, and authorize colonels to raise volunteers by bounty.[77]

There are reports of ballots being held in Tyrone, Co. Dublin, Carlow, Leitrim, Arklow (Co. Wicklow), Sligo, and Roscrea (Co. Tipperary). There was a first report of raising men by 'beat of drum' in Waterford, 'Yesterday a party beat up in this city for men to serve in the militia. This mode of procuring men seems to have entirely changed the terrific form of the Militia Act, for notwithstanding no bounty was offered, twenty-five fine young fellows entered in the course of a few hours.'[78] At first sight, the fact that this change in approach followed so closely on the heels of the militia riots might be taken as confirmation of a connection between the violent protests against the ballot and its subsequent abandonment. However, the detailed evidence of the operation of recruiting in the localities suggests a more complex picture. Practical difficulties, rather than political decision-making, caused the downgrading of the ballot. A number of expedients were put into effect to circumvent these difficulties, and the experimentation with different methods of recruitment was staggered over quite a long period.

One of these was an alternative to insurance against the ballot, which provided the same result (that is, substitutes), but was cheaper and non-profit making. Lieutenant-Colonel Lord O'Neill of the Antrim Regiment provided

74 William Wickham to Lord Clements, 24 Nov. 1802 (NLI, PC 630, Clements papers).   75 John Boyd, Ballymacool, to Lord Clements, 8 Dec. 1802 (ibid.).   76 Andrew Knox, Prehen, to Lord Clements, 4 Dec. 1802 (ibid.).   77 Richard Maxwell, Birdstown, to Lord Clements, 8 Dec. 1802 (ibid.).   78 *Faulkner's Journal*, 22 June 1793.

a typical example: he raised a general subscription of 3s. per man, from those subject to the ballot, which allowed a bounty of three guineas for each recruit, and as a result, there were hardly any balloted men in the regiment.[79] Variations on this were carried out in other regiments. It is worth noting that the motives underlying modification of recruitment practices were varied, and did not arise solely from a desire to avoid public protest. The militia needed a steady supply of good recruits; while landowners might be reluctant to lose good tenants, and farmers' able-bodied labourers, so that they would willingly pay for substitutes or for the exemption of their men.

No other regiment apparently tried the douceur offered by Lord Kingsborough, lieutenant-colonel commandant of the North Cork regiment who, on 12 October 1793 offered a small farm in the province of Munster to the first 244 men to volunteer for his regiment. The farms were to be held at reasonable rent, but the men had to be Protestants. The *Sentimental and Masonic Magazine* commented, 'The benign intention of the Sovereign seems to have for its object a generous fraternization of his people. This distinction ... does not square with such an intention, and so far deviates from the intention of the father of his people.'[80]

The popular perception of the reasons for the abandonment of the ballot has been focussed on the militia riots, and the effect they had throughout the country. These riots are seen as the principal reason for the failure of the ballot, yet it has been clearly shown here that the riots affected no more than half of the Irish counties, and bad as the riots may have been, there have to be other reasons, principally the fact that the Militia Act was designed to create a part-time force, but was being applied to a full-time one. This resulted in two major problems that reveal the act to be inadequate for what it was being asked to do. The first of these, from the evidence of Dublin and Donegal, is that because of the large number of categories of exemption, it was very hard to get the required numbers of men either from a particularly populous area, or a particularly remote one. The militia, in fact, was slow to fill up at first despite all the claims on embodiment. The act was passed in March, but it had only 2,500 men by July, 5,000 by 1 August, and 6,000 by 1 September 1793[81] It was not until other methods of enlistment were tried, that numbers increased rapidly, and returns show that, from 1795 approximately, the militia was well able to recruit to establishment.

Second, the ballot was slow, expensive, and inefficient. To ballot above 2,000 names to get only 280 out of a target of 420 was clearly not an efficient way to raise men. In order to remain operational, a regiment constantly

79 Ibid., 12 Apr. 1794.   80 *Sentimental and Masonic Magazine*, July–Dec. 1793, iii, p. 383. It may have worked, though. The North Cork suffered very few desertions and in 1800, the least number of volunteers to the line of any regiment.   81 Thomas Pelham to Col. Brownrigg, 26 Oct. 1796 (PRONI, T/755/3/153.)

needed recruits to replace those who had died, deserted, or were discharged. These 'casualties' (the generic term) were a continual drain on manpower when on full-time service. The ballot could replace men when the period of service was 28 days a year, but it could not do so when the regiment was permanently embodied.

A fourth reason why the ballot was better designed for part time service, rather than full time, was the question of the rate of cess. Balloted men were a drain on the parish cess, which substitutes and volunteers were not. For part-time service, this would not cost much, and could be collected over a period of time, but full-time service was a different matter. Again, with substitutes, there was less fear of families being a charge on the parish, which encouraged substitution. Thus abandonment of the ballot suited all sides, the landowner liable for cess, and the tenant anxious to avoid service, and it also offered an opportunity for gainful work at home for unemployed young men.

Finally the replies to Lord Clements from Donegal show that if the deputy governors would not do their job, the ballot could not be held. There could be many reasons for this, from fear of intimidation, to laziness, but landowners were usually aware of the needs of their tenants, and were often very reluctant to lose a good one. A Mr Henry Hamilton of Ballymacool in Co. Meath demonstrated a good example of this. One of his tenants, a Michael Boylan, had been drawn to serve in the Royal Meath Militia. Although Boylan had insurance with Brett Smith who was willing to pay for a substitute, he had received a notice to join the regiment or he would be posted as a deserter, and a warrant would be issued for his arrest. Despite the insurance, Hamilton requested the governors to apply to his Dublin address where whatever sum needed to pay for a substitute would be paid.[82] Hamilton obviously thought highly of Boylan. Landlords would have known of the dislike of compulsory service, of the trouble that there had been, and indeed, many among the gentry had started subscriptions to pay for substitutes, thus nullifying the effects of the ballot.

Historians who treat the militia riots simply as an episode in Irish political history are in essence looking at the raising of the militia from the perspective of an event that happened five years later. In 1793 the problems faced by the government were immediate. It sought to defend the country and to counter the practical problems in raising a new force. Those counties worst affected by the militia riots had witnessed violent incidents long before the militia was proposed, and this violence continued long after the militia had been embodied; indeed, the new militia was used in its suppression. The protests on the formation of the militia were a transient phenomenon: the

---

82 Henry Hamilton to the Governors of the County of Meath, 7 Aug. 1795 (NLI, MS/8029, Fingall Papers).

Militia Act was used as yet another grievance, and when protests failed to prevent the formation of the force, the grievance was discarded as it had outlived its usefulness. Nor did the militia riots cause a breakdown in social order in Ireland. The administration of the country continued, the assizes were held, grand juries met. The militia itself was duly embodied.

The ballot itself was a hopelessly inadequate and expensive means of keeping a full-time force supplied with men. It may have been adequate for a force that was to serve for only 28 days a year, but after the militia was embodied for full-time service parliament did not amend the original balloting legislation in the almost annual amendments to the rest of the act, despite evidence that it was being used less and less. The militia riots certainly revealed a popular revulsion at the method of balloting, and probably for a militia generally, but the principal reasons for the decline of the ballot were practical, and, of course, financial. Thus the militia riots are most usefully seen in the immediate context of 1793. The government was faced with particular problems of external defence and internal security, which it sought to solve by the establishment of a militia. The militia became its principal military arm, assisted by the fencibles and the yeomanry, as the London government steadily withdrew the regular army from Ireland. The story of the formation of this alternative army should be regarded, not as the first episode of the '98, but rather as the first step in the suppression of that rebellion.

EMBODIMENT

This small but important step has already been touched upon. The Act created the militia, and once it had become law, the government had to order the commandants of the different regiments to 'embody', or organize their regiments and raise the men. When the commandants had done this, they reported the fact to the commander-in-chief, and the day they did this became their embodiment date. There was no set time for embodiment, because each county was different in size, geography, and population. Nor, it appears, was there a set number of men to be recruited for the regiment to be regarded as 'embodied'. In fact, we know from the returns that several regiments when 'embodied' existed only in cadre form. For example, the Armagh Regiment was ordered to embody on 3 May 1793, it was embodied on 16 September 1793, 130 days later, and on 31 March 1794, it had 362 rank-and-file out of an establishment of 420.[83] The Donegal were ordered to embody on 29 April 1793, and had complied by 23 August 1793, 122 days later, when they had 216 rank-and-file out of 560.[84] As we have seen, the

[83] Pay Lists and Muster Rolls, Armagh Militia (NA, WO/13/2603). [84] Pay Lists and Muster

militia was slow to fill up at first, and some regiments had smaller proportions than these.

As soon as a regiment was embodied, it had to be 'called out' for service, usually within a few days. The Armagh, for example, was called out on 19 September 1793.[85] The Donegal were called out on the day of their embodiment on 23 August 1793.[86] When a regiment was called out, it received instructions from the adjutant general, placing it under orders of the commander-in-chief, it was sent the standing orders of the army in Ireland, and the *Rules and regulations for the field exercise*, instructions for submitting returns of manpower, pay, leave for officers, equipment, and any additional instructions and orders peculiar to the area in which they were serving.[87] The regiment also received a letter from the quartermaster general giving instructions on the quartering of the regiment, together with 'routes' to get there. It contained instructions about equipment, and instructions for the use of money for lodgings.[88] We know too that at this stage Lord Downshire asked for his regiment to be allowed to remain at Killough and Newry,[89] and that Lord Gosford asked for the Armagh to be quartered in Dundalk.[90] Other commandants did the same, which suggests that at this early stage, the commandants considered they were operating under an act for part-time service, and that, some time between the autumn and winter of 1793, the commander-in-chief had decided that they were to be a full-time force for the duration of the war. No record of such a decision has been found.

Regiments formed up at a place chosen by the lieutenant-colonel commandant. Lord Downshire chose Killough, a small village on the Co. Down coast, south of Ardglass. The reason remains unclear, although Downshire had property in the area, and was responsible for the building and commissioning of the nearby South Rock, or Kilwarlin lighthouse in 1798. He received authority to hire buildings, a barrack containing 85 beds, officers' rooms, a hospital, a large stable, and a garret which could hold another 44 beds, whilst having a large storehouse nearby which could accommodate the whole regiment.[91] The ballot in county Down worked well, and when the regiment was embodied it had 747 men, out of an establishment of 770.[92] It was here that the regiment carried out its initial training, and in 1801 the barracks were described by the Army Medical Board as being in good order,

---

Rolls, Donegal Militia (ibid., WO/13/2751). 85 Cunninghame to Hobart, 24 Sept. 1793 (NLI, KP/1012/217). 86 Ibid., 23 Aug. 1793 (ibid., KP/1012/197). 87 For example, see Adjutant General to Lord Gosford, 20 Sept. 1793 (PRONI, D/3574/D/4 Armagh Militia Letter Book). 88 For example, see Quartermaster General to Lord Gosford, 21 Sept. 1793 (ibid., D/3574/D/5, Armagh Militia Letter Book). 89 Cunninghame to Downshire, 2 Dec. 1793 (ibid., D/607/C/177). 90 Gosford to Quartermaster General, 3 Oct. 1793 (ibid., D/3574/D/6). 91 Charles Handfield to Lord Downshire, 30 Aug. 1793 (NLI, KP/1080). 92 Pay Lists and Muster Rolls, Royal Downshire Regiment (NA, WO/13/2776).

except for the stables, able to accommodate 200 men, facing the sea, but lacking a fresh water supply.[93]

In the late eighteenth century Ireland rank and precedence were all-important. There was naturally competition between the lieutenant-colonels commandant to have the 'senior' regiment, the best turned-out band, a different uniform, and so on. Because groups of counties received orders to embody on different dates, the first regiment to do so could hardly be called the 'senior.' On 8 August 1793, a ballot was held in Dublin to decide on the order of precedence, which was signified by a number to be worn on uniforms, and equipment, along with the regimental badge, usually the county coat of arms. The Monaghan came out of the draw first, the Tyrone second, and so on, down to the 38th, which was the Wexford.[94] Regiments, however, were always known by their county title. This numbering was slightly changed in 1800, when the 24th, the Drogheda, was amalgamated with the Louth, and its old number assumed by the newly created Royal North Downs, on the division of the Royal Downshire Regiment in that year. Otherwise the numbering was unchanged until 1881.

Another connected matter was the presentation of colours to each regiment. In this period colours were carried into battle, and were the rallying point for the men of the regiment. The presentation of 'colours' was a partly religious, partly secular ceremony, and was one of the most important acts in the creation of regimental pride and loyalty: a symbolic form of 'bonding'. Regulations regarding colours dated from the Royal Warrant of 1751.[95] There were two colours in each regiment, the 'King's' colour, a pre-Union flag with the regimental number in the centre, and a 'regimental' colour, which had the regimental number, and county badge, as well as other devices on it. In 'royal' regiments, such as the Downshire or the Meath, this colour would have a dark blue background, but in non-royal regiments the background could be buff, red or black. 'The colours of British Regiments became something like the Ark of the Covenant, and were invested with more than earthly significance ... where they stood, the regiment stood, come what might, and if necessary the last man would be expected to give his life to keep them from the enemy.'[96] Not surprisingly, the presentation of 'colours' was a religious ceremony, with a suitable sermon from the clergy, and a party afterwards. One of the first militia regiments to be presented with colours, was the Louth, at Drogheda, on 31 August 1793, when Colonel Thomas Foster, son of the Speaker, presented new colours to Ensigns Bellingham and Brabazon. The regiment was reported 500 strong, and possessed a regimen-

---

93 *Report of the Army Medical Board on the State of Barracks in Ireland*, 12 Nov. 1801 (NAS, GD/364/1/1125).   94 *Freeman's Journal*, 14 Aug. 1793.   95 R. Money Barnes, *A history of the regiments and uniforms of the British Army* (4th ed., London, 1957), pp 19–20.   96 Ibid.

tal band.[97] On 16 May 1794 colours were presented to the Royal Downshire Regiment at Youghal by the lieutenant-colonel commandant, the marquess of Downshire. Major George Matthews commanded the men on parade. Downshire is reported to have spoken 'at considerable length' about loyalty to the sovereign and duty to the regiment. 'Under these standards', said his lordship, 'none must refuse to yield obedience and from them none must ever presume to fly; but faithfully as good soldiers, defend them with the last drop of their blood.' The chaplain delivered a 'truly feeling and excellent discourse' following which there were three volleys and cheers. Later there was a ball for the officers and their ladies, and beer for the men.[98]

It should not be assumed that once the ballot had been completed, and the regiments mustered, problems were at an end. This was a disturbing and unsettled period as regiments sorted themselves out. Officers and non-commissioned officers discovered what their duties were, while getting to know their men, and vice versa. Several officers and many soldiers found the transfer from civilian to military life extremely difficult. Officers could, and did, resign, but private men did not have this option, for if they did not like military life, they could only stay or 'run' (desert). Desertion will be considered later, but it is worth pointing out at this stage that in the returns of the regiments there was at first a high rate of desertion in some regiments. In the first six months, to 31 March 1794, the Wexford lost 27 men out of 207 by desertion, the Downshire 14 out of 649, the Tipperary 16 out of 480, the Meath 45 out of 298, and the City of Dublin 33 out of 291.[99] The Meath had one of the highest rates of desertion in this period in the entire militia force, and the City of Dublin was only slightly better. None of these regiments ever lost so many in a single period again, so it is not unreasonable to attribute these figures to the first shock of military service.

A mixture of beat of drum, balloting, and substitution raised the Waterford Regiment. In 1794 the lieutenant-colonel commandant, the marquess of Waterford, gave a clear picture of how the system worked. He announced to the press that he would make good subscriptions for substitutes to bring the regiment to its established strength, but he would not make good vacancies caused by death, desertion or discharges – these would be charged to the respective district to which they were appropriated. He pointed out that deserters were mainly hidden in their home areas, and quoted the example of Private Power, who, when bringing in the deserter Private Leonard, was beaten for his efforts by local people and Leonard duly rescued.[1] In other words a casualty (the generic term for those who had died,

---

97 *Freeman's Journal*, 6 Sept. 1793. 98 *Sentimental and Masonic Magazine*, Jan.–June 1794, pp 5, 191. 99 Pay Lists and Muster Rolls (NA, WO/1 3/2815, 3330, 2776, 3243, 3141).
1 *Freeman's Journal*, 29 Aug. 1794.

been discharged, or had deserted) would be a charge on the parish from which he came, and it would have to pay for a substitute, or provide a volunteer, or pay a fine, or hold a ballot, to find a replacement. With regard to other unfilled vacancies, for which men had not been recruited, Lord Waterford would use his fund to pay for substitutes.

As soon as the regiments formed up and were called out, they received notice that they were to be inspected by a general officer. Units were informed in advance by the adjutant-general of what details of training they had to be able to perform. A good example of this is to be found in the orders to the Carlow Battalion. On 7 September 1793 they received an order that they would be inspected before 1 October 1793 by a general officer, and that the battalion had to be able to perform the 'evolutions agreeable to the directions contained in the System for Field Exercise, under the head, 'Inspections or Reviews', the first seven pages,' and that this comprised; marching past the general; forming into line; the manual exercise; platoon exercise; firing by wings; retreating in line; firing by battalion; the advance; firing by companies; advancing in line; open ranks; and the general salute.[2]

This was a lot to learn in a very short time, in fact it comprised a large part of the 200 pages of instructions which precede 'Inspections or Reviews' in *Rules and regulations for the formations, field-exercise, and movements of His Majesty's Forces*. The assumption is made that the men had been taught basic foot drill (Part 1), the platoon exercise (Part 2), and at least some battalion manoeuvres (Part 3). The inspecting general in turn was to 'particularly observe and specify' whether or not, among other things:

> The original formation of the battalion is according to order.
> The marches are made with accuracy, at the required times and length of step, and on such objects as are given.
> The proper distances in column and echelon, are at all times preserved.
> The wheelings are made just, and in the manner prescribed.
> The formations into line are made true, without false openings, or necessity of correction.
> The officers are alert in their changes of situation, exact in their own personal movements, and loud, decided, and pointed in their words of command.
> The march in line is uniformly steady, without floating, opening or closing.[3]

---

2 General Order, 7 Sept. 1793 (NA, WO/6 8/2 9 6/7). 3 *Rules and regulations for the formations, field-exercise, and movements of His Majesty's Forces* (London, 1793), 1–7 following parts 1–3.

These 'observations' mean the troops had a lot to learn in a very short time for this was a mixture of individual and collective training. It was an almost impossible task for a newly raised regiment to acquire the necessary expertise in all of these areas in the time allowed to them, which in the case of the Carlow was three and a half months.

TRAINING

There is almost no contemporary literature on the basic and advanced training undertaken by the Irish militia. Much can be deduced from orders and regulations, while conclusions can be drawn from the known military requirements of the time, and the textbooks used. Unfortunately, none of the inspection returns, save one, have been found – and that includes the inspection returns that would have been made by the very first inspecting generals. They exist for the regular army regiments serving at the time in Ireland, but not for the Irish militia. Training, however, was not neglected in the eighteenth-century army, and, by the 1790s had developed into a pattern that the Irish militia would have followed.[4] I intend to look at what the men were required to be able to do, the time in which they had to learn how to do it, and the problems, tensions, and stresses which they faced. It was all very well for the Castle to prescribe the end result, but how that end result was achieved was left to the (inexperienced) lieutenant-colonels commandant. Moreover it is most important never to forget that the performance of the militia in all of its tasks throughout our period, depended on the quality of its training.

The syllabus for infantry training laid down by David Dundas became the official manual for the army in 1793.[5] In this Dundas wrote, 'The recruit must be carried on progressively; he should comprehend one thing before he proceeds to another.' This 'progressive' method of training is the forerunner of the modern concept of 'individual', and 'collective' training. The recruit was issued with his clothing and equipment. The first thing he had to learn was how to wear it, including 'small' clothes or underwear, which he might never have seen before. He would have to learn how to keep it clean, and himself as well, how to powder his hair, and how to present his kit and equipment for inspection.

At the same time, he would be introduced to foot drill, and taught the intricacies of 'standing at ease,' 'attention,' and turning to the right, left, and

---

4 On the subject of training, see Houlding, *Fit for service*, chapters 4 and 5. 5 David Dundas, *Rules and regulations for the formation, field exercise, and movements of HM Forces* (NA, WO/68/383).

about. These were called the 'facings'. The purpose of foot drill was twofold, to train the man so that he could take part in larger formation movements, and to instil instant obedience to orders. The recruit was then taught how to march, the thirty-inch step, at 75 paces to the minute. He was taught how to halt, and then moved on to training with a squad.

Here the recruit learned to operate with a colleague on each side, one in front, and another to the rear. He learnt 'dressing,' 'marking time,' marching, halting, and the different 'steps,' to the side, or back. He learnt to march in quick time, and quicker. 'Quickstep' was 108 paces to the minute, or 270 feet per minute, it was used for moving from line to column, or vice versa. 'Quickest' step was 120 paces to the minute, which is 300 feet. It was used for wheeling.[6] The recruits were also taught to march in file, in column, in line, and how to wheel, and turn.

Having mastered all this, the recruit had to learn arms drill, then known as the 'manual exercise'. First, he learnt as an individual how to handle his firelock – clean it, and carry it in the approved military manner. Then he moved to doing all this in a squad, including marching, and the 'firings,' which were the ways of firing his piece – to the front, obliquely to the left and right, and by files. He would also have practice in actually firing it, but the allowance of powder and ball for this purpose was miserly, which is surprising given the British belief in the effectiveness of heavy fire. (This was volley fire, which was considered more important than individual aimed fire.) Accuracy was not at a premium – a battalion of Norfolk Militia in 1779, fired two volleys at a target 70 yards distant, which measured about eight feet by two feet. They fired 632 rounds, and scored 126 hits on the target – a score of twenty per cent, which was considered good.[7]

Having mastered individual and platoon training, the recruit moved to battalion training. Here, along with all the other officers and men, he had to learn how to form up in line of battle, the places of the officers and non commissioned officers, the structure of the battalion so formed up, the 'grand divisions' (a 'grand division' was two companies), and what were called the 'firings'. Fire was given by platoons, and in such a way that the line was continually spouting flame, as one platoon fired after another according to a set pattern. When the battalion was so drawn up, the grenadier company was 'right of the line,' and the light company was on the left. The line companies were numbered, and were placed by seniority of their captains from left to right.

When the men had learnt how to do all of this, and practised it, they had to learn how to move from column to line, and vice versa. They had to learn

6 To put this into perspective, the modern army moves at about 120 paces to the minute. The Guards at the annual 'Trooping of the Colour' ceremony, at about 110 or 112.   7 Houlding, *Fit for service*, p. 262.

to advance in line, without 'bunching,' and to turn to the right, or left, and retire. All this took time, and was complicated. The eighteenth-century soldier may have the reputation of being an automaton, but, in fact, he had to think about what he was doing in the field, or on the barrack square, all the time.

The next question to be asked when considering the amount of training a soldier had to undergo, is the amount of time it took to produce a trained battalion. As Houlding says in relation to the regular army: 'In the normal routine of service, therefore, it required from two to three years for a corps to amass sufficient concentration-time during which it might prepare itself to take the field. New raised regiments, too, generally, took two to three years to complete their training, even with the advantage of concentration and camps of exercise.'[8] These are figures for the regular army, yet the Irish militia, to all intents and purposes serving in just the same way as the regular infantry, was rarely to be given the luxury of the 'concentration-time' necessary to produce a properly trained battalion.

Earlier, we saw that orders were given to the newly raised regiments, that they were to be inspected by a general officer on or about 1 October 1793, and that they had had their orders detailing what they had to be able to perform before him. The Donegal Regiment received similar orders to the Carlow; they were to be reviewed on 1 October 1793, and had only been embodied on 30 September, one month before![9] This was an impossibly short period in which to train the men. Unfortunately, no report exists of what happened. Other examples of the amount of training time allowed, show that the Longford, embodied 6 June 1793, had nearly four months, as did the City of Limerick, and the Wexford had three, but the Downshire –the largest regiment – had only two months. These periods are woefully short, and the manoeuvres witnessed by the inspecting generals must have been pretty dreadful, despite honeyed words and encouraging reports to the press. Their reports to the Castle are not to be found.

From what we do know, Generals Crosby and Massey carried out the inspections in the prescribed period. On 1 October 1793 Massey reviewed the Longford and Kilkenny Battalions, and remarked, 'that military knowledge was much sooner acquired by Irishmen than by people of any other country.'[10] Massey was himself an Irishman, and had served his entire regimental career in the 27th Inniskillings.[11] He went on to review the Leitrim Battalion,[12] and on 23 October 1793 the City of Limerick at Parsonstown (Birr), where he is reported to have said, 'that if occasion offered, he should

8 Ibid., p. 296. 9 Adjutant General to Commanding Officer, Donegal Militia, 23 Aug. 1793 (NA, WO/6 8/2 2 1). 10 *Faulkner's Journal*, 3 Oct. 1793. 11 Memorial of Gen. Massey, 23 Nov. 1796 (NA, HO/1 0 0/6 1/2 1 1). Massey had been commissioned in 1739. It was unusual for a regular officer to spend all his career in the same regiment in the eighteenth and early nineteenth century. 12 *Faulkner's Journal*, 16 Oct. 1793.

be happy to have command of such troops.'[13] Massey, as an old soldier, knew the value of praise and encouragement. He continued his tour, and on 5 November 1793, he reviewed the Wicklow Regiment at Lambarton, near Arklow, and considered their progress in four months to be 'excellent'.[14]

These were impossibly short periods, and we do have the candid opinion of Major George Matthews when his regiment, the Downshire, were marched out of their county to Youghal, arriving on 5 April 1794, some seven months after embodiment. Matthews, one of the best officers in the Irish militia (as we shall see), had four companies immediately detached to Clonmel. He complained to Lord Annesley, his lieutenant-colonel, 'I hope in God Lord Downshire will prevent our being hacked about in this manner until we get the regiment properly disciplined and then let them drive us about as much as they like.'[15] On the same day, he wrote to Lord Downshire, 'I believe there never was better men; not a word, not a murmur this morning on the parade, although it was as bad a morning as you ever saw. They were all ready at five o'clock, and marched off with the greatest cheerfulness. It goes to my heart to see such men undisciplined, and I curse the author of it from my heart.'[16] This gives us a better perspective of the training situation because the Downshires had been in the hands of an enthusiastic and dedicated officer.[17] Although the detached companies were only away for a few days, it is obvious that Matthews did not consider them fit for service. Yet there is nothing unusual about this, most of the regiments were marched out of their counties in late 1793, and early 1794, and probably in a similar state of discipline.

The question of training, therefore, became a problem as the demands of detached service meant that units found it difficult to get sufficient time to train together as a formation. This, in turn, was bound up with the wider question of the purpose of the militia: was it to be a police force countering internal dissension, and in consequence, quite likely to be divided into small detachments, or was it to be an army to counter invasion? Although this is a problem to be considered in a later chapter, it is worth pointing out here that the establishment of the yeomanry in 1796 suggests that the purpose was the latter, and at no time was there any suggestion of training suitable for a police role. Dispersed service made formation training difficult. This was a problem recognized by the Castle, and Lord Camden established camps of instruction in 1795.[18] It is easy in these circumstances to concentrate on platoon and company training, forgetting the necessity of larger formation

13 Ibid., 1 Nov. 1793. 14 Ibid., 7 Nov. 1793. 15 Matthews to Lord Annesley, 8 Apr. 1794 (PRONI, D/607/C/31). 16 Same to Lord Downshire, 8 Apr. 1794 (ibid., D/607/C/32). 17 Major George Matthews (1756-1839), lived at Springvale, Co. Down (now Ballywalter Park), having married Miss Echlin, sister of Charles Echlin, of Echlinville (now Rubane, in the same county). 18 Camden to Portland, 17 Apr. 1795 (NA, HO/100/54/29).

training. One of the reasons for the failure of the ballot, remember, was the 'revolving' nature of a regiment: men were constantly needed, and had to be trained, to replace those who were casualties, and, in 1797 a large number of men were needed to replace those men discharged on the termination of their service. This constant necessity for recruit and platoon, and company training, obscured the need for training at battalion level, and higher.

There are two aspects to this need for concentration of the whole unit for training. The first is that regiments moved every year, with the attendant disruption of moving men, equipment, wives, and children, to a new location where they had to settle in and learn their new duties. The second was the question of detached service, and the difficulties this created for company and battalion training. Many of the problems experienced by the militia in the 1798 rebellion, stemmed from disrupted and inadequate training in the years beforehand.

On 15 August 1794, the Donegal Regiment – ten companies – marched some 30 miles from Birr to a new station at Athlone.[19] Immediately, on 23 August 1794, a company was detached to Castlerea, Co. Roscommon, some 50 miles away, and another to Roscommon itself, somewhat nearer Athlone only 20 miles distant. In September, and again in November, detachments were sent to Lough Glyn in Co. Roscommon. Lough Glyn was some ten miles beyond Castlerea. The remaining eight companies were together for four months before major disruptions. On 30 June 1795, the regiment marched to Drogheda; in July, a company went to Trim (Co. Meath); in August, another to Carrickmacross (Co. Monaghan); in September, two companies went to Navan (Co. Meath), and another to Ardee (Co. Louth); in October, a fifth company was detached to Balbriggan (Co. Dublin), these places were all no more than 25 miles of Drogheda, and so it remained until 2 April 1796, when the regiment marched to Loughlinstown (in south Dublin). This tour at Loughlinstown was attendance at summer camp, which did allow complete formation training. At no time during the tour in Drogheda were more than three or four companies present together, yet the four months in which eight companies were together in Athlone, was the longest period, as well as the largest grouping of the regiment between 23 August 1794, and 20 April 1796, a period of 20 months. This made it almost impossible for the regiment to do any constructive training as a body.

To take another example: the Longford Battalion consisted of six companies, and was one of the two militia regiments which did not behave well at Castlebar in 1798 when they were deployed to fight a set-piece battle against the French. This battalion had been stationed in Dublin from November 1794 to April 1796. In that month they moved to Carlow – and

19 Donegal Militia Order Book (ibid., WO/68/221/60.)

had detachments at the Curragh Camp (Co. Kildare), Castlecomer (Co. Kilkenny), Roscrea (Co. Tipperary), Maryborough, Ballinakill, Ballyroan, Doonan (all Queen's County), and Athy (Co. Kildare). In January 1797, they moved to Rathkeale (Co. Limerick), with detachments in Kilkenny, and Limerick; in August 1797 they moved to Limerick, with detachments at O'Brien's Bridge, and Killaloe; in May 1798 moved to Ennis, with detachments at Clarecastle, Kilrush, Tuamgraney, Sixmilebridge, Newmarket, Bradford, and Tullo (all in Co. Clare). In January 1797, they lost their Light Company to the 1st Battalion Light Infantry at Kilkenny.[20]

Headquarters	Company locations	Distance in miles
Carlow	Curragh	23
	Castlecomer	11
	Roscrea	37
	Athy	11
Rathkeale	Kilkenny	90
	Limerick	15
Limerick	O'Brien's Bridge	8
	Killaloe	11
Ennis	Clarecastle	3
	Kilrush	27
	Tuamgraney	19
	Sixmilebridge	12
	Newmarket	9
	Tullo (Tulla)	8

Table 4: Longford Battalion. Location distances, 1796–7

In August 1798, the Longford marched to Castlebar to fight as a four-company formation. Thus in a period of two years, they had changed headquarters four times, and would never have had the opportunity to train as a battalion. They did have this opportunity during a tour in Dublin in 1794-6, but it is important to recall that there would have been a constant turnover of men, for Dublin duty was like London duty, with a heavy requirement for guards for ceremonial duties.[21] This treatment is typical of what happened to many of the militia regiments, and there can be no doubt that this

---

20 General Order, 24 Jan. 1797 (PRONI, T/7 5 5/4/1/59). The order establishing the Light Battalions.   21 H.A. Richey, *A short history of the Royal Longford Militia* (Dublin, 1894), Appendix.

detached service materially affected their ability to fight as formations, as it prevented proper advanced training. Again, the purpose of the militia was a question not properly addressed, even after the 'march to Bantry' in December 1796, or on the formation of the yeomanry earlier in that year. And, of course, the whole thing came to a head with the appointment of General Abercromby as commander-in-chief in 1798. As we shall see, Abercromby wanted the army to be concentrated, and not divided into small detachments or 'penny packets'.

Larger formation training did take place, but finding evidence of it is difficult. Annual summer camps were to be a feature of militia training but it is unlikely any were held before 1795. In April of that year the new lord lieutenant, Lord Camden, outlined his plans for the defence of Ireland to the duke of Portland.[22] These plans included summer camps for the infantry, regular, fencible, and militia. He ordered camp stores for 20,000 men as there were only enough for 10,000 in store. In fact he had 41,000 men but only barracks to accommodate 8,000, which was a problem in itself. He was sending reconnaissance parties to find the best places for camps in the north and in Dublin. His proposal was that there should be 5,000 men in camp near Dublin, 4,000 in the south, and 3,000 in camp in the north. Later that summer, it was reported that in the 'camp near Dublin', probably Loughlinstown, were the Downshire, Drogheda, Fermanagh, Londonderry, South Mayo, Sligo, Westmeath, and Longford regiments and battalions, in the northern camp near Belfast, probably Blaris near Lisburn, Co. Antrim, were the Clare, South Cork, Limerick County, and Wexford, and in the southern camp near Cork, the Antrim, Armagh, Donegal, Dublin County, Galway, Leitrim, North Mayo, Monaghan and Waterford. There are no details, however, of what training these units carried out. It should also be noted that there is no record in the existing letter and order books of the Donegal Regiment of the regiment being at a camp at Ardfinnan in 1795.

In 1796 Camden reported that camps were to be established at Loughlinstown, Co. Dublin, Ardfinnan, Co. Tipperary, and Blaris, near Lisburn, Co. Antrim.[23] In June of that year Camden complained that although there were near 40,000 men in Ireland, they were so scattered that only 6,700 could be spared for the different camps throughout the country.[24] At his time of writing, the Kildare and Clare battalions, and the Donegal Regiment were in camp at Loughlinstown, the Wexford, Louth and Armagh Regiments were at Ardfinnan, and the Westmeath, Queen's County, Limerick City, and Cavan Battalions at Blaris.[25]

---

[22] Camden to Portland, 17 Apr. 1795 (NA, HO/100/54/29). [23] Camden to Portland, 21 Mar. 1796 (ibid., HO/100/60/67). [24] Camden to Pelham, 28 June 1796 (ibid., HO/100/64/129). [25] *Faulkner's Journal*, 2 June 1795.

There are some details of the camps at Loughlinstown and at Blaris. At the former, General Crosby, commanding the Dublin Garrison, reviewed the Clare, Kildare, and Donegal regiments on 23 June 1796. At this review, the regiments went through a series of manoeuvres before the general. The day was bad, and the general excused the Clare Militia from going through all their manoeuvres, as they were last on to the parade ground.[26] The camp at Blaris lasted from the beginning of June to 22 October 1796.[27] There is no information on the command structure of the camp, and the units involved were all stationed in the Belfast – Lisburn area in any case. The copies of orders and instructions that exist are mostly to do with administration. They include camp standing orders, with a prohibition on 'marauding', enforcing cleanliness, inspection of messes by the orderly officer, details of guard mounting and dismounting, the construction of 'necessaries', and the establishment of a general hospital in Lisburn. Other orders dealt with 'revilly' at break of day, morning and evening parades, prohibitions on gaming, booths selling drink to close at 8p.m., and not open until 'revilly' (that is, about 5a.m.). These orders also gave the daily 'parole', or password.

On 26 June, men were allowed to build 'hutts', and on 29 June, Sergeant William Anderson of the Cavans was appointed deputy provost marshal. Permission to build huts implies permanent residence as does the employment of women, one as a nurse in the hospital, and three per company to draw bread daily. Details of actual training and other activities are sparse. Soldiers had to perform their normal duties, and normal military tasks. On 23 June a detachment of the Cavans was ordered to Gilford, another to Hillsborough to meet Mr Lane (presumably Thomas Lane, Lord Downshire's agent for his Hillsborough estates). Another party was sent to Hillsborough to escort prisoners to Downpatrick gaol. On 31 July orders were given for regimental drill to be from 7 to 9 in the morning, and commanding officers were to practice the 18 manoeuvres for a review. There is no other evidence of what the troops did. The camps at Loughlinstown and Blaris did indeed become permanent, for the Kildare, Clare, Donegal, Limerick City, and Wexford were ordered to winter at the former, and at the latter, the Carlow, Wicklow, and Kerry regiments.[28]

There may have been camping in 1797, but the only record is in newspaper accounts of a three day exercise by the troops at Loughlinstown and the Dublin Garrison. Troops from Loughlinstown included the Romney Fencible Cavalry, the City of Limerick, Cavan and Kilkenny Battalions, and from the Dublin garrison, Fraser's Fencibles, York Fencibles, Suffolk Fencibles, 1st Battalion Light Infantry, and the Antrim Militia.[29]

---

26 *Freeman's Journal*, 25 June 1796. 27 General Orders for encamping, 20 June 1796 (NA, WO/68/402/102, Cavan Battalion letter book). 28 *Faulkner's Journal*, 27 Oct. 1796. 29 *Freeman's Journal*, 13 Oct. 1797.

This was a major exercises that had entailed considerable planning by the staff, and much rehearsal by the troops taking part. It was all essential training and experience, since it was precisely what they would have to do should an invasion take place. The only problem is that these are the only detailed accounts to be found in contemporary documents of major exercises, and newspapers, especially those which supported the government, such as the *Freeman's Journal*, were keen to publish such stories because they showed the crown forces practising their duties, with the added bonus of a social occasion. Indeed, there is no evidence of camping in 1797 other than at Loughlinstown, because there are no documents showing the locations of the troops in Ireland for that year. Thus if there was no other camping in 1797, twenty-seven militia regiments had trained together in 1795, 96, and 97. Of these, only the Clare, Donegal, Wexford, Armagh, Westmeath, Limerick City and Cavan had attended twice. No regiment attended a camp in all three years which was the original intention of the Castle. The numbers of units available to attend camps, 21 in 1795, ten in 1796 and only three in 1797, so far as is known, amply demonstrates the dispersal of the militia.

In December 1797, Abercromby, who did not run any major exercises, replaced Carhampton and he in turn was replaced by Gerard Lake just before the outbreak of the rebellion. If these were the only major exercises to have taken place, then it is evidence of a neglect of advanced training which the militia, as an army, needed to practise. It did not augur well for the future.

BARRACKS

The whole question of accommodating the militia in barracks, lodgings, and billets was a bone of contention from the raising of the militia in 1793, until well after the 1798 rebellion, when the reforms of Lord Cornwallis took place. The principal barracks in Ireland were at Carrickfergus (Co. Antrim), Dublin, Waterford, Cork, Kinsale (Co. Cork), the Forts in Cork Harbour, Limerick, Galway, and Londonderry. By far the biggest were at Dublin, and Cork. Smaller barracks were to be found at Athlone, Cashel (Co. Tipperary), Wicklow, Youghal (Co. Cork), Duncannon (Co. Waterford), Ross Castle, Dingle (both Co. Kerry), Clarecastle (Co. Clare), Belleek (Co. Fermanagh), and Ballyshannon (Co. Donegal).[30] In the 1790s, many smaller barracks were created, such as Clifton House in Belfast.[31] Barracks, however, might be regarded as the biggest business organization in eighteenth-century Ireland.[32]

---

30 Houlding, *Fit for service*, p. 53, has a map of the Quarters in Ireland in 1753. 31 Returned to the Belfast Charitable Society on 15 Nov.1798, Lord Castlereagh was to indemnify them for its use. Letter to Maj.-Gen. Nugent, 15 Nov. 1798 (NLI, KP/134/200). 32 R.B. McDowell, 'Ireland in the eighteenth-century British Empire', in J.G. Barry (ed.), *Historical*

Barrackmasters were appointed to administer these barracks. They had to provide firing and candles, beds, clean bedding, fire irons, cooking utensils, and facilities, whilst keeping the barracks in good order. Where necessary, they had to hire buildings to be used as barracks, and if they were on a main highway, had to provide accommodation for troops moving from one location to another. This meant putting soldiers in billets (private houses), in public houses and inns. It was a responsible, and extremely important task, given that so many bodies of soldiers were always on the move. No doubt many barrackmasters performed their duties perfectly adequately, but there were some spectacular failures, caused, as ever in eighteenth-century Ireland, by inadequate organization, neglect, lack of supervision and liaison. Barracks were the responsibility of the commissioners of the Barrack Board, until Lord Tyrawley was appointed barrackmaster-general in 1799.[33] They were not the responsibility of the commander-in-chief, who could only request the barrack board to take action, and there was little he could do if they refused, other than appeal to the lord lieutenant. For example, there were complaints about the poor quality of coals in Belfast in October 1797, made by the regiments stationed there, including the Monaghan Militia. Lord Carhampton, the commander-in-chief, could only request that the barrack board improve their quality.[34] That was the nub of the problem. Until the crisis caused by the outbreak of war with France in 1793, the position of barrackmaster was given to civilians without any necessity of military experience, and was regarded as something of a sinecure. As we shall see, barrackmasters could act as contractors to their own barracks for fire and candles, but inspectors of barracks and architects could also act as contractors, which was both useful and profitable to them, as they decided on contracts, the acceptability of goods, services, buildings, and repairs.

The first hint of the problems to come appeared in July 1793, when Lord Glandore, lieutenant-colonel commandant of the Kerry Regiment, complained about the conduct of the barrackmaster at Ross Castle, and Colonel Handfield noted that there had been frequent complaints about neglect of barrackmasters throughout the kingdom.[35] Then Lieutenant-Colonel Montgomery of the Monaghan Militia complained about the work being done in the barrack yard in Monaghan. The men doing it, he averred, 'are as fit for the execution of it as they are to command a squadron of men o' war.'[36] Five months later, Mr Donelan was ordered to complete the work, and was informed that he would not be paid until the work was done properly.[37]

Studies, 9 (1974), p. 58. 33 Cornwallis to Portland, 17 Mar. 1799 (NA, HO/100/83/188). 34 Carhampton to Pelham, 24 Oct. 1797 (NLI, KP/1014/31). 35 Charles Handfield to Richard Thwaites, 25 June 1793 (ibid., KP/1115/56.) 36 Charles Handfield to Richard Thwaites, 12 Nov. 1793 (ibid., KP/1115/80). 37 Charles Handfield to J.B. Roberts, 4 Feb. 1794 (ibid., KP/1115/99).

The institution

In the meantime, in April 1794, Major George Matthews marched his regiment, the Royal Downshire, from Killough and Newry to Youghal. He provided one of the few contemporary reports on the standard of accommodation arranged for them on their route by local barrackmasters.

Ardee (Co. Louth) – Waiter wouldn't drink the King's health, and got beaten.
Navan (Co. Meath) – bad.
Trim (Co. Meath) – very bad.
Clonard (Co. Westmeath) – well.
Edenderry (Co. Kildare) – very well.
Portarlington (King's County) – well.
Maryborough (Queen's County) – well.
Castle Durrow (Queen's County) – well.
Johnstown (Co. Kilkenny) – horrid bad.
Cashel (Co. Tipperary) – bad for men.
Clogheen (Co. Tipperary) – well.
Kilworth (Co. Cork) – well.
Tullow (Co. Cork) – well.

Table 5: Accommodation for the Royal Downshire Militia, Newry to Youghal

He also reported that the barracks in Youghal were bad, and infested with rats, one of which had reportedly eaten an ear off a man of the 55th Regiment, and due to this infestation, the men dreaded the 'black hole' (solitary confinement).[38]

Bad though some of the places were in which troops had to lodge while on the march, the established barracks could be a problem, and this could be known for some considerable time before any action was taken. Lieutenant-Colonel Montgomery commented on the work being done in Monaghan Barracks in 1793, but it was not until January 1796 that action was ordered to be taken, and this was as a result of an inspection by the quartermaster of the Clare Battalion. Barracks housed militiamen, their wives and children, and sickness was a problem that was much feared, even though the health of the Irish militia throughout this period was good.[39] The quartermaster of the Clare Battalion found that the barrackmaster would not go round with him and make an inventory, the rooms were dismal, the garret had holes in the roof, there were eight beds in it, the rain came in incessantly, the windows were all broken, as a result the battalion had to take a large room in the town at 3 2s. per month chargeable to them, in several rooms there was no window glass, outside doors had no locks, there were no fire irons, pot hooks, or coal tubs. Some of the floors were so rotten as to be a danger to those walking on them. Since the Clares took possession on 26 October 1795, they had never received clean straw or clean sheets.[40]

38 Maj. Matthews to Lord Annesley, 8 Apr. 1794 (PRONI, D/607/C/31). 39 A statement of deaths in the Irish militia for five years ending 31 Dec. 1800 (NAS, GD/ 364/1/1129/2). 40 Lt.-Col. Quin John Freeman to R. Uniacke, Esq., 23 Jan. 1796 (NLI, KP/1116/53).

Complaints continued steadily, it was patently obvious that the system did not work well – if a barrackmaster refused to do his duty, for whatever reason, there was no system of supervision, nor any form of sanction. Action, when it came, was as a result of persistent complaints from the army. In June 1795 the barrackmaster at Birr sent a bill to the Donegal Regiment for 'barrack damages.'[41] Lieutenant-Colonel Richard Maxwell replied smartly that when the detachment arrived at Lough Glynn House – the 'barrack' in question – there had been no-one there to hand it over to them, and on quitting, no-one to receive it back, which was 'exceedingly irregular.'[42]

In 1797 there does not seem to have been any real improvement. In May a depot for furniture was established at Armagh.[43] Five months later a letter from Lord Carhampton to Thomas Pelham reveals the tension between the army and the barrack board. In answering a complaint from the board about great depredations carried out in barracks, Carhampton retorted that if the board had done its duty under 'Article 1 of the Order of Government of 28 June 1789,' such things would not have happened.[44]

General Sir Ralph Abercromby replaced Lord Carhampton in December 1797. In February 1798 Abercromby, as a result of his initial inspections throughout the country, reported to Pelham that at Loughlinstown, he would station no more that 500 troops; at Blaris (Co. Antrim), an inconvenient location, 1,200; and at Tarbert, on the Shannon near Limerick, he would make no change because of its importance as an artillery position. Needless to say, there were considerably more than these numbers at these locations.

Abercromby did not stay long enough to make any impression. It was not until the arrival of Lord Cornwallis on 20 June 1798 that things began to improve. In August 1798, the members of the barrack board, Ponsonby Moore, John Townsend, Lieutenant-Colonel Sir J.M. O'Reilly, and the Hon. A.C. Hamilton, were ordered to Dublin to do their duty.[45] In September, Robert Fenwick, the barrackmaster at Drogheda, was superseded, and in the same month, the barrack board was told to make specific complaints, and not general ones, as troops had to know their duties, and officers must be named if they were to be charged with neglect. The affair, which brought matters to a head, was failure to supervise the barracks at St Stephen's Green.[46]

In October 1798, Cornwallis made his views known to the barrack board in an order outlining the state of barrack accommodation, and the future requirements, together with names of those who had offered accommodation

---

[41] John Stevens to Officer Commanding, Donegal Regiment, 2 June 1795 (NA, WO/68/221, Donegal Militia Letter Book). [42] Richard Maxwell to John Stevens, 7 June 1795 (ibid.). [43] Handfield to R. Uniacke, 9 May 1797 (NLI, KP/1116/90). [44] Carhampton to Pelham, 30 Oct. 1797 (ibid., KP/1014/39). [45] Secretary of the Barrack Board to the Members, 3 Aug. 1798 (ibid., KP/1116/143). [46] H. Taylor to R. Uniacke, 28 Sept. 1798 (ibid., KP/1116, no pagination). Taylor was aide de camp to Cornwallis.

to the army in the southern part of the kingdom. He specifically demanded action on the accommodation for troops stationed on the Grand Canal, and made a request for an additional 6,346 new bed spaces in counties Kildare and Wicklow.[47]

The barracks at New Geneva was an important location because it was from there that soldiers convicted of crimes, and sentenced to serve abroad for life, were sent out of Ireland to New South Wales, the West Indies, and elsewhere. New Geneva was located at Passage, near the confluence of the rivers Barrow and Nore, and opposite the fortress of Duncannon in Co. Waterford. Major-General Johnston, who commanded there, forwarded a report made by the commanding officer of the Dunbarton Fencibles in which the barracks were described as being filthy, bedding being issued which had been condemned, walls filthy, needing whitewash, eighty convicts in each house instead of seventy, broken windows everywhere, the officers quarters being without tables, chairs, or fire irons, and that Mr Hendy, an inspector of barracks, had visited recently, but had not gone into any barrack room. It was after this that things began to change rapidly.[48]

In the same month, Isaac Corry, MP for Newry, recommended a Mr Samuel Reed as the new barrackmaster for Newry. This was not accepted, as Cornwallis believed that barrackmasters should be deserving old soldiers, and not persons 'in a civil line.'[49] In 1801, Captain Snowe of the North Cork Militia was appointed barrackmaster at Carrick-on-Shannon, Co. Roscommon, at 7s. 6d. a day.[50] On the same day Captain Chambers of the Longford Militia, who had been very badly wounded at the defence of the bridge in Castlebar, was offered a similar position in Roscommon, at the same rate of pay.[51] In May 1801, Chambers unsuccessfully requested a pay rise to 10s. per day.[52]

Cornwallis took complaints seriously. In November 1798, there were complaints about the barrackmaster in Carrick-on-Suir.[53] A few days later, there were complaints about accommodation for the North Corks on the (Grand) canal, despite specific instructions a month earlier.[54] On 17 November, Mr Lyster, the barrackmaster of Naas was dismissed, and he was the first of several.[55]

Cornwallis obviously felt that the 'Commissioners of the Barrack Board' constituted too amorphous a body for anyone to take responsibility, to act promptly, and decisively, so in 1799, Lord Tyrawley was appointed barrackmaster-general, with Lieutenant-Colonel Quin John Freeman of the 16th

---

[47] H. Taylor to the Commissioners of the Barracks, 9 Oct. 1798 (ibid., KP/1116, no pagination). [48] Ibid., 15 Oct. 1798. [49] H. Taylor to Rt. Hon. Isaac Corry, 10 Oct. 1798 (ibid., KP/1205/174). [50] H. Taylor to Capt. Snowe, 19 Mar. 1801 (ibid., KP/1092/210). [51] H. Taylor to Capt. Chambers, 19 Mar. 1801 (ibid., KP/1092/211). [52] Ibid., 1 May 1801 (ibid., KP/1093/20). [53] H. Taylor to Commissioners of the Barrack Board, 5 Nov. 1798 (ibid., KP/1116, No pagination, or numbering). [54] Ibid., 7 Nov. 1798 [55] H. Taylor to Lord Tyrawley, 17 Nov. 1798 (ibid.).

Regiment as his deputy.[56] In November of the same year, barrackmasters were ordered to cease acting as contractors to their barracks, as were inspectors and architects.[57] In December the Donegall Arms, departure point in Belfast for the Dublin Mail, was given up as a barracks.[58]

Cornwallis, as a soldier, was well aware of the important linkage between the effectiveness of the soldier, and the quality of his accommodation. Poor accommodation led to illness and disease, and reduced the effectiveness of the troops. In November 1801, the Army Medical Board reported on the state of barracks in Ireland. Evidently more attention was being paid to the medical aspects of accommodation, and the Medical Board was acquiring more influence in the administration of barracks. The board criticized the new infantry barracks in Belfast, built to accommodate 2,000 troops, but completed for only half that. The chimneys were reported as not good, there were too many huts, and an inadequate water supply. Three pumps had been provided in the square, two were not working, and men were being admitted to hospital with fever and disease, but they reported that such admissions were not in the proportion of one to six of men admitted who lodged in the town.[59] This gives a fair indication of the general state of barracks in Ireland, and the efforts of Cornwallis to improve things, by reforming a system previously run for the benefit of its operatives.

In many ways, the conduct of barrackmasters epitomizes much of what has been discussed in this chapter. There was reluctance among many of the members of the Barrack Board, and many barrackmasters, to perform their duties, since they regarded their appointments as being virtually a sinecure, with the facility of being able to act as a contractor. This was so even after the tremendous increase in troops following the declaration of war with revolutionary France. It is something that can be compared with the indecision evident in 1793, when the militia was called out for full-time service, about whether or not regiments should serve in their home counties – despite it being specifically mentioned in the act that they would – with the general indecision over the actual purpose of the militia. All of this badly affected the training of the soldiers, particularly in formations larger than a company. It is almost as if the government, having decided on a course of action, and having put it into effect, did not think of the next stage of implementation, or of supervision of what they had directed. A characteristic of the Irish government of the time, seems to be that it was always totally reactive, and rarely, if ever, proactive.

---

56 Cornwallis to Portland, 17 Mar. 1799 (NA, HO/100/83/188). 57 E.B. Littlehales to Lord Tyrawley, 9 Nov. 1799 (NLI, KP/1137/346). 58 E.B. Littlehales to Lt.-Col. Q.J. Freeman, 26 Dec. 1799 (ibid., KP/1121/5). 59 *Report on the state of barracks in Ireland*, 12 Nov. 1801 (NAS, GD/ 364/1/1125).

CHAPTER FOUR

Officers

Colonel John Moore arrived in Ireland on 2 December 1797 and was posted first to command the forts in Cork Harbour, but before long he had been promoted to the rank of brigadier-general and given command of a brigade of Irish light infantry. He was not impressed by the quality of his officers:

> When the militia was first formed, had pains been taken to select proper officers and to introduce discipline, they might, by this time, have been respectable troops but like everything else in this country the giving of regiments was made an instrument of influence with the colonels, and they made their appointments to suit electioneering purposes.[1]

Moore's first impressions of the Irish militia accord with several other oft-quoted first impressions, made with great confidence in private diaries and letters, but from short acquaintance and little experience of the Irish soldier, and the situation in Ireland. The problem we face in forming a truly objective opinion about the officer corps of the militia generally is the lack of contemporary evidence. If the half-yearly inspection reports of the militia regiments could be found, they would reveal a great deal about the quality of the officers in general, and the state of training of the men. Since all of these reports, save that of the King's County Regiment in Guernsey in 1799 are missing, much of what we can glean comes from a wide variety of sources, and tends to provide us with 'snapshots' from which to draw conclusions. This can be effective, but the great disadvantage is that the vast majority of officers who do their duty in an unspectacular fashion, never get any mention, and tend to be forgotten. The point has been made before, that for all the bad or inefficient officers in the militia, every regiment had some good ones, who had a considerable influence on the performance of their units in the field and in barracks.

The half yearly inspection reports may be missing but the requirements of the inspections are well known and most of what was being inspected was the responsibility of the officers of the regiment. The best example is the order to the Donegal Regiment on 22 May 1799, that they were to be

---

1 Sir J.F. Maurice (ed.), *Diary of Sir John Moore*, 2 vols. (London, 1904), i, ch. 11.

inspected by Major-General Sir Robert Ross, and that he would be looking at all aspects of the regiment's work, including the established and effective strengths (which shows the efficiency of the regiment's recruiting), the commanding officer's attendance at quarters, and his attention to discipline, the instruction and attention to duty of officers and NCOs, whether or not the regiment adhered to King's Regulations, the regiment's performance at the field and manual exercise, the size, age and nationality of the men, and recruits, the state of clothing and arms, numbers of men who had died, been discharged, or had deserted in the previous six months, the regiment's accounts, the regimental books, how the regiment dealt with complaints, the management of the regimental hospital, the arrangements for feeding the men, the recording of regimental courts martial, and the turnout and dress of the officers and men.[2]

Much of this is also highly relevant when discussing the men, but all of these things were the responsibility of the officers of the regiment. If the general reported unfavourably on any of them, then that was failure in an officer to have done his duty. As Major Matthews of the Royal Downshire commented to his colonel, Lord Downshire, about the officers in the regiment, 'The men are everything you could wish them, and you have some good officers ... having spirit enough to meet the enemy in the field is by many people thought sufficient for an officer, in my opinion it is the least part of his duty'.[3] In other words, the perception of many people was that an officer's duty was to lead his men gallantly against an enemy, and nothing else, whereas Matthews was pointing out that an officer was responsible for his men, for their training, welfare, discipline, and dress and these matters comprised the major part of an officer's duty. In trying to form a judgment on the officers of the militia, we will look at the militia commission and its peculiarities, the attitude of officers to duty, and discipline, and the question of absence, with or without leave. It is obvious, already, from what both Moore and Matthews had to say, that there were divergent views among the officers themselves, as to what they were supposed to do.

THE MILITIA COMMISSION

We have already looked at the general background of senior army officers posted to Ireland, with reference to the mental adjustment they had to make over the question of the religion of their soldiers. These officers belonged to a tried and trusted system, which, in their eyes, all understood. Officers in

2 General Order, Cove, 22 May 1799 (NA, WO/68/222. Donegal Militia general order book).
3 Matthews to Downshire, 7 Jan. 1797 (PRONI, D/607/E/14). (A comment made on the 'road to Bantry', 1797.)

the infantry and cavalry in the main purchased their commissions, although as much as one third of the officer corps were promoted from the ranks or commissioned without purchase. This system had the reputation for being haphazard, but was in fact strictly controlled. All new commissions were signed by the king, and had to be approved first by the commanding officer of the regiment, then by the colonel, before reaching the king. Both George II and George III took a great interest in the commissioning of officers. All exchanges to another regiment, promotions, and 'selling out,' could only be done with the authority of Horse Guards. Officers exchanged regiments frequently on promotion, as, for example, General Robert Craufurd, who was commissioned into the 25th Foot in 1779, promoted captain in the 75th Foot in 1783, and lieutenant-colonel in the 60th Royal Americans in 1798, when he came to Ireland.[4] It is important to realize that all officers were commanded by regimental or staff officers, and all had come through the same system, so that the army could always ensure that it had a body of officers acceptable to itself.

When the government raised the militia, the system of creating officers was different. The lieutenant-colonels commandant were appointed by the Castle – the lord lieutenant represented the king. Moore complained that the appointments were political, but this is not necessarily correct. The Castle would be extremely unlikely to appoint someone who was actively against the government, but did appoint people who were not necessarily government supporters. Many colonels were county governors, such as Lord Abercorn in Tyrone, and Lord Portarlington in Queen's County, and they were government supporters, but 'supporter' is a matter of interpretation. In 1796 Camden wrote to Pelham about the vacancy in the Donegal Regiment as the lieutenant-colonel commandant had died. He said he was going to offer it to Lord Clements because of his weight and property in the county, provided he supported the government.[5] Clements, who took his duties seriously, accepted the appointment, and there is a note in his own hand, which might have been a draft of his reply to Camden, setting out his views.[6] It is clear that he was not a supporter of the government (he opposed the Act of Union in 1 7 9 9), and he said that acceptance of the appointment would not make him a supporter, but he did support the government in its prosecution of the war against France. He did not regard the appointment as an office

---

4 Lieutenant-Colonel Robert Craufurd (1764–1812), was deputy quartermaster general of the forces in Ireland in 1798. He commanded the Light Division in the Peninsular War, and was killed leading the assault on Cuidad Rodrigo in 1 8 1 2. He was impetuous, opinionated, and ambitious, as well as being possibly an over zealous disciplinarian, and was very unpopular with his officers. The manner of his death created a legend perpetuated by officers of the 60th and 9 5th Rifles in post-war literature.   5 Camden to Pelham, n.d., but soon after 15 June 1796 (PRONI, T/755/3/18).   6 Note, n.d., but 1796 (NLI, Clements papers, P.C. 630).

under the government (which would have compromised his principles), but one that was offered to 'independent gentlemen of fortune selected for their consequence and influence in the country'.[7] Undoubtedly Clements was right, but the very fact that the note was written is proof that such appointments were made in other cases for political reasons, and certainly it is worth noting that the duke of Leinster resigned from the Kildare Militia in 1797 because he could no longer support the government.[8]

The newly appointed lieutenant-colonels commandant had the task of appointing the officers to their regiments. A study of the dates of officers' commissions shows that they did this with despatch. Moore claimed that these appointments were made for electioneering purposes, and Robert Craufurd observed that 'only a proportion of the captains and none of the subalterns ... are gentlemen'.[9] Craufurd watched the militia closely, and made a number of suggestions for improvements in discipline and training, many of which were subsequently acted upon. However, these comments by Craufurd and Moore are based on what they had seen in particular parts of Ireland in a short space of time in 1798.Whilst undoubtedly electioneering or other interest may have influenced appointments of captains and subalterns, and that many may not have been 'gentlemen,' nepotism and family interest were of far greater importance. Almost every regiment had a relative of the lieutenant-colonel commandant in it, or a relative of some or all of the field officers. We have already mentioned Lord O'Neill's sons in the Antrims, but, to give some examples: Lord Gosford appointed his sons, Archibald and Edward Acheson, as ensigns in the Armagh Regiment;[10] in the City of Cork the Hon. Richard Longfield appointed Mountifort Longfield as his lieutenant-colonel; in the City of Dublin Henry Gore Sankey appointed his son and his own brother as captains. In the North Cork relationships were labyrinthine. Lord Kingsborough, the lieutenant-colonel commandant was related to Lord Kingston, his lieutenant-colonel; Major Thomas Newenham was the son-in-law of Captain-Lieutenant Edward Hoare; Captains Richard Foote and Edward Heard were related; and Captain James Lombard was married into the Kingston family.[11] In the Downshire Major Matthews was related to Captain John Echlin; Captain David Hamilton Boyd to Ensign John Keown; and of course, in the Londonderry Thomas Conolly appointed as his lieutenant-colonel his nephew, Robert Stewart, Lord Castlereagh.

The social status of the junior officers is much more difficult to access, Lord Downshire, as an example, appointed eight captains, all of whom were

---

7 Ibid.   8 Camden to Portland, 19 May 1798 (NA, HO/100/69/317).   9 Craufurd to Wickham, 19 Nov. 1798 (ibid., HO/100/79/116).   10 Archibald became a captain in 1795, major in 1798, colonel in 1801, but at least he came through the officer ranks. Edward transferred to the 85th Foot on 22 February 1800, and later to the Coldstream Guards.   11 I am grateful to Mr Stawell St Leger Heard of East Sussex for this information.

landowners or who had an interest in land in accordance with the Act – Sir Richard Johnston at Gilford, Cromwell Price at Saintfield, Francis and Andrew Savage at Portaferry, D.H. Boyd at Kircubbin, John Echlin at Rubane, and Arthur Annesley at Castlewellan. Of his lieutenants, eleven out of fourteen, and of his ensigns, seven out of ten, had property in the county.

On the question of political allegiances, Lord Downshire seems to have appointed a fairly broad spectrum of county landowners to his regiment, and political allegiances do not seem to have been of great importance. No doubt he was assisted by the fact that the Stewarts, his great rivals in the county, were connected with the Londonderry Regiment. However, no Blackwood served before 1800, despite overtures made by Sir George Dallas MP from 1798 onwards, and several officers resigned after minimal service, such as Robert Waddell, Edward Southwell Trotter, and the Hon. Robert Ward. Verifiable Downshire supporters in the regiment included Lord Annesley, Major George Matthews, Sir Richard Johnston, Robert Montgomery, Cromwell Price, Sir George Stephenson, and the Revd Holt Waring, the chaplain, and Stewart supporters included the Hon. Robert Ward, John Gordon, Pringle Hall, and Andrew Savage.[12] But of course, this is only the case of the Downshire Regiment, which admittedly had a colonel who was very conscious of his status, which would have to be reflected in his regiment. Other colonels may well have been less scrupulous.

Other anomalies in commissions given to Irish militia officers should be considered. At first, dual commissions, both regular army and militia, were allowed, but how officers were able to fulfil the duties of one or the other is difficult to know. The practice was stopped in 1795, and officers had to choose which they wished to retain.[13] This is why Captain the Hon. Robert Ward had considerable problems in the Downshire Militia in 1796. He had raised a regiment for the King's service, and as their colonel, could not remain as a militia officer, so resigned when he moved to England with them.[14]

Officers who were surgeons, and mates, also held dual commissions, and were expected to be both regimental officers and surgeons. The most famous example would perhaps be that of Lieutenant David McAnally, surgeon of the Armagh Regiment, and great-grandfather of Sir Henry McAnally.[15] Another example is Lieutenant Daniel Williams, surgeon of the North Cork Regiment, who was killed at Oulart Hill in 1798, acting as a regimental officer.[16] According to Sir Henry McAnally, the Army Medical Board condemned this practice, and added, 'on service the joint discharge of the mil-

12 P.J. Jupp, 'County Down elections 1783-1831,' in *IHS*, 18:70 (1972), 201-2. 13 Longford Militia, General and Standing Orders (NAI, M3480). 14 C. Handfield to Lt. Col. Ward, 7 July 1797 (NLI, KP/1081/142). 15 McAnally, *Irish Militia*, reproduced as the frontispiece. 16 Pay Lists and Muster Rolls, North Cork Militia (NA, WO/13/2706).

itary and medical duties has ever been found impracticable, and ... we have never as yet met with a single individual who could act the part of the soldier and the surgeon at the same time without being good for nothing in the latter capacity'.[17] Nevertheless, the practice was not stopped until after the rebellion in 1798.[18] This was followed by another order, defining the position of surgeons and mates – the former had the standing of captains, and the latter, that of lieutenants, but without rank.[19] Surgeons and mates had to be qualified, and were not allowed to serve both in a civilian hospital, and the army.[20] Surgeons, and mates, incidentally, like adjutants, did not require a property qualification to be eligible for a commission.

Militia commissions were signed by the lieutenant-colonel commandant, not by the lord lieutenant, or the king. This made them an inferior commission to that of the regular officer. Future promotions were the responsibility of the lieutenant-colonel commandant, or the commanding officer of the regiment. Commissions were not purchased, although there is evidence that sometimes they were. In May 1793, a notice appeared in the *Freeman's Journal* offering a £400 'douceur' for an adjutancy in a militia regiment.[21] In 1798, Lieutenant James Harrison applied to Lord Downshire for authority to sell his adjutancy of the Downshires to Mr Smollett Holden, the bandmaster, for £700.[22] He did not wish to sell his commission, as he wanted to remain as paymaster. Holden confirmed that he wished to purchase.[23] There is no evidence that Downshire ever did anything about this most unusual request, and it is worth remembering that in the army generally, if a rank was not purchased, then it could not be sold. Harrison was not trying to sell his commission, but his appointment as adjutant to Holden, who was a civilian.

In 1799 Major Woodward of the Cavan Battalion paid the 'late' major to induce him to resign. Colonel Littlehales informed him that militia commissions were 'under no circumstances vendible, and private pecuniary transactions highly irregular'.[24] However, Littlehales may have been acting on false information, or have been a little hasty, because Woodward's predecessor, James Platt, had not been induced to resign, but had been promoted to lieutenant-colonel at the same time.[25] Another example was that of Captain Fitzmaurice of the Queen's County Regiment who purchased the adjutancy

---

17 McAnally, *Irish Militia*, p. 23. 18 Castlereagh to Clements, 10 Oct. 1798 (NA, WO/68/221, Donegal Militia Order Book). 19 Adjutant General's Order, 24 June 1799 (ibid.). 20 35 Geo. III, c.8, xxvi (1795). 21 *Freeman's Journal*, 9 May 1793. 22 Harrison to Downshire, 4 Mar. 1798 (PRONI, D/607/F/147). 23 Holden to Downshire, n.d. (ibid., D/607/F/147). Holden did become adjutant of the Royal South Down Militia in 1800. 24 Littlehales to Maj. B.B. Woodward, 14 Aug. 1799 (NLI, KP/1086/68). Woodward's son, Benjamin (1816–59), became the distinguished architect. 25 *A list of the officers of the several regiments and battalions of militia and of the several regiments of fencible cavalry and infantry*, 8 Aug. 1800 (PRONI, T/3367/1).

from Captain St Clair for £550. The brigade commander of the Queen's County Regiment was informed that the clerk of the peace of the county signed militia commissions, and that they were not vendible.[26] There is sporadic evidence of this nature, showing that from time to time commissions and appointments were bought and sold, including those of surgeon and mate, but no evidence of a general trade in them.

At first there was no minimum age for ensigns, nor were there any formal educational qualifications (there were none for any army officer), as the sons of the gentry were expected to have received a modicum of the latter. In 1794, a general order directed that all newly appointed ensigns were not to be under sixteen years of age, and to be fit to do duty.[27] Obviously, this was aimed at those who commissioned younger sons, still at school or university. In September 1793, for example, Patrick Savage of Portaferry thanked Lord Downshire for appointing his son, another Patrick, to the Royal Downshire Militia, and noted, 'wherever he may be quartered, he probably will have opportunity of pursuing his school learning (which his late illness has interrupted) and your Lordship will, I am certain, allow him to take advantage of it'.[28] There is more than a suggestion here that the very young ensigns may have been young men who did not have an aptitude for learning, and that their education may have been neglected or avoided, so that a commission in the militia was seen as a way of providing gainful employment, and removing them from other temptations. In support of this suggestion, one may cite evidence of an attitude to education, 'One of the officers present with the Sligo Regiment at Vinegar Hill used to recount the circumstances attending his debut into military life, which occurred shortly before that event. A sergeant, entering the school room in Sligo, where he was attending at his lessons, saluted and noted the adjutant's request that the youthful ensign should forthwith join his regiment. The schoolboy thereupon, flinging his books at the head of his pedagogue, rushed out of the classroom cheering for the army.'[29] The second part of the quotation from Colonel Craufurd, above, says, 'everyone knows what a brute the uneducated son of an Irish farmer or middleman is',[30] but Craufurd does not elaborate, or provide any concrete evidence, so that we do not know if this is a comment on 'education' as such, or on 'class', as he exempted all the field officers from his strictures. In 1801, Lieutenant-Colonel Richard Maxwell of the Donegal Regiment, writing to his colonel, Lord Clements, about Captain Colhoun, who was to be sent to command the light company which was detached to

---

26 Littlehales to Brig.-Gen. Barnett, 29 Aug. 1799 (NLI, KP/1137/10).   27 General Order, Adjutant General's Office, 6 Mar. 1794 (NLI, KP/1086/68).   28 Savage to Downshire, 9 Sept. 1793 (PRONI, D/607/B/428).   29 *Digest of services of the Sligo Militia* (NA, WO/68/76).   30 Craufurd to Wickham, 19 Nov. 1798 (ibid., HO/100/79/116).

the flank battalions, described the posting as, 'an arduous undertaking for a young man who has been most dreadfully neglected in his education ... and who at the same time is so totally ignorant of the service ... instead of taking care of a company, it would almost require a company to take care of him'.[31] A doubt must persist about the educational standards of some of the officers commissioned at a very young age. On the other hand, a subaltern or captain who was an heir to a landed estate, as many of the militia officers were, would be extremely unlikely not to have an education to fit him to manage his inheritance in due course.

Earlier, it was mentioned that lieutenant-colonels commandant were responsible for filling officer 'casualties' as they occurred. A study of the muster rolls shows that resignations were common, and, also that these vacancies were filled quickly. The most glaring exception was Lord Downshire. Whatever credit he may be given for choosing his officers from a broad political spectrum, and for his work in easing the passage of the Militia Act, he can only be described as negligent in the care and attention he paid to his regiment afterwards. In particular, he was extremely slow to fill vacancies for officers, and his papers contain many pleas from Major Matthews for the colonel to come to the regiment, concern over the quality of the men's' clothing, and slowness in filling officer vacancies. Indeed, after the death of Cromwell Price in 1798 and the resignations of Captains Waddell and Trotter, three companies had no commander for eighteen months. This was scandalous, and would not go unobserved in the six-monthly inspections, so that when Downshire fell foul of Cornwallis in 1800, his inattention to his regiment would have been one of the things counting against him.

These are but a few of the anomalies and peculiarities of the militia commission. They were more than enough to cause a certain antipathy between regular and militia commissioned officers when the militia was called out for full-time service. In the eighteenth century there was no professional training for any army officer, other than artillery and engineers, and new officers had to learn their duties from more experienced colleagues. In the militia, however, there was no such reservoir of service, other than most of the adjutants who happened to be former sergeant-majors. Of the eleven officers in the Armagh Regiment in 1796, three had served more than twelve years (they were ex-regulars), five had served three years, and the remainder less than three. The youngest officer was the Hon. Edward Acheson.[32] His father, Lord Gosford, was 50, as was Captain Michael Obins, Captain Richard Johnston was 38, Major Thomas Stewart, and Captain Edward Obre were

---

31 Maxwell to Clements, 17 Oct. 1801 (NLI, Clements papers, PC 945).   32 After transferring to the Coldstream Guards, he was involved as a lieutenant-colonel in the defence of Hougoumont Farm at the battle of Waterloo in 1815.

both 30, and the remaining five, including Lieutenant-Colonel Robert Camden Cope, were 25 or under.[33] There is no evidence that the broad general experience of the regular army was ever put at the disposal of the militia, other than to lend sergeants to teach the manual and platoon exercise. Furthermore, the army commanders had no powers of recommendation in the selection of the colonels commandant, or of promotions within regiments, or on the filling of vacancies, or on the quality of any officer. Not only this, militia colonels were appointed by the lord lieutenant, to serve under the commander-in-chief. Almost without exception, they were men of territorial power, which also meant political power. If they did not like the policies of the commander-in-chief, they could circumvent him by going through parliament to the lord lieutenant, and this almost certainly happened with General Abercromby in 1798. This severely limited the powers of the commander-in-chief, as well as taxing whatever diplomatic ability he may have had. The militia was 'difficult' to deal with, and the English militia was even more troublesome in this regard as Cornwallis found in 1798-9. The army commanders, few of whom were Irish, were well able to complain about the quality of militia officers, almost all of whom were Irish, but there is no evidence that any of them ever did anything to make officer appointments more accountable to the military establishment, or to ensure that the officer corps of the militia was of a standard acceptable to them.

One of the problems faced by almost all the field officers of the militia regiments, and a substantial number of the junior officers, was how to balance the demands of regimental service with their positions as landowners and public officials. Many officers were magistrates, others high sheriff, members of grand juries, and of parliament. These appointments required their presence in their counties, or in Dublin, and also made demands on that precious commodity, time. No less than twenty-one peers were colonels commandant of the militia, a further three were lieutenant-colonels, and two were members of the house of commons , as younger sons – Lords Castlereagh and Tyrone. This means that 61 per cent of militia colonels had to attend parliament, which, in those days, was supposedly compulsory. As well as this, some 18 per cent of members of the house of commons were also militia officers.

The problem was compounded when a regiment had more than one field officer who was a public official. Nine regiments had two field officers who were members of one or other house of parliament, which meant that two out of three field officers might be absent when parliament was sitting. If the third field officer was absent, a very junior officer might command the regiment indeed. A very good example may be found in the Downshires, where Lords Downshire and Annesley were members of the house of lords,

---

[33] Muster Roll of the Armagh Regiment, 1793–1801 (PRONI, D/183/1).

and Major Matthews a member of the County Down grand jury. Indeed, in this instance, as many as seven out of 23 grand jurymen in 1796 were Downshire Militia officers, including the foreman, Francis Savage, and the Hon. Robert Ward, who were also MPs.[34] The leave rules required at least one field officer to be present at all times, and this 'one' tended to be the norm in many regiments. Between 1793 and 1798, in the regiments to which we have paid most attention, the Armagh and the Longford did not once have all three field officers serving together at the same time, the Downshire had all three once only, and the Donegal had two of the three once only. The North Cork had no field officers present at all between 1 October 1794 and 31 March 1797, some thirty months. Moreover, despite the order from the Castle that one field officer was to be present at all times, the Longfords lost Major Sandys, and the Antrims Major Hardy, to staff duties in Dublin and Wicklow respectively, for almost all of this period.[35] The burden of public office fell heaviest on the more senior officers, who were also the men who held the executive positions in a regiment. In 1793, of the nine captains and above in the Armagh Regiment, no less than seven held public office – Lord Gosford was governor of the county, Major William Brownlow a member of parliament and a member of the grand jury; Lieutenant-Colonel William Richardson, Major William Brownlow, and Captain Michael Obins also members of the grand jury; Obins and James Verner justices of the peace; and Captain-Lieutenant John Pringle high sheriff.[36] This situation continued in the following years, as individuals were replaced, their successors held public office of one kind or another. The consequence for the running of militia regiments was that junior officers frequently had responsibilities beyond their age and experience, regiments were short-staffed, with the concomitant effect on discipline and training of the men. In 1796–7 when the regiments had so much detached service, it was particularly noticeable and it is a point that cannot be emphasized enough.

Militia officers were not unaffected by the social standards of the time, and regarded defence of their 'honour' as an essential part of the duty of an officer. Duelling was but a small part of the persona of the eighteenth-century militia officer, who, in this respect, was no different to anyone else of his class. There is no evidence – at this stage – of commanding officers ever forbidding duelling. A very good example of how easy it was to see offence where none was intended, was to be found in a small, potentially very dangerous, disagreement between Lord Llandaff and Major Hobart, the chief secretary, in

[34] Thomas Lane to Lord Downshire, 16 July 1796 (PRONI, D/607/C/102). Lane was Downshire's agent for his Hillsborough estates. [35] Sandys was brother-in-law of Edward Cooke, under secretary at the Castle. As militia officers were prohibited from taking staff appointments, this was undoubtedly the result of 'influence'. [36] *History of the Irish parliament, 1690–1800*. Electoral facts volume, author's unpublished notes.

1793. Llandaff, because of his rank and position in society, considered that he should have been offered the lieutenant-colonelcy as commandant of the Tipperary Militia. Instead, the Castle offered it to John Bagwell, of Marlfield, near Clonmel. Llandaff regarded this as a slight; Bagwell was only a lowly country gentleman and what was more, had been 'in trade' as a miller. Llandaff believed his honour had been slighted. However, he transferred his 'dishonour' to his son, as the chief secretary said in a letter to the under-secretary in the Home department, Evan Nepean, 'I believe I told you that Lord Llandaff was to kill me, because he did not get command of the Tipperary Regiment. The quarrel however it was thought advisable to transfer to the son the father having reserved himself for the lord lieutenant.'[37] The son, Francis Matthew, took up the challenge and requested an 'explicit answer' from Hobart, which could only mean one thing.[38] Hobart replied, diplomatically, that his duty to the King's government precluded giving an answer,[39] which caused Matthew to ask for a reconsideration as he had appealed to Hobart as a man, and not as a minister. If not, he would feel *'really concerned'* [sic].[40] Hobart then demonstrated his verbal dexterity by saying that as a minister he had given the only answer he could; as a man he could not be responsible for the appointments made by executive government; and he regretted mortification caused by such measures.[41] Matthew accepted the logic, and, as regret had been expressed, was satisfied.[42] There is no question that Matthew had been willing, perhaps more than willing, to call Hobart out.

The first record of a duel between militia officers was between two officers of the South Mayo Militia in 1794. Neither was injured, and the matter was settled.[43] On 23 October of the same year, a duel was fought over the parliamentary election for Co. Kerry, between Sir Barry Denny, lieutenant-colonel of the Kerry Regiment, and Mr John Crosbie. Sir Barry's pistol missed fire, and Crosbie's ball hit him in the eye, mortally wounding him. This left a vacancy for a lieutenant-colonel in the Kerry that went to Captain James Crosbie.[44] The coroner's verdict, incidentally, was 'manslaughter in his own defence', which seems to have been usual in cases of duelling.

Reports of duels are only found in the press, and they seem to be the affairs where one of the participants is killed. This presumes that duels in which both parties satisfied honour without loss of life, went unreported. For example, Major John Sankey challenged Captain John Giffard in 1799 – Sankey fired, Giffard did not, and honour was not satisfied. Both were officers in the City of Dublin Regiment, but this affair was not reported in the

37 Robert Hobart to 'E.N.' (probably Evan Nepean), 17 June 1793 (NA, HO/100/44/147).
38 Matthew to Hobart, 2 June 1793 (ibid.). 39 Hobart to Matthew, 3 June 1793 (ibid.). 40 Matthew to Hobart, 5 June 1793 (ibid.). 41 Hobart to Matthew, 7 June 1793 (ibid.). 42 Matthew to Hobart, 8 June 1793 (ibid.). 43 *Freeman's Journal*, 25 Jan. 1794. 44 *Faulkner's Journal*, 28 Oct. 1794.

press.[45] The reason for this is unclear since Giffard was the lessee of the *Dublin Journal*, and such discretion was not in his character.[46]

What was much more common, was officers being 'sent to Coventry' for alleged ungentlemanlike behaviour. In this period, the concept of the officers' 'mess' was in its infancy, and such behaviour was perfectly possible. Giffard, for example, was sent to Coventry after his duel with John Sankey. In the Downshire, Lieutenant Courtney became embroiled in a dispute with a man named Huey, and got out of it so badly that his brother officers considered that he had not 'supported the character of an officer and a gentleman,' and would not mess with him,[47] The matter went further and, although Courtney later apologized, a petition from the officers requested Lord Downshire to bring him to court martial. Fifteen out of the nineteen officers present with the regiment signed it.[48] Courtney was not court martialled, but did resign his commission on 6 February 1797.[49] In yet another case, in a dispute between Lieutenant-Colonel Henry O'Hara and Major Joseph Hardy, both of the Antrim Regiment, the Castle ordered each officer to appoint a field officer as a referee, and these two officers to appoint a third field officer, and both parties to agree to their judgment. Unfortunately, we do not know the nature of the dispute, nor the verdict of these 'three wise men'.[50]

It is obvious that officers of the militia did attempt to maintain the standards of gentlemen, and to behave as they perceived officers should. The problem was that there was no military standard for them to follow; the regiments were all new, and so, too, were most of the officers. It is very easy to criticize, and most of the criticism of these military novices – for that is what they were – was destructive. However, Craufurd was writing after seeing militia officers in action, not in peacetime cantonments, and without question, some of the behaviour of militia officers was not what was expected of any army officer, as we shall see. It is pertinent, therefore, to look at attitudes to duty, for this is by far more important than having the attributes of a gentleman, although, of course, it was expected of a gentleman always to do his duty, and to do his duty to those for whom he was responsible.

PERCEPTIONS OF DUTY

Robert Craufurd, the one critic of the Irish militia who also tried to be constructive, compared the attitude to duty of the regular and the militia officer.

---

45 Giffard to Sir William Medows, Commander-of-the-Forces, n.d., almost certainly 1801 (NA, HO/100/102). 46 Brian Inglis, *The freedom of the press in Ireland, 1784-1841* (London, 1954). 47 Matthews to Downshire, 31 Aug. 1796 (PRONI, D/607/D/143). 48 Officers of the Royal Downshire Regiment to Lord Downshire, 5 Dec. 1796 (ibid., D/607/D/373). 49 Pay Lists and Muster Rolls, Downshire Militia (NA, WO/13/2776). 50 Charles Handfield to Lord O'Neill, 10 Nov. 1795 (NLI, KP/1080/53).

> The officers, too, in the Line, *are obliged*, to behave like gentlemen, and men of honour, even if they are not naturally so, for a man who enters as an officer, into a regiment of the Line, makes the army his profession, he gets out of all other habits and conditions in life, and feels that if he were to lose the hold he has in the army, he would be plunged into the depths of misery and ruin ... In the militia, the case is widely different ... militia officers do not feel the necessity of endeavouring to imitate the conduct of men of honour, because they know that at most you can only take from them that situation which at any rate they will lose in a year or two.[51]

Craufurd was referring to the junior officers in particular. He had ample evidence of poor behaviour, and outlined some of it: captains cheating the men, failing to enforce discipline, making themselves hated, Craufurd says he heard a soldier's reply to an officer who threatened to have him punished, 'By Jasus, I should like to see the man who will have me punished now that I have 60 ball cartridges in my pouch.'[52] (Which raises the unanswered question; what did Craufurd do about it?) But Craufurd failed to appreciate that the condition of the militia, during and after the rebellion had as much to do with the dispersed nature of their service, and the free quarters in 1797-8, as with the quality of its officers. He also failed to appreciate that officers of the regular army had given up their civic responsibilities during their years of service, whereas militia officers had not. Craufurd was also a regular officer looking at militia officers, and their attitudes were often worlds apart.

It is obvious that the regular officers were using their own standards to judge the officers of militia units, most of whom were military novices, with no training system other than what they could observe. The problem was compounded by adverse comment on officers who did not do their duty well, while those that did were ignored. This perception of duty on the part of the militia officer can be divided into three parts, first, personal, second, to operations and training, and third, to administration.

The personal aspect is perhaps the most difficult to define, because it depended so much on the qualities, and character of the officer concerned, and his knowledge of military affairs. He had to dress properly, and appropriately, adhere to the unwritten code of a 'gentleman', set an example, know his men, and be known by them, lead and manage his men, enforce discipline, encourage loyalty, and, above all, be present in the unit when he was supposed to be. Much of the duty of an officer was laid down in 'standing orders', both for the army as a whole, and also for the individual regiments.

---

51 Craufurd to Wickham, 19 Nov. 1798 (NA, HO/100/79/116). 52 Craufurd to Wickham, 19 Nov. 1798 (ibid., HO/100/79/116).

The only regimental 'standing orders' remaining in existence are those for the Armagh Regiment, but others would have been roughly similar, and they laid down quite specifically what the duty of an officer was to be.[53] The standing orders of the Armagh Regiment deal primarily with the relationship between officers and men. They follow a pattern – starting with what the officer himself must be, then dealing with the non-commissioned officers, the discipline of the private men, and finally matters of administration. Standing orders also dealt with similar categories for non-commissioned officers, and also with the behaviour of the private men to those set in authority above them. In effect, they regulated behaviour between the ranks.

The standing orders of the Armagh Regiment began with the command that officers, by their dress, alertness, and obedience to orders, had to set an example to non-commissioned officers, the 'eyes and springs of a regiment'.[54] Non-commissioned officers were to be treated with the 'most exact, impartial, and strict authority', tempered with courtesy and civility, so that they might carry equal command and enforce obedience from the private men.[55] Then officers must always ensure that they were saluted (as holders of the lord lieutenant's commission), and that they were not to tolerate 'answering back' when on parade. They were to teach the men the 'attitude' of soldiers, enforce discipline, correct errors, ensure that they were properly clothed and fed, and maintain impartial justice, punishing offenders. Most of this was the 'core' of an officer's duty – training, discipline, and welfare of the men. Officers were also enjoined to know the names and characters of their men.

These standing orders state quite clearly what an officer must be, and what he must do. In effect an officer would have had to spend a lot of his time on administration of his men, but an officer's task, in modern parlance, was to manage, and an aspect of management is leadership. It is a military 'truism' that it is possible to gauge the happiness and efficiency of a regiment within minutes of entering its barracks. In the eighteenth-century army, the first thing a visiting officer looked for was the obedience of the men to their officers. For example, Lord Ancram arrived in Dublin on 19 May 1797, to take command of the Midlothian Fencible Cavalry. He was posted to Dundalk, under command of Colonel Sankey of the City of Dublin Regiment, 'a very pleasant gentlemanlike man, and as were many of the officers, but the soldiers were not very subordinate'.[56] When the King's County were in Guernsey in 1799 Sir Hew Dalrymple found a spirit of insubordination in the men which the field officers could not suppress, although he did not refer to it again when he wrote the one half-yearly inspection report that still exists, in which he was complementary to the regiment and its officers.[57]

53 McAnally, *Irish Militia*, Appendix v.   54 Ibid.   55 Ibid.   56 Uncompleted diary of Lord Ancram, 19 May 1797 (NAS, GD/40/10/24).   57 Sir H. Dalrymple to Adjutant General

Setting an example is always difficult, and just as there were numerous examples of officers, such as Major Matthews of the Downshire, Lord Granard of the Longford, or Lieutenant Gardner of the Antrims, who did set an example, there are others who did not. Sir Harry Hayes of the South Cork is a very good example of what would happen when an officer disregarded his duty, considering himself to be above such an encumbrance. He was court-martialled on 12 February 1796, charged with disobedience of orders, striking his colonel (Lord Doneraile) on 2 September 1795, breaches of the articles of war and standing orders of his regiment, making an improper addition to a record of a regimental court martial and signing for it, calling a meeting of officers of the regiment in order to censure the conduct and orders of the colonel and finally, not resigning his commission when he had agreed to do so. He was found guilty of the first of the charges, not guilty of the remainder, and sentenced to be dismissed the service with the verdict to be read at the head of the regiment.[58] In February 1798, Lord Annesley reported that Lieutenants Montgomery and Bradford could not leave their houses because the sheriff was after them for debt.[59] So far as Montgomery was concerned, there were repeated references in the Downshire papers to his being persistently drunk, which culminated in his court martial and dismissal at Castlebar in 1798.[60] Finally, after the battle of New Ross, in which the Donegal Regiment was involved, three officers applied to resign their commissions – Lieutenant Edward Fawcett and Ensigns Henry Downs and John Whittaker. These could well be the men seen by Craufurd, who was at the battle, and commented on adversely by him. Then the Castle said that their resignations could only be accepted if it was also stated in the *Dublin Gazette* that they had been dismissed for 'improper behaviour before the enemy at New Ross'.[61] They were superseded in November 1798, when it was reiterated that the details of their behaviour had to be printed in the *Dublin Gazette*.[62]

Craufurd criticized the personal discipline of the officers. This was a much wider field than the few officers who may have attempted to cheat their men out of their pay, and some of the affairs reveal not only a lack of commitment, but also putting self before duty to the king and constitution. There are three events which no discussion on the Irish militia can avoid: the

---

(Horse Guards), 9 Apr. 1800 (NA, HO/ 100/90/224). 58 General Court Martial, 12 Feb. 1796 (ibid., WO/68/411). Hayes was an impetuous man: he abducted a Miss Pike, absconded (without her), was arrested, sentenced to death, commuted to transportation to New South Wales, pardoned by the Prince of Wales in 1812. In Sydney, he is reputed to have imported 40 barrels of Irish earth to keep the snakes out of his home, Vacluz House. 59 Annesley to Downshire, 26 Feb. 1798 (PRONI. D/607/F/68). 60 Assistant Adjutant General's Order, Castlebar, 12 Nov. 1798 (ibid., D/3574/D/1, Armagh Regiment Letter Book). 61 H. Taylor to Lord Clements, 8 Nov. 1798 (NLI, KP/1083/269). This had not been done by the end of 1799. 62 Castlereagh to Lord Clements, 26 Nov. 1798 (NA, WO/68/22).

Vennel–Lawler affair, the courts martial of Lieutenant Nicholas Cole Bowen, and Lord Kingsborough, all in 1798, and the Giffard – Sankey dispute, 1799–1801. The first was one of the acts of licentiousness referred to by General Abercromby in his famous order of 26 February 1798. A Miss Catherine Finn was taken into protective custody as a witness to the murder of a Mr Jasper Uniacke of Arraglyn, Co. Cork. While there, Lieutenant William Vennel of the 89th Foot, Lieutenant Thady Lawler of the Clare Militia, and the 'centinel' or sentry, raped her. The latter was arrested, but the two officers absconded.[63] It is not known if they were ever caught, despite rewards being posted in the newspapers by the officers of the two regiments.[64]

The second incident concerns counter charges made between Lord Kingsborough, colonel commandant of the North Cork, and Lieutenant Nicholas Cole Bowen, one of his officers. (The North Cork Regiment will be discussed more fully in chapter 6.) Lieutenant Bowen was charged in October 1798, by Lord Kingsborough – who had been captured and detained in Wexford when it was occupied by the rebels in 1798 – with deserting his post and going on board a vessel in Wexford harbour, leaving his men to fend for themselves (the North Cork had suffered severe losses at this stage, and the men on the retreat from Wexford were poorly disciplined). He was found guilty, and sentenced to be dismissed. Bowen had counter-charged Lord Kingsborough, who was court martialled on 4 October 1798, charged with ungentlemanly conduct, theft of government and private property, disloyalty, discharging men without court martial, throwing salt on a flogged man's wounds, and sending two sergeants and fifteen privates to Duncannon, for service outside Ireland, without trial.[65] Kingsborough was found not guilty but the suspicion exists that some of these practices did go on in his regiment, and that discipline among the officers, as well as the men, was not what it might have been. The disaster which the regiment suffered at the hands of the rebels at Oulart a few weeks earlier had been due to disobedience of orders, as much as the impetuosity of the men in attacking the rebels. Both officers seemed to have a perception of duty which placed themselves first and and the army second. Kingsborough resigned on 3 November 1798, twelve days after the promulgation of the result of his court martial.

The third incident sheds most light on the internal officer discipline of a militia regiment, and how its officers perceived their duty. In 1799 Captain John Giffard was in command of the Grenadier Company of the City of Dublin Militia. Giffard was a former high sheriff of Dublin, and was the lessee of *Faulkner's Dublin Journal*. He was virulently anti-Catholic, and pos-

---

63 Maj.-Gen. Henry Johnson to Lt.-Gen. Abercromby, 19 Feb. 1798 (ibid., HO/100/73/63).
64 *Dublin Journal*, 3 Mar. 1798.   65 General Order, 23 Oct. 1798 (NA, WO/68/221, Donegal Militia Order Book).

sessed of a very short temper, as well as a strong sense of his own importance. Because of his activities in the service of the Castle he was known as the 'dog-in-office'. In May of that year the lieutenant-colonelcy became vacant and Major Crampton, the most senior officer, was passed over in favour of Captain Edward Sankey, son of the colonel, Henry Gore Sankey. As a consequence, Crampton resigned, leaving the majority vacant. Giffard was ordered to do duty as major, which he did, and he applied to the colonel for appointment to that rank (as commander of the Grenadier Company, he was the senior captain). Colonel Sankey, however, appointed his brother John instead. John Sankey had been the most senior captain, but had resigned before the rebellion. He was a wine merchant, and had been declared bankrupt on 6 December 1798, which meant that by law his property belonged to his creditors, and he was not legally qualified to hold a commission in the militia.[66] This led Giffard to 'disrespectful conduct' to his colonel on 14 April 1799.[67] He was charged with this, as well as with defrauding his men, and found guilty, but his sentence to be reprimanded was to be 'slight'.[68] Giffard was still left with an acute sense of injustice. He had publicly insulted John Sankey, who challenged him to a duel. When Sankey fired, Giffard did not, as related earlier. This would have endeared Giffard still less to the Sankey family, and they sent him to Coventry, but then Lord Cornwallis intervened, and gave Giffard twelve months' leave to allow matters to cool down.

Captain Giffard rejoined his regiment on 1 December 1801, at Arklow, but found that circumstances had not changed. Every night, there was howling and barking under his windows, 'Dog, dog, God damn you dog, bow, wow, wow.'[69] On 17 December 1801, Giffard dined with Mr Sherwood, his next door neighbour, Captain Purcell of the Artillery, and Lieutenant Noble, who was the officer of the guard, and an officer in Giffard's company. The howling started under Sherwood's windows, Giffard went home, lifted a fowling piece, and went outside to get Sherwood back inside. The officer of the guard arrived with a file of men. Then Lieutenant-Colonel Sankey arrived, and sent away the guard, cursing and swearing, according to Giffard, who bundled Sherwood into his house, and closed the door. Sankey and eight others then broke the door down, dragged Giffard outside, discharged and broke his fowling piece, beat him, and left him for dead.[70] Subsequently Sankey brought Giffard to a court martial.

The court sat on 29 December 1801. Giffard was charged with lifting a weapon and firing at his commanding officer, and disrespectful conduct

66 *Dublin Gazette*, 6 Dec. 1798. 67 Giffard to Sir William Medows, n.d., almost certainly 1801 (NA, HO/100/102). 68 *Dublin Journal*, 13 Aug. 1799. The general order promulgating Giffard's sentence was printed in full. See also I.F. Nelson, 'John Giffard and the City of Dublin Militia' in *Irish Sword*, 23:93, 321–34. 69 Giffard to Medows, n.d., almost certainly 1801 (NA, HO/100/102). 70 Ibid.

towards his superior officer. He was found guilty of striking his commanding officer, and of disrespectful conduct, and not guilty of the other charges. The court considered that the events of 17 December had degenerated into a riot, which could have been avoided had Colonel Sankey used the guard. It considered Giffard had suffered considerable ill treatment, and gave him a mild sentence, by suspending him from rank and pay for twelve months.[71]

The matter did not end there. In confirming the sentence, Cornwallis directed the court to re-convene and his opinion to be read to them, 'that the tumultuous scene ... betrays such a total want of discipline and ordinary demeanour among the officers of the corps, that His Excellency thinks it expedient for the preservation of good order and military discipline, to lay their names severally before His Majesty, in order to receive his Royal commands with respect to any further proceedings'.[72] On 2 October 1801 Lieutenant-Colonel Edward Sankey was dismissed for countenancing a 'party' in the regiment, and sanctioning a riot at Arklow on 17 December 1800.[73] Cornwallis's comments on this unfortunate affair sum up the relevant points, that discipline among the officers of the City of Dublin was disgracefully low, and, indeed, also show that he himself was well aware of what had been going on. It is also very difficult to understand how this affair – which had dragged on from 14 April 1799 to 2 October 1801 – could possibly have remained a secret within the regiment. It was an appalling example to set to the men, and it is difficult to imagine that it did not affect the discipline of the men, and their obedience to their officers.

It was expected that all officers were loyal to king and constitution, and hard evidence of disloyalty is difficult to find. Officers could claim to be disloyal for a specific purpose such as in the well-known case of Captain J.W. Armstrong of the King's County Regiment, who infiltrated the United Irish movement and subsequently implicated the Sheares brothers, which, in military terms, can be regarded as intelligence gathering.[74] The only case of active disloyalty on the part of an officer, was that of Captain Alcock of the Wexford Regiment. He was court martialled, and found guilty of drinking treasonable toasts with 'Mr Patrick Twomey of the Cloyne Yeomanry', declaring that he would join the French when they landed, and aiding and abetting the swearing of United Irishmen. Alcock was found not guilty of concealing a conspiracy to murder, adherence to the United Irishmen, and of trying to seduce Twomey from his loyalty.[75] He was found guilty of other charges, and sentenced to be transported to Botany Bay for life. This one

---

[71] Court Martial Proceedings, 29 Dec. 1801 (NLI, KP/1 2 0 1), no pagination or paragraphing. [72] E.B. Littlehales to Lt.-Gen. Craig, 20 Feb. 1801 (ibid., KP/1 2 0 1). [73] General Order, 2 Oct. 1801 (PRONI, D/3574/D/2). [74] Bartlett and Jeffery (eds), *A military history of Ireland*, p. 278. [75] General Order, 25 Nov. 1798 (NA, WO/68/221, Donegal Militia Order Book).

case is unique. The United Irish movement placed great store on seduction of the militia to their cause, but in order to create a viable 'army' they had to recruit officers and, in this, they seem to have utterly failed.

An officer gave his loyalty to his regiment and to his men, who could not be expected to maintain high morale if they did not have confidence in their officers. There are, in fact, numerous examples of this loyalty to the men being demonstrated, none better than that by Lieutenant-Colonel Herbert of the Kerry Regiment at Athlone in May 1796. This is a case where local connections accustomed the magistracy and the law officers to act together, and to getting their own way, because there was no other local combination strong enough to counter them. However, the Kerry Regiment was stationed in Athlone, and their colonel was not prepared to have his men browbeaten by authority, or bullied by the magistracy. What is interesting about this case is the potential division in the forces of law and order, of which both the magistracy and the militia were both supposed to be a part.

The facts are these.[76] The Revd Annesley Strain, a magistrate, stopped a riot in the streets of Athlone, between two persons in 'coloured clothes'. One of the two turned out to be a soldier in the Kerry Regiment, whereupon his comrades, who had seen what had happened, rescued him. Strain went to the barracks, and said that he wanted to bring to punishment the man who had twice rallied the rescue party. The men were paraded, and eventually two men were brought for questioning. Strain wanted to question them in secret, with the sovereign of the town, but Herbert would not allow this to happen, nor would he allow the men to be questioned on hearsay evidence. As a result, Strain claimed that everything had been done by the regiment to screen or protect the men, and to frustrate the law.

The upshot of all this was that Colonel Herbert was charged with not giving assistance to the sovereign and the Revd Strain, in discovering persons in the Kerry Militia who had rescued a prisoner on 7 May 1796. This was a serious charge. Herbert could have been cashiered if found guilty, and rendered unfit to hold public office. The case was heard on 15 May 1796, and dismissed.[77] In July Herbert was granted £50 towards the case in the crown solicitor's bill, and was authorized to charge the balance to the regimental contingency account,[78] 'in the case of the groundless prosecution of you by Rev. Annesley Strain'.

It is not hard to imagine the increasing fury of the magistrate who was unsure when confronted with the men of the regiment, and unable to identify the rescuer of the man he had detained. Equally it is not hard to recognize the

---

[76] Account of a transaction, 7–15 May 1796 (ibid., WO/68/411,Order Book, Kerry Militia).
[77] Herbert to Johnston, 15 May 1796 (ibid., WO/68/411/89, Order Book, Kerry Militia).   [78] C. Handfield to Herbert, 11 July 1796 (ibid., WO/68/411/92).

defence of the commanding officer, which was perfectly proper. Strain, the accuser, had to identify the rescuer, and when he attempted to use a system which had obviously worked before – secret interrogation – the colonel would not hear of it. Colonel Herbert's conduct in this whole affair was entirely proper, and it is obvious he would protect any soldier from wrongful accusation and would not agree to be a 'magistrate's lackey.' This affair must have had a considerable beneficial effect on the morale of the regiment.

Then we come to the vexed question of absence from the regiment, either with, or without, leave. This is one of the most serious problems in any discussion of the officers of the Irish militia. The rules for officers' leave were laid down shortly after the regiments were called out. Lord Granard received his on 17 October 1793.[79] They stated that one field officer, and not less than two thirds of the captains and subalterns in proportion, would be required on duty at all times, and leave could be given to the remainder at the colonel's discretion. This would seem simple enough; everything depended on the colonel but if he was absent, which was usual, to whom did the power of granting leave fall? If memorials – the method of application – were forwarded to the colonel, how was he to know the numbers at quarters if the commanding officer did not tell him? At this stage, numbers at quarters did not have to be put on the memorial. In fact the system did not work at all well. Leave tended to be given indiscriminately, so that some corps were perpetually short of officers, a considerable problem in cantonments where there were many detachments which required an officer in command. Some stations required the presence of the whole regiment, such as Dublin and Loughlinstown.

The Donegal were in Loughlinstown in March 1796, and had one field officer, three captains and twelve subalterns present. Absent were two field officers, which was acceptable according to the rules, four captains', which was not, and eight subalterns', which was.[80] The Downshire were in Dublin in March 1795, and had all three field officers present, two captains, and nine subalterns. The Dublin Garrison had many public guard mountings, reviews, and was very much in the public eye, which would have suited Lord Downshire. Seven captains were absent, and thirteen subalterns, neither figure acceptable according to the rules.[81] Another cantonment, with few permanent detachments, was Carrickfergus. On 1 February 1795 the muster return for the Kilkenny shows that they had no field officers present, only two captains and four subalterns on duty, with three captains and five subalterns absent, which according to the rules, was not permissable.[82]

---

[79] Adjutant General's Office to Lord Granard, 17 Oct. 1793 (NAI, M₅474, letter, order, and court martial books, Longford Militia). [80] Pay lists and muster rolls, Donegal Regiment (NA, WO/13/2751). [81] Pay lists and muster rolls, Downshire Militia (ibid., WO/13/2776). [82] Pay lists and muster rolls, Kilkenny Militia (ibid., WO/13/2942).

In 1795 the rule for leave was tightened: applications had now to be made through commanding officers to the district commander, then to the commander-in-chief, but the rule about attendance at quarters by the different ranks remained the same. On 27 February 1796 the commander-in-chief restated the rules, and added that on memorials for leave, the commanding officer had to certify the numbers of captains and subalterns remaining on duty.[83] From this point on, the Castle enforced the rules rigidly, and the Kilmainham Papers are full of refusals for leave, usually because the numbers remaining on duty were not enclosed or, perhaps because there had been a wilful disregard for the correct procedure. In December 1795 Colonel Fitzgerald of the North Mayo applied for leave '(with the consent of Major-General Craig), for leave of absence to Captain Atkinson to 14 January, Lieutenant Molloy to 1 March, Ensign Fleming to 1 April'. He stated that one field officer, two captains, and four ensigns remained with the regiment. The leave was approved.[84] On the other hand, an example of a refusal made to Colonel Sir Lawrence Parsons of the King's County in 1797, shows that in applying for leave for a Lieutenant Hobbs, Parsons certified that 17 subalterns remained at duty, which was the figure he had certified shortly before in respect of leave for Ensign Doolan. He was asked to recheck and say how many officers remained, and to note that applications for leave for officers of the flank battalions were to be made through the commanding officer of the battalion, and not through the regimental commanding officer. (Note the confusion on lines of communication where a regiment's light company was detached to the battalions of light infantry.)[85] Another very good example of what could happen when the Castle enforced the rules is provided by the case of Major Matthews, when the Downshire were in Birr in 1797. It also throws light on other issues.

On 27 January 1797 Major Matthews applied for leave of three months (leave was usually from one to four months), because his estate was small, his expenses high, and he could only make ends meet by having three months leave each year. He wanted to go in the first week of March.[86] Then on 4 February 1797, he repeated his request, saying that advantage had been taken of his absence to ruin his brother-in-law, John Echlin.[87] On 19 February 1797 Matthews again wrote to Downshire, and said that it was vital that he be in Dublin during the first week of March.[88] In the meantime Downshire had obviously forwarded the application to the Castle, and Matthews was informed that he could have his leave if the lieutenant-colonel rejoined to

---

83 General Order, 27 Feb. 1796 (NLI, KP/1080). 84 Memorial of Col. Fitzgerald, 5 Dec. 1795 (ibid., KP/1192). 85 Maitland to Col. Sir Lawrence Parsons, King's County Militia (ibid., KP/1081?276). 86 Matthews to Downshire, 27 Jan. 1797 (PRONI, D/607/E/72). 87 Matthews to Downshire, 4 Feb. 1797 (ibid., D/607/E/81). 88 Matthews to Downshire, 19 Feb. 1797 (ibid., D/607/E/109).

relieve him.[89] Matthews forwarded this letter to Lord Downshire on 27 February 1797,[90] and on 5 March 1797 Handfield informed Downshire.[91]

On 12 March 1797, Matthews wrote to Downshire again, reiterating that he needed leave immediately: his wife and children were with him in Birr and he wanted to take them home. If the regiment moved, he had no money to leave them, as 'paper' was not acceptable in Birr.[92] ('Paper' money in which the troops were paid, was not universally accepted, and could only be exchanged for coin at a discount.) On 19 March 1797 Matthews finally received his leave when Lord Annesley arrived to join the regiment. He blamed the delay on the commander-in-chief.[93] In fact, the delay was caused almost certainly by Downshire, who did not act on his major's behalf with any degree of despatch, a typical example of Downshire's cavalier attitude to his regiment after 1794. A lesser man than Matthews would simply have gone on leave without permission and been posted 'absent.'

As the commander-in-chief, Lord Carhampton, wrote to Lieutenant-Colonel Sir Edward O'Brien MP, of the Clare Militia in 1797, 'I cannot hesitate to say that the order of 23 September does affect you, it has been represented to me that without leave you set off for your country seat one hundred miles both from camp and parliament, therefore, permit me to say the question is not which duty is to be preferred for if I understand the latter part of your letter right, you did not mean to attend either.'[94] Absence without leave was a major problem. After 1795 there were numerous examples of officers being superseded for persistent absence. Between July 1797 and April 1802 no less than 21 officers were superseded for absence alone, of whom three were subsequently reinstated, and 14 officers were superseded for unspecified reasons, some of which were undoubtedly absence.[95] There were also continual threats of superssion. In 1799 an order was issued for absent officers to return to duty or face supersession. Twenty-five of the officers named were from the militia.[96] The problem, however, predates the use of the power of supersession, and some of the punishments for absence were tactlessly harsh. For example, in July 1794 Captain John Browne of the South Mayo, who had been absent without leave from 25 February to 1 May of that year, and found guilty by court martial was sentenced to be reprimanded at the head of the regiment, and was suspended from rank and pay for three months. The court observed that never less than four officers of the regi-

---

89 C. Handfield to Maj. Matthews, 23 Feb. 1797 (ibid., D/607/E/121). 90 Matthews to Downshire, 27 Feb. 1797 (ibid., D/607/E/129). 91 Handfield to Downshire, 5 Mar. 1797 (ibid., D/607/E/155). 92 Matthews to Downshire, 12 Mar. 1797 (ibid., D/607/E/183). 93 Same to same, 19 Mar. 1797 (ibid., D/607/E/209). 94 Carhampton to Sir Edward O'Brien, [Nov. 1797](NLI, KP/1080). 95 Compiled from the Kilmainham papers. 96 Circular, 2 Nov. 1799 (NLI, KP/1137/305).

ment were absent without leave at the same time as Browne.[97] Being reprimanded at the head of the regiment, in front of the assembled soldiers, was a pernicious punishment that discredited the officer in the eyes of his men, and thus reduced their respect and obedience.

Perhaps one of the worst examples of wilful and persistent absence that could not be dealt with effectively, concerned Lieutenant-Colonel Samuel Ahmuty of the Longford Battalion. Bear in mind that the Longford were at the battle of Castlebar in 1798; that for two years beforehand, they had had no opportunity to train as a formation; and that Major Sandys, one of their field officers, was removed to the staff and was absent for most of our period. With the considerable absence of Ahmuty, the burden of command fell on Lord Granard, and could not be properly shared by the field officers. This meant that other officers could not have leave because of Ahmuty, and junior officers had to command the battalion. The whole business flared up in 1803, on the re-mustering of the Longford Battalion, in which Ahmuty continued as lieutenant-colonel. On 8 September 1803 Lord Granard's patience finally ran out. He sent a memorial to General Fox, the commander-of-the-forces, which drew the general's attention to the problem. Ahmuty had been given leave that was to expire on 20 August 1803, and nothing had been heard of him. As a result, he had been posted absent. Granard, however, outlined, with dates, the nineteen times his lieutenant-colonel had been returned absent without leave from 14 November 1796, when he had been promoted to his rank, to 14 February 1802.[98] Ahmuty pleaded family illness, was forgiven, and rejoined the battalion. The problem with absence without leave, was that there was no adequate sanction, and no means of getting officers back to duty quickly: there were no military police; absent officers could not be arrested by local magistrates (who were probably uninformed that an officer was absent); and the whole apparatus was clumsy. At this time, there was no distinction between absence without leave and desertion.

Much of what has been said of the personal component of the militia officers' attitude to duty appears negative, and supportive of the criticism of regular officers. However, many of the accounts recorded here are examples of situations of which the Castle was well aware, and did very little to counter. The procedure for applying for leave, for example, was regularized and enforced, but the reasons for the problem were never properly addressed; the punishment never fitted the crime; 'honour' was never extended to include the concept that officers simply did not go absent as it was a betrayal of their men. This lack of will to enforce standards in the militia is as impor-

---

97 General Court Martial, 1 July 1794 (NA, WO/68/402/58, Cavan Regiment Letter Book).
98 Memorial of Lord Granard to Gen. Fox, 8 Sept. 1803 (NAI, M₿475, Royal Longford Militia Letter Book).

tant as criticism of their behaviour. Furthermore, the point has to be made, and remade, that all regiments had some good officers.

The second aspect of a militia officer's attitude to duty relates to operations and training. Operations as such will be considered in an overall context in chapter 6. Here we are really concerned with what the officer perceived to be his duty. Of course, many officers had quite clear ideas of where their duties lay, but others seemed unsure, as Lieutenant-Colonel the Hon. Robert Ward found out when he didn't 'march to Bantry' with the Royal Downshire Regiment in 1796. He received a letter from Lord Carhampton, who, as we know from his missive to Sir Edward O'Brien, did not mince his words:

> It is my duty to take care that every officer in this kingdom does his duty. You are pleased to reply to a letter I wrote ordering you to quarters, to express a doubt that the letter was authentic. You are a captain in the Royal Downshire Regiment, you receive pay as such, you have neglected doing duty with the regiment for some time past. This neglect of yours has not been noticed as it ought to have been, but it was not to be supposed that a gentleman of your rank should have heard that the regiment in which he was a captain, and received pay of it, was marching towards an enemy, threatening every hour to invade his country and that you should hesitate a moment to fly to join it. Therefore, whether the letter you received under any signature was really mine or not the obligation of which you was (sic) reminded was the same. Every moment you remain at Castle Ward after the receipt of my order is (I must take the liberty of telling you) an aggravation of your neglect of duty and disobedience of my orders and without any personal disrespect to you I will vindicate the orders I have given.[99]

Ward was placed under arrest, but never court martialled. In fact, Ward had raised a regiment of (regular) infantry, and so held a double commission; hence being addressed by Carhampton as 'lieutenant-colonel' although only a captain in the militia where Lord Annesley was the lieutenant-colonel. He had to choose which commission to follow, and he opted for his regiment.[1] Nevertheless, this remains the strongest rebuke to a militia officer short of a court martial, between 1793 and 1802.

Essentially, the officer had to command and lead his men, not always an easy task when under pressure and outnumbered, as the militia almost always were. It is when in this situation that clear thinking proved most difficult, especially for a military novice. A very good example of what could go wrong

---

[99] Carhampton to Lt.-Col. Ward, 2 Jan. 1797 (NLI, KP/1081/24). [1] Same to same, 7 July 1797 (ibid., KP/1081/142).

happened to Major Ker of the Monaghan Regiment at Ballybay, Co. Monaghan, on or about 13 April 1797. This revealed the military naiveté of an inexperienced officer, torn between his duty and a desire to preserve peace, which had the most sanguine consequences. Ker was also a magistrate, and in that capacity had become involved. A party of twenty soldiers of the Armagh Regiment had accompanied a Mr Breaky, a revenue officer, in a search for illegal stills in the Ballybay area. They had been involved in a fracas with local people, a number of whom had been killed. Ker set off to find the party, accompanied by some eight or nine of the principal inhabitants of the area. They found Breaky and ten privates of the Armagh confronting a mob of about 300 people, who were about 150 yards off. Ker spoke to them, and it was agreed that the soldiers should go to gaol pending an investigation into their conduct. Ker made to move off, but the mob demanded that if the prisoners – the soldiers – were to go to gaol, they ought not to retain their arms. Ker said that the gentlemen with him agreed with this, and that if the soldiers gave them up (to them), they would be protected. Ker agreed. The soldiers were disarmed. They were immediately attacked by the mob: two ran off, three were killed, including a corporal, one died of wounds, three were seriously wounded, and two were slightly wounded.[2] Ker then found that the 'gentlemen' who had accompanied him, and who had recommended that the soldiers hand in their arms, all positively refused to give any assistance in identifying any of the mob, as they believed their lives or properties would not be safe.[3]

It was obvious that the mob represented a threat. Assisting the revenue in searching for illegal stills was a part of a soldier's duty, for which he received extra pay, since it was recognized as dangerous. Ker was trying to do his duty as a magistrate without exacerbating the situation, as was correct, but as a militia officer he should not have considered it his duty to order the soldiers to disarm, the 'gentlemen' who agreed to take the arms were neither soldiers nor police, and Ker had no guarantee that they would protect the disarmed men. In the event, they did nothing. It is a military principle that soldiers never give up their arms because, without them, they lose their moral authority, and cannot do their duty or defend themselves. Ker, who was devastated by the outcome of this affair, should have known this.

Another example of the perception of duty, or the lack of it, is the murder of Edward Birch in 1799. Here is an example where an officer made little effort to command his men, but went along with them instead. Fortunately, such examples are rare. The officer, Lieutenant Edward Hogg, with a party of the Antrim Regiment, came to the house of the Revd Gill

---

2 Lord Gosford to Thomas Pelham, [– June 1797] (NAI, RP/6 2 0/3 1/1 8 4). Gosford names all the soldiers, and the 'gentlemen.'   3 Ker to Pelham, 27 Apr. 1797 (ibid., RP/620/31/326).

near Arklow, and demanded whiskey. He was refused, but his men broke into the house anyway, and took it. They accosted Edward Birch, and accused him of being a rebel, and took him away. He was later found murdered. Four men were charged with the murder: two were found guilty, and sentenced to death, and two acquitted.[4] Lieutenant Hogg, who led the demand for whiskey, and who had had a woman behind him on his horse, was himself court martialled on 28 March 1799, but acquitted, a result deplored by Lord Cornwallis, even though it was highly likely that Birch had been a rebel (he had belonged to a Yeomanry Corps disbanded for dissent).[5] Hogg was later described by Lieutenant-Colonel O'Hara of his regiment, as a desperate Orangeman who caused religious dissension within the regiment.[6] He was eventually superseded, but it is plainly obvious that he had little concept of his duty, and was using his military power for his own ends.

The problems of command over private men could also be exacerbated by drink. We have already seen that Lieutenant Montgomery of the Downshire was dismissed for persistent drunkenness. Other examples are harder to find, as this is a topic that could be covered up as in the case of Captain Hyacinth Bodkin of the Galway Regiment. Bodkin was court martialled in Youghal on 26 August 1800, charged with beating and imprisoning a yeoman, ordering soldiers of his regiment to fix bayonets and disperse a lawful crowd when neither garrison commander nor officer of the day, and for drawing his sword in a public street, whetting it, and declaring 'The first Orange rascal I meet, I'll split him' or words to that effect. He was acquitted but he was undoubtedly drunk.[7] When things got out of hand, other explanations could be given, as in the assault on Captain Giffard at Arklow in 1800.

When the King's County Regiment under Colonel L'Estrange was in Guernsey in April 1800, Lieutenant-General Sir Hew Dalrymple ordered a board of enquiry into the strange behaviour of Lieutenant Palmer, officer of the guard, on 3 April 1800. When Lieutenant Hazard of the Royal Engineers, commanding officer of the 'fort' (not specified, either Fort George, or Castle Cornet), went to get the keys from Palmer, he would not give them to him, claiming he did not recognize Hazard, or Lieutenant Ross of the Invalids, and would read neither the guard-orders, nor their commissions. They thought Palmer was drunk. According to the lady in charge of the canteen, Palmer and another officer had dined there that evening, and had consumed a bottle of wine and some gin punch. She thought they were drunk when they left, but could not swear to it. Palmer called witnesses, including Colonel

---

4 Court martial, Privates Disney, Kean, Doherty, and Quinn, of the Antrim Regiment, 28 Mar. 1799 (ibid., RP/620/17/30). 5 General court martial, 28 Mar. 1799 (ibid., RP/620/17/30/74). 6 Court martial proceedings, 28 Mar. 1799 (NA, HO/100/84/14). This is the report sent to London of Hogg's court martial. 7 Court Martial, Youghal, Lt.-Col. Peyton, Leitrim Regt., President (NLI, KP/1201).

L'Estrange, his commanding officer, all of whom said he had been sober.[8] Dalrymple forwarded the proceedings to the adjutant general in London with the comment that he would not trust keys to this guard because he found a spirit of insubordination in the regiment, which the field officers could not suppress, and believed an example was necessary.[9] When the King's County left Guernsey in July 1800, Dalrymple did not write to Cornwallis commending their behaviour, and attention to duty. This was a normal military courtesy and did happen in the case of the Wexford Regiment when they left Jersey at the same time. Cornwallis forwarded the proceedings to Portland, with a request that Palmer be superseded for reprehensible conduct.[10] There was little doubt that Palmer had been inebriated, but there may well have been tensions between the subalterns of different units, which the board of enquiry did not elicit from those involved. Certainly, we know that the men of the King's County did not get on well with the local people.[11] (It is worth pointing out that both the King's County, and the Wexford went to the Channel Islands with almost a full complement of officers.)

Earlier, we looked at the unfortunate consequences of decisions made by an officer under stress. Officers also suffered from frustrations in the performance of their duties, and sometimes this frustration led to excessive behaviour. The case of Captain Kay of the Armagh Regiment is pertinent here, because Kay's actions, which were quite illegal, led to his prosecution, and a term in gaol, which shows us that officers were not above the law. Kay had been sergeant-major of the 2 3rd (Royal Welch) Fusiliers and, according to the Blacker Papers, quoted by Sir Henry McAnally, for whom he was something of a hero,[12] 'His character and appearance led to his being appointed adjutant to the young regiment, and, being in fact the only drilled soldier in it from the colonel down, he soon had the management of literally everything, and may be said to have been colonel, paymaster, quartermaster, and adjutant, all in one.' The appointment of adjutant was tied to the rank of lieutenant but Kay was an exceptional officer, and in 1798 had risen to be captain-lieutenant (an old rank, still used in the militia, and the equivalent of senior lieutenant), and a captain by 1800, which meant that he commanded a company. However, in August 1797, one Patrick Murphy, a weaver in Drogheda, was seized by two sergeants of the Armagh Regiment and brought to the barracks. Here, under the orders of Captain Kay, Murphy had his left eyebrow and the left side of his head shaved, and was marched to the Tholsel, where he was 'pumped' (put under the pump, and water pumped over him).

---

8 Proceedings of a Board of Enquiry held at Fort George, Guernsey, 5 Apr. 1800 (NA, HO/100/90/226). 9 Dalrymple to the Adjutant General, 9 Apr. 1800 (ibid., HO/100/90/224). 10 Cornwallis to Portland, 3 May 1800 (ibid., HO/100/90/222). 11 Dalrymple to the Adjutant General, 8 Mar. 1800 (ibid., WO/100/27/83). 12 McAnally, *Irish Militia*, p. 55.

Later, he was again detained and confined in the 'black hole' for 60 hours, before being freed. Kay and the two sergeants, were arraigned before Chief Baron Yelverton, and Mr Justice Tankerville Chamberlain.[13] The jury found the men guilty, Kay was fined 30 marks, and sentenced to three months' imprisonment, and the sergeants to a fine of one mark, and also three months' imprisonment. All three served their sentences, although Kay insisted that Murphy was a United Irishman who had attempted to seduce soldiers,[14] but couldn't prove his allegations, and the chief baron felt an exemplary sentence was needed. Kay was plainly frustrated at his inability to convict those whom he regarded as United Irishmen, but having done wrong, he paid the price.

No regiment could operate efficiently without an adjutant, a quartermaster, a paymaster and a surgeon, yet from time to time, some or even all of them might be absent, other than on leave. In 1799, Lieutenant-Colonel Robert Camden Cope of the Armagh, when writing to Lord Gosford, his colonel, said that three officers did not deserve any indulgence, and that one of them, Lieutenant Jephson had been guilty of 'unpardonable' neglect of the duties of quartermaster.[15] One order book has survived: that of Lieutenant Peter Hurst, adjutant of the Donegal Regiment.[16] It gives a good impression of the duties of an adjutant, and covers the period from 5 May to 11 August 1794. It has entries for each day, and gives the 'parole' for that day (this is the officers' password), the name of the duty officer, and in a 'remarks' column, instructions as to transfers and promotions of the men, turnout (dress), and different parades. It details the firing of a 'feu de joye', preparations for field days, payment of the men, making cartridges (by the sick), divine service, deliveries of turf, powdering of hair, servicing of ramrods, reviews of arms, mending of clothes, instructions to the men to 'turn their coats' when going to market, punishment for 'accidental discharges', and arrangements for courts martial. It concludes with instructions for a review of the regiment by General Crosbie, for the men to be steady, since 'appearance before the reviewing general determines reputation'.[17] The behaviour of the men in Birr had been good, and, after the review General Crosbie assured the commanding officer of his approbation on their appearance and drill, 'most particularly for their steadiness under arms by which the discipline of a regiments is so strongly marked.'[18]

The adjutant was the commanding officer's principal staff officer – he was responsible for the administration of the unit, as well as ensuring everyone knew of the commanding officer's orders. No such document has been

[13] Lord Yelverton and Mr Justice Tankerville Chamberlain, *Report to Edward Cooke on the Armagh business*, 30 Aug. 1797 (NAI, RP/620/32/90). [14] Kay to Lord Gosford, 30 Aug. 1797 (ibid., RP/620/32/90). [15] Cope to Gosford, 16 June 1799 (PRONI, D/1606/1, Gosford Papers). Jephson was another notorious absentee. [16] Order Book of a regiment stationed in Birr, 1794 (NLI, MS 9889). This book can be identified positively as belonging to Hurst. [17] Ibid. [18] Ibid.

found for quartermasters or paymasters, the latter were called to Dublin when their accounts were not well kept, and indeed, this happened to Lieutenant Walpole of the Armagh.[19]

ORANGEISM

The spread of the Orange Order into the militia was very much in the hands of its officers. The Castle gave no orders or instructions about the subject. Indeed, the commanders in the north were only too glad to use Orangemen in guarding installations in Belfast during the 1798 Rebellion, and Brigadier-General Knox, commanding in Tyrone, felt that they were the 'only description of men in the north of Ireland that can be depended upon'.[20]

Aiken McClelland, historian of the Order, claimed that by March 1798 there were lodges in the Tyrone, Fermanagh, Monaghan, North Cork, Donegal, Cavan (2), Armagh (3), Regiments and Battalions, and that by May 1798, also in the Downshire, City of Dublin, Sligo, and Tipperary Regiments.[21] McClelland wrote for an Orange Order audience and is not always a reliable authority, but certainly in March 1798 when Lodge 176 was brought to Dublin, its members included Lord Annesley (Royal Downshire), Major Sandys (Longford Battalion), Captain John Giffard (City of Dublin Regiment), Major BB Woodward (Cavan Battalion), Lieutenant-Colonel Joseph Platt of the same battalion, Viscount Kingsborough (North Cork Regiment), John Maxwell Barry, colonel of the Cavan Battalion with three sergeants of his battalion, three of the Fermanagh, and three of the Armagh.[22] This does not represent widespread penetration of the militia by the order. There could be several reasons for this, not least the preponderance of Roman Catholic soldiers in almost all regiments, but active discouragement must have played a part. Brigadier-General John Moore, commanding the Light Brigade said to his men on St Patrick's Day 1798

> I made a speech yesterday to the troops. I reprobated some meetings of Orange boys (Protestants) which, as I heard, had taken place. I said if by such meetings they intended to form a union to defend their country, they were unnecessary, as every good man was already determined in his heart to do so, and they, as soldiers, had already sworn to do it; but if it was to create a distinction and separate interest from the Catholics, it was wicked and must be punished.[23]

19 E.B. Littlehales to Lt. Walpole, Armagh Regiment, 28 Sept. 1799 (NLI, KP/1086/253). 20 Brig.-Gen. Knox to Thomas Pelham, 19 Apr. 1797 (PRONI, T/755/4/2/284). 21 Aiken McClelland, *The formation of the Orange Order*, no date, no place of publication. 22 Cecil Kirkpatrick (ed.), *The formation of the Orange Order, 1795–98* (Belfast 1994), p. 117. 23 Maurice, *Diary of Sir John Moore*, I, 79.

In May 1798, General Dalyrmple, commanding the Southern District, also made an order to stop the spread of lodges in his command,

> A representation being made that several clubs of particular distinctions existed in several regiments under the denomination of Orangemen, the General and commanding officers of regiments seeing the impropriety of such associations (as must no doubt appear evident to them) it is expected that they will take the most effectual and immediate means to put a stop to it, and impress on the minds of the soldiers that no distinction should exist among His Majesty's loyal subjects, and that the character of a soldier rests on the faithful discharge of his duty, and the obedience he pays to the orders he receives, and not in making improper distinctions which the Legislature and the laws of the country have now set aside.[24]

Dalrymple was more concerned about Orangeism causing disputes within his regiments between Protestants and Roman Catholics. (In his last phrase he is referring to the repeal of the laws against Catholics in 1792.) Moore feared this as well, but he was also concerned to keep his light battalions working as teams, especially as the companies came from different regiments.

In July 1796 Edward Cooke reported that the Queen's County Militia had attacked an Orange parade in Drogheda in which an Orangeman had been bayoneted. The soldier who did it was under arrest.[25] In December 1796, Major George Matthews of the Royal Downshire Regiment reported to his colonel, the marquess of Downshire, that Orange clubs had taken place in the regiment led by Sergeants Balmer and Kerr. They had insinuated that they had Lord Downshire's approval but Matthews said that he would put a stop to it.[26] He was not happy with sharing his barracks with the Queen's County Battalion and a few days later reported that 'But there is nothing surer than that Orangemen ... will be the means of making United men, and our neighbours the Queen's are I believe very willing to undertake the business'.[27]

The fears expressed by Matthews do not seem to have been realized, Orangeism was never put forward as a reason for militiamen becoming members of the United Irishmen. There were no disputes within regiments arising out of the formation or the activities of Orange lodges. However, some officers were involved in the creation of Orange lodges, none more so than Captain John Giffard of the City of Dublin Regiment.

Giffard was detached with his company from Newry to Portadown in May 1794 and during his time there he was involved in the creation of the Order.

---

24 H.A. Richey, *A short history of the Royal Longford Militia, 1793–1893* (Dublin, 1894), ch. 2. 25 Edward Cooke to Thomas Pelham, 14 July 1796 (PRONI, T/755/3/31). 26 Maj. G. Matthews to Lord Downshire, 3 Dec. 1796 (Ibid., D/607/D/366). 27 Ibid. (D/607/D/367).

Plate 1: Colonel William Blacker's crossbelt badge

The popular perception is that he was involved directly after the battle of the Diamond at Loughgall in Co. Armagh on 21 September 1795. This was the affray between Defenders and 'orange boys' that led directly to the establishment of the Orange Order shortly afterwards. Colonel R.H. Wallace in his *History of the Orange Order* states that Captain Gifford (*sic*) and his company of the Royal Dublin Militia were sent to Loughgall after the battle of the Diamond where Captain Gifford was 'then and there admitted to the order'.[28] According to Aiken McClelland, the City of Dublin were in Portadown from November 1794 to August 1798, and he quoted Francis Plowden on Giffard, 'To him are attributed the adoption of the title of Orangemen their original oath and obligation, and the first regulations by which they were organized into a society.'[29] He also quoted John Best, Master of Lodge 41, in 1803, who said that Giffard made the oath and drew up the rules. Edward Giffard, a grandson of John Giffard, stated that his grandfather's company of the Royal Dublin Militia separated the contestants at the battle of the Diamond, but this is hearsay.[30] Colonel William Blacker, who was present at the battle, mentions no military involvement at all.[31] The problem with all of this is that with the exception of Best and Blacker, none of it is contemporary. Furthermore, the Orange Order did not magically spring into existence after the battle of the Diamond. Long before the official formation of the order, 'Peep o' Day' boys had clashed with Defenders in Co. Armagh. There were 'Boyne' and 'Aughrim' clubs, the 'Royal Boyne Society', and the 'Aldermen of Skinner's alley'. Giffard could have belonged to any of these organizations before he went to Portadown, although once there he was involved in some way with the formation of the order.

The difficulty over Giffard's involvement in the actual formation of the order is that the dates given for his company being in Portadown are not correct. The regiment certainly went to Newry in late 1794, with Giffard's company being detached to Portadown. However, in July 1795, the regiment moved to Hillsborough to train as a complete formation, and in any case, Giffard had been

---

28 Kirkpatrick, *Formation of the Orange Order*, p. 30. 29 McClelland, *Formation of the Orange Order*, p. 31. 30 Sir A.H. Giffard, *Who was my grandfather?* (London, 1865), p. 40. 31 Kilpatrick, *Formation of the Orange Order*.

given lord lieutenant's leave from 1 April to 30 September 1795.[32] It would be extremely unlikely that he would have spent his leave in his or another company's sphere of operations, although not impossible. There is a report of his company being called out near Portadown on 12 June 1795 to disperse a riot between 'Break o' Day' men and Defenders.[33] The report does not actually say Giffard was present, but Colonel Blacker in a letter to Stanley Lees Giffard (youngest son of John Giffard) said in 1837 that he (Blacker), was present with a Mr Obins, a magistrate. Blacker also stated quite categorically that Giffard was not present on 21 September 1795 at the battle of the Diamond as his company had left Portadown 'some time before'.[34] On 8 July 1795 Giffard was in Dublin because that was the day in which he appeared in court charged with an assault on John Potts, editor of *Saunders News Letter*.[35] Giffard, therefore, was extremely unlikely to have been in Portadown in September 1795. It could be that Wallace, McClelland, and Plowden are confusing John with his son, Ambrose Harding Giffard, who was also an Orangeman. When the Grand Lodge of Ireland was formed in Dublin on 9 April 1798, Ambrose Harding Giffard was one of those detailed to produce the rules and regulations.[36]

The fact that a regiment contained an Orange Lodge does not seem to have affected its performance in any way. Evidence of the existence of lodges is sparse, and it is difficult to find any evidence that Orangeism was a factor in their performance. Or in the performance of those officers who were members of the order

I have attempted in this chapter to give some ideas on the concept of duty among militia officers in the first phase of the Irish militia, before the peace of Amiens in 1802, in the face of strong criticism from some regular officers. It is significant that the regular officers whose opinions have been quoted were men of ability who showed their mettle in the war against Napoleon that followed in 1803. The pattern revealed of militia officers is a very mixed one: some officers' keen; some anything but; and none as well trained as they ought to be. For this state of affairs, the general staff must shoulder some of the responsibility. At the end of the 1798 rebellion, Major Matthews said of the officers in his regiment,

> The more I see of the Irish militia the more I am convinced that they are totally unfit to take the field against regular troops, we have not

---

[32] Pay lists and muster rolls, City of Dublin Militia (NA, WO/1 3/2817). [33] *Faulkner's Journal*, 22 June 1795. [34] Lt.-Col. William Blacker to Stanley Lees Giffard, 4 Oct. [postmarked 1 8 3 7]. (Papers of T.L.G. Landon, box file 18th–19th century. Envelope Stanley Lees Giffard to/from/between children). I am grateful to Professor Jackie Hill of NUI Maynooth for this information. [35] *Freeman's Journal*, 10 July 1795. [36] Kilpatrick, *Formation of the Orange Order*, p. 118. For a fuller account of Giffard's career in the militia, see I.F. Nelson, 'John Giffard and the City of Dublin Militia' in the *Irish Sword*, 23:93, 321–34.

officers, for my own part I am at our own officers every day about their duty, but all in vain. Nature never intended them for war, except for a few they are not worth their salt. I can't get anything done as it ought to be, all your last batch are worse than useless.[37]

But Matthews was looking at his own situation. The quality of officers in the militia as a whole was, in many ways, comparable with the quality of the officers in the regular army, and it is pertinent to point out that this period from 1793 to 1802 marked the nadir of British regular infantry. The criticisms levelled against the militia officers could have been levelled with equal candour against the regulars. The opinion of Major Matthews may have been only too typical, but the militia cannot be divorced from the regular army. This seems to have been a period of confusion such as often accompanies the early stages of war, and was characterized by the waste of men to disease in the West Indies, and the disastrous campaigns in the Low Countries. If officers in the regular army were learning their trade the hard way, by bitter experience, then the officers of the militia were doing the same.

---

37 Matthews to Downshire, 15 Sept. 1798 (PRONI, D/607/F/410).

CHAPTER FIVE

The militiamen

When historians comment on the Irish militia, they are usually referring to what the soldiers, the private soldiers, did or did not do. Yet the Irish militia was a military body under officers who were themselves under the command of the Irish general staff. This point has been made before, but it must not be forgotten. The private soldiers were not a force to be seen in isolation. Their behaviour mirrored not just the degree of training they had received, but also the administrative, social, and economic ethos of the army as a whole and the government that controlled it. This in itself raises questions at the level of the private man, about background, discipline, and loyalty.

BACKGROUND AND RECRUITMENT

> The men who had enlisted were mechanics, and inhabitants of towns ... peasants could seldom be persuaded under any circumstances to quit their families and place of nativity ... I could hardly believe ... that even in the militia they were chiefly manufacturers and mechanics. To ascertain the facts, I called for a return from the regiments in garrison who happened to come from the different provinces in the kingdom, and I found that two-thirds or three-fourths of each regiment were of that description.[1]

At this remove, it is very difficult to prove or disprove the chief secretary, Thomas Pelham's observations, but some hard evidence does exist in the shape of the Carlow Militia enrolment book.[2] This is an impressive, if somewhat imperfect, record. Enrolments of men are listed alphabetically, and all the pages up to, and including, 'G', are missing. The book gives the recruit's name, his height, age, description, place of birth, trade, former service (if any), enlisted (by whom, when, where), casualties (dead, discharged, deserted), and adds further 'observations'. The book is complete up to 1801. The total number of men enlisted was 325. It included Privates Thomas Newman, 27

---

[1] Pelham to Camden, 14 Nov. 1796 quoted in Gilbert, *Documents relating to Ireland*, p. 100.
[2] NA, WO/68/302.

years old, a hosier from Lancashire, who enlisted in Dublin in 1797, 'Paterick' Prendergast, 22 years old, a shoemaker born in Newfoundland, who enlisted at Carlow in 1800, John Strahan, 20 years old, black, a servant born in Bridgetown, Barbados, who enlisted at Carlow in 1 8 0 0, and three children, Peter Smith, aged 1 1, George Talbot, aged 1 2, and Alexander Wilson, also aged 1 2. The last named were probably enlisted as drummers because they were well below the minimum age.

Of the 325 men who enlisted, 124 were born in Co. Carlow and 173 men enlisted in that county. The remainder joined in Dublin, Longford, Robertstown (Co. Kildare), Blaris (Co. Antrim), Tallow (Co. Waterford), Nenagh (Co. Tipperary), Wilson's Hospital,[3] Fermoy (Co. Cork), Cork, Roscrea (Co. Tipperary), Stradbally (Queen's County), Mullingar (Co. Westmeath), and Trim (Co. Meath). With the exception of Longford, these were all places where the regiment had served, and it helps to confirm the belief that regiments recruited vigorously in the places where they were stationed. The average age of the recruits was 24, and their average height was five feet five inches (height will be discussed later, in reference to recruiting). Occupations included 146 labourers, 23 weavers, and 12 shoemakers but of the 237 occupations given, men with skilled trades (referred to at that time as mechanics), comprised 38 per cent of the total, while labourers, and other unskilled trades were in the majority at 62 percent. On the surface, this would appear to be the reverse of what Pelham claimed, in that almost two thirds were unskilled men, but whether 'labourer' means agricultural or urban, is not clear. It must be noted, however, that none had an interest in land, either as a tenant, or an owner. The matter must remain unproven, but if Pelham is correct, then it is possible that the people who rebelled in 1798 were small farmers, and from a rural background, whereas those who enlisted in the militia, were mainly from the towns.

This is the only contemporary enrolment book that seems to have survived. Another, for the North Mayo Militia exists, but was compiled after 1803.[4] It is not as complete as the Carlow book, and could well be a summary of information compiled from a variety of sources, but it does give information that in many ways is not much different from a decade earlier. Almost all the men were volunteers from County Mayo, or enlisted there. They included two black men – one from St John's, West Indies, and the other an American from Rhode Island, and four boys, the youngest being thirteen. Of the men, 194 listed 'no occupation,' and the remainder comprised 197 men with a trade, 54 labourers, and one farmer. When consid-

---

[3] The hospital and school at Multyfarnham, Co. Westmeath, founded in 1761 for old Protestant men, and 150 Protestant male children. It is now a co-educational school. [4] NA, WO/68/325.
[5] Wakefield, *An account of Ireland*, table of religious sects, no pagination.

ered with the Carlow book, this evidence suggests that militiamen did not come from any class that possessed land – unless balloted – and that Pelham was largely correct in his generalization.

There is no record of the men's religion in either of these enrolment books, nor in the pay and muster rolls. It remains a matter of conjecture that the county regiments reflected the religious make-up of the parent county. The only evidence of religious affiliation is that provided by Edward Wakefield who compiled his statistics before 1800, although they were not published until 1812. Wakefield's evidence must be treated with care, because we do not know how he obtained his information, and the suspicion must be that much of it was hearsay.[5] Accepting that Wakefield's evidence is somewhat suspect, a comparison of his figures for the proportions of Catholics to Protestants in the county, and in the militia, is most revealing:

Regiment	Militia Proportion	County Proportion
Carlow	5:2	9:1
Cork County[6]	7:2	11:1
Fermanagh	2:13	2:1
Galway	5:1	39:1
Kerry	5:1	79:1
Kilkenny	7:1	22:1
King's County	6:1	7:1
Leitrim	2:1	29:1
Limerick County	14:1	79:1
Louth	5:4	14:1
Monaghan	3:4	4:1
Roscommon	7:1	79:1
Tipperary	19:1	11:1
Sligo	2:1	30:1
Westmeath	2:1	29:1
Wexford	2:1	9:1

Table 6: Proportion of Catholics to Protestants in the Irish militia

In all cases, the ratio of Catholics to Protestants in the militia does not accord with the ratio in the county. This suggests that, in proportion, more Protestants joined the militia than Catholics. This would hardly be surpris-

6 The North Cork, and the South Cork Regiments.

ing in many ways, because the restrictions of Catholics serving in the British Army had been lifted so recently. In two counties, Fermanagh, and Monaghan, more Protestants than Catholics were privates in the militia, in contradiction to the proportions in the county. In Wexford, the proportion of Catholics in the militia was much smaller than in the county at large, and in Tipperary, the opposite was true, the proportion of Catholics in the militia, being much greater than in the county. Of particular interest are the proportions in Roscommon – which had a much smaller proportion of Catholics in the militia, as compared to the massive preponderance in the county – since Roscommon was the most disaffected county in the 1790–3 period.

What cannot be answered is whether or not colonels deliberately recruited Protestants. We have already seen that Lord Kingsborough in Cork was reported to have done so by offering a small farm in Co. Cork to each of the first 244 men to volunteer, provided they were Protestants.[7] Lord Enniskillen of the Fermanagh Battalion is another. He became a keen Orangeman later, though he can hardly have been one in 1793, before the formation of the order. It should be remembered that the militia had filled slowly when it was first raised because of the inadequacy of the ballot, which suggests that the colonels were only too pleased to accept what they could get. The real truth of the matter is probably that the army hierarchy were not really interested in the religion of the troops, the Catholic Relief Act of 1793 having removed almost all barriers to recruitment and advancement of officers and men. It had always been a policy of the army to provide for the religious beliefs of the men, and not to interfere with them.

Some places in the country did not welcome Catholic soldiers. Contemporary accounts at the level of the private soldier at this time are extremely rare, and only one letter from a friend or relative to a private soldier is known to exist. It makes reference to this very problem. Bridget Brennan of Strabane wrote to her friend Pat Kerr of the Royal Tyrone Regiment, stationed in Dublin, in August 1796.[8] In it, she refers to the difficulties faced by Catholics in Co. Armagh, and by the County of Limerick Militia in Derry:

> In Derry they awe the people although no army ever behaved better than they do and yet some of our inhabitants hates them and would wish them elsewhere. Justices gives no hearing or redress to the Catholics even if a mans goods and property be found in a protestants custody he is acquitted and no law against murder and robbery. But if a papist indeavour to save or defend himself is either transported or hanged.

7 *Sentimental and Masonic Magazine*, July–Dec. 1793, iii, 383. 8 Bridget Brennan to Pat Kerr, Dublin, 14 Aug. 1796 (NAI, RP/620/24/131a).

Bridget was quite right about distrust of the Limericks in Derry. Sir George Fitzgerald Hill, a Derry magistrate, and subsequently clerk to the house of commons in Dublin, wrote 'I perceive that (Major) Loyd is an excellent worthy man, and a good officer, he is over-partial to his regiment, and is persuaded that people here have a prejudice against them because they are mostly Roman Catholics and march with musick to mass.'[9]

Nevertheless, the Castle authorities remained very sensitive to the subject of religion of the men, and could be guaranteed to intervene if they suspected that the soldiers were being denied freedom of worship. From Ardfinnan Camp in 1796 Sir Edward Bellew, a Catholic officer in the Louth Regiment, one of those encamped there in that year, wrote to a 'Mr Strange', saying that Catholic soldiers had to attend a Protestant service. His comments reached the ears of the lord lieutenant, and a correspondence ensued between the chief secretary, Thomas Pelham, Major-General Sir James Duff, commanding the Centre District, and the commanding officers of the regiments; it even involved the Speaker, John Foster, the colonel of the Louth. The commanding officers, however, insisted that they had taken the 'sense' of the men, and that all were agreeable to what was taking place, because all could attend their denominational services as well. They wished to continue with the arrangement, and were allowed to do so. Not only was the Castle sensitive to this matter, but the regiments were as well. Finally Bellew wrote to Lord Louth, his commanding officer, saying that his authority for complaining that the men found great discontent in assisting at a Protestant service had been Mr Fennessy, the parish priest. He himself had found this assertion to be untrue, and he had never said the men were prevented from seeing their priest.[10] As Major General Eyre Coote said, 'Sir Edward, I am told, is much alarmed in consequence of the steps he has taken – all in camp, poor wretch, are against him.'[11]

There is no question that this incident was blown out of proportion, but its importance lies in the seriousness with which those in authority too the claim, even though it had emanated from a junior officer. Much effort was made to resolve the situation, as the Castle was well aware of the implications for the morale and loyalty of the men. It is also a comment on channels of communication; Bellew would have been 'on parade' on Sundays and he would thus have known what actually happened; so did he intend his remarks to be private, or were they taken out of context? It is highly likely that they were, for if he had had a complaint he could have raised it through the proper military channels.

9 G.F. Hill to Edward Cooke, 'Friday' (NAI, RP/6 2 o/2 4/112). Lloyd or Loyd was the major of the Limericks. 10 Capt. Sir Edward Bellew to officer commanding, Louth Regiment, 10 Oct. 1796 (PRONI, T/755/3/145). 11 Maj.-Gen. Eyre Coote, Clogheen, to Thomas Pelham, 10 Oct. 1796 (ibid., T/755/3/146). Ardfinnan is in south Tipperary.

An undated order issued in 1795 or 1796 gave instructions to recruiting officers of the Roscommon Regiment on the type of men they were to enlist. This would presumably be common to all the other regiments. At this stage, in the Roscommon, recruits were raised mainly by 'beat of drum', which meant sending recruiting parties under the command of an officer into the home county on a regular basis, and in competition with other recruiting parties from the regular army, and whichever militia regiments were stationed there.[12] The parties were required to get men not less than five feet six inches tall, and not over 36 years old, but boys could be five-feet-five-and-a-half inches tall, and aged between 16 and 18. Every week the recruiting officer had to send a return of the number of recruits he had enlisted to Lord Kingston, the colonel commandant, and monthly to the adjutant. Recruits were to be sent to the regiment in 'tens,' and to come complete with their attestation papers, and their 'accounts'. There were rules for the payment of bounties, and the 'marching guinea', as well as the 'necessaries' each man was required to possess.[13]

These rules were never strictly followed. Men were accepted under age and under size. But once the militia had surmounted the initial difficulties of raising men, it did not really have any recruiting problems, and could get men of the requisite size and age. Every half-yearly return submitted by the regiments contained tables of age and height, as well as length of service and nationality. Unfortunately, we no longer have these in general, but do have the result of a return from all militia regiments called for by the Castle in 1802, as well as the individual returns from the King's County, Donegal, and Armagh Regiments, which were a part of this return. The figures given for the whole militia are collated below:[14]

Age

Under 18	18	20	25	30	35	40	Over 40
392	1714	7553	7361	3916	1625	569	672

Total = 23,802 men. Average age = 25.08 years.

Height

Less	5'4"	5'4¼"	5'5"	5'6"	5'7"	5'8"	5'9"	5'10"	5'11"	6'0"	Over
753	1128	1164	3617	5060	4186	3213	2094	1475	661	246	207

Total = 23,804 men. Average height = 5ft 6¾ins.

Table 7: Ages and heights of militiamen, 1802

12 Instructions for recruiting officers (NA, WO/7 9/4 5, Roscommon Militia, standing orders). (In fact, not 'standing orders' as such, but army and district general orders.) 13 Ibid. 14 Return of ages and heights of the Irish militia, 12 Jan. 1802 (NLI, KP/1131).

The mean height of the Irish people in the period, 1800–15, has been estimated at 5 feet 5¼ inches, which shows that militiamen were 1½ inches taller than the average.[15] Such a difference is hardly surprising, since militiamen were young, and in the prime of life, were well fed, and had plenty of exercise. The average age is hardly surprising either, as the majority of men fell into the age bracket 20 to 25, as can be seen in the table.

This age bracket infers that they could well have been married, and the Irish militia was very much a married force. As a rule, the army did not like to have to deal with wives and families: they were a necessary nuisance at best, and a source of continuing trouble at worst; wives had the reputation of being the worst marauders, and children the most liable to spread fever among the men living as they did in such close proximity. The regular army had strict rule: when serving in Great Britain and Ireland soldiers could be accompanied, but when posted overseas only a small number, six or ten wives per company would be allowed to travel, and they would be employed as cooks and washerwomen in their husband's companies (and, owing to the vicissitudes of war, could marry, and remarry, several times). The militia was not a part of the regular army and did not serve outside Ireland until after the Act of Union, except for the King's County and the Wexford in 1799 –1800, and in this case the rule did not seem to apply. One of the reasons for trouble on the formation of the militia had been the lack of any provision for wives and families if the unit were to be called out for full-time service. This had been remedied by Foster's Family bill, rushed through parliament after the Militia Act,[16] which allowed one shilling per week for each child born in wedlock, and 2s. for each wife, provided that she did not follow the regiment, the money was to be raised by the parish cess. The allowance was only to be paid to balloted men, and, therefore, the families of substitutes had no option but to follow the regiment.

Foster's Act was repealed in 1795, and a new statute limited the allowance to children under ten, but included the father and mother, if supported by the militiaman, at 2s. a week each, and 1s. for each brother and sister.[17] The family allowance was to be not more than 4s. a week in total, and the money was to be paid from the county rather than the parish cess. In 1801 these allowances were authorized for all militiamen, should their regiments volunteer for service outside Ireland, and actually depart from the country, something that happened in the following decade.[18] The changes in the regulations, along with the introduction of allowances to pay for wives to return home when their husbands went overseas, show that the government and the

15 Cormac O'Grada, *Ireland, a new economic history* (Oxford, 1994), p. 21.   16 33 Geo. III, c.28.   17 35 Geo. III, c.2.   18 *Regulations for making provision for wives and children of soldiers of militia regiments which volunteer for service outside Ireland* (NA, HO/100/102/108).

army, were slowly coming to accept that some provision had to be made for the families of both the regular and the militia soldier. Soldiering, even then, was a way of life, which involved all ranks, their wives and children. A barracks or cantonment was a hive of activity, with soldiers going about their business, civilians working for the army, running canteens, or acting as contractors, wives employed as cooks and washerwomen, quite possibly a children's school, and a regimental hospital. Official recognition of this fact came painfully slowly, because it involved additional expenditure.

Figures for the numbers of wives and children attached to regular and fencible units are easily ascertained,[19] but the same cannot be said of the Irish militia. Only a few surviving returns give the necessary information, and all of these are from the latter part of the period. When the King's County went to Guernsey on 10 July 1799, they were 682 rank-and-file strong, and had 285 women and 254 children with them.[20] When they returned, and disembarked at Monkstown on 13 May 1800, they had 665 rank-and-file, 271 women, and 222 children,[21] representing a married rate of 44 and 40 per cent. When the Wexford Regiment returned from Jersey on 4 July 1800 they were 655 rank-and-file strong, and had 232 wives, and 236 children,[22] representing a married rate of 35 per cent. A return of the Armagh Regiment in 1801 or 1802 shows that the strength of that regiment was then just over 800.[23] There were 232 wives, and 298 children, which gives a married personnel rate of 29 per cent.[24] These figures suggest that the Irish militia had a high percentage of married men, and it could well be that the attraction of military service, with regular pay, allowances, prospects of promotion, but no risk of service outside Ireland, or later the British Isles (except as a volunteer), was an attraction for the unskilled, or semi-skilled married man. In addition, the prospects of securing an education for children, the possibility of a pension, and other advantages, would be an added attraction.

The Army Medical Board issued reports on the health of the troops in Ireland for the period 1796 to 1800, and made very pertinent comments on wives and children in a report on the health of two English militia regiments, stationed in the same barracks in Dublin for the same length of time,[25] one of which was an observation which was directly applicable to the Irish militia:[26]

---

19 In NA WO/27 series.   20 Cornwallis to Portland, 14 July 1799 (NA, HO/100/84/173). 21 Disembarkation return of the King's County Regiment, 13 May 1800 (ibid., HO/100/92/60).   22 Disembarkation return of the Wexford Regiment, 4 July 1800 (ibid., HO/100/91/134).   23 Historical register of the 3rd Battalion, Royal Irish Fusiliers (PRONI, D/3574/D/3A and 3B). The return is undated, but one of the company commanders was Captain William Blacker, who entered the Armagh Regiment from the 60th Royal Americans in 1801. He became major in 1806, and lieutenant-colonel in 1812.   24 Return of mens' wives of the Armagh Regiment (ibid., D/3574/D/2).   25 A comparison of the health of the Warwicks. and West Yorks. Militia, Dublin 1798 (NAS, GD/364/1/1129/16).   26 The two

> Our official experience enables us to state with some confidence that a multitude of women and children attached to any corps produce many formidable inconveniences; they are generally the medium through which contagious diseases are first introduced among the soldiery, and they invariably preserve the [forms] of infection until by repeated irruptions it has exhausted its virulent effects; the filth and unventilated state of a barrackroom in which the wives and children of soldiers are lodged can only be conceived by those who have frequently visited such apartments before cleansing day, when every sense is violated in the greatest possible degree. We know ... that the Irish militia have so great a proportion [of married soldiers], as absolutely to render barrack cleanliness and ventilation nearly impracticable. But in the present state of the army in Ireland we confess ourselves at a loss to point out any efficacious regulation to remedy this evil.

Nevertheless, despite the dismal picture of basic hygiene revealed by this extract, the Army Medical Board were concerned enough to produce a report on all the regiments of militia, based on a survey of deaths from disease, and other causes in the period 1795–1800. The average number of effective soldiers in the militia during this period was 22,038. The total number of deaths was 1,885, and, of that, the total of deaths from disease as 1,373. This gives an annual proportion of effectives to death of 1:79, and the Board commented that compared to all classes of mankind, aged 20 to 50 years, this figure was unusually favourable.[27] The most favourable ratio in the militia was the Waterford Regiment, with 1:196; in five years they lost only 18 men, fourteen to disease. This complements the earlier statistics on age and height: the Irish militia, despite having a large contingent of wives and children, was thus a remarkably healthy force for its time. The board considered that the reasons for this were, first, that the militia was composed of 'natives', that is, Irishmen in the prime of life; second, that the majority of the men were from the peasantry, 'as stout and hardy a race of men as any in Europe'; third, that they were seldom exposed to severe fatigue, or the vicissitudes of inclement weather, or collected in very large bodies; fourth, that they were well fed, well clothed, tolerably well accommodated, and finally, a compliment to the board itself and the regimental medical officers, 'during the entire period alluded to, a vigilant and laudable attention has, to our knowledge, been paid to the treatment of the sick'.[28]

---

regiments were in the Royal, now Collins Barracks in Dublin. These barracks were built in 1701, and are now open to the public. When built, they had no internal sanitation, and no internal plumbing. They are four storeys high. Families shared the same accommodation as the single men, a curtain or sheet providing 'privacy'.   **27** A statement on deaths in the Irish militia for five years, ending 31 Dec. 1800 (NAS, GD/364/1/1129/2).   **28** Ibid.

Another Medical Board report, made slightly earlier in 1800, had condemned the recruiting system, which was full of abuses, and outlined the failure to inspect recruits properly, be they for the regular army, fencibles, or militia.[29] The militia contained 1,344 incurably diseased soldiers, 118 children and boys, 84 of them under size. But these abuses were not confined to the militia. To put things in perspective, remembering that the 1790s mark a nadir in British military prowess, particularly in expeditions to the continent of Europe, in March 1796 the fencibles had 1,849 incurably diseased men and 1,062 boys not fit for service, out of a total strength of 8,537 men (34 per cent of their strength). Ten regiments of the Line destined for the West Indies, and sent to Ireland in 1794 and 1795, were 6,336 strong. Of these 974 died in Ireland, and upwards of 600 were left behind in Cork, many of whom had to be discharged. This represents one quarter of the force.[30] In comparison, the figures, above, for the militia, represent 6.6 per cent not fit for duty, which is incomparably better than either.

DISCIPLINE

Leadership was the most important aspect of the management of the army, but discipline was the glue that held it together, that produced orderliness, obedience, and self-control. There was a direct relationship between leadership and discipline. Many of the failures of discipline in the Irish militia can be shown to have been the direct result of failures of leadership at sub-unit, regimental, or general staff level. Discipline, itself, can be divided into three linked spheres, the first of these being discipline imposed from above. This is a very broad subject, ranging from the training of the recruit to the rules and regulations of the army expressed in the annual Mutiny Act, regimental standing orders, and the general orders issued regularly by army commands and districts. The second sphere is the discipline of the individual soldier, which is a summation of his character, and the care with which he has been trained and led; and the third aspect is the discipline of the group, the battalion or regiment. Each of these separate spheres will be considered in turn.

The Mutiny Act and the articles of war regulated the regiments themselves, and the men they contained, annually. The individual soldier was affected by five of the twenty sections in the articles of war, which included disrespect to the royal family, or the commanding general, mutinous behaviour, desertion, deliberate loss or damage of arms, ammunition, accoutrements, clothing, dereliction of duty, misbehaviour in the field, plundering, and giv-

---

29 *Observations annexed to the Army Medical Board's report of the sick of the Army in Ireland dated Dublin, 1 June 1800* (NAS, GD/364/1/1129/3). 30 Ibid.

ing information or assistance to the enemy. Regimental practice and necessary rules could be added to these because the final section included the 'catch all' phrase 'conduct prejudicial to good order and military discipline'.[31] Both regimental standing orders and the articles of war had the sanction of a court martial. There were two types of court martial, the general, which tried serious offences against the articles of war, and which could convict capitally, and the regimental, which tried 'crime' within the regiment itself. In the eighteenth century a regimental court martial was presided over by a field officer, who sat with four younger officers. They tried cases of theft, misbehaviour on duty, absence, drunkenness, and so on. Punishment, when found guilty, was loss of rank, or suspension, or public apology, and or flogging. The concept of imprisonment was in its infancy, except for debt, a civil offence, and the punishment of 'confined to barracks,' was coming into vogue.

The court martial book of the Royal Downshire Regiment is the only record of regimental courts martial extant for the Irish militia.[32] It began on 31 October 1793, and ran, albeit with five pages missing, to 24 August 1796 giving the dates of offences, the location, the names of the accused, their company, the crime, verdict, and punishment, all of which makes it a detailed and valuable record. However, it is a somewhat inconsistent record. Since officers had to have a property qualification in order to be commissioned, it would be expected that offences against property, both real and personal, would have been dealt with severely. G.A. Steppler, who has made a study of regimental courts martial in the eighteenth-century, considered theft to be a crime that military officers deemed to merit very severe punishment, even more severe than striking a non-commissioned officer, but in the Downshire, this is not quite the case.[33] Of those found guilty of theft, sentences varied between 'stoppages of pay', and/or suspension from rank, to 200-300 lashes. The most severe punishments were those connected with theft of arms or ammunition; for example, pledging (or pawning) a firelock merited 1,000 lashes. In fact, drunkenness, which was a much more prevalent crime, merited on average 150 lashes; six sergeants, and six corporals were reduced to the ranks for it, but otherwise there were no suspensions from rank, or any other sentence than flogging. Again, there was inconsistency. Private Hugh McKeevers received 100 lashes for being drunk on the firing ranges in charge of a loaded weapon, but being drunk on guard merited 100 to 300, with one award of 500 lashes. Drunk on guard duty may have been a very serious offence, but scarcely more serious than drunk in charge of a loaded weapon. There does not seem to have been any consis-

---

31 G.A. Steppler, 'British military law, discipline, and the conduct of regimental courts martial in the later eighteenth century,' in *English Historical Review*, 102 (1987), 863. 32 Court martial book of the Royal Downshire Regiment, 1793-6 (PRONI, D/374/4). 33 Steppler, 'British military law', p. 879.

tency, or indeed a regimental policy on sentencing, which presumably would have been easy to organize.

Absence from duty was another problem area; four sergeants and three corporals were reduced to the ranks for it, and three corporals were suspended from rank and pay, for one, three, and six months respectively. Extra guard duty was also a punishment (for seventeen men, all married, who were absent from 2 p.m. drill on Sunday, 7 July 1795 as it happens), and two periods in the 'black hole' (solitary confinement on bread and water for anything up to three days) were awarded. Of all punishments, the 'black hole' seems to have been the most dreaded. Again, however there was inconsistency. One soldier, absent for two years, received 200 lashes; another, absent for seven months, received 500, which were not in fact administered, a third also received 500, but was given 100 for three months' absence; and one man received an award of 1,000 for twelve days' absence, of which he received only 150.

Many of these cases were a result of the scrapes into which feckless soldiers got themselves. On 9 September 1794, Private Roger Roney received a night in the 'black hole' for insolence to a sergeant; on 18 June 1795 Private Andrew McCann, of Captain Waddell's Company, having been found drunk on a march from Cork was sentenced to 300 lashes; while on the same date Private William White went absent without leave, having spent the day at the races and also lost his firelock, for which he was ordered to receive 200 lashes. On 8 September 1795, Corporal Pekin was reduced to the ranks, and received 300 lashes for being drunk, abusive, and found in an officer's room, asleep in his bed (alone).

Several men were court martialled more than once. Moses Higginson became a sergeant, was suspended in one incident, reduced to the ranks in another, and was one of the first to receive the punishment of 'confined to barracks'. Yet, on 2 July 1800 he became an 'in-pensioner' at the Royal Hospital, Kilmainham.[34] The worst offender, however, was Private Daniel Doran, who was a regimental tailor. He was court martialled no less than six times for a list of offences ranging from theft, drunkenness, absence, and playing cards. He received a total of 975 lashes, not all of which were administered, and together with Charles Christie and James Shaw, in March 1795 was the first to be given one weeks' 'confined to barracks'. Their crime was absence, and gambling in 'Simon's the dram shop'.

Some 324 men were charged in the period with these minor offences, of whom fifty-five, or seventeen per cent were found 'not guilty' and acquitted. Of the remaining 83 per cent, 21 per cent were guilty of drunkenness, 25 per cent of absence from place of duty, and 6 per cent of theft. The remainder were guilty of such offences as assault, fraud, embezzlement, and

---

34 Royal Hospital, Kilmainham, register of pensioners (NA, WO/118/36).

robbery, threatening behaviour, neglect of duty, rioting, and disobedience. The figure for absence from place of duty is interesting as it suggests an imperfect understanding among the men of the importance of attending such duty, a casual attitude to it, or, perhaps the most likely, lack of adequate officer supervision.

The principal punishment was flogging. In this period, guilty men in the Royal Downshire Regiment were sentenced to:

Lashes	21,625 (in total)
Remitted	8,526 (39.43 per cent)
Administered	9,078 (42 per cent)
No data	4,021

Table 8: Royal Downshire Regiment, punishment by flogging, 1793–6

Steppler says of flogging, 'Perhaps nothing more characterizes the popular notion of British military discipline in the eighteenth century than the image of some hapless wretch undergoing a flogging sentence resulting from a capricious decision by haughty officers completely indifferent to his fate.'[35] The facts show this to be wide of the truth as far as the Irish militia was concerned; yet Steppler is correct in his statement as a reflection of twenty-first-century opinion. In the 1790s, whether in the regular or auxiliary forces, the range of punishments available was limited, since there was no concept of confinement for a period of time, one of the most common punishments in the modern army. At that time all servicemen, and civilians, knew flogging to be the principal punishment, and the widespread use of flogging to obtain information – as in 1798 – is thus not surprising. In the armed forces of the Crown, command had to be backed by sanction, and in the eighteenth century, sanction was very imperfect, not only in relation to the gravity of the offence, but also in the maintenance of discipline. Hence there came about the gradual introduction of confinement, and a movement in this direction. It must be said, however, that from the point of view of the commanding officer, flogging was a useful deterrent, and a quick punishment, so that the offender returned to duty without the necessity of having to employ good men in guarding prisoners.

A court martial book such as this tells much about the types of trouble that men got into, and these represent lapses in personal discipline. There were other matters which represented lapses in personal discipline, but which

35 Steppler, 'British military law', 859.

were tried at a higher level. However, militiamen committed very little rape or murder (for which they could be charged). We know for example, that Lieutenant Vennel and Ensign Lawler involved the 'centinel', or sentry, in the rape of Catherine Finn. The only other incident of a rape involving militiamen to be recorded occurred in October 1798 when Privates Henry Grady and William Fitzgerald, of the Limerick Militia, were convicted at Kilkenny assizes of raping a Mrs Joan Doyle. On 20 August 1798, on the march after Vinegar Hill, these men halted at Gowran, Co. Kilkenny, went into Doyle's house and demanded a drink of milk. When she went to get it, they carried her into a haggard and 'abused' her, holding off her husband with their firelocks. Found guilty, they were reported to be 'for execution on the 17th'.[36]

Despite Cornwallis' notorious claim about the militia – 'in short, murder appears to be their favourite pastime' – outside the period of the rebellion itself, there are very few accounts of deliberate murder.[37] We have already considered the case of Edward Hogg, and the murder of Birch by soldiers of the Antrim Regiment, which is certainly one example; another, and one of the worst, was the murder of John McCarthy and Margaret, his wife, who lived at Ballinvostig in the Union of Ahada, near Carlisle Fort in Cork by three privates of the Cavan Battalion. This was an atrocious murder for which Privates William Stacey, Thomas Hamilton, and Joseph Cook were capitally convicted and executed on 3 December 1800.[38]

On the other hand, there are attested examples of soldiers who, under provocation, kept their heads, and acted calmly, remembering their duty as in the case of the behaviour of Sergeant Power of the Clare Militia in Limerick on 15 September 1800. This matter came to light with the court martial on 6 October 1800 of Captains Elwin and Hawker of the 2nd Battalion, 46th Regiment. Hawker was charged with impersonating the officer of the guard, in Limerick, and disarming and imprisoning Sergeant Power, who was the sergeant of the ordnance store guard. Elwin was charged with abusing and striking Sergeant Power, and endeavouring to wrest from the 'centinel' his firelock and bayonet.[39] They were both found guilty but the court thought the charges exaggerated, and the conduct of Sergeant Power very officious, so much so, that he had provoked the two officers to act as they had done. Their sentence was lenient, to be publicly reprimanded by the general officer commanding the district.

36 Grady and Fitzgerald were executed. *Freeman's Journal*, 2 Oct. 1798. A 'haggard' is an enclosed yard usually near a farmyard containing hay and other barns, chicken runs and houses for farm equipment.   37 Marquess Cornwallis to Portland, 8 July 1798 quoted in *Cornwallis Corresp.*, ii, 359. At this date, Cornwallis had been in Ireland less than three weeks.   38 E.B. Littlehales to Maj.-Gen. Myers, 24 Nov. 1800 (NLI, KP/1 4 1/2 8 5). Also *Hibernian Chronicle*, 24 and 27 Nov. 1800, 1 and 4 Dec. 1800.   39 Hawker and Elwin court martial, 6 Oct. 1800 (ibid., KP/1201).

Cornwallis, however, took great exception to this verdict.[40] He thought that Sergeant Power had 'acted throughout the whole business as a faithful and good soldier, that he in no instance overstepped the strict line of his duty and that he would have been highly reprehensible if he had taken a less active part to preserve the peace of the city and to secure the important post committed to his charge.' Cornwallis obviously considered that the court had been deliberately lenient, and had tried to traduce the good name of a militia unit when trying officers of the regular army. He wrote a second letter on this subject to General Duff, on the same day, 'You should call in Sergeant Power of the Clare Militia, and in the presence of all the officers inform him that the Lord Lieutenant entirely approves of his conduct ... which was that of a good and faithful soldier, and that it gave ... particular pleasure to see that although the sergeant could not be overawed into a dereliction of his duty yet he never in the whole course of the business, forgot the degree of respect which was due to persons who wore the badge of the King's Commission.' Duff was also ordered to acknowledge the part played by Colonel the Hon. Nathaniel Burton, who had supported his sergeant, 'so necessary for the maintenance of discipline ... and so essential for the future harmony and co-operation of the different descriptions of troops of which ... the army is composed.'[41] The importance of this incident is not just Sergeant Power's devotion to duty, but also the support he received from his colonel, and the public recognition of this by the commander-in-chief. This had an excellent effect on the morale of the men of the Clare Battalion.

Numerous other examples can be found of soldiers exhibiting good discipline in the performance of their duties. To a very large extent, the overall discipline of a unit was a summation of the degree of discipline exhibited by its individual members. But each unit was subjected to different pressures, and given tasks where individuals were subsumed into the impersonal whole. This was where leadership had to be shown by their commanders. If it was not, discipline would inevitably suffer, and this is indeed what gradually happened to the militia in 1796 and 1797. When the United Irishmen became a secret revolutionary movement in 1795, sought an alliance with the Defenders, and began to attempt the seduction of militia soldiers from their allegiance, their campaign brought tremendous strains upon militia units comprised largely of Catholic rank-and-file, particularly on the discipline of the men. It is from this period that the claims of illegal and 'licentious' behaviour of militia units emanate.

In 1796 the commander-in-chief, Lord Carhampton, pacified northern Connacht in a swift and thorough campaign in which he sent to the fleet

---

40 E.B. Littlehales to Maj.-Gen. Sir James Duff, 23 Oct. 1800 (ibid., KP/1141/181). 41 E.B. Littlehales to Maj.-Gen. Sir James Duff, 23 Oct. 1800 (ibid.).

local men suspected of any disaffection, without any semblance of a trial, and in contravention of the law. Then, in response to growing unrest, and the inadequacy of the magistrates, who were really unable to act when an area was disaffected, on 17 May 1797, a proclamation was issued, repeated to the army on 18 May 1797, authorizing the military to act without waiting for the direction of a civil magistrate in dispersing 'tumultuous or unlawful assemblies.'[42] This order only applied when no magistrate was present; if there was one, the troops could not act on their own but had to obey him.[43] At the same time troops were dispersed in small detachments throughout the country to maintain law and order. In March 1797 General Lake was given 'full authority' to disarm the north, which he and Brigadier General Knox made full use of.[44] Colonel John Moore, newly arrived in Ireland, summed up the government's attitude by noting in his diary that their mode of quieting a district where there was trouble was to let loose the military, who were encouraged to act violently, arrest without trial, and send men out of the country, an oblique reference to Carhampton in Connacht the previous year, but also to the men being sent overseas from Duncannon and New Geneva.[45] This type of service, where the men were away from the control of officers, and often non-commissioned officers as well, encouraged them to act as they pleased, and was ruinous to discipline, both of the men themselves, and their units.

Lieutenant-General Sir Ralph Abercromby was appointed on 10 November 1797 to succeed Carhampton as commander-in-chief.[46] He was no stranger to Ireland; having served there for more than twenty years with the 6th Dragoon Guards, and during the American war he had commanded the 103rd (or King's Own) Regiment, which had been raised in Ireland.[47] Abercromby was much more of a soldier than a politician: he travelled over Ireland, and he did not like what he found.

As a soldier, Abercromby had well defined principles. He believed that the defence of Ireland was against external threat rather than internal insurrection, that the army had to act under the authority of civil government, and wanted to be able to train his troops in formed bodies. Instead he found the troops dispersed in small detachments around the country for the protection of individuals. Discipline had deteriorated because of lack of officer

---

42 General order, 18 May 1797 (ibid., KP/1 0 1 3/3 52). The proclamation of 17 May was signed by seven privy councillors who were colonels of militia regiments, Lords Waterford, Westmeath, Glandore, Portarlington, and Gosford, John Foster, and Denis Browne.   43 Samuel Reed, lord mayor of Dublin, to Thomas Pelham, 19 May 1797 (NAI, RP/ 620/3 0/1 1 2).   44 Pelham to Lake, 3 Mar. 1797 (PRONI, D/607/ E /1 48).   45 Maurice, *Diary of Sir John Moore*, i, p. 271.   46 Camden to Portland, 21 Nov. 1797 (NA, HO/100/68/273).   47 *Freeman's Journal*, 6 Dec. 1797.(One of his officers had been Capt. Ryan, mortally wounded in the arrest of Lord Edward Fitzgerald in May 1798.)

supervision. Troops in these small detachments were exposed to corruption and were disorganized, while morale was low. In general they were in no condition to fight the French.[48] These strictures, it must be added, applied to the whole army, not just the militia.

In an attempt to halt what he saw as a decline in the army, Abercromby issued his famous general order of 26 February 1798.[49]

> The very disgraceful frequency of Courts Martial and the many complaints of irregularities in the conduct of the troops in this Kingdom having so unfortunately proved the army to be in a state of licentiousness which must render it formidable to everyone but the enemy

It is important to remember that this order applied to the whole army, including the militia. Several commentators have taken it to apply to the militia alone, but the inference is incorrect, and probably originated in the subsequent efforts of Lord Camden to deflect criticism of the whole army on to the militia in particular. Nevertheless, there were problems that affected the militia particularly and the discipline of its men. The regiments were dispersed and had to provide so many detachments that there were often not enough officers to command them; at times, not enough non-commissioned officers either. In January 1798 off-duty men of the City of Cork Militia and the Romney Fencibles during the absence of their officers, Captain Swayne and Lieutenant Diebling, burnt the houses of people who had murdered a sergeant of the Romney Fencibles at Newbridge, Co. Kildare.[50] One example among many of what could happen in these circumstances.

Other problems of unit discipline had already manifested themselves before Abercromby highlighted them. Units of the regulars, fencibles and militia, did not always get on well together, nor did they always get on well with local people. As a result, there could be outbreaks of violence. A quarrel between the Limerick City Militia and the Reay Fencibles in Belfast in June 1796 led to the Limericks being removed to Derry, where, as has been seen earlier in this chapter, they continued to have problems with the local people.[51] In May 1797 an affray took place in Dundalk between the City of Dublin Regiment and the 'Antient Britons,' a Welsh Fencible cavalry regiment, in which one of the Dublins was killed, and two very seriously injured. Two troopers were found guilty of manslaughter, and sentenced to be burnt on the hand.[52] Earlier, in 1794, there had been cases of ill discipline, and

---

48 P.C. Stoddart, 'Counter insurgency and defence in Ireland, 1790–1805' (DPhil, Oxford, 1972). 49 General order, 26 Feb. 1798 (NA, WO/68/221/37, Donegal Militia order book). The order appears in numerous other regimental books. 50 Officer commanding, Royal Cork Militia, to Maj.-Gen. Needham, 5 June 1798 (PRONI, Lake–Hewitt correspondence, MIC/67/8). 51 Camden to Pelham, 1 July 1796 (ibid., T/755/3/10). 52 Memorial from

even incitement to mutiny arising from quarrels between the Kerry and Waterford Regiments.[53] In 1796, a brawl between men of the Roscommon and the Waterford led to a resort to arms, but the men were separated by their officers, and returned to duty.[54]

There were also many examples of ill feeling between regiments and local people. In 1795 a serious affray in Loughbrickland, Co. Down, occurred in which the Westmeath Militia killed three local people. A landlord ordering soldiers out of an unlicensed public house had caused it.[55] In July 1797 a very serious riot took place between the Kerry Regiment and the people of Stewartstown, County Tyrone, provoked by the locals wearing orange cockades. The Kerrymen (predominantly, if not entirely, Catholic) took exception to this, and a riot ensued in which eight or nine of the regiment were killed, and their march to Galway halted. Lord Blayney, colonel of the 89th Foot, was sent with some dragoons to restore order. He met a sergeant and three men of the Kerry, and promptly attacked them, killing three of them. Blayney was later dismissed for this precipitate action.[56] A few days later Colonel Leslie, commanding in Cookstown, issued orders that no one in the town was to wear orange cockades until the Kerry Regiment had marched through.[57] Orangeism caused dissension in the militia, and, just as some of the officers and men were in favour of the movement, others were strongly against it. Major Matthews, hoping to stop Orange clubs in the Downshire Regiment wrote, 'there is nothing surer than that Orangemen will be the means of making United men, and our neighbours the Queen's [County Regiment], are I believe very willing to undertake the business.'[58]

Overall, unit discipline suffered severe trauma in the period between 1795 and the outbreak of the rebellion on 23 May 1798. Lord Castlereagh, the only government office-holder with actual experience of militia service, summed up the militia experience in a letter to William Wickham in September 1798:

> The Duke of Portland may depend on every exertion of mine in seconding the salutary military regulations ... the Lord Lieutenant is about to adopt for restoring the discipline of the Irish Army, particularly of the native Irish Militia which has suffered more from the irregular service in which the troops have necessarily been engaged than any other force ... there is little to fear from disaffection, much

---

Col. H.G. Sankey, City of Dublin Militia, [n.d.] (NLI, KP/1142/116). 53 Court martial, 31 Dec. 1794 (NA, WO/68/402, Cavan Battalion letter book). 54 Gen. W. Dalrymple to Thomas Pelham, 4 Dec. 1796 (PRONI, T/755/3/200). 55 Thomas Lane to Lord Downshire, [Nov. 1795] (ibid., D/607/C/164A). 56 Camden to Portland, 17 July 1797 (NA, HO/100/71/109). 57 General order, Cookstown, 15 July 1797 (NAS, GD/26/9/527/1/117). 58 Maj. Matthews to Lord Downshire, 5 Dec. 1796 (PRONI, D/607/D/366).

from insubordination and religious distinction. A disposition to plunder has grown out of the unfortunate warfare in which they have been engaged, which the measure of free quartering, however well regulated, was calculated to countenance.[59]

Castlereagh, then lieutenant-colonel of the Londonderry, thus expressed very well the problem as it stood in September 1798. As chief secretary, he was in a position to see the overall picture of how the discipline of the militia, both individual and collective, had stood the strain of the rebellion.

That leads to the third subject covered in the present chapter, the loyalty of the men. Despite all the problems the dispersed service created in 1797 and 1798, the loyalty of the men was part and parcel of what brought them through the rebellion. Not everyone thought that it would. Robert Craufurd was one: 'And as to its loyalty, I much fear there is not in it such a fund of steady, determined, loyalty as would carry them through, and make them hang steadily together, when surrounded by their own countrymen in rebellion, and opposed to a formidable foreign enemy, professing in their usual way, that they come not to conquer, but emancipate Ireland.'[60] He was to be proved wrong.

LOYALTY

Loyalty is by far and away the most difficult aspect of any discussion on the men of the Irish militia: there is no direct evidence of what the men themselves thought, and we can only surmise what influenced them and motivated them to remain loyal. Undoubtedly, military discipline played a very important part in encouraging loyalty by compulsion, but how strong this was depended also on leadership. There are numerous oft-quoted examples of adverse comment on the leadership qualities of militia officers but (the point has been made before), at the same time almost every regiment had some good officers. Even more important than the officers in this question of leadership and management of the regiment, were the non-commissioned officers. Unfortunately, with few exceptions – such as Sergeant Power – we know little about the quality of non-commissioned officers. This is an unfortunate impediment to any understanding of the loyalty in the private men, because the non-commissioned officers were the 'nerves and sinews of the corps'.[61] The point cannot be underestimated: officers directed, organized,

---

[59] Castlereagh to Wickham, 17 Sept. 1798 (NA, HO/100/78/355). [60] Craufurd to Wickham, 19 Mar. 1798 (ibid., HO/100/66/76). [61] John Williamson, *The elements of military arrangement, and of the discipline of war; adapted to the practice of the British infantry*, 2 vols (1782), quoted in Houlding, *Fit for service*, p. 270.

and controlled, but non-commissioned officers put their commands into practice; in modern parlance, they were the first line of management.

When the regiments were raised the establishment of non-commissioned officers was very quickly filled, and every regiment maintained this establishment thereafter. When the militia was invited to volunteer to the line in 1800, non-commissioned officers were forbidden to take part.[62] In common with other infantry regiments, regular and fencible, the ratio of non-commissioned officers to men was between one to seven and one to twelve. For example, in the Armagh, in March 1797, it was one to seven; in the North Cork, March 1798, it was one-to-twelve; in the Donegal, March 1801, it was one to nine; and in the Downshire, in March 1798, it was one to eight.[63] For the whole militia, on 31 October 1801, the figure was one to eight.[64] There were more non-commissioned officers to private men in the British Army than in the Prussian.[65] One of the defining principles of the British Army in the eighteenth century was the degree of reliance and responsibility placed upon its non-commissioned officers. This must have had a considerable effect on retaining the loyalty of the men. It is worth noting that very few non-commissioned officers deserted, and few ever faced a general court martial (as opposed to a regimental court martial). One of the problems faced by the United Irishmen, when attempting to seduce militiamen from their allegiance, in 1795, was their almost total failure to suborn non-commissioned officers.

Non-commissioned officers were promoted from the ranks, which meant that, by and large, they were from the same strata of society as the private men. Non-commissioned officers also lived in close proximity to the men, and their very numbers made them a powerful group for the enforcement of discipline. In no way could non-commissioned officers be threatened by groups of private men; for it was quite the reverse, the non-commissioned officers could strongly influence the loyalty of the men, and indeed, weld together the men into the powerful group loyalty that characterized the British regimental system. Sir Hew Dalrymple, in his half-yearly report on the King's County Regiment in Guernsey, on 5 March 1800, wrote 'I have also communicated the very extraordinary unanimity which seems to prevail in screening certain sorts of offenders from punishment', and 'individuals have in certain instances shown much zeal in prosecuting to conviction men of their own nation, but in other regiments, who have held republican or improper political language of any sort'.[66] Thus we have prima facie evidence

---

62 Sgt. Scott, and Cpls McFadden and Connelly, of the Clare Battalion, volunteered into the 27th Inniskillings. Maj.-Gen. Sir James Duff was ordered to return them to their battalion as no N.C.O.s were allowed to volunteer to the Line. 27 Feb. 1800 (NLI, RP/1139/5 5). **63** Figures extracted from pay lists and muster rolls (NA, WO/1 3 series). **64** *Abstract of the returns received from the several regiments of militia, 31 Oct. 1801* (NAS GD 364/1/1128/5). **65** Houlding, *Fit for service*, p. 271. **66** Lt.-Gen. Hew Dalyrmple to Adjutant General, 8 Mar.

of a strong group loyalty, created by the system. This is but one aspect of loyalty, the other is the degree of loyalty displayed by the individual. The army was described as a way of life that contained a number of elements that actively encouraged the individual private men, and non-commissioned officers to remain loyal. The first of these was pay.

Between 1793 and 1797 a soldier's pay was adequate, but facing the problem of increasing inflation because of the war, even though corn prices in Dublin fell from around 40s. a barrel in July 1796, and again to 23 shillings a year later (remaining fairly steady until the end of 1798).[67] The problems with a soldier's pay were twofold. First, he was increasingly paid in paper money – which was not trusted in country districts, and could only be exchanged for specie at a discount. Paymasters attempted to alleviate this by exchanging paper money before paying the men, and the Kilmainham Papers are full of requests for authority to exchange at a discount, particularly in 1798 and 1799. The problem here was obviously that no one would wish to be paid their wages, and immediately lose up to ten per cent because of what amounted to a local 'exchange rate'. The second problem was 'stoppages.' Soldiers paid for their 'necessaries' – small clothes, hair powder, pipe clay, repairs to uniform, and so on – as well as 'barrack damages' (damage to living quarters, paid for by all at a flat rate), and voluntary contributions, from deductions made from their pay, with their consent, by the paymaster. When 'stoppages' had been taken out the private man had very little to live on, although he was accommodated and fed. In May 1797 a petition from the soldiers of the Dublin garrison asked for an increase in pay, and they threatened not to leave barracks unless it was granted. The North Mayo and Limerick City Regiments thanked them for this stand, but as such petitions could be regarded as very close to mutiny, they declared their loyalty to the king, and the constitution.[68] A pay rise was awarded in 1797, and this petition did not lead to considerations of mutiny. (This was the year of the naval mutinies at the Nore, and Spithead.)

A comparison of pay rates for all ranks in 1795 and 1799 is at Table 9.[69]

The first comment to be made is that colonels held their rank by brevet until 1797, which means that they held a rank one step higher than the one for which they were paid. The second is that the regimental staff officers – chaplain, quartermaster, adjutant, surgeon, and surgeon's mate – received pay of their appointment in addition to pay for their rank. The third is that the private soldier received the biggest percentage increase at ninety-two per cent.

1800 (NA, WO/27/83). 67 *Freeman's Journal*, and *Faulkner's Journal*, extracted corn returns, 1793 to 1802. Figures extracted from pay lists and muster rolls (ibid., WO/13 series). 68 Petition, 16 May 1797 (NAI, RP/620/30/93). 69 Sources: 1795, Willow to Hickson, 9 June 1795 (NA, WO/68/41 1/66, Kerry Militia order book). (Willow was the regimental agent, Hickson the paymaster.) 1799, Pay lists and muster rolls, Royal Downshire Militia (PRONI, T/1115/4A).

Rank	Daily Rate, 1795 £. s. d.	Daily Rate, 1799 £. s. d.
Colonel	13 1	1 2 6
Lieutenant-Colonel	13 1	15 11
Major	11 7	14 1
Captain	7 7	9 4¼
Captain-Lieutenant	3 6	5 8
Lieutenant	3 6	5 8
Ensign	3 0	4 8
Chaplain	5 0	5 0
Quartermaster	3 6	4 0
Adjutant	3 0	4 0
Surgeon	3 0	5 0
Mate	3 0	4 6
Sergeant-Major	1 7½	2 0¼
R.Q.M.S.[70]	1 7½	2 0¼
Sergeant	1 1½	1 6¾
Corporal	10½	1 2¼
Drummer	9½	1 1¼
Private	6¼	1 0

Table 9: A comparison of rates of pay 1795 and 1799

Insofar as the private men were concerned, a comparison with rates of pay for unskilled workers in civil life may be apposite. Arthur Young estimated that the wage paid to agricultural labourers in the late 1770s was about 7*d.* per day, Wakefield, in about 1810 (although his research had been made ten years earlier), at 10–1 3*d.*[71] Skilled men may have been paid much more, for bricklayers in Dublin received 1 5*d.* a day.[72] Militia soldiers, as we have seen, came from an unskilled, and semi-skilled background, so their military pay before 1797 would have been about 'average' in amount, but favourable because it was 'all found', and also because any promotion would have raised it above the average. After 1797 it can be said that militiamen were well paid in comparison with civil life. The only problem, perhaps, was that the government's generosity in increasing the private soldier's pay to 1*s.* a day left it unable to make a further increase until 1871.[73]

70 Regimental-Quartermaster-Sergeant.   71 Wakefield, *Account of Ireland*.   72 Rates of pay for unskilled and skilled men, and the opinion of Arthur Young, are to be found in Cormac O'Grada, *Ireland, a new economic history* (Oxford, 1994), pp 16–17.   73 Ferguson, 'Army in Ireland', p. 88.

Moreover, all soldiers had an opportunity to earn additional pay. Provided permission was obtained, soldiers could take on civilian work outside duty hours, and married militiamen, selected by ballot, received the family supplement from 1793, widened to include parents and siblings in 1795. This was used as a recruiting tool by the Royal Dublin Militia in 1795 in an advertisement for recruits, taking advantage of the removal of the ballot requirement, but not mentioning that such allowances were only payable if the family did not 'follow the drum'.[74] 'Applications are to be made to Colonel Sankey, Clare Street, Sergeant Montgomery, No 9, Horse Barrack Gate, and the officers commanding at Newry, Dundalk, Rathfriland, Portadown, Kilkeel, and Rostrevor.' The rate for wives, children, fathers and mothers was two shillings each per week, and brothers and sisters, one shilling a week, provided that the whole did not exceed 4s. a week. All of these had to be dependent on the militiaman for subsistence.

There were other allowances. The two most important, and most common, were for the duties of assisting 'the revenue' to search for illicit distillation, and providing escorts for prisoners. Both could be very dangerous, the Ballybay affair, in which several soldiers of the Armagh Regiment had been killed and wounded, was caused by searching for illegal stills in county Monaghan, and Sergeant Kirkus of the City of Dublin when on escort duty had to kill a prisoner to prevent rescue by a mob.[75] In April 1795 ten revenue officers, having made a 'seizure' six miles from Carrick-on-Shannon, were murdered by Defenders. No militia were involved on this occasion, but it gives an idea of just how dangerous searching for stills could be.[76] On the other hand, this did not stop soldiers accepting the challenge, and they could be very resourceful in doing so. In 1796 three privates of the Drogheda Battalion, under a sergeant, found an illegal still on an island in Lough Erne, and the distillers threatened to shoot in its defence. The three privates, Christopher Newcomen, Matthew Gibbons, and Thomas Reilly, tied pistols to the top of their heads, swam to the island, arrested the distillers, destroyed the mash, and recovered the still, head, and worm.[77] The three privates would have received 5s. 5d. for this, and the sergeant 1 1s. 4½d. more than ten times their daily pay. The rates for this service, when equipment was captured, are at Table 10.[78]

The rates for escorting deserters were also laid down in standing orders for the army.[79] They were based on the mileage the men had to march, and the men would also have been entitled to a subsistence (or food), and accommodation allowance. Escort duty involved guarding deserters and prisoners of all sorts, many of whom were accused of treason. In this case, soldiers

---

[74] *Faulkner's Journal*, 5 May 1795.   [75] Sgt. Robert Kirkus to Col. Sankey [Mar. 1797], (PRONI, T/755/2/198).   [76] Camden to Portland, 24 July 1795 (NA, HO/100/58/157).   [77] *Freeman's Journal*, 20 Aug. 1796.   [78] *Standing orders and regulations for the army in Ireland* (copy in Q.U.B.library, hqUB/627).   [79] Ibid.

The militiamen

	Still, head worm	Still, head	Still and worm	Still	Head and worm	Head or worm
	s. d.	s. d.	s. d.	s. d.	s. d.	s. d.
Sergeant	11 4½	8 1½	8 1½	4 10½	6 6	3 3
Corporal	8 1½	5 11½	5 11½	3 9½	4 4	2 2
Private	5 5	3 9½	3 ½	3 3	3 3	1 7½

Table 10: Rewards for capturing illegal stills

were paid their allowances from the secret service funds. For example, Lieutenant Atkinson of the Louth Militia was paid expenses of £16 14s. 10d. for bringing La Roche and Teeling, French prisoners, to Dublin on 14 September 1798, and Sergeant Gleeson, of the Limerick County Militia, who brought a prisoner from Cork, was paid £3 8s. 3d. for his expenses.[80] The set allowance for escorting prisoners was:[81]

Distance marched miles	Each man s. d.
6–15	1 1
15–39	2 2
39–78	4 4
78–117	5 5
117–156	6 6
Above 156	8 1½

Table 11: Travel allowances for escort duty

Beyond purely financial incentives to loyalty, there were other less tangible advantages, of great use to soldiers and their families. In 1796, soldiers, but not officers, were allowed to send letters at a concessionary rate of one penny a letter.[82] The charter of the 'Lying-in hospital', in Dublin specifically gave priority to 'wives and widows of soldiers and sailors',[83] and on the foundation of the Hibernian Military Institute in 1764 – predating a similar institution at Chelsea by nearly forty years – the sponsors declared 'that upon the death of non-commissioned officers and private men ... and upon the removal of regiments and of drafts from regiments to foreign service great

---

80 Gilbert, *Documents*, 20-1.   81 *Standing Orders and Regulations for the Army in Ireland, 1794.*
82 John Lees, secretary of the post office, to all postmasters [Mar. 1796] (NA, WO/68/221, Donegal Militia letter book).   83 Ferguson, 'Army in Ireland', p. 93.

numbers of children had been left destitute of all means of subsistence.'[84] The Institute, which in due course became the Royal Hibernian Military School (1764–1922), employed a sergeant-major of instruction, a matron, eight or nine teachers, and other craftsmen. It catered for both boys and girls, and the children of militiamen were eligible to be admitted to it. This co-educational boarding school, which in effect was what the Hibernian Military Institute really was, provided the first formal provision for the education of the children of other ranks in the British Army.[85] In the period 1793 to 1799, 18 per cent of school leavers went into the army themselves, 62 per cent became apprentices, 14 per cent returned to their families, 0.6 per cent ran away, and 5 per cent died.[86]

Militia parents could send their children to this institution, and there is evidence that there was unofficial provision of education for children in the militia regiments themselves. The best known was the school in the Cavan Battalion, supported by subscription from the officers.[87] The boys of this school wore a uniform made by the regimental tailor, and learned reading, writing, arithmetic, catechism, and spelling. They had two masters, both sergeants in the battalion, and they used the 'monitor' system: those that had 'passed' a lesson then taught it to a pupil who was attached to them for that purpose. There were about seventy boys, Protestants and Catholics in the school, which was supported entirely by the officers, who subscribed £121 10s. a month between them for its upkeep. There were other schools in other regiments, such as the school in the Tipperary Regiment that was established by Colonel John Bagwell, while its headmaster was Sergeant Chris Fox, who went to train at Chelsea in 1812, but who had been running the school long before that.[88] There was also a school for the children of private soldiers to be educated and 'instructed in the principles of the Christian religion gratis', at 45 Barrack Street, Dublin. It was supported by public and private subscription.[89]

Militiamen were eligible for a pension after 16 years service. The rate for a private soldier was 1s. a day.[90] Pensioners were of two types, 'in-pensioners,' who lived in the Royal Hospital at Kilmainham (and who dressed in a similar fashion to modern day Chelsea Pensioners), and 'out-pensioners', the vast majority, who lived at home. Between 1793 and April 1802, 466 militiamen became pensioners – these men would have had previous military service, but in 1801-2, the number of militia pensioners slowed to a trickle.[91] The reason is unclear; eligibility because of the war, which at this stage had

84 Ibid.   85 In 1922, it was amalgamated with the Duke of York's Royal Military School, which now is once again co-educational, and situated in Dover.   86 *CJI*, vols 15–18, appendices.   87 Wakefield, *Account of Ireland*, ii, 443–6.   88 Digest of services, Tipperary Militia (NA, WO/68/88).   89 *Faulkner's Journal*, 10 Dec. 1795. (Barrack Street was in front of the Royal Barracks, and is now named Benburb Street.)   90 Charles Handfield to the earl of Granard, 28 Apr. 1801 (NLI, KP/1093/1).   91 Pensioners at Kilmainham (NA, WO/118/36).

been going for nine years, may have had something to do with it. The numbers of former soldiers in the militia may have declined and militiamen themselves would not have completed 16 years' service at that time. However, by 1822, there were no less than 22,000 pensioners on the Kilmainham 'bounty', many of whom would presumably have been militiamen.[92]

If the militia soldier did not live to achieve a pension, but was killed in action, there was the possibility of organized charity. In September 1798 a 'Subscription for the relief of the soldiers wounded, and the widows and orphans of those killed', was opened in Dublin. The secretary was the barrister, Harding Giffard (eldest son of Captain John Giffard of the City of Dublin Regiment), who published a notice in the press, organizing collection of subscriptions in the different parishes of the city.[93] This subscription list was later published. The Camdens gave £2 0 0, Thomas Newenham £5 1 3s. 9d. (for the widows of the North Cork Regiment), Lord Castlereagh £5 0, Lord Kenmare, £2 0, and Dr Troy (Roman Catholic archbishop of Dublin), £5 1 3s. 9d.[94] A considerable sum was raised, and it is reported that there had been 9 9 applications from widows of the North Cork, and seventy from the widows of the Meath.[95]

Private men had the opportunity of promotion to corporal, sergeant or sergeant-major. There was only one sergeant-major in each regiment. Some militia non-commissioned officers were promoted to commissioned rank. In 1794, for example, Sergeant Major Neil Cockburn was promoted ensign in Colonel Hewitt's Regiment, from the Tipperary Militia.[96] This may have been something of a rarity from the Irish militia at this time, but a large number of officers of the regular army were commissioned from the ranks, about one third according to some estimates.[97] In the case of the militia, by far the most interesting is that of John Hamilton, who was promoted from the ranks as a reward for brave and distinguished conduct.

At the battle of New Ross, on 5 June 1 7 9 8, two persons above all were responsible for the defeat of the rebels: one was the commander, Major General Henry Johnston (an Irishman), and the other was Sergeant John Hamilton of the Donegal Militia. Musgrave described the advance of the rebels into the town:

> A numerous body of them, supposed to amount to five hundred, went down a great part of Mary Street, which is on a declivity, to attack

---

[92] Ferguson, 'Army in Ireland', p. 94.   [93] *Freeman's Journal*, 15 Sept. 1798.   [94] *Faulkner's Journal*, 12 June 1798.   [95] Ferguson, 'Army in Ireland', p. 188. The North Cork lost a total of 119 men in action in the rebellion, and the Meath 115 men. These could represent phenomenally high married rates, of 83 per cent and 61 per cent respectively. However, they might have included applications from parents and siblings.   [96] *Freeman's Journal*, 25 Mar. 1794.
[97] G.A. Steppler, 'The British Army on the eve of war,' in A.J. Guy (ed.), *The road to Waterloo* (London, 1990).

the main guard, ably defended by Sergeant Hamilton of the Donegal, and sixteen men only, with two ship guns, which were very badly mounted, and yet they were served with such effect as to occasion a prodigious slaughter.[98]

Lord Clements, colonel of the Donegal Regiment, recommended Hamilton for a commission in the line as a reward for his actions. He was advised that he should commission him into the Donegal, and Hamilton could then be transferred to the line when a vacancy occurred.[99] This sounds like a way of avoiding making a decision, but as far as is known Hamilton was not eligible for a militia commission. Clements was not to be deterred, so in October 1799, Hamilton was commissioned as an ensign in the Northampton Fencibles, then serving in Ireland.[1] In February 1800, when soldiers from the militia could volunteer into the line, one ensigncy without purchase was offered to militia subalterns for every forty men of their regiment who volunteered for unlimited service. The Donegal had a substantial number, so Hamilton was transferred back to the Donegal as an ensign, and on 18 March 1800 was given an ensigncy in the 1st Battalion, 1st Foot (the Royals).[2] We know that he served with the Royals at Swinley Camp, near Windsor in July 1800 where he wrote to Lord Clements asking for a 'stay' on a loan, as his wife had been ill,[3] and a year later, he wrote again from Saint Martins, a small Dutch island in the Leeward Islands in the West Indies, saying that his financial circumstances had improved, and that he hoped to purchase his next 'step' with his prize money (promotion by purchase to the rank of lieutenant). He also reported that above three hundred 'brave Irish Hearoes [*sic*]' in the 1st and the 64th Regiments, had been lost to disease.[4] However, Hamilton was placed on half pay in 1802, which suggests he had been was wounded or incapacitated in the West Indies, and he thereafter disappears from view.[5]

Another non-commissioned officer promoted for distinguished conduct was Sergeant Collins of the Armagh Regiment. According to Captain William Blacker he rallied the men attacked by the mob at Ballybay, Co. Monaghan, and made a stand at the churchyard until help arrived (the churchyard was a defensible position on the top of a hill in the town). Blacker mentions this promotion in his diary when the light company, which he commanded, halted at Ballybay on their way to be disbanded in 1802.[6] Lord Gosford did not

---

98 Musgrave, *Memoirs*, p. 389.   99 E.B. Littlehales to Lord Clements, 1 July 1799 (NLI, KP/1082/52).   1 Cornwallis to Portland, 6 July 1799 (NA, HO/100/84/14).   2 Cornwallis to Portland, 18 Mar. 1800 (ibid., HO/100/90/159). The Royals are now the Royal Scots.   3 Ens. John Hamilton to Lord Clements, 24 July 1800 (Clements papers, P.C. 945).   4 Ens. John Hamilton to Lord Clements, 12 June 1801 (ibid.). These were former militiamen.   5 *Army List*, 1803.   6 T.G.F. Patterson (ed.), 'Armagh Militia extracts from the diary of Lt.-Col. William Blacker', vol. iii, p. 240 (unpublished MSS in the Royal Irish Fusiliers museum).

mention the promotion in his account of the action,[7] but Collins was appointed an ensign in the Armagh Regiment in July 1797.[8] This could be an example of an officer being appointed who had no property qualification, and Ensign Collins was not promoted further.

The colonels in a variety of ways actively encouraged collective loyalty. There are numerous examples of regimental medals awarded to soldiers 'for merit', and of medals awarded to soldiers for gallant actions. The National Museum of Ireland has a collection of the former, and an example of a medal awarded to the City of Limerick Militia for their action at Collooney in 1798, in silver (The officers received a gold version.) The Ulster Museum possesses several similar medals awarded 'for merit', as well as one for the defence of Hacketstown in the 1798 rebellion (defended by a party of the Antrim Regiment under Lieutenant Gardner on 25 June 1798).[9] Medals were also given for 'restoring order', such as that given to the men of the Wicklow Regiment for restoring order in Westmeath in 1797.[10]

Teaching the men the importance of the regimental colours, and the connections between the regiment and its parent county also created regimental pride. County pride and loyalty was very strong in Ireland, and it is quite possible that the linking of regular regiments of the line with counties later in the nineteenth century was influenced by the experience of both the English and Irish militia. Another point of pride was the approbations that regiments received for their service in various areas of the country. These approbations were published in the press; for example, when the Wexford Regiment left Enniskillen in 1794 the burgesses and freemen expressed their highest approbation of their conduct, and regret at their departure.[11] There are many other examples of this type of approbation: Co. Mayo to the Tyrone Militia on 25 August 1795, Carrick-on-Shannon to the North Cork on 7 May 1796, and Armagh to the Queen's County on 6 January 1798.[12] There are examples, too, of regiments offering rewards for the apprehension of people attempting to seduce their soldiers from their allegiance. A good example would be the Antrim, and Wexford, in north Cork, and Carlow, all in May 1797.[13] It would be easy to be cynical about such advertisements, but it must not be forgotten that in 1797 soldiers had seen their comrades executed and punished for allowing themselves to be seduced by the United Irishmen or Defenders. The clannishness of the King's County Regiment, cited by General Dalyrmple in Guernsey, is hardly surprising, nor is their willingness to bring to punishment Irishmen in other regiments who harboured treacherous ideas. Men of the Monaghan Regiment destroyed

7 Gosford to Camden, [n.d.] (NAI, RP/620/31/184). 8 Pay lists and muster rolls, Armagh Regiment (NA, WO/13/2603). 9 Lt. R.W. Gardner to Lord Castlereagh, 26 June 1798 (NAI, RP/620/41/79/239). 10 Oliver Snoddy, 'Two military medals by William Mossop, 1751–1805' in *Irish Sword*, 6:25 (1964), 252-6. 11 *Freeman's Journal*, 2 Dec. 1794 12 Ibid., 25 Aug. 1795, 7 May 1796, 6 Jan. 1798. 13 Ibid., 16 May 1797, 27 May 1797,

the offices and press of the *Northern Star* in Belfast after the execution of four of their comrades. It is just as likely that this was done on the initiative of the men, as opposed to that of the officers, still less that of the Castle. As Thomas Pelham wrote, 'The destruction of the Northern Star at Belfast and the attack on Mr Gregg's house ... by the soldiers of the Monaghan Militia were outrages not to be justified, and were punished.'[14]

Yet some militiamen were disloyal. The way in which the authorities dealt with this, and the ruthlessness with which dissident men were punished, had the effect, to paraphrase Voltaire, of encouraging the others to remain loyal. The type of service on which the men were engaged gave encouragement to those who wanted to seduce men from their allegiance, and at the same time, left militiamen open and vulnerable to their blandishments. It would be appropriate here to look at the numbers of men who succumbed to these attempts, in comparison with those who did not. It is difficult to quantify the number of men executed for taking the United oath, and the larger number who were involved but were pardoned or sent overseas to serve abroad for life. At the very least seventeen men were executed, and over 150 punished in various ways, from being 'drummed out,' to being sent abroad, or forgiven. Men known to have been executed included two from the Wexford, two from the Kildare, four from the Monaghan, two from the Louth, three from the City of Dublin, two from the County of Dublin and one each from the Roscommon and the Westmeath regiments, in 1797.[15] McAnally's conclusion is appropriate for the 1797 period. 'There was in progress a struggle for the soul of the Irish militia. The contention was between Irishman and Irishman and not between Irishmen and aliens ... In leaflet and in the columns of the press, they were the targets of the written word; they were also the targets of the whispered word.'[16]

The Castle was well aware of the seriousness of the problem, and a considerable degree of rumour, which caused a certain amount of panic, is to be found in the official correspondence. It even affected Portland, who was able to advise Pelham that the Limericks were distrusted by their officers, that the City of Limerick were disaffected, as were the Queen's County and the Westmeath. There is no record of how Portland himself obtained this information.[17] In September 1796 General Nugent, in the north, was able to report on the militiaman found murdered in the Lagan Canal at Stranmillis, Co. Antrim, on subversion in the Queen's County, and in the City of Limerick, as well as about the arrest of civilians. This would have corroborated Portland's information of a month earlier, but the lines of communication are unclear.[18] However, the gen-

---

[14] Pelham to —, 2 Nov. 1797 (HMC, *Dropmore MSS*, iii, 385). [15] Extracted from newspaper reports, 1796–7, and NA, HO/100 series. [16] McAnally, *Irish Militia*, p. 112. [17] Portland to Thomas Pelham, 28 Aug. 1796 (PRONI, T/755/3/71). [18] Nugent to Pelham,

eral staff conducted executions of convicted militiamen in front of the troops, some of the firing parties were from the companies of the convicted men, and the whole business was conducted with the utmost military solemnity, which could not fail to impress the soldiery, this being the intention.

There is no question that stern measures had to be taken to restore order – but the total number of men tainted by the United Irish conspiracy seems to have been no more than a small fraction of the total in the force. Moreover, very few non-commissioned officers were involved, while apart from taking oaths, and subverting colleagues, there does not seem to have been much of an effort to organize subverted men into an effective force.[19] Without organization, such men were of little use to the United movement, and could easily have been dispersed in action. The colonels of the regiments, their officers, and non-commissioned officers, took pains to declare the loyalty of their units, and published notices widely, offering rewards for information, both oral and written, about seditious papers, and persons. For example, the Antrim non-commissioned officers, drummers, and privates, offered two guineas to a soldier who could offer private information, and ten guineas for a conviction of any person 'known to circulate seditious papers, or attempting to administer unlawful oaths, or to endeavour by any means whatsoever, to withdraw any of the army from their allegiance to the best of Kings'.[20] The sergeants, corporals, drummers, and privates of the Wexford Regiment did the same thing, offering five guineas.[21] The ultimate test of loyalty, of course, was behaviour in action, and in 1798, the militia showed that subversion had only been superficial, and that distrust of their loyalty was misplaced.

The soldiers of the Irish militia were probably little different to any others of the period. We have shown that they tended to have no 'interest' in land, that they came from a wide variety of backgrounds and that there may have been more Protestants in the ranks than the ratio of Catholics to Protestants in the counties would have suggested. Many of the trades represented in the ranks were those with employment problems, such as weaving. Sectarianism does not seem to have been a problem within the units themselves despite the reservations expressed by many outside their ranks. Once the issues of pay and family allowances had been sorted out, the regiments were well able to recruit to establishment.

Discipline is much more difficult to summarize. The regiments had all the organizational and administrative systems to maintain discipline. There was an adequate (and important) ratio of non-commissioned-officers to private men. However, the regiments had to cope with two factors that mitigated against strict discipline. The first was the attempts at subversion by

30 Sept. 1796 (ibid., T/755/3/106). **19** Details of the numbers of men who were subverted are to be found in chapter 6, p. 129 ff. **20** *Freeman's Journal*, 16 May 1797. **21** Ibid.

the United Irish movement which did lead to executions and punishment of many militiamen, a small proportion of the whole perhaps but these attempts would be known within the units and would have had an unsettling effect. The second factor was the use of soldiers in small detachments and on 'free quarters', often without an officer in command, and this made the maintenance of the bonds of discipline extremely difficult. Not only that, it prevented meaningful regimental training, evidenced, for example, in the decline in numbers of regiments able to attend camps from 1795 to 1797.

However, loyalty must be the most difficult aspect of a study of militiamen to summarize. There can be no question that the benefits of pay, the opportunity of extra pay, marriage allowance, accommodation, food, prospects of promotion, pensions, education for children, medical care, and outward marks of approbation all played a part. Indeed, it can be argued that the private soldier in the militia was much better off than his regular army counterpart. The difficulty lies in assessing the aspects of loyalty that are intangible. Again, the ratio of non-commissioned-officers to privates had an influence as had the group loyalty to one's friends and comrades. There was also the belief the men had in their cause, their confidence in their ability, and the contempt they had for those in rebellion, which they continually exhibited. They knew they were a part of a large and powerful system, which was more powerful than perhaps those who rebelled, realized.

There can be no question that the men themselves were of a high calibre, and ultimately serious steps were taken to get them to transfer to the regular army in 1800 and thereafter. But however important the calibre of the men might be, it is in the quality of leadership exhibited by those set in command of them that is even more important. Each company had a captain, a lieutenant, and an ensign, except the grenadiers and the light company, which had an extra lieutenant. This number was totally inadequate when the soldiers were acting in small detachments. Not only that, but the colonel, the lieutenant-colonel, and the major were also company commanders as well as regimental or battalion commanders and as a consequence their companies had to operate with only two effective officers. No attempt was made to remedy this deficiency and if the officers were of very mixed ability, as indeed militia officers were, then the stresses of active service could and sometimes did lead to the loosening of the bonds of discipline with the result that in the advance or the retreat, the behaviour of the soldiers was often far from satisfactory. If the Irish militia was truly a 'licentious' force, as many historians unfairly depict it, then the fault lies with command and control by regimental and superior officers. Irish soldiers have the reputation for being 'spirited'. Soldiers who are 'spirited' need firm command and control both in the barracks and in the field.

CHAPTER SIX

'But our militia brave our country will save'[1]

The militia was employed in preserving the peace from its embodiment in 1793 until the French expedition to Bantry Bay in December 1796. This was a difficult task because it meant that units were split up into 'penny packets', or small detachments, with consequent problems of discipline and training. Nevertheless it did give the officers and men time to get to know each other and to discover the nature of their duties before the force faced the more real difficulties of subversion, actual rebellion and invasion.

In 1796 the militia became the target for subversion by the United Irishmen; the following year the authorities having become aware of this 'purged' the militia. In 1798 efforts to reform the army system were frustrated by both opposition to the commander-in-chief's proposals, as well as the outbreak of the rebellion. The campaigns of the army against the French in 1796, and the rebellion in 1798, were piecemeal reactions to events, and although it is possible to argue that primarily the militia defeated them, the 'esprit de corps' of the militia regiments was as much responsible as good management by their generals.

Militia involvement in the battles and actions of the rebellion has not been examined to any great extent in modern times. The current fashion in historical writing on this period of Irish history has been to concentrate on the performance of the rebels, and to slant consideration of the rebellion towards the ideals of the United Irishmen. However, there is another side to the story that deserves consideration in its own right; after all, Irishmen suppressed the rebellion, and these Irishmen were primarily in the Irish militia.

PRESERVING THE PEACE

At some stage in the spring and early summer of 1793, a decision was taken to call the militia out for full-time service.[2] No record exists now of how this decision was reached between the Castle and the commander-in-chief. We do know that the latter, General Robert Cunninghame, was quite happy at

---

1 Contemporary song, *Brown's Square Delight* (NAI, RP/620/54/64). About the Limerick City Militia when stationed in Belfast.   2 The English Militia had been embodied for full-time service on 1 Dec. 1792. Beckett, *Amateur military tradition*, p. 71.

first to allow regiments to be stationed in their home counties. Then, sometime in the autumn, we find the regiments marching out of their counties, never to serve there, or in an adjacent county, again, which proved to be both a good and a bad thing. It removed men from the danger of subversion by disaffected friends and relations, but it also removed them from proximity to their homes and families. This, in turn, made it inevitable that the families of volunteers and substitutes would 'follow the drum'.

At first the militia was slow to fill. In July 1793 strength of the regular army in Ireland was 11,094, but from then on, it steadily declined. In January 1794 it stood at 8,514, and in July of that year, 4,134. In January 1795 the strength increased to 6,708, and six months later it was augmented by regiments destined for the West Indies, sent to Ireland to recruit, and stood at 13,335. However, with the departure of these regiments by January 1796, the strength of the regulars declined to 1,676 men. In the same period, from 1793 to 1796, the militia increased steadily in numbers. The first return in July 1793, showed that it stood at 5,150 men; by January 1794, it had almost doubled to 9,495; and by July 1796, it stood at 18,093.[3] The militia was the largest part of the army in Ireland until 1800, comprising 63 per cent of the total armed forces of the crown, excluding the yeomanry in July 1796. By March 1794, some regiments were especially well recruited indeed; for example, the Limerick City Battalion was only five men under strength, the King's County six, the Carlow none, and the Queen's County three. Unsurprisingly, some regiments spoilt this picture; the Galway was 243 men under strength, the Cork City 285, and the North Cork 336.[4] Overall, the militia was 26 per cent under strength, but the situation rapidly improved after this, and in 1795 the first augmentation took place.

When the militia was raised, companies had a strength of 50 men each, including corporals and sergeants, and the established strength of the whole was 14,150. This was deemed insufficient for the defence of Ireland. In 1795, therefore, the militia was increased, or augmented, by 5,630 men, making the new establishment 22,699, including officers. This gave a ratio of non-commissioned officers to men of one to five, which was well within the parameters of the British Army of the time.[5]

Throughout the period, from 1793 to the beginning of 1796, the principal task of the militia was in countering the depredations of the Defenders. In addition, from 1795, the militia had to intervene to prevent outrages between the Defenders and the newly formed 'Orange-boys' in Co. Armagh. The outrages committed by the Defenders did not end with the formation of a militia but continued for a considerable period thereafter. It was not

---

[3] Sources for these figures: Ferguson, 'Army in Ireland'; NLI, RP/ 620/50/56; NA, WO/1 3, Pay Lists and Muster Rolls series. [4] Strength of the Army and Militia in Ireland, 1 Mar. 1794 (NA, HO/100/50/392). [5] *CJI*, xvi, Jan.–Apr. 1796, Appendix 88.

until 1796, however, that the connection between the Defenders and the United Irishmen began to be made by the Castle.

The militia were involved in counter-Defender actions very soon after their formation. One of the first engagements has already been mentioned: the affair at Bruff, Co. Limerick, involving the County of Limerick Militia, on or about 21 July 1793, when an unsuccessful attempt was made to liberate prisoners being escorted from Kilfinnane Bridewell to Limerick;[6] another was at Cashel on 3 October 1793, when a party of the Meath prevented rioters attacking the police, captured arms and pikes, and took 12 prisoners.[7]

Trouble continued into 1794. In June the City of Dublin Regiment was involved in an affray with Defenders in Co. Cavan in which it was reported that at least sixty people were killed, for the loss of two soldiers.[8] Another report of the same incident claimed that trouble arose between the Defenders and Presbyterians, and that they were separated by the City of Dublin, reports said that casualties were eighty of the Defenders.[9] More details are known about another incident in Co. Cavan near Ballyna, or Ballinaugh. On 13 May 1794 at a fair day in Kilnaleck 32 Defenders were reported to have been killed in a fight with 'Scotchmen'. On 14 May, there was another riot and the Defenders retired to a hill near Ballyna. The Grenadier and Light Companies of the City of Dublin Regiment under the command of Captains Medlicott and O'Meara, with Lieutenants Sankey and Thwaites, arrived from Killeshandra. In the ensuing affray the town was set on fire, 40 houses were destroyed and 30 Defenders killed. More of the regiment arrived, the leader of the Defender band was captured, and a further 40 were detained in gaol.[10] In July 1794, the City of Dublin arrested a leader of the Defenders named Kelly, who had a reward of £200 on his head.[11] In March 1795, the Leitrim Militia captured eight Defenders in Co. Meath.[12] On 8 May 1795, the Londonderry Regiment killed some 50 Defenders who attacked them in Co. Roscommon. This was a sequel to one of the worst incidents of the period, when two preventive officers, and nine Revenue police, searching for illegal stills between Mohill and Cashkargan (or Cashkerrigan), were attacked by armed Defenders and killed.[13] Camden's reaction to this was to send Lord Carhampton to the west to quieten the country. This Carhampton proceeded to do with such disregard for the law that it was noticed by Camden who thought his 'doctrine' did great good but was carried out too publicly: he was certain Carhampton would have actions brought against him for his 'conduct in Roscommon'. Camden thought it very likely Carhampton would be

6 John Straton, Rathkeale, to Hon. Revd P. Jocelyn, 21 July 1793 (PRONI, MIC 147/9/146).
7 *Freeman's Journal*, 18 Oct. 1793. 8 Ibid., 20 May 1794. 9 Ibid. 10 *Freeman's Journal*, 24 May 1794, and Seamus O'Loingsigh, 'The burning of Ballinaugh' in *Breifne, journal of Cumman Seanchas Bhreifne*, 2:7 (1964), 359-65. 11 Ibid., 26 July 1794. 12 Ibid., 6 Mar 1795. 13 *Faulkner's Journal*, 5 May 1795.

the subject of a parliamentary enquiry, and an act of indemnity might be required to cover the magistrates who had acted 'so zealously and indiscreetly' – which is exactly what happened.[14] The counties most affected were Roscommon, Leitrim, Sligo, Galway, and Longford. The Londonderry Militia was a part of Carhampton's force.[15] The lord lieutenant made the point that when one area became quiet, another was sure to erupt. Thus when Leitrim and Cavan were quiet, disturbances arose in Meath; when Meath became quiet, then disturbances arose in Kildare, and so on.[16]

It was at this time that Camden began to see the connection between the Defenders and the United Irishmen, and the beginning of attempts to suborn the militia. In July 1795, he wrote, 'The militia are the finest troops it is possible to see, and have universally behaved well.' In the same letter, he compared the aims of the Defenders and the United Irishmen, and noted that both organizations intended to provide themselves with pikes and firelocks, and to subvert the military.[17] By September he was able to report that militiamen found by themselves were being robbed of their weapons; that nine men of the South Cork had been found guilty at a court martial of Defenderism, and that one, Hanlon, the fife major of the Fermanagh, was a captain of the Defenders; he was under arrest, but refused to say anything.[18]

Mention has already been made of the sudden increase in the numbers of regular soldiers in July 1795. This was because four regiments were sent to Ireland. They were destined to be re-numbered, and sent to the West Indies, but this was kept a secret from them in order to prevent desertion. Word got out, however, and the 104th and the 111th Regiments, stationed in Dublin, mutinied. Companies of the Westmeath, Londonderry, and Longford Militia, together with the Essex and Breadalbane Fencibles, and artillery, were deployed against them, and the mutiny was quelled.[19] When word got out of what had happened in Dublin, the 105th and 113th Regiments, in Cork, also destined for the West Indies, mutinied for the same reasons. The cause was blamed on 'Jacobinism' in Cork but the true reason was posting to the West Indies, the graveyard of so many soldiers in this period. The Louth, Meath, King's County, and Roscommon Militia together with the 32nd Foot, artillery, and the 7th Dragoon Guards were deployed against them causing the mutiny to collapse.[20]

Efforts were being made to suborn the militia, to attack its soldiers on the march, or when escorting prisoners. On 30 January 1794, a notice

14 Camden to Pelham, 30 Oct. 1795 (PRONI, T/755/2/240). 15 Camden to Portland, 28 May 1795 (NA, HO/100/57/336). 16 Same to same, 25 Sept. 1795 (ibid., HO/100/58/334). 17 Same to same, 24 July 1795 (ibid., HO/100/58/157). 18 Same to same, 25 Sept. 1795 (ibid., HO/100/58/334). 19 One of the officers involved in this affair was Lt.-Col. Robert Stewart of the Londonderry Regiment, later Lord Castlereagh. 20 Edward Cooke to Thomas Pelham, 7 Sept. 1795 (PRONI, T/755/2/182).

appeared in *Faulkner's Journal*, signed by the principal people (mayor, councillors, and magistrates) of Cavan, testifying to the sobriety and good behaviour of the Wexford Regiment. Ten days earlier, soldiers of this regiment guarding prisoners in the gaol had been offered whiskey, which they drank. The whiskey was poisoned, and one soldier died as a result.[21] This attempt to liberate prisoners did not succeed.

Approbations of militia regiments, which appeared in the press, were nearly always put there by the upper classes of the county. Yet although behaviour of the regiments concerned may have been all that was claimed, relations with local people could still be very difficult. The fact that a man wore a red coat may have been acceptable to many, but to others it was not, irrespective of the wearer's religion or status. In December 1794, for example, a private in the Galway Regiment went to mass at Drumcondra, Co. Meath. He was drunk and behaved in such a manner that the people took exception and turned him out, giving him a beating in the process. A corporal and a private, also at that mass, were abused and turned out as well. A party of the Galway Regiment arrived from the guard to protect their comrades, and the priest prevailed on the sergeant to take his men away peacefully, to which he agreed. However, when marching off, a stone was thrown, which knocked the sergeant down, and other missiles were thrown at his men. The sergeant ordered his men to protect themselves, they fired on the crowd, killed four on the spot, and two more died of wounds the following day.[22] This was the sort of behaviour faced from time to time by non-commissioned officers and private men, but it is worth noting the strong bond of regimental loyalty, even if misplaced at times, that characterized militia regiments.

Despite the difficulty we have in discerning anything about plans for the defence of Ireland from what was happening to the militia in this early period, Lord Camden did have a plan. It was based on the establishment of the army in Ireland of 20,000 regulars, plus another 20,000 militia. There was to be a camp at Loughlinstown, Co. Dublin, and a garrison in Dublin, both comprising 10,000 men, with the aim of acting against a landing north or south of the capital. In the north of Ireland, 4,900 men were to be based near Belfast to resist both foreign and 'domestic' attack, and in the south, 9,500 men to protect Cork and Waterford with a reserve at Clonmel. Camden also planned camps of instruction for the infantry at Loughlinstown, Ardfinnan (Co. Tipperary), and Blaris (Co. Antrim). He allocated 10,500 men to static garrisons, and 4,910 men to a stationary force 'for the purposes of police' in Mayo, Sligo, Leitrim, Roscommon, Cavan, Meath, Westmeath, Longford, Louth, Wexford, Kilkenny, Kerry and parts of Cork.[23] His plan had weak-

---

[21] *Faulkner's Journal*, 30 Jan. 1794.   [22] *Faulkner's Journal*, 27 Dec. 1794.   [23] Camden to Portland, 17 Apr. 1795 (NA, HO/100/54/29).

nesses; it was inflexible in that it was reactive to invasion, numbers of troops were based on supposition not reality, and therefore it required more troops than he had available, or was likely to have. It was not until 1799 that a realistic plan was devised by Cornwallis, which required 50,000 men. In December 1795, the militia had 595 officers present, 988 sergeants, 552 drummers, 13,162 rank-and-file, 1,081 men sick (6.3 per cent), 2,913 men detached on duty, recruiting, or on furlough (17 per cent). It needed 20 sergeants, one drummer, and 2,648 men to complete to establishment.[24]

If 1793–5 was a period of uncertainty in the role of the militia, it was nevertheless one of comparative calm. This allowed recruitment to proceed apace, by the partial abandonment of the ballot, enrolment of substitutes, and by 'beat of drum'. It allowed regiments time to settle down, recruit to strength, receive colours, and establish an 'esprit de corps' reinforced by attendance at summer camps. The militia might not have been able to stand the strain of the following two-and-a-half years without the benefit of this period of grace. By December 1795 the militia was recruited to 87 per cent of its established strength. Up to this time, it had been used as a 'police force' guarding private houses, commercial installations, and public utilities. However, things were about to change.

'TARGET OF THE WHISPERED WORD'[25]

The problem with subversion was that it went on quietly at first so that a considerable number of people would be suborned before any kind of action could be taken. There was no shortage of rumours, but little solid evidence. Certain prolific correspondents of the 1790s were notorious spreaders of rumour – Robert Ross MP, and Thomas Lane, in letters to Lord Downshire, and Sir George Fitzgerald Hill in Derry, writing to Under-secretary Edward Cooke (Hill was a magistrate, and later clerk to the house of commons; there was a germ of truth in what he said, but he tended to report everything without discrimination).

Sometime in the middle of 1796 Hill wrote to Cooke expressing his reservations about the County of Limerick Battalion, then stationed in Derry. He was collecting evidence of disaffection, and believed the Limericks to have been subverted. Certain incidents had suggested this to him, and he believed the defence of Derry should not be left to 'men suspected'.[26] Hill had 'heard' that some soldiers had beaten witnesses who gave evidence against Defenders. He spoke to their commanding officer, Major Lloyd, or Loyd, about this subversion, but Lloyd did not agree, believing that his men mixed with 'coun-

---

24 *CJI*, xvii, 9 Jan. 1798 to 6 Oct. 1798, appendix 188. 25 McAnally, *Irish Militia*, p. 112.
26 Sir G.F. Hill to Edward Cooke, n.d. (NAI, RP/620/24/112).

try people' for the sake of drink. Hill thought Lloyd was over partial to his men, because he believed that there was a prejudice against them since they were 'mostly Roman Catholic and march with musick to mass'.[27] This much-quoted remark has often been taken out of context, referring only to the religion of the men, but it is also part of Hill's suspicions of subversion.

Hill followed up this letter with a report that an officer of the Limericks had told a friend of Hill's 'privately' that he could not depend on the private soldiers, and if they were 'called out', two thirds would desert.[28] He claimed that there was to be a disturbance in the first or second week of October 1796, and that Major Lloyd was a 'well intentioned, good natured man unsuspicious of his men, and too indulgent. I believe a strong friend of the Catholics, and attributes the faults found to his regiment to Protestant jealousy'.[29] However, there was a germ of truth in Hill's assertions, when he reported that a soldier named Burke had purchased his discharge, for which he had been given money by people in Belfast, and that he had gone there accompanied by four or five of the grenadiers.[30] Some of this was true, as we shall see: Burke had gone to Belfast, but he went alone, and had not purchased his discharge.

Edward Cooke followed up Hill's report on Burke. In August 1796 Lord Clare, whose estate lay at Castleconnell, Co. Limerick, was able to report that Burke had not been discharged, but had been given leave for sixty days to procure 200 men for the regiment, upon which he had a promise of his own discharge. Clare thought Burke was in Limerick, as he knew his 'connections', and they were 'respectable'.[31] In fact, Burke, who had authority to raise two men, not 200, had not gone to Limerick as he was supposed to but to Belfast. Major Lloyd in Derry described Burke or Bourke as being married to a Miss McInally whose father sold old clothes opposite Knox's house where Lloyd himself lodged. Burke had been given a pass to go to Limerick but had gone to Belfast where he was doing 'no good'.[32] General Nugent, commanding in the north, reported that Burke was to be ordered back to his regiment,[33] but on 6 September Nugent said that the sovereign of Belfast had arrested Burke as a deserter.[34] Corporal Burke was sent to Dublin, and then on to Duncannon, Co. Waterford, the holding place for soldiers being sent to serve overseas. There is no record of a court martial of Burke, however, or any authorization to send him there.

Whilst he was in Belfast, Burke became heavily involved in the United Irish conspiracy. He wore civilian clothes, talked publicly that the militia

27 Ibid.   28 Sir G.F. Hill to Edward Cooke, n.d. (ibid., RP/620/24/118).   29 Ibid.   30 Ibid.
31 Lord Clare to Edward Cooke, 25 Aug. 1796 (NAI, RP/620/24/155).   32 Maj. Loyd to 'Dear colonel', 24 Aug. 1796 (ibid., RP/620/25/27).   33 Gen. Nugent to (Edward Cooke), 29 Aug. 1796 (ibid., RP/620/24/170).   34 Nugent to Cooke, 6 Sept. 1796 (ibid., RP/620/25/27).

would be ordered to serve overseas with 20 guineas offered as a bounty, and that the militia in Armagh were ready to disarm the Orangemen. He was reported to have said that 15,000 stand of arms had been landed, with 35,000 more to come. Future laws had already been framed, and the combined force of the United Irishmen, Defenders, and militia amounted to 200,000 men with arms for more than half.[35] This was the sort of rumour spread deliberately by the United Irishmen, which was to have bloody results in 1798.

However, at Duncannon, General Fawcett, using the well-known interrogation technique of 'hard' and 'soft' questioning, closely interrogated Burke. Fawcett persuaded Burke to divulge information, including where he was suborned (in North Street, Belfast by a cotton spinner named Hamill), and he reported that Burke was willing to return as a spy. Fawcett did not recommend this, however, as Burke was 'easily led although a big strapping lad'. Burke also incriminated two men in his regiment as suborned, and had given the names of local civilians.[36] The soldiers were arrested, and four others deserted.[37]

This affair has been considered in detail because it is typical of much that took place. When all the exaggerated rumour is stripped away, it was obvious that Burke was a low-level operative, who could well have been exploited to spread false information about the French and the United Irishmen, although he was not entirely an innocent dupe for he was reportedly involved in murder. As it happened, the County of Limerick Battalion never wavered in its loyalty, despite encountering such difficulties.

Studies of the disposition of the secret service funds reveal much about subversion and counter-espionage. Edward Cooke, one of the under-secretaries at the Castle, was responsible for administration of this fund. In July 1796, he was reporting attacks on Roman Catholics by Orangemen in county Armagh, and attempts by them to seduce the militia. At this stage even Lord Camden, the lord lieutenant, who had been so complimentary about the militia in 1795, was beginning to have doubts: 'it is impossible to have much confidence in some of the militia regiments', he said.[38] The body of a private in the City of Limerick Militia had been found in the Lagan Canal at Stranmillis, near Belfast.[39] Some days later, Cooke was able to report that the murdered private had been employed by General Nugent to collect information.[40] Later, Nugent reported more about him. The man's name was Connell; he had given twenty names of soldiers sworn as United Irishmen, and he had gone voluntarily to Belfast to find out more about their activities.[41] However, Connell's actions became known to Corporal Smills of the

35 'Report of a spy', 19 July 1796 (NA, HO/100/62/139 and 143). 36 Fawcett to Pelham, 30 Nov. 1796 (NAI, RP/620/25/109). 37 Fawcett to Cooke, 19 Dec. 1796 (ibid., RP/620/25/138). 38 Camden to Cooke, 30 July 1796 (PRONI, T/755/3/43). 39 Cooke to Camden, 19 Dec. 1797 (ibid., T/755/3/39). 40 Ibid., 10 Aug. 1796 (ibid., T/755/3/55). 41 Maj.-Gen. Nugent to Cooke, 30 Sept. 1796 (ibid., T/755/3/106).

City of Limerick Militia, who wrote to Henry Joy McCracken, telling him about Connell, and pointing out the necessity of stopping him which could have led directly to Connell's murder.[42] In 1797, Edward Newell, an artist, United Irishman, and a spy, reported that Connell had been murdered and thrown over the bridge in Belfast by Corporal Burke and six other men.[43]

It is hardly surprising that all these reports involve troops stationed in the north of Ireland, for it was there that the most determined attempts were made to seduce militiamen from their allegiance. The United Irish movement was strongest in Ulster (and Defenderism weakest, except on the Ulster borders), and members of the organization there tried hardest to implement its policy towards the militia. There were other examples: another private in the City of Limerick named Hayes, was sworn at Lisburn on 20 September 1796; the Revd Johnston, rector of Derriaghy, who was also a magistrate, arrested a deserter from the Queen's County who swore against four in his regiment; and Lord Portarlington sent one Morrison to gaol for administering oaths.[44] Even so, it was likely that Camden was not yet convinced of the seriousness of the situation. In December 1796 Colonel John Bagwell of the Tipperary Regiment, stationed in Derry, where they had relieved the County of Limerick, complained that attempts were being made to corrupt his regiment, mainly by the better sort of people, shopkeepers, and so on. He was asking for advice because he had near 400 men in billets in the town, who were especially vulnerable.[45] Pelham replied a few days later saying that he had not heard from Sir George Hill – to whom he obviously referred the letter – but that he had no fears for a regiment so well disciplined as the Tipperary, with Colonel Bagwell in command.[46] What Bagwell thought about this patronising reply is not recorded.

On the other hand, it is not clear why Bagwell wrote to Pelham, for this was a matter which he could have taken up with his army commander, who could then fight his battle for accommodation with the Castle. Pelham must have known by this time what the official policy of the United movement was. Hill did reply (to Cooke), saying he thought Colonel Bagwell was over-anxious, but that putting men in barracks would be advisable, and that the 'bishop's house' should be commandeered.[47] Hill recognized that much of the trouble was caused by inattention to the men by officers and non-commissioned officers, and that the practice of billeting in towns could be ruinous to discipline.

---

[42] Lord Portarlington to Edward Cooke, 10 Oct. 1796 (NAI, RP/620/25/156). Portarlington was colonel of the Queen's County Militia, then stationed at Blaris.   [43] Secret report of Edward John Newell, [1797] (NA, HO/100/69/202).   [44] Maj.-Gen. Nugent to Thomas Pelham, 30 Sept. 1796 (PRONI, T/755/3/106).   [45] John Bagwell to Thomas Pelham, 7 Dec. 1796 (NAI, RP/620/26/104).   [46] Ibid.   [47] G.F. Hill to Edward Cooke, 'Wednesday night' (NAI, RP/620/26/107). This was the house of the earl-bishop of Derry.

There were more reports of subversive activities in this period, again, all from the north of Ireland. We do know from what happened in 1797, that there was subversion in other parts of Ireland, but the reports from 1796 only refer to the north. In June 1796, a party of the City of Dublin, commanded by Captain John Giffard, and accompanying Mr Soden, a magistrate, arrested 'Switcher' Donnelly near Maghera. Donnelly was a leader of the Defenders and the United Irishmen, and had a price of £200 on his head.[48] In November Lord Glandore, colonel of the Kerry Regiment, placed an advertisement in the newspapers denying that his men had given up arms and ammunition, or that they had been corrupted in any way. They were stationed at Coleraine.[49]

However undecided the Castle may have been about the degree of infiltration of the militia by the United Irishmen in 1796, it did make some important military reforms on the appointment of Lord Carhampton as commander-in-chief in place of General Robert Cunninghame. In October Ireland was at last divided into military districts, which simplified management of the army.[50] There followed two interesting coincidences. On 12 November 1796, another general order was issued for the swift collection of units to act together in the event of an invasion, and on 1 December 1796, Brigadier-General Eyre Coote wrote to his commander, Lieutenant-General William Dalrymple, offering his opinion that Bantry Bay offered a very suitable and strategic place for an invasion fleet to land.[51] The following week, however, Major Brown of the Royal Engineers outlined the problems of defending Cork: there were insufficient artillerymen, not enough infantry, and the defences were incomplete.[52]

Does this mean that the Castle had prior knowledge of the French intention to land at Bantry? It could well be, for the British government was well aware of French intentions through its system of spies; the gathering of a French fleet at Brest and the loading of nearly 15,000 troops was something that could not go unnoticed. The general order of 12 November was comprehensive;[53] it covered assembly, disposal of heavy baggage, families, equipment to be carried by the soldier, hire of cars (or horse drawn carts), foraging, advance parties, order of march, orders for camping, and timings. Coincidence, forewarning, or not, it was given at an opportune moment, for on 21 December 1796 the French started to arrive in Bantry Bay. Immediately plans were set afoot to counter the expected invasion.

Unfortunately, only one regimental route or order for movement survives, but obviously the militia was heavily involved. Troops in the north of Ireland, and most of the Dublin garrison, remained at their stations. Of the remainder

---

48 *Faulkner's Journal*, 16 June 1796. 49 *Freeman's Journal*, 14 Nov. 1796. 50 General Order, 26 Oct. 1796 (NA, WO/68/221/28, Donegal Militia Letter Book). 51 Coote to Dalrymple, 1 Dec. 1796 (PRONI, T/755/3/199). 52 John Brown, Major of Engineers to Lt.-Gen. Dalyrmple, 12 Dec. 1796 (ibid., T/755/3/209). 53 General Order, 12 Nov. 1796 (NA, WO/68/221/29, Donegal Militia Letter Book).

who might have had to face the French, 67 per cent of the infantry were Irish militia, so that if the French had landed the forces assembled to oppose them would have been very largely composed of militia. It is arguable of course that in December 1796 the Irish militia was fitter for this type of action that it was to be seventeen months later, in 1798. In detail, a total of 5,630 effective rank-and-file were available in the southern district, which included Bantry, and a further 4,222 were at Limerick and in north Kerry. However, 1,000 of these men were not so readily available because they were in Waterford and Duncannon, and the troops from Limerick had to cross the mountains to get to west Cork. Of these forces, 62 per cent were militia. Troops were ordered to concentrate in west Cork, and the regulars, fencibles, and militia were set in motion. Insofar as the militia is concerned, ten regiments in the north of Ireland, and the Dublin garrison were not ordered to move. Twelve regiments in the southern district, which stretched from Duncannon to Bantry, either moved to Cork, or stayed put, and 16 others were ordered to move as follows:

Regiment	From	To	Strength
Waterford	Mullingar	Clonakilty	420
Wexford	Loughlinstown	Inniskeen	500
South Cork	Ennis	Limerick	470
Cork City	Galway	Limerick	450
Donegal	Loughlinstown	Carlow	530
South Mayo	Naas	Kilkenny	400
North Mayo	Dublin	Kilkenny	300
Limerick City	Loughlinstown	Tipperary	370
Clare	"	"	350
Kildare	"	"	270
Tyrone	Kells	"	650
Wicklow	Blaris	"	300
Downshire	Drogheda	Athlone	616
Armagh	Ardfinnan	"	497
North Cork	Sligo	Galway	470
King's County	Athlone	Galway	490
		TOTAL	7,083

Table 12: Troop movements, December 1796

From this table, the strategy of the commander-in-chief is not difficult to understand. The regiments in the southern district and those in Limerick were concentrated in Cork. They were replaced by those in the table above, but as it was not known if the French intended another landing somewhere else, the commander-in-chief had to have a reserve ready to move to any other trouble-spot, hence movement to Carlow, Limerick, Galway, Athlone, and Tipperary, places for the concentration of his forces (which also included regulars, and fencibles).[54] When the French left Bantry, regiments were halted at the point they had reached, but were not ordered back until it was certain that the French were not going to land somewhere else. For example, the one regiment for which we do have a route (the Longford) was ordered to Cork from Athy. They were to march by Leighlinbridge, Kilkenny, Callan, Clonmel, Clogheen, and Kilworth to Cork.[55] However, by the time the French departed, they were at Rathkeale in Co. Limerick. Their movement order, or route, directed that the sick and heavy baggage were to be left behind, and that wives were not to accompany husbands, but that each wife was to receive fourpence a day during their absence.[56]

Camden, reporting on 17 January 1797 that the French had gone, praised the fidelity of the militia (citing the Antrim and the Downshire in particular). Had a landing taken place, he wrote, he did not doubt their loyalty. He also praised the attitude and actions of the country people, who had supported the army wholeheartedly. He said that if the enemy had landed, they would not have been supported.[57] In view of what was to happen in 1797, some of this loyalty may have been ephemeral, but, nonetheless, the response to the French threat was wholehearted and could have been effective. The new year of 1797 had started auspiciously, but it was not long before some of the unresolved problems of 1796 came to the fore, particularly the battle for the soul of the militia.

PURGING SUBVERSION

This battle continued unabated into 1797, but in the middle of the year the Castle had to take drastic steps to curb the spread of disaffection. This was not the only matter of note. After the scare at Bantry, steps were taken to improve the efficiency of the army, although the major problem, of exactly how to defend the country from invasion and internal subversion, was no nearer solution. Military efficiency was bedevilled by a lack of confidence between the lord lieutenant, Camden, and his commander-in-chief, Carhampton. Camden had wanted David Dundas as commander-in-chief instead, but Dundas had refused the appointment. Camden believed that Carhampton was not a master of detail, and lacked the confidence of the

---

[54] The computation of militia units is taken from a comparison of the winter quarters of the militia, 1796 (*Faulkner's Journal*, 27 Oct. 1796), and the general distribution of the columns of the army, 30 Dec. 1796 (NAI, RP).   [55] Q.M.G. Order, 25 Dec. 1796 (NAI, M3474,Royal Longford Militia Letter Book).   [56] Ibid.   [57] Camden to Portland, 10 Jan. 1797 (published in *Freeman's Journal*, 17 Jan. 1797).

'gentlemen of the country', as, indeed, he did of the other generals,[58] particularly Lake and Knox.

On 10 January 1797 Carhampton made his proposals for the disposition of the force he required (4,280 cavalry, and 28,030 infantry), for brigading the troops, the formation of light infantry battalions, a commissariat (which did not exist at all), and arrangements for ordnance, ammunition, and so on.[59] Apart from being the largest component of the infantry, the Irish militia were involved in these plans in two ways: to provide extra gunners for the forts in Cork; and in surrendering their light companies to the new light battalions,[60] an important and significant event for both the Irish and English militia.

The formation of the new light battalions was ordered before the end of January 1797. There were to be four, each formed around the nucleus of a regular battalion, and commanded by a regular officer, with the companies made up by the light companies of the militia. These battalions were to assemble at Kilkenny (1st), Bandon (2nd), Blaris, near Lisburn in Co. Antrim (3rd), and at Loughlinstown, Co. Dublin (4th). The men were to be between 5ft 6ins. and 5ft 9ins. in height, and under 30 years of age; the officers 'such as will be equal to a service in which in the event of invasion, much exertion may be required'.[61] The 1st Battalion was to be commanded by Lieutenant-Colonel Campbell of the 65th Foot, based on a detachment of 210 men of his regiment, and the light companies of the Tyrone, South Mayo, Louth, Longford, Downshire, Wicklow, Cork City, King's County, North and South Cork Militias, some 910 men in total. The 2nd Battalion was to be commanded by Lieutenant-Colonel Williamson of the 30th Foot, with a detachment of 259 men of his regiment, and the light companies of the Galway, Leitrim, Westmeath, Sligo, Dublin County, Waterford, Roscommon, Wexford, Londonderry, Meath, Fermanagh, and Limerick County Militias, and was 1,099 strong. The 3rd Battalion was to be commanded by Lieutenant-Colonel Innis of the 64th Foot with 115 men of his regiment, and the light companies of the Tipperary, Kerry, Monaghan, Cavan, Dublin City, Carlow, and Armagh Militias, and was 605 strong. The 4th Battalion was to be commanded by Lieutenant-Colonel Stewart of the 89th Foot with 342 men of his regiment, and the North Mayo, Kilkenny, Antrim, Clare, Donegal, Kildare, Limerick City, and Queen's County light companies, 902 men. Each light company was 70 rank-and-file strong.[62]

58 Camden to Portland, 30 Jan. 1797 (NA, HO/100/67/35).   59 'Commissariat': the organization for supplying the army with transport, food, clothing, and equipment. Without it, troops had to forage, with consequent opposition from local people, or make regimental arrangements.   60 Carhampton to Camden, 10 Jan. 1797 (NA, HO/100/67/45).   61 General Order, 24 Jan. 1797 (PRONI, T/755/4/1/59).   62 Order for forming light infantry battalions, 24 Jan. 1797 (ibid., T/755/4/1/59).

The concept of amalgamating light companies into battalions was not new. It had been done in America in both the Seven Years War, and in the revolution. Light companies had several roles; they could fight in the line the same as other companies but their specialities were scouting, acting in detached formations, and in action, disrupting the rhythm of an attacker by targeting officers and non-commissioned officers. They were supposed to be young and fit; they were regarded as the 'crack' troops of the period.[63] Nevertheless, the creation of such a 'crack' force was something of a mixed blessing. The militia colonels did not like losing one of their best companies, which had to be kept up to strength with both officers and men. There are many examples of colonels having substituted inferior men for those selected for the light battalions, and it became the norm for each light infantryman to furnish a written physical description of himself. There was another, more serious, reason why it was a mixed blessing: regiments that lost their light companies lost their sharpshooters, scouts, and men trained to fight independently. It also left the battalion companies vulnerable to the light troops of an enemy in a 'set-piece' battle. Captain William Blacker, who commanded the Armagh Light Company in 1801–2, gave more prosaic reasons. The men detached were separated from their friends, and had reduced chances of promotion. There were administrative inconveniences, and the officer commanding a light company had difficulties in reconciling the demands of two colonels.[64]

The light companies remained 'brigaded' in the light brigade until well after the peace of Amiens in 1802. The regular army component varied as regiments of foot were posted into and out of Ireland, but the staff of the battalions was drawn from a much wider background than the militia, something that brought the benefits of broad experience to them. For example, in March 1799 the battalion staff is at Table 13, with only a regular component of one company of the 6th Foot in the 1st Battalion:

The army had been 'brigaded' earlier. Each district, commanded by a lieutenant or major-general, was subdivided into smaller areas commanded by a brigadier-general. Each general was to remain with his 'brigade' to enforce attendance of officers, promote instruction, and get to know the officers and men under his command, 'so as to be able to supply their wants, check their irregularities, and reward their merits'.[66] Reportedly the militia colonels did not like this new organization of the army, but it had been ordered by the king, and applied to the whole army.[67]

---

63 Houlding, *Fit for service*, pp 336–7. 64 T.G.F. Patterson (ed.), 'Armagh Militia extracts from the diaries of Lt.-Col. William Blacker', iii, 171 (unpublished MS in the Royal Irish Fusiliers Museum, Armagh). 65 Kilmainham papers 199 (back of book). 66 Thomas Pelham to Lord Carhampton, – Jan. 1797 (PRONI, T/755/4/1/95). 67 William Elliott to Thomas Pelham, 6 Feb. 1797 (ibid., T/755/4/1/121).

1st Battalion	Lt.-Col.	Bowen	6th Foot
Athlone	Major	Fitzgerald	107th Foot
	Adjutant	Sergeant-Major	6th Foot
	Quartermaster	Lt. McNeill	Louth Regiment
2nd Battalion	Lt.-Col.	Sir William Cockburn	Royals
Athlone	Major	Aylmer	Manx Fencibles
	Adjutant	Lt. Ferguson	Londonderry Regt.
	Quartermaster	Lt. Davis	"
3rd Battalion	Lt.-Col.	Crofton Vandeleur	107th Foot
Lifford	Adjutant	Lt. Bennett	Armagh Regiment
	Quartermaster	Ensign Thomas Butler	7th West Indies Regiment
4th Battalion	CO	Major Sharp	22nd Foot
Athlone	Major	Ramsey	92nd Foot
	Adjutant	Ensign Cameron	"
	Quartermaster	Ensign Cummings	Gordon Fencibles[65]

Table 13: Battalion staff, Light Brigade, 27 March 1799

There was an almost permanent shortage of artillerymen in Ireland throughout the 1790s. Indeed, militiamen had been drafted to man the guns in Cork harbour in 1794, as there was 'no artillerist in Ireland', according to General Cunninghame.[68] This move had been a success, and the militia continually manned the Cork forts. In February 1797, however, militiamen who were trained in the 'artillery exercise' augmented the artillery. Again, it was reported that the colonels were not happy that the 321 men detailed for this duty had been removed from their regiments. (Interestingly throughout the period 1793 to 1802 there was a small but steady trickle of militia officers transferring to the Royal Irish Artillery.)

These changes occurred piecemeal: brigading took place at different times during the year in different districts. There does not seem to have been any sense of urgency and, for whatever reason, the enthusiasm displayed by Carhampton on his appointment seemed to evaporate. This gradual loss of enthusiasm reflected itself in several ways, one of which was loosening of discipline because of the type of service the men were engaged upon: the troubles in the Irish countryside continued unabated, as did attempts to suborn the militia and the other troops.

Indeed, if anything, the intensity of violence increased. In April 1797 three soldiers of the Armagh were killed at Ballybay, Co. Monaghan (an inci-

---

68 Cunninghame to Douglas, 24 Feb. 1794 (NLI, KP/1012/278).

dent considered in detail in an earlier chapter).[69] In May a party of about 250 Defenders attacked the house of a Mr Sparks at Carberry, Co. Kildare. Sparks defended his property vigorously, and a detachment of the Wicklow Militia marched to his aid under the command of Lieutenant Edward Hepenstall. The soldiers drove off the raiders with the loss of one man, and captured two rebels, one of whom turned 'king's evidence', the other was convicted at Athy assizes in September.[70] At the trial, it transpired that Lieutenant Hepenstall had attempted to get information by putting a rope around the neck of the accused, and, throwing it over his shoulder, had drawn the prisoner up. The judge reprobated Hepenstall's conduct: 'it was an error, but such as a young and gallant officer might fall into, warmed with resentment'.[71] Thereafter, the officer was known as 'half-hanged Hepenstall', or 'the walking gallows'.[72]

There were other incidents involving militia units. In May, the Antrim's publicly offered ten guineas for the conviction of any person circulating seditious papers, and the Wexford offered five guineas for the same.[73] In the same month a private in the light company of the Waterford Militia was stoned to death near Bandon, and General Eyre Coote offered £50 for information leading to a conviction.[74] At the end of the month, a party of the Monaghan raided the cotton manufactory of Robert Armstrong on the Falls Road in Belfast, and surprised a blacksmith making pike heads. He was arrested, and the Monaghans destroyed his smithy.[75] Again, in May, which certainly was a bad month for the forces of law and order, the Wicklow Regiment shot two Defenders near Carberry, Co. Kildare, and a desperate attempt was made to capture the barracks at Philipstown in King's County which was only foiled by the vigilance of the sentry. The North Corks at Sligo, because of repeated attempts to suborn the men, publicly took the oath of allegiance on the town square.[76]

In June Captain John Giffard and the City of Dublin Militia brought 'several cars' loaded with arms into Dundalk, which they had captured in the Carlingford area.[77] In August Captain Kay, adjutant of the Armagh, was found guilty of assaulting one Patrick Murphy and sentenced to three months' imprisonment, showing that members of the armed forces were not above the law.[78] In November, Thomas Pelham summed up what had been happening:

---

[69] Thomas Dawson and George Holdercroft to John Lees, 13 Apr. 1797 (NAI, RP/620/29/245/240). Dawson and Holdercroft were postmasters, Lees the secretary to the Post Office Board. [70] *Freeman's Journal*, 10 May 1797. [71] Ibid., 24 Sept. 1797. [72] Lt. E.L. Hepenstall transferred to the 6 8th Foot on the volunteering to the Line in 1800, but died of a 'dropsical complaint', before assuming the appointment (ibid., 8 Aug. 1800). [73] *Freeman's Journal*, 16 May 1797. [74] *Faulkner's Journal*, 18 May 1797. [75] Ibid., 28 May 1797. [76] *Freeman's Journal*, 27 May 1797. [77] *Faulkner's Journal*, 18 June 1797. [78] *Freeman's Journal*, 1 Sept. 1797. One of the very few examples, this case has been considered earlier.

Since the outrages began in the south, one magistrate has been killed, another wounded, a constable murdered, and his limbs cut to pieces and afterwards placed on a hill with a label in his hand threatening the same treatment to anyone who would bury him; in another case, a farmer, his wife, maidservant, all pigs and dogs were killed. Houses were burnt, but in nearly all cases arms and pikes were concealed.[79]

Yet while the Defenders continued their depredations in 1797, the government was attempting to do something to stop them. The problem was that, apart from Ulster, there does not seem to have been any kind of overall plan. Counter-measures were piecemeal, and General Moore's description of the government's actions seems appropriate: 'The mode of quieting the country is to proclaim districts where people are most violent and let loose the military who are encouraged in acts of greater violence against all supposed to be affected.'[80] Before this was written in November 1797 the duke of Leinster had resigned as colonel of the Kildare Militia, because he disapproved of the methods used by the administration in governing Ireland.[81] Indeed, in the following year, one of General Abercromby's reasons for resigning was his distaste for the methods of Camden's government. As he wrote to his friend, Colonel the Hon. Alexander Hope, 'I rejoice in quitting a country where the government is more despotic than that of Russia and where the troops are employed in the way that the Cossacks and Calmucks are accustomed to act. Nothing but the [—] of the times should ever induce me to remain one day longer as a soldier.'[82]

The government had been taking action on two fronts, one against dissension in the countryside and the other against subversion in the army, which was the 'purge' of the militia. On 17 May 1797 a proclamation from the lord lieutenant and the privy council authorized the military to act without waiting for direction from a magistrate in dispersing assemblies that threatened the peace. It was given to the army a day later.[83] The lord mayor of Dublin clarified the position further the following day, by asking whether or not troops had to obey a magistrate if he was with them. The answer was that they did.[84] The importance of this order for the militia was that it loosened the strings of strict discipline. Not only was the militia very thinly dispersed in the protection of individuals in the countryside; officers did not command many of these detachments. It gave the men the opportunity to act with violence against the civil population (whether this was justified or

---

79 Thomas Pelham to —, 2 Nov. 1797, HMC, *Fortescue MSS*, iii, 1899, 335.　80 Maurice, *Diary of Sir John Moore*, i, 271.　81 Camden to Portland, 19 May 1797 (NA, HO/100/69/317).　82 Gen. Abercromby to Col. the Hon. Alexander Hope, 15 May 1798 (NAS, GD/ 364/1/1082/3). Word illegible.　83 General Order, 18 May 1797 (NLI, KP/1013/352).　84 Samuel Reed to Thomas Pelham, 19 May 1797 (NAI, RP/620/30/112).

not), and moreover to come to accept this behaviour as the norm, with little chance of having to answer for it. As Lady Louisa Conolly said to her father in 1798:

> The free quarters, whipping the people and burning the houses have just been stopped ... for although in some places ... the object did answer discovering the pikes and arms, yet upon the whole it was a dangerous method in regard to the licentiousness that it produced among the soldiers, the fury and madness it drove the insurgents to, and the lukewarmth that it threw upon the well disposed persons who found themselves equally aggrieved by the free quarters as the rebels were.[85]

This would have bad consequences in 1798.

In March 1797 the government's patience finally gave out. General Lake, the commanding general, was given orders to reduce the north to peace and to disarm the populace. The order gave Lake virtually carte blanche to act as he thought fit,[86] with the only restriction placed upon him being not to disarm Belfast. Lake believed that strenuous efforts had been made to suborn the militia. For this reason the least number of militia regiments were stationed in Ulster: the Dublin City were in Monaghan, the Monaghan in Belfast, 3rd Light Infantry at Blaris near Lisburn, Tipperary in Derry, Carlow in Downpatrick, Kerry in Coleraine, Drogheda in Ballyshannon, Co. Donegal, and the Cavan in Newry: 2,609 men out of a total force of 8,975. (Still, nearly a third of his force.) Nevertheless, Lake wanted them exchanged for fencibles: 'nothing but coercive measures in the strongest degree can have any weight in this country', he said.[87] In April, he recommended burning a town to make an example.[88] In the same month, Brigadier-General Knox, commanding in west Ulster, wrote to Pelham complaining that Carhampton did not:

> Seem sensible to the danger of employing the militia in the north ... If they are troops to be depended upon they are as good elsewhere as in the north. If on the contrary they are not to be depended upon, the danger arising from them is a thousand times greater by keeping them in the north than it would be were they employed in any other part of the kingdom. There is not a day passes that does not bring me an account of the Dublin City Militia having become United – but Lord Carhampton will not believe it.[89]

---

[85] Lady Louisa Conolly to the duke of Richmond, 18 June 1798 (PRONI, T/3048/B/27).
[86] Thomas Pelham to Gen. Lake, 3 Mar. 1797 (ibid., D/607/E/148). [87] Lake to Pelham, 13 Mar. 1797 (ibid. T/755/4/2/165). [88] Same to same, 16 Apr. 1797 (ibid., T/755/4/2/264).
[89] Knox to Pelham, 19 Apr. 1797 (ibid., T/755/4/2/287).

Knox worked well with Lake: both believed in a coercive policy, and neither got on well with Carhampton. Knox, too, was an Ulsterman, from Dungannon, so he had personal knowledge of his area of operations. Yet he offered no evidence of corruption of the militia, and his letter was highly irregular, if not disloyal, since Carhampton was his superior officer. Still, Lake's operations did have an effect, producing 4,654 guns, and 823 pikes along with other weapons by August 1797.[90]

But there was subversion in some parts of the militia, and between May and August 1797 much of it was revealed. On 25 April 1797 Colonel Charles Leslie of the Monaghan Militia informed General Lake of a conspiracy in his regiment and that Pat McCanna of the Grenadier Company, Pat Ryan of the colonel's, John Wilson of Captain James's, Owen McCanna of the major's, Peter McCarron of Captain Richardson's, Daniel Gillan of Captain Lucas's, and William McCanna of the lieutenant-colonel's had all been arrested. Lake proposed that Leslie proceeded cautiously.[91] The result of the investigations into the Monaghan Regiment resulted in the court martial of four men, and the pardoning of a further 70. The court martial sat on Monday 8 May 1797, under the presidency of Colonel Henry Gore Sankey of the City of Dublin Militia, with fourteen militia officers as members. The accused were Daniel Gillan, Owen McCanna, William McCanna, and Peter McCarron. They were accused of mutiny, found guilty, and sentenced to death. There can be little doubt that they were guilty, but the suspicion remains that this verdict was inevitable, that it had been decided in advance that these men were to be made an example of the government's determination to stamp out subversion. The men defended themselves, but not very well, and two members of the court, Captain James, and Captain-Lieutenant Minnett, officers in the Monaghan Regiment, were sitting in judgment of their own men.[92] The four privates were executed at Blaris on 16 May 1797, with due ceremony, witnessed by the artillery, the 64th Regiment, the Breadalbane Argyle Fencibles, and three militia regiments: the 3rd Light Infantry, the Monaghan and the Carlow. This example of the determination of the government to counter subversion in the military was made for all to see and heed.

During the remainder of the year there followed other executions, pardons, and men sentenced to serve abroad for life. Table 13 summarizes the details:

---

[90] Return of arms seized in the northern district, 9 Aug. 1797 (NLI, KP/1013/325). [91] Lake to Pelham, 1 May 1797 (PRONI, T/755/5/1). Lake communicated with Pelham throughout this affair, further evidence of a bad relationship with Carhampton. [92] *Proceedings of a court martial held in the town of Belfast*, 8 May 1797 (NA, HO/ 100/70/199). This is a complete transcript of the trial, printed for circulation.

Date of Court Martial	Regiment	Name	Crime	Punishment
11 Oct 1796	Queen's County	Thos. Callaghan	Defenderism	Verdict not known
		Pat. O'Brien	"	"
16 May 1797	Monaghan	Wm McKenna	Mutiny	Executed
		Owen McKenna	"	"
		Danl Gillan	"	"
		Peter McCavan	"	"
20 May 1797	Wexford	James Neil	Swearing men to be United	Executed, by men of own company who requested the duty
		Hugh Sherry		600 lashes
20 May 1797	Wexford	James Clarke	Sedition	1000 lashes
		James McCall	"	Not guilty
7 June 1797	N. Mayo Lt Coy	James Henigan	Seduction of Inverness Fen.	Executed on the '15 acres'
	Kildare	— Carty	"	"
		— Mahon		
12 June 1797	Louth	James O'Neill	Taking United oaths	Executed at Adare
		Peter Murneen	"	"
18 June 1797	South Cork	Danl Connors	Taking United Oaths	Serve overseas for life
		John Luny	"	"
		Michael Farrell	"	"
25 June 1797	City of Dublin Light Company (Part of 3rd Battalion Light Infantry at Blaris)	James Matthews	Taking United oaths	Executed
		— Sheridan		Not known
		Sgt Rochfort		"
		Danl Proud		Sent on board tender
		John Matthews		"
		— Masterson		"
		— Ward		Not known
		Patk Carr		"
		47 Rank and file		Confessed and pardoned

'But our militia brave our country will save'   173

Date	County	Name	Offence	Sentence
25 June 179-	Limerick	— Wing	Taking United oaths	Not known for all these men were from 2nd Battalion Light Infantry at Bandon
	Leitrim	— Costello	"	"
	Roscommon	— Fitzgerald	"	"
		— Fitzgerald	"	"
	Meath	Cpl O'Connor		
27 June 1797	Louth	10 private men	Taking United oaths	Serve overseas for life
1 July 1797	Roscommon	James Howard	Taking United oaths	550 lashes, given 425
		— Fitzgerald	"	600 lashes, " 300
		— Fitzmorris	"	550 lashes, " 300
	Wexford	John Clancy	Taking United oaths	999 lashes, given 425
				Serve abroad for life
	Meath	James Kelsh/Kelly	Taking United oaths	800 lashes, given 325
		Patk Maguire	"	Acquitted
		— Bermingham	"	550 lashes, given 300
		— Mulvaney	"	Acquitted
	Sligo	— Scully	Taking United oaths	550 lashes, given 300
4 July 1797	Tipperary	5 private men	Taking United oaths	Not known
9 July 1797	City of Dublin	— Ward	Taking United oaths	Executed
		— Law	"	Executed
	Tipperary	3 private men	Taking United oaths	Guilty, punishment not known
12 July 1797	Roscommon	Dominic Gillan	Taking United oaths	Executed at Bandon
	Westmeath	Patk Drumgold	"	"
	County of Dublin	James Murphy	Taking United oaths	Executed
		Patk Halvey	"	Executed
		Henry Hodgins	"	800 lashes
		Valentine Cooke	"	1000 lashes
		Matt Toole	"	800 lashes
		Charles Kelly	"	Pardoned
Date not known		Daniel Condron	"	1000 lashes[93]

Table 14: Militia sentences for subversion in 1797

The figures for men charged cannot be entirely accurate, but that for executions is as accurate as it is possible to be at this remove. Seventeen executions in all were reported in the press and in private correspondence. The total number of men found guilty was 98, and even allowing for inaccuracies, this was a miniscule proportion of the 20,753 men serving in the militia in the summer of 1797. The table does not include the large number of men who were pardoned, probably several hundred. The point to be made is the 'purge' was effective. The Monaghan Regiment, enraged by the execution of their comrades, blamed the newspaper, the *Northern Star*, for fomenting the trouble, and on 20 May 1797 they wrecked the presses. They also damaged the house of a Mr Gregg, whose sisters had sent sustenance to the four soldiers confined for court martial, and who were supporters of the United Irishmen.[94]

By May 1797 Camden, who had been 'singing the praises' of the militia the preceding January was showing his vacillating nature. He wrote: 'The want of attention on the part of the officers, and the very great difficulty to enforce discipline are reasons for discontinuing this force after the present war.'[95] However, if the militia had had a traumatic time in 1797, it was nothing compared to what was in store.

---

[93] Sources for these figures: Pelham MSS (PRONI, T/755); NA, HO/100 series; Roscommon Militia Standing Orders (ibid., WO/75/44); NLI, Kilmainham papers, 1013; *Faulkner's Journal*, and *Freeman's Journal*, May to July 1798. [94] Thomas Pelham to – , 2 Nov. 1797 (HMC, *Fortescue MSS*, iii, 385–9). [95] Camden to Portland, 6 May 1797 (NA. HO/100/69/275).

CHAPTER SEVEN

Rebellion

Three things dominated the year 1798, before the arrival of the French in Connacht in August. First was the deplorable state of the army, which had been exacerbated by the practice of 'free quarters'; second was the effect on the army, and country at large, of the short stewardship of Lieutenant-General Sir Ralph Abercromby as commander-in-chief; and the third was the 1798 rebellion. They are obviously interconnected. Abercromby acted as a catalyst; he brought to a head all that was wrong with the army, but his attempts to do something about the problem were taken out of context by politicians and others who thought he was politically motivated, thus frustrating his efforts. What Abercromby was really asking for again, without perhaps realizing it, was a definition of the strategic purpose of the army, whether or not it was to be a police force or an army to counter invasion.
On his arrival in November 1797,[1] he found a force much affected by the dispersed service in which it had been engaged. Indeed, if the army was following the plan devised by Camden, it had become dangerously skewed. There was too much 'police work' and insufficient concentration of forces. Abercromby was a disciplinarian, who believed that the army should be kept together for the sake of its discipline and effectiveness. He also believed that it had always to be subordinate to the civil power. Abercromby relied on his own judgment, but the appointment of commander-in-chief was anything but an isolated one, it being essential that he should retain the confidence of his political masters, and, at the same time, meet and retain the confidence of his senior military officers. Carhampton had not retained the confidence of either, and it is unfortunate that Abercromby, possibly because of his long service in Ireland, and with Irish soldiers, did not appreciate the necessity of discussing his plans with his political masters, or of consulting his district commanders when making these plans. Even so, his disaffection with his new command was not a secret. Thomas Lane, Lord Downshire's agent in Hillsborough, was able to report to his master in January 1798 that 'Sir R. Abercromby is ashamed, it is said, of the state of the soldiery.'[2]

---

[1] Camden to Portland, 21 Nov. 1797 (ibid., HO/100/68/273). The date of his commission was 10 Nov. 1797.   [2] Lane to Downshire, 25 Jan. 1798 (PRONI, D/607/F/28).

Abercromby issued his famous order on 26 February 1798, which summed up his experience of his command:

> The very disgraceful frequency of courts martial, and the many complaints of irregularities in the conduct of the troops in this Kingdom having so unfortunately proved the army to be in a state of licentiousness which must render it formidable to everyone but the enemy.
>
> The commander-in-chief thinks it necessary to demand from all generals commanding districts and brigades, as well as commanding officers of regiments, that they exert for themselves, and compel from all officers under their command, the strictest and most unremitting attention to the discipline, good order and conduct of their men, such as may restore the high and distinguished reputation which the British troops have been accustomed to enjoy in every part of the world. It becomes necessary to recur, and most pointedly to attend to the standing orders of the kingdom, which, at the same time that they direct military assistance to be given at the requisition of the civil magistrate, positively forbid the troops to act (but in case of attack) without his presence and authority, and the most clear and precise orders are to be given to the officer commanding the party for this purpose.
>
> The utmost prudence and precaution are also to be used in granting parties to revenue officers, both with regard to the person requiring such assistance, and those employed on the duty. Whenever a guard is mounted, patrols must be frequently sent out to take up any soldier who may be found out of his quarters after his hours.
>
> A very culpable remissness having also appeared on the part of the officers respecting the necessary inspection of barracks, quarters, messes etc. as well as attendance at roll-calls and other hours, commanding officers must enforce the attention of those under his command to these points and the general regulations for all which the strictest responsibility will be expected for themselves.
>
> It is of the utmost importance that the discipline of the dragoon regiments should be minutely attended to, for the facilitating of which the Commander-in-chief has dispensed with the attendance of orderly dragoons on himself, and desires that they be not employed by any general or commanding officer, but on military and indispensable business.[3]

Much comment on this order is based on political considerations, and the effect the order had on the ruling classes. While it undoubtedly did have a political effect, the causes of the order being made were entirely military. Abercromby

---

3 General Order, 26 Feb. 1798 (NA, WO/68/221. Donegal Militia Order Book).

believed in the principle of concentration, of keeping the army together, hence his refusal the split it into small groups for the protection of individuals or public or private buildings. For example, he refused Lord Courtown's request for troops to be stationed in Co. Wexford (which in fact might have been a wrong decision!). He said, 'I do not see sufficient reasons for detaching troops to the places named – and that their removal at this season ought to be avoided – and I trust no event will arise to make it necessary.'[4]

Just over a week later, he outlined some of his problems to his friend Andrew Wauchop in Scotland:

> This country is at present in a perfect state of tranquillity, whether it is overawed by a superior force or whether there is any policy in the matter I know not. That a great part of the inhabitants are disaffected is clear. The militia is inferior to that of England and the fencible regiments are weak in numbers as well as in bodily strength. The cavalry much fallen off since I was in this country. The regiments of the line are mere skeletons, the artillery bad beyond description. In that with an army of 40,000 we have little to depend on.[5]

The first part of this quotation shows a certain political innocence, but in the following month many more details of the abuses he found came to the surface. A general order of 13 February detailed some of them – illegal commutation of forage, turning horses to grazing, and then claiming full feed, the purchase of horses under size, under value, and under age and then charging full value to the state, the misemployment of musicians, drummers, tailors, servants, and pioneers (every officer was entitled to a servant, but they were not excused from military duties). Arms had been damaged by carelessness, and battalion gun limbers were being used as farm carts with the gun horses being ridden by officers.[6] On 17 February he commented on the neglect of the accounts of the South Mayo Battalion, 'which certainly must not pass unnoticed'.[7]

But the "straw that broke the camel's back", the one incident that seemed to sum up all that was wrong with the army in Ireland, was when Abercromby recommended to Pelham that Lieutenant Vennell of the 89th Regiment, and Lieutenant Lawlor of the Clare Militia be superseded for desertion, and infamous conduct, after raping Catherine Finn, the maid of a Mr Jasper Uniacke, of Arraglyn, near Kilworth, Co. Cork, in February 1798.[8]

---

[4] Abercromby to William Eliot, 28 Dec. 1797 (NLI, KP/1 0 1 4/8 3). [5] Sir R. Abercromby to Andrew Wauchop, 1 Jan. 1798 (NAS, GD/247/192/4). [6] General Order, 13 Feb. 1798 (NA, WO/79/44/168. Roscommon Militia Standing Orders). Not 'standing orders' as such but general orders and letters. [7] Abercromby to Pelham, 17 Feb. 1798 (NLI, KP/1 0 1 4/1 1 4). In fact, this neglect led to a Board of Enquiry in 1799. [8] Abercromby to Pelham, 21 Feb. 1798 (NLI,

Catherine was a witness to the murder of Uniacke, and had been taken into protective custody where she was molested by the two officers and the 'centinel' or sentry, who had since been confined. 'I cannot help considering their infamous conduct as a mark of the want of discipline in the army calling for vigorous exertions to get the better of.'[9] Five days later, Abercromby issued the order which was addressed to the whole army, and did not mention any one particular part of it, other than the cavalry.

The order of 26 February 1798, however it may have been seen in the army, caused a furore. The gentry regarded it as a slur on the militia and the yeomanry, but were more horrified at Abercromby's intention to ensure that the regulars, fencibles, and militia were to be an army for the defence of the country, and not a protection force for individuals. The army was not happy with it either. Major-General Sir James Duff, commanding in Limerick had this to say: 'I cannot express the mortification the Regiments feel, on the commander-in-chief's order of the 26th Feby. being made known to them. The six Regiments in this District have been upwards of *Ten months* [*sic*] under my command. No men could have conducted themselves with greater propriety during the above period'. He then went on to contradict himself when he asked for some method to compel the attendance of field officers with their regiments as the Tyrone and South Mayo Regiments had none present.[10] The deputy quartermaster general, Lieutenant-Colonel Robert Craufurd, an admirer of Abercromby, gave a more reasoned opinion: 'The order which has occasioned so much dissatisfaction was given out ... immediately after Sir Ralph's return from a tour of the southern and western parts of the Kingdom, during which he had been forcibly struck with the great want of discipline in several regiments', and, 'feeling strongly, Sir Ralph gave this famous order, which certainly was unguarded, and very unfortunately worded'.[11] Portland regarded the order as a 'triumph' for Lord Moira, a noted proponent of Catholic emancipation, and other critics of the government.[12] Camden lacking in moral courage, sat on the fence. This really does mark the nadir of his administration. He told Portland that the order was a military one only, which was true, but 'called for by the relaxation of discipline in the army, composed as it is of very bad militia and fencible officers', which was not true.[13] The order applied to all: regular, fencible, militia, yeomanry, and the officers from general to private. Abercromby, on the other hand, felt he had been accused by Portland of a political manoeuvre. He made it very clear to Camden that he had to take action against the 'loose texture' of the

---

KP/1014/120). 9 Ibid. 10 Sir James Duff to Maj.-Gen. Hewitt, Limerick, 10 Mar. 1798 (PRONI, MIC 67. Lake–Hewitt correspondence). 11 Robert Craufurd to William Wyckham, 19 Mar. 1798 (NA, HO/100/66/76). 12 Portland to Camden, 11 Mar. 1798 (ibid., HO/100/75/193). 13 Camden to Portland, 15 Mar. 1798 (ibid., HO/100/75/224).

Irish army, and did not consider the proclamation of 18 March 1797 to be still in force, as he felt he could not leave such an order to be executed by officers of all ranks and by men of all descriptions. (This was the proclamation authorizing troops to act without a magistrate being present.) Despite Camden's attempts to placate Abercromby, and to ensure that he retained Abercromby's services, and the latter's protestations that his order was a military one only; the discussion became a 'dialogue of the deaf'. Camden wanted Abercromby to remain as commander-in-chief, but to acknowledge that his order was injudicious and wounding to the public of Ireland. Abercromby would do no such thing and resigned.[14]

The effect on the militia must be considered as the teeth had been drawn from Abercromby's order and things continued very much as before. In March 1798 Kildare, King's County, and Queen's County were disarmed, and so, too, were parts of Cork. The method used in disarming counties was to proclaim them to be in insurrection, and then to billet the troops on the people at no cost to the government, but at considerable cost to their unwilling hosts. Unless strictly controlled, this system could easily lead to 'licentious' behaviour on the part of the troops, it was iniquitous: all suffered, loyalist and disaffected alike. One who operated 'free quarters', but understood perfectly how to do it, was Brigadier-General John Moore. He wrote to Major James Nugent of the Westmeath in Cork on 4 May:

> I hope you will be cautious of giving tickets of safety until you see a real disposition to surrender all the arms. As yet I understand you have received no muskets. The language I have been obliged uniformly to hold in the west is that the troops will continue to live upon them until every arm is delivered and therefore the good – or those who have surrendered arms – must force the others to do the same, otherwise their troubles will continue. The least lenity does harm, and the remedy we have adopted is too violent to be repeated. We must therefore make it effectual.[15]

On 6th May he wrote to Major Nugent again, urging him to stay until every arm was given in since the people were being obdurate, but he warned at the same time, 'Endeavour to prevent your people from committing excesses, by sending them always under officers to forage, and preventing such as remain from straggling.'[16] Moore thought privately that Camden and his advisers wished the army to act violently, but were too timorous to say so. He did not like the government's methods of operation, or the treatment of the lower

---

14 Camden to Portland, 26 Mar. 1798 (NA, HO/100/75/299).   15 Moore to Nugent, 4 May 1798 (PRONI, D/2620/5/7).   16 Ibid., 6 May 1798 (ibid., D/2620/5/8).

orders of people by the upper. However, Major Nugent and the Westmeath Militia did obtain the surrender of 800 pikes and 3,400 stand of arms in the Carberries in west Co. Cork.[17]

Essentially there were three problems with the discipline of the army, which included the militia, on the outbreak of the rebellion. Soldiers had been accustomed to acting in small parties, not necessarily commanded by a commissioned officer or NCO, and found that they could do more or less as they pleased with little prospect of punishment for wrongdoing. Second, the bonds of discipline between officers and men were weakened, the soldiers could become less obedient, and open to attempts at subversion as well as the temptations of theft and drink. Third, regiments did not get time to train as complete formations. This affected not only discipline, but also fighting ability. Camden had intended that all militia regiments and battalions should go to an annual summer camp. In 1795, 27 regiments had been encamped, in 1796 there were 10, but in 1797 only three. In the rebellion the cumulative effect can be seen in the initial unsteadiness of militia regiments in the face of the enemy. Although all raw troops were initially unsteady, the militia had simply not practised enough, and officers and NCOs had great difficulty in controlling their men after an action when 'loose' discipline became 'looser'. In a civil war, it was very difficult to distinguish between friend and foe, and the soldiers tended at times to regard everyone as the latter. This was not unusual, of the American revolutionary war it was observed that:

> Like all civil wars, it had made the soldiery more ferocious, and less easy to control, and, like all wars abounding in defeats, had deprived them of confidence in victory; and at the beginning of the French war they had no strong feelings to animate them, and no "esprit de corps" to take the place of strong feelings.[18]

The same observation could easily be applied to the militia in Ireland in May 1798, not forgetting that very many of their commanding generals had fought in the American war.

Professor G.A. Hayes-McCoy, when discussing the mixed opinions of the Irish militia, wrote that 'events were to show that mistrust of the militia was quite unjustified. In fact it would not be difficult to make out a case for the militia units as those which put down the revolt.'[19] Hayes-McCoy's point is worth considering. On the outbreak of the rebellion on 23 May 1798 the disposition of the troops in Ireland was much the same as it had been in 1797. In January 1798 there were 1,830 regular infantry in Ireland; by July, this

---

17 Maurice, *Diary of Sir John Moore*, i, p. 289.   18 *Dictionary of national biography*, 'Gen. Sir Ralph Abercromby'.   19 G.A. Hayes-McCoy, *Irish battles* (Belfast, 1990), p. 277.

Map 1: Ireland in 1798

had increased to 2,380. The fencibles stood at 10,751 in January 1798, and 13,247 by July; the Irish militia 22,728 in January 1798 and at 22,930 by July. In addition there were 2,516 British Militia in Ireland in July 1798.[20]

In other words, in January 1798, the Irish militia comprised 80 per cent of the infantry, and even after reinforcement in July 1798, the percentage still stood at 56. To all intents and purposes the rebellion was over by July, and it is after that month that the large reinforcement of infantry took place.

The militia regiments were not stationed throughout Ireland in any kind of pattern, except in the north, where Lake and his generals did not want the militia to be because of their supposed susceptibility to subversion. There are no returns for the numbers and stations of the army in Ireland in 1798, but it would not have been very different to a year previously as units changed on an individual basis. In 1797 the militia comprised 35 per cent of the army in the north, 61 per cent in the eastern district and 77 per cent in the southern district. However, outside the north the rebellion chiefly affected the counties in the east and southeast, where the militia comprised 63 per cent of the forces available to the government.

These are raw statistics but they do put into perspective the dependence of the government on the militia, and reinforce Hayes-McCoy's argument. The government and the army commanders may not have liked this dependence because they were uncertain of the men, and inexperienced in defending the kingdoms of Ireland and Great Britain with Roman Catholic soldiers. Moreover, the quality of the generals was not high.

The rebellion itself was a campaign of small encounters, of ambush, and surprise, and of little mercy, conducted mainly in the counties of Dublin, Meath, Queen's County, Kilkenny, Carlow, Wicklow, and Wexford, together with Down and Antrim in the north. The United Irishmen's plan was a rebellion with French assistance in order to overthrow the government. However, the conspiracy was riddled with government spies, and in the early part of 1798 large numbers of the chief conspirators had been arrested, including the putative commander-in-chief, Lord Edward Fitzgerald who had been seized on 19 May 1798, just before the planned date of the insurrection. The remnants of the United Irish leadership determined on a rebellion with or without French assistance and fixed on 23 May 1798 as the day on which it was to start. Much of their strategy has to be surmised from actions of the rebels in the field, and the writings of those who were involved after the rebellion was over.[21]

The principal sources for the actions of the government forces are to be found in newspaper reports, government proclamations about military actions,

---

20 Ferguson, 'Army in Ireland', p. 149.   21 For an analysis of rebel intentions, see Daniel Gahan, *The peoples' rising* (London, 1995), p. 7.

the surviving letter books of militia units, the Kilmainham and Rebellion papers, and the published letters and diaries of participants such as Lord Cornwallis the lord lieutenant, and Brigadier-General John Moore. There are many contemporary accounts of the rebellion published in the aftermath, the most famous of these being Sir Richard Musgrave's *Memoirs of the different rebellions in Ireland* published in 1801. Musgrave thought the rebellion a Catholic conspiracy, and a re-run of the failed rebellion of 1641. However, disregarding the polemic, Musgrave culled his facts from official sources and in consequence his work is a valuable source of factual information.

The prime aim of the United Irishmen was to seize Dublin, and the counties around the capital – north Co. Dublin, Meath, Kildare, and Wicklow – would then form a shield around it. This would prevent reinforcement of the crown forces in the city. The United Irish forces then in the individual counties would seize control of them.[22] The rebellion did break out on 23 May as planned, but the arrest of Lord Edward Fitzgerald, the putative commander-in-chief, on 19 May and the arrest of other members of the Leinster Directory badly upset the plans of the insurgents. At the same time it alerted the government to the fact that something was afoot. They may not have known the proposed date of the rising but the army and the yeomanry had been mobilized and were guarding every important location in Dublin. The mail coaches were stopped (the signal for the rising), and it did take place in the surrounding counties of Kildare, Meath, and north Wicklow. It was defeated within a week but only after some ferocious fighting. The insurgents suffered reverses in Co. Kildare at Naas, Clane and Rathangan, but enjoyed some success at Prosperous, also in Co. Kildare.

All the infantry engaged at Naas were Armagh Militia under the command of Lord Gosford, their colonel. He described the action:

> They made their attack upon our troops posted near the gaol with great violence but after three desperate onslaughts were repulsed – They then made a general attack in almost every direction as they got possession of almost every avenue into the town – They continued to engage the troops for near ? of an hour when they gave way and fled on all sides.[23]

At Prosperous on the same night of Monday 23 May 1798 all the infantry engaged were from the City of Cork Militia under the command of Captain John Swayne. They were not so fortunate as the Armagh because the insur-

---

22 Daniel Gahan, 'The military strategy of the Wexford United Irishmen in 1798' in *History Ireland*, 1:4, Winter 1993 (http://www.iol.ie-fagann/1798) (26 Aug. 2004). 23 Lord Gosford to Lt.-Gen. Lake, 24 May 1798 (NAI, RP/620/37/152).

gents adopted a stratagem in order to put the soldiers off their guard. The local parish priest and a Yeomanry officer, Dr Esmond, persuaded Swayne that the people of Prosperous wished to surrender arms and weapons in order to prove their allegiance to the crown, they wished to do it in the evening, but were afraid of the sentries. Captain Swayne and his company relaxed their guard and as a result were surprised during the night by the insurgents. Swayne was murdered in his bed, his men were driven upstairs in their barrack, which was then set on fire, and the soldiers killed as they attempted to escape.

The fight at Clane (in Co. Kildare) proved to be another desperate affair. The infantry involved were from the Armagh Regiment under Lieutenant Jephson. His men were in billets throughout the village which laid them open to an assault which duly happened. The soldiers fought their way to the officer in small groups losing two killed and five wounded. They rallied and drove off their assailants. The following day Jephson abandoned Clane and retreated to Naas. At the same time, in Ballymore Eustace, Co. Wicklow, in another hard fought contest a detachment of the Tyrone Regiment fought off the insurgents, losing an officer and four men in the process.

The rebels captured Rathangan on 23 May 1798, but on the following day they were attacked by the City of Cork Regiment under the command of Colonel Longfield, defeated and dispersed.[24] On 23 and 24 May, General Dundas was driven out of Kilcullen. However, after committing many depredations, and no doubt discouraged by the news from Dublin and the rest of the county, or else engaged on a massive deception (it is not known which), the rebels sent a message to Dundas signifying their wish to surrender their arms and return to their allegiance. Dundas detailed General Wilford to take this surrender. In the meantime, Major-General Duff, commanding in Limerick, had set off for Dublin without orders to do so, leaving his rear comparatively unprotected and without its commander. He had under his command the 'Dublin Regiment' (the City of Dublin Regiment), and was joined on the way by the South Cork Regiment with their curricle guns and a detachment of the 4th Dragoon Guards. When they got to Kildare they found the body of Lieutenant William Giffard of the 82nd Regiment who had been murdered whilst on his way to rejoin his regiment in England. Giffard had been with his father, Captain John Giffard of the City of Dublin Regiment, in Limerick before setting out on his fateful journey. In fact when Captain Giffard heard of the death of his nephew, Captain Daniel Ryan, mortally wounded in the arrest of Lord Edward Fitzgerald on 19 May 1798, he took the first stage to Dublin, which his son was to have taken. Lieutenant Giffard took the next one, which his father was to have been on, with fate-

---

24 Lt.-Col. Longfield to Lt.-Gen. Dundas, 29 May 1798 (NAI, RP/620/37/208).

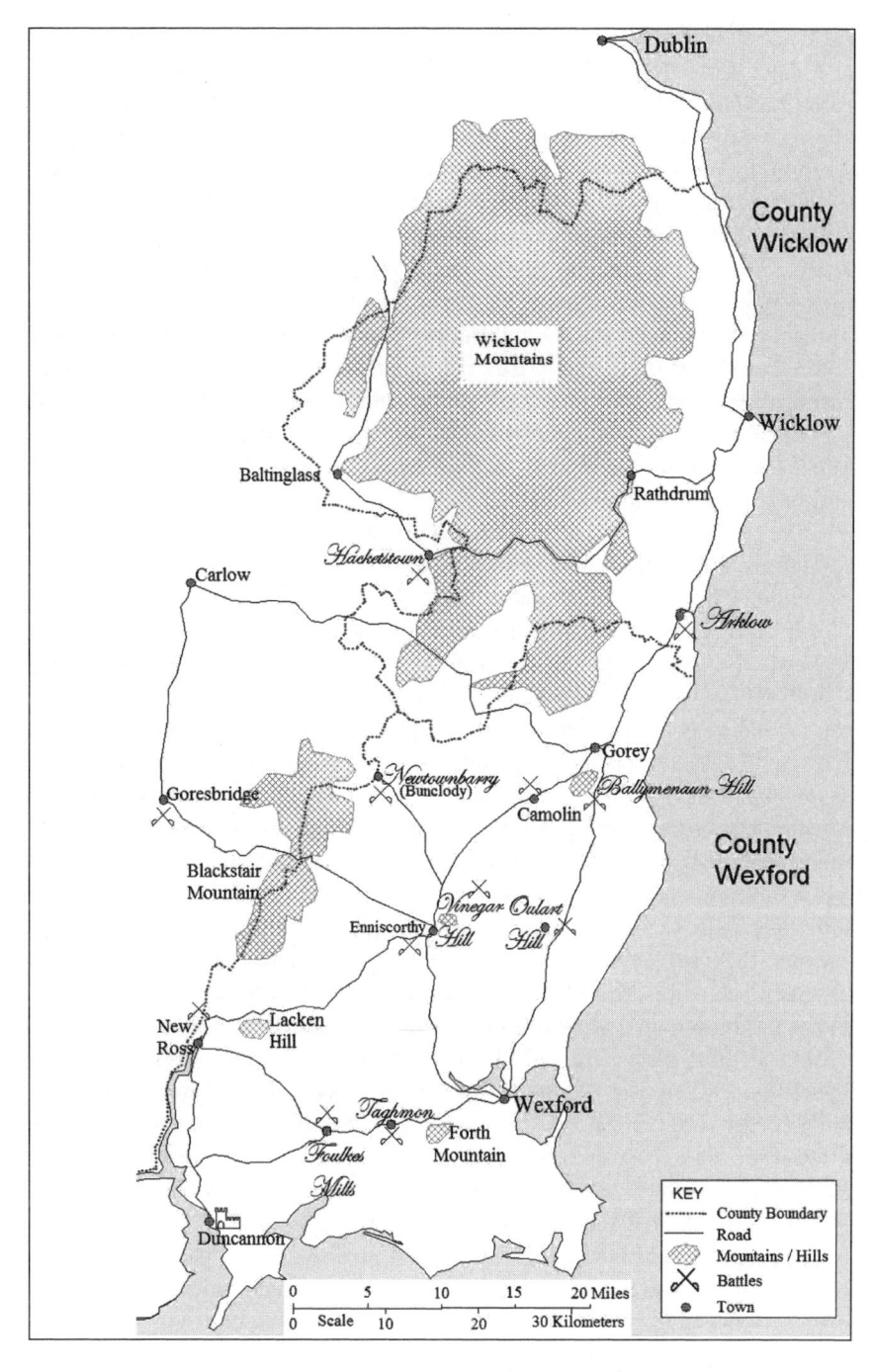

Map 2: Counties Wicklow and Wexford showing principal actions

ful consequences. When Duff's force came up with the surrendering rebels at Gibbet Rath, they killed many with little loss. This was a confused action, caused either by the troops firing on the rebels or the rebels firing on the troops who were anxious to avenge young Giffard, who, according to Musgrave, 'most of them knew and loved'.[25]

There was further fighting at Edenderry on 30 May where the City of Limerick Militia under the command of Lieutenant-Colonel Gough dispersed rebels. This marks the end of the initial phase of the rebellion. The brunt of the fighting had been borne by the militia as they were the only infantry available. In the main the militia regiments and their detachments were well commanded, but it is equally true that their opponents had no overall command, their attacks were unco-ordinated, and in consequence were defeated piecemeal. Initially it was the same in Wicklow and Wexford. However, in Wexford the rebels were able to form a vast army that took a determined and organized response to defeat.

The rebels in Wexford mobilized when word reached them of the rising in and around Dublin, and this county became the epicentre of the whole rebellion. Partly this was because the only soldiers in the county were the North Cork Regiment at Wexford town, Enniscorthy, and a small detachment at Ferns. In April 1798 the North Cork had been stationed on the Grand Canal, with companies at Ponsonby Bridge, Sallins, Kilmurry, Hazlehatch, and the 11th lock. It was an eight-company regiment, but the light company under Captain Edward Heard was detached to the Light Battalion at Athlone. Sometime in early May (the actual date is uncertain), the regiment was ordered to counties Wicklow and Wexford to look for arms. The strength of the regiment less the light company was 24 officers, and 524 rank-and-file.[26] It is difficult to know exactly what the dispositions of the regiment were when they left the canal. According to Musgrave, who gleaned his facts from official sources, they arrived in Wexford on 26 April 1798, and had three companies at that place, with others, numbers unspecified, at Enniscorthy, Gorey and Ferns.[27] These figures do not add up when the numbers of men involved in actions at these places are considered. Nor do they sound militarily correct. Much more likely the regiment was sent to Wexford, with detachments at Enniscorthy (Captain Snowe's company, and one subaltern and 30 men from Captain de Courcy's), at Gorey (one subaltern and 30 rank-and-file), and at Ferns (one subaltern and 30 rank-and-file).[28] The strength of the regiment in Wexford would have been 19 officers and 369 rank-and-file.

The government forces in Wexford had received news that a strong force of rebels was congregating on Oulart Hill, some fifteen miles to the north.

---

25 Musgrave, *Rebellions*, p. 242.   26 Pay Lists and Muster Rolls, North Cork Militia (NA, WO/13/2706).   27 Musgrave, *Rebellions*, p. 306.   28 Ibid., 326, 370, 409.

Colonel Foote, commanding the North Corks organized a force to march against them.

The force that went to Oulart was essentially an enlarged company. Why so many officers went with it is difficult to understand: two field officers, one captain, three lieutenants, and an ensign. Normally, one would have expected a commander of the force, the company commander, usually a captain, one or possibly two lieutenants, and an ensign. The only reason that can be suggested is that the officers were very keen to settle accounts with the insurgents. The action at Oulart Hill is well known and well documented, although few historians describe the 'ground' on which the battle was fought, yet this is usually the best clue as to what happened in any affray. Oulart Hill rises above the surrounding countryside and dominates it. It is steep on its southern face but more gently sloping on the others. When Colonel Foote saw the rebel position on the hill, he advised caution, and expressed a wish to wait for reinforcements before offering battle. A single company force was far too small in numbers to mount an attack on such a large edifice, it would be attacking up a very steep hill, and had the danger of being outflanked. But Major Lombard and his officers were very keen to get to grips with the rebels and advanced against them. What Colonel Foote feared happened, for they were outflanked. They were attacking up a very steep hill – in fact it was a stiff climb – and after discharging their firelocks against the rebels they were in no position to withstand a carefully thought out ferocious attack that had the impetus of being made downhill. It was a foolhardy attack and the North Cork paid a heavy price for their enthusiasm.

Morale in the regiment collapsed after the trauma of Oulart, six officers and 106 men had lost their lives, reducing the regiment to 13 officers and 273 rank-and-file.[29] The unreliability of the regiment was one of the reasons why Lieutenant-Colonel Maxwell of the Donegal Regiment, evacuated Wexford on 30 May 1798.[30] The questions raised about the quality of the officers are highlighted by such incidents as Lieutenant Nicholas Cole Bowen deserting his men to go on board a ship to escape (for which he was court martialled and dismissed the service). Nevertheless, the men fought well at Enniscorthy and later at Arklow.

The North Cork had a reputation for extreme cruelty in the methods they used when searching for arms in Wexford. They were also described as being 'Orange.' The former seems likely to have been exaggerated, for there were not enough of them to cover more than a very small part of the county, and they were not there long. On the second point, the regiment certainly had an Orange lodge, but could not be described as an 'Orange' one, since we

[29] Which tallies with Musgrave, 'not three hundred men.' [30] Maj.-Gen. Ross to Lake, 2 June 1798 (NAI, RP/ 620/38/29).

know it had Roman Catholic soldiers, some of whom raised their missals on surrendering at Oulart (but were killed nonetheless). In those days, no record of the religion of the men was kept by the army, but a study of the names of those killed at Oulart reveals some presumably Irish Catholic surnames such as Bourke, Mahony, Murphy, Reagan, Kelleher, and Docherty, and others presumably Protestant, such as Kirby, Hudson, Lloyd, Lane, and Barrett. Of course, such evidence proves nothing by itself, though taken together with other evidence it carries some weight. Some of the officers could well have been Orangemen: their colonel, Lord Kingsborough, most certainly was one, and there were very strong family links between the regiment and Co. Armagh. There were family connections between the Kings of Mitchelstown, including the colonel of the regiment Lord Kingsborough, and the Charlemont family in county Armagh; Lieutenant Roe, an officer in the regiment, was from Mount Roe in Armagh; while Lieutenant Jephson of the Armagh Regiment was from the Cork family. The officers of the North Cork were a close-knit body with many family ties uniting them.[31] Lord Kingsborough, himself, was an original member of Orange Lodge No. 176 in Dublin.[32] Regiments certainly bore the stamp of the character of their colonel, and when 'Big George' Kingsborough was court martialled in 1798, he was accused by Lieutenant Nicholas Cole Bowen, among other things, of only promoting Protestants in his regiment[33] No evidence was offered by Bowen to prove his accusations, but it may be suggestive that the names of the non-commissioned officers killed at Oulart were Sergeants Miller, Parker, Bradshaw, Lombard, Caulfield, and Dee, and Corporals Grant, Flanagan, Francis, Homan, and Caulfield. Lombard was the major's surname, and Caulfield was the family name of the Charlemont family.

Keyed up by their success at Oulart Hill the insurgents attacked Enniscorthy the following day, 28 May. The defence of the town was entrusted to Captain Snowe of the North Cork, with his own company, and a detachment of Captain de Courcy's together with three detachments of yeomen. (De Courcy was one of the officers killed at Oulart.) In all it was a force of about 300 men, opposed by about 6,000 rebels. Enniscorthy is a small town on the River Slaney, where there is a bridge. The ground rises steeply from the river. There was a Norman Castle, but no town walls. Captain Snowe had no artillery. The rebels divided their force into three divisions to attack the town from the west, south and east, but the main assault was from the west through the Duffry Gate. This assault, which included the use of

---

[31] I am indebted to Mr Stawell St Leger Heard of East Sussex for this genealogical information. [32] Grand Orange Lodge of Ireland, *The formation of the Orange Order, 1795–1798* (Belfast, 1994), p. 117. [33] Court martial of Lord Kingsborough, 4 Oct. 1798 (NA, WO/68/221/54, Donegal Militia Order Book).

Plate 2: Enniscorthy: from the Duffry Gate, the rebels attacked down this hill

stampeding cattle, was made downhill, and once the attackers had a momentum going they were impossible to stop. The town had been successfully defended to this point but Captain Snowe recognized that it could not be defended further, and successfully extricated his force and retreated to Wexford. The combined loss of the small force was 74 men killed and 17 wounded, which was almost a third of its strength.[34] The total number killed and wounded was the second highest in the rebellion, after New Ross.

The officer commanding in Wexford was Lieutenant-Colonel Richard Maxwell of the Donegal Regiment. He left a graphic account of the impossibility of the situation he was now in because of the paucity of soldiers, low morale, disaffected townspeople, lack of provisions, and a failure of promised reinforcements to arrive. The reinforcement Maxwell was expecting comprised the Meath Militia and the 13th Foot, who were to assemble at Taghmon, some three and a half miles west of Wexford town, and advance on Wexford. General Fawcett, on his march to Wexford, ordered Lord Bective, with four companies of his Meath militia, and 70 men of the 60th Foot to meet him at 'Fox Mills' (Foulkes Mills). He described what happened to the Meath under Captain Adams of the advance guard, 'Owing to extreme ignorance, and a total inexperience of any service – or his duty as

---

34 Musgrave, *Rebellions*, p. 331.

an officer – instead of waiting to receive any orders from me proceeded. Adams, with no precaution taken, or weapons loaded, was ambushed and cut to pieces.'[35]

On receiving news of what had happened to the Meath battalion, Maxwell immediately marched at the head of 200 of the Donegal, and 120 Yeoman cavalry to attempt a junction with the 13th Foot, but after continual opposition at Three Rocks he could see that this was impossible and he retreated back to Wexford. Morale in the town was low, and many in positions of responsibility advised evacuation. But Maxwell was made of sterner stuff: 'Notwithstanding this unfavourable situation of the garrison I could not prevail upon myself to acquiesce in the opinion of the meeting, and ordered all the troops to their respective stations for the defence of the place.' Then Maxwell found out the strength of his little garrison:

> I visited the different barriers and to my astonishment and concern, I found that two yeomanry corps had quitted their posts; in one instance where I had every reason to expect 60 or 70 I found but three privates and in another nearly a like number, not a single individual where there became in a retired part of the town an open and safe approach for the rebels.

Maxwell did not know if this defection was deliberate or if it was due to timidity, but then he received news 'that men of the North Cork Regiment refused to obey their officers or take any further part against the rebels; the state of the place became in my own opinion so truly alarming that I could not reconcile to myself further opposing the evacuation'. On Wednesday 30 May 1798, Maxwell successfully evacuated the garrison to Duncannon.[36] Mrs Brownrigg, who remained in Wexford, described it thus: 'The North Cork Militia was at various posts guarding the entrance to the town when every one of their officers but a young lad of 14 (of the name of Little) left them there and went on board the ships', and as a result, 'the North Corks deserted by their officers and seeing the retreat of the Donegals quitted their posts immediately'. However, 'Several of the North Cork officers went back to Wexford from the ships, and as I afterwards found, joined their men, who, with the Donegal's, Mr Ogle and corps, and some few loyalists who knew of the retreat, fought their way, and after incredible hardships arrived at Duncannon Fort.'[37] One of the officers who did not return to his men was

---

35 Maj.-Gen. Fawcett to Lt.-Gen. Lake (PRONI, MIC/6 7/4 3. Lake–Hewitt correspondence). 36 Maj.-Gen. Eustace to Lt.-Gen. Lake, 2 June 1798 (NAI, RP/620/38/29. Enclosing Lt.-Col. Maxwell's account of the retreat from Wexford. An 'officer of some note'.). 37 H.F.B. Wheeler & A.M. Broadley, *The war in Wexford* (London, 1910), p. 168

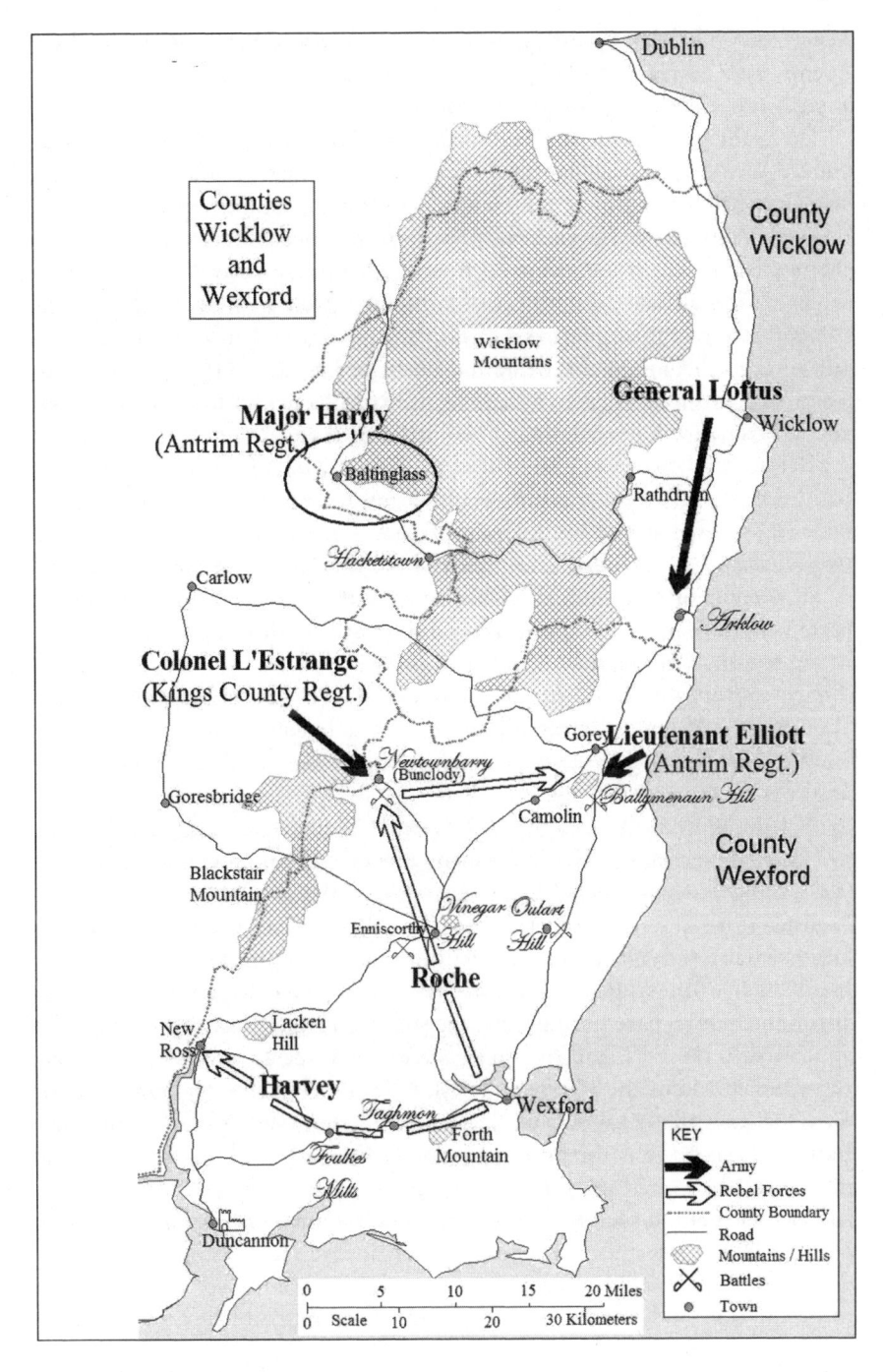

Map 3: Plans of insurgent and government forces, 30 May 1798

Lieutenant Nicholas Cole-Bowen for which he was court martialled subsequently and dismissed from the service as we have seen. Incidentally, Ensign John Little was more than 14 years old.

After their successes at Enniscorthy and Wexford, the largest towns in county Wexford, the insurgents decided to divide their forces into two divisions in order to complete the conquest of the county. The southern force under its commander Bagenal Harvey was to advance against New Ross, and the northern force under Edward Roche was to attack Newtownbarry and Gorey. If these attacks were successful, not only would the county have been cleared of government forces but also the way would have been open to spread the rebellion to the west, and north to Dublin. (After all, the invasion route into Ireland taken by the Normans had been up the Barrow Valley and across to the Liffey Basin.) The northern force moved off immediately.

Before the North Cork were sent to Wexford in April 1798, the county had been devoid of any kind of regular army force. The same was not true of Wicklow, which had been disaffected for some time. The geography of Co. Wicklow was responsible for much of the character of the county because of the mountains more or less in the centre of the county. The northernmost barony of Rathdrum had more in common with south Co. Dublin, Arklow in the south, with north Wexford, and Shillelagh in the west, with Carlow. Thus geography meant that any incursion northward by the rebels from Wexford was bound to bring Wicklow into prominence.

Wicklow had been well organized by the United Irish movement who used anti-orange propaganda to inflame passions and terrify Catholics into joining the movement. As Ruan O'Donnell, the historian of the rebellion in Wicklow, has observed, 'by skilful manipulation and a well crafted structure, the United Irishmen of Wicklow grew to be the largest county army in Leinster in 1798'.[38] The government was well aware of the strategic importance of the county, and on 27 September 1797 had appointed Major Joseph Hardy of the Antrim Regiment as garrison commander. This was an unusual appointment. We have already seen that militia officers were forbidden to be appointed to the staff, and this was a staff appointment, even though Hardy remained in command of a detachment of 300 men of his regiment. There were two exceptions to the rule, Hardy, and Major Sandys of the Longford Battalion. Sandys was the brother-in-law of Edward Cooke, something that may have had a bearing on his appointment. Hardy does not seem to have had any such advantage of birth so it must be assumed that he was appointed on his reputation as a former regular soldier. Joseph Hardy is one of the most under-estimated army commanders of the rebellion period, yet he has a claim to be the one soldier who knew what he was doing and how to suppress

38 Ruan O'Donnell, *The rebellion in Wicklow* (Dublin, 1998), p. 47.

insurgency. He was commissioned at the age of seventeen after distinguishing himself as a Volunteer in the 65th Foot at the battle of Bunker Hill in the American Revolution.[39] He transferred to the 93rd Foot in 1780, but resigned his commission in 1783 when that regiment was disbanded. He had married well, and was re-commissioned as major in the Antrim Regiment in 1793. In 1796 he commanded the flank companies of the Dublin garrison that marched against the French, which means he was preferred over regular army officers. Hardy claimed he had been given the local rank of brigadier-general but there is no independent written evidence for this assertion – without written authority he would not have been obeyed by colonels, and after rallying the remnants of Colonel Walpole's defeated force, he requested supercession because there were colonels in that body.[40] He would not have needed to do this if he were a brigadier-general.

On arrival in Wicklow with his 'flying camp' of 300 Antrim Militiamen, Hardy distributed them over the '40 Irish miles between Blessington and Enniscorthy'.[41] Hardy also had family connections with Co. Wicklow as he had spent part of his youth at Hillbrook in southern Wicklow, and his brother, Thomas lived at Hacketstown, which helped to give him a valuable insight into county affairs and friendship with the county gentry.

Hardy was conscientious, fair, and experienced in the ways of soldiers. By November 1797, he had seized over 700 stand of arms that had increased to over 1,300 by the outbreak of the rebellion together with about 4,000 pikes. He mixed the yeomanry with the soldiery in all duties, 'thereby inspiring the former with confidence, and the latter with local Knowledge'.[42] He established a night curfew and was neither unafraid to take hostages for future good behaviour, nor to confine one of his officers for flogging civilians in Dunlavin (Lieutenant Hogg, whom we encountered in an earlier chapter). As garrison commander he had the power to order arms searches and sweeps, and to co-ordinate them himself. He was also responsible for the deployment of the Antrim Regiment soldiers. On the outbreak of the rebellion he had his headquarters at Baltinglass, but moved to Rathdrum on 7 June, a more strategic location, at the same time as Captain John Giffard and 220 men of the City of Dublin Regiment. 'Thus after five skirmishes, hundreds against thousands, was this intricate mountainous country kept secure without murder or torture, or even free quarters, with one militia regiment and detach-

---

[39] A 'Volunteer officer' served without pay in the hope of being appointed to a commission without purchase by reason of distinguished conduct in action. The 65th Foot later became the York and Lancaster Regiment. [40] Memorial of Joseph Hardy to Charles Lennox, duke of Richmond, nd [but after 1802] (NLI, M/S 55/217, Melville papers). [41] Maj. Joseph Hardy, *Journal of the principal occurrences in Ireland and principally in the Co Wicklow between September 1797 and September 1798 when the French surrendered at Ballinamuck in which Major Hardy was engaged.* (NLI, p 5641). [42] Ibid.

ments of 300 men besides the yeomanry whose conduct was gallant and vigilant, while Wexford on one side was sacrificed to the horrors of rebellion', he said with some asperity.[43]

In the meantime, Newtownbarry had been reinforced by a detachment of the King's County Regiment under the command of Colonel Henry L'Estrange. At the same time, Lieutenant-General Loftus moved to Arklow as a prelude to advancing down the coastal route to Wexford. At this stage, neither the government forces nor the rebels were aware of each other's intentions. Newtownbarry was the first to be attacked on 1 June 1798. L'Estrange had no more than 350 men including yeomanry. He withdrew from the town, which the rebels then set about plundering. However, L'Estrange was only concentrating his force, and reinforced by another detachment of the King's County, he attacked the rebels and defeated them at the point of the bayonet. The Yeomen cavalry completed the defeat. 'This victory is of the utmost consequence', said Edward Cooke, 'to the operations in Wexford as it will prevent the escape of the rebels into Carlow or Kilkenny – Newtownbarry is at the source of the Slaney which flows into Wexford.'[44]

On the same day a detachment of the Antrim Regiment of about 200 men under Lieutenant Elliott reinforced Gorey. Elliott took command of all the forces in the town, and on receiving information that rebel forces were on Carrigrew Hill, about five miles off, he marched out to meet them. The insurgents were taken completely by surprise and at Ballymenaun Hill were defeated in an attack in open field. As at Newtownbarry, the Yeoman cavalry completed the rout.[45] Lord Camden received an account of this action from General Loftus, 'By an account just received from General Loftus it appears that the troops in Gorey consisting of 30 of the Antrim Militia, a subaltern's detachment of the North Cork and some others attacked the rebels at Ballycanoe and killed one hundred of them, some of the arms of the North Corks were retaken'.[46]

Lieutenant-General Lake, the commander-in-chief, planned to recapture Wexford. He had General Asgill in Kilkenny, Colonel L'Estrange in Newtownbarry, General Loftus on his way to Arklow, and he was sending General Johnston to reinforce New Ross. They were to advance simultaneously and trap the rebels in Wexford. On 2 June 1798 General Loftus was informed that a force of troops collected in Kildare by Colonel L.T. Walpole was to join him at Gorey. This force, or rather the commander of this force was to cause Loftus considerable problems.

Walpole was a well-connected staff officer in Dublin. He was a relative of the duke of Portland, the home secretary in London. Portland had shame-

---

[43] Hardy, *Journal*, 29 May 1798. [44] Edward Cooke to William Wickham, 2 June 1798 (NA, HO/100/77/2 1). [45] Gahan, *Military strategy*, p. 90. [46] Camden to 'My dear Lord', 4 June 1798 (NA, HO/100/77/28).

lessly attempted to have Walpole promoted to the rank of brigadier-general whilst he was still only a brevet colonel in 1796. His regiment was in the West Indies, but Portland claimed 'his health was not good enough for that station'.[47] Camden diplomatically refused, but did agree to find a reason for Walpole not to go to the West Indies.[48] It is obvious from this, and from the way Loftus treated Walpole, that Walpole was very well connected, and that his military colleagues, including his force commander, were wary of him.

Walpole was to march to Gorey and then hand over his command to General Loftus. Colonel Walpole had different ideas. He refused to do this, arguing that he could attack the rebels encamped on Carnew Hill, near Newtownbarry, and then march on Enniscorthy. Loftus expressly forbade this but did agree that Walpole and his force should march towards Ballymore on the Gorey to Enniscorthy road. Colonel Lord Ancram and the Midlothian Fencible Cavalry were ordered to Scarawalsh Bridge supported by 250 men of the King's County Regiment. General Loftus would move south on the Arklow Road to the crossroads near Ballymore, and a detachment of the Antrim Regiment was posted on Ballymenaun Hill under Captain McManus, in a position to support either Walpole or Loftus should the necessity arise.[49] Colonel Walpole was under orders not to attack unless he had reconnoitred the rebel position first.

This plan was eminently sensible; unfortunately it depended on the experience and judgement of an officer who was more concerned with fame, glory, and personal advancement. On 4 June, Walpole did find the rebels on Ballymore Hill but instead of deploying and informing Loftus as he had been ordered to do, he marched on without either an advance guard or flankers.[50] When he reached Tubberneering where the road was deep and had high banks on either side, he was ambushed. His troops could not deploy. Walpole himself was killed, and his force began to retreat in great confusion. Lieutenant-Colonel Robert Camden Cope with a detachment of the Armagh Regiment towards the rear of the column took command and extricated the force from its predicament, covering a retreat to Gorey. Since Walpole had not informed any of the supporting columns of his impending action, confusion ensued resulting in the entire force retreating back to Gorey, then to Arklow and finally back to Wicklow. Major Hardy commented that the troops abandoned Arklow without his knowledge or consent and retired on him in Wicklow. Obviously he regarded the abandonment of Gorey and Arklow to be the result of panic.

Nevertheless he knew how to deal with the situation. 'I met them', he said, 'formed them up on a hill, amused them with temporary intrenchments

---

[47] Portland to Camden, 31 Oct. 1796 (ibid., HO/100/62/308). [48] Camden to Portland, 7 Nov. 1796 (ibid., HO/100/62/325). [49] Musgrave, *Rebellions*, p. 373. [50] Ibid.

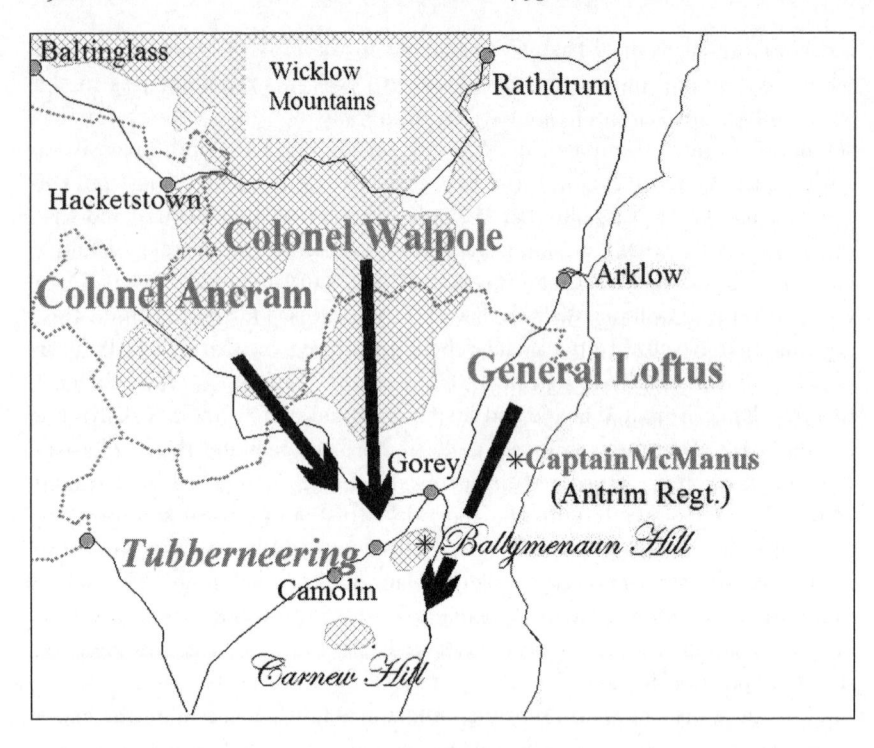

Map 4: Tubberneering, 4 June 1798

while I provided spare houses for them in Wicklow to prevent them sacking the town, dissipated their panic, found a colonel and two lieutenant-colonels with them so requested Lord Camden to relieve me'.[51] In fact, he did not ask Camden to relieve him, he asked the commander-in-chief, General Lake instead, who said to him:

> I am much obliged to you for your hints respecting proper officers being sent to command in Wicklow ... when I selected General Loftus for that command it appears to me that I had taken care of that country by sending an officer of experience ... Unfortunately by the failure in one division of his force he has been obliged to take a different route by means the command devolves to the officer next in rank. I am sorry to hear so bad an account of the insubordination of the troops under command of you both which I should hope may be rectified with a little management – I am quite clear that when troops

---

51 Hardy, *Journal*, 3 June 1798. He asked to be relieved or superseded as these officers were senior in rank to him so he could not give them orders.

are struck with a Panick the best mode to relieve them from it, is to reason and not to abuse them, by which means they may be brought to act against an enemy with great success.[52]

Hardy had obviously said more to Lake than he admits to in his *Journal*, and it is obvious that Lake knew what Hardy's role was in Wicklow. Lake refused to supersede him, but General Needham was sent down. The losses at Tubberneering were 28 of the Armagh Regiment killed, 10 of the Tyrone, 10 of the Londonderry, and three of the Suffolk Fencibles.[53] These were serious losses, and Camden mourned the loss of Walpole: 'Colonel Walpole was one of my oldest friends and one for whom I had the sincerest regard. I feel infinite affliction at his death.'[54]

On 5 June 1798, the southern division of the rebels under Bagenal Harvey attacked New Ross. Harvey was a Protestant landlord and United Irishman who lived at Bargy Castle in the south of Co. Wexford. A ferocious battle ensued in which all the government infantry were Irish militia, a battle that really marked the turning point of the rebellion. For some time after 23 May New Ross had been virtually undefended, the only troops being the Ross Yeomanry, about 150 strong, under the command of Charles Tottenham, the local landlord. Tottenham attempted to put the town in a state of defence, hoping for reinforcement. On 3 June Major-General Henry Johnson arrived with Major-General Eustace, a detachment of 4th Light Infantry, the Donegal, Meath, and Clare regiments of militia together with artillery and cavalry. General Johnson was an Irishman, who had not had a particularly distinguished career up to this moment. Cornwallis regarded him as a bit of a blockhead – probably because when he commanded the 17th Foot he had been surprised and captured by 'Mad' Anthony Wayne at Stony Point in the American war.[55] On 4 June the County of Dublin Battalion under Colonel Lord Mountjoy arrived as a further reinforcement.

New Ross lies on the River Barrow, which flows from north to south. The major part of the town lies on the east bank with the small suburb of Rosbercon on the west bank. On both sides the town is built on steep slopes that lead down to the river. The streets are narrow and winding, ideal for defence with cannon, otherwise equally difficult for defence or attack. General Johnson had a total force of 1,400 men. He was opposed by a massive force of 10–15,000 rebels,[56] or as many as 30,000.[57] The lower figure is more likely

---

52 Gen. Lake to Maj. Hardy, 6 June 1798 (NLI, KP/1081/373). 53 Sir Watkin Williams Wynne to Lt.-Gen. Lake, 4 June 1798 (NAI, RP/620/38/43). 54 Camden to [—], 4 June 1798 (NA, HO/100/77/36). 55 Born in Kilternan, Co. Dublin, 1748, died in Bath 1835. There is a memorial to him in Bath Abbey, just inside the door into the nave, on the right. 56 Keogh and Furlong, p. 121. 57 Musgrave, *Rebellions*, p. 384.

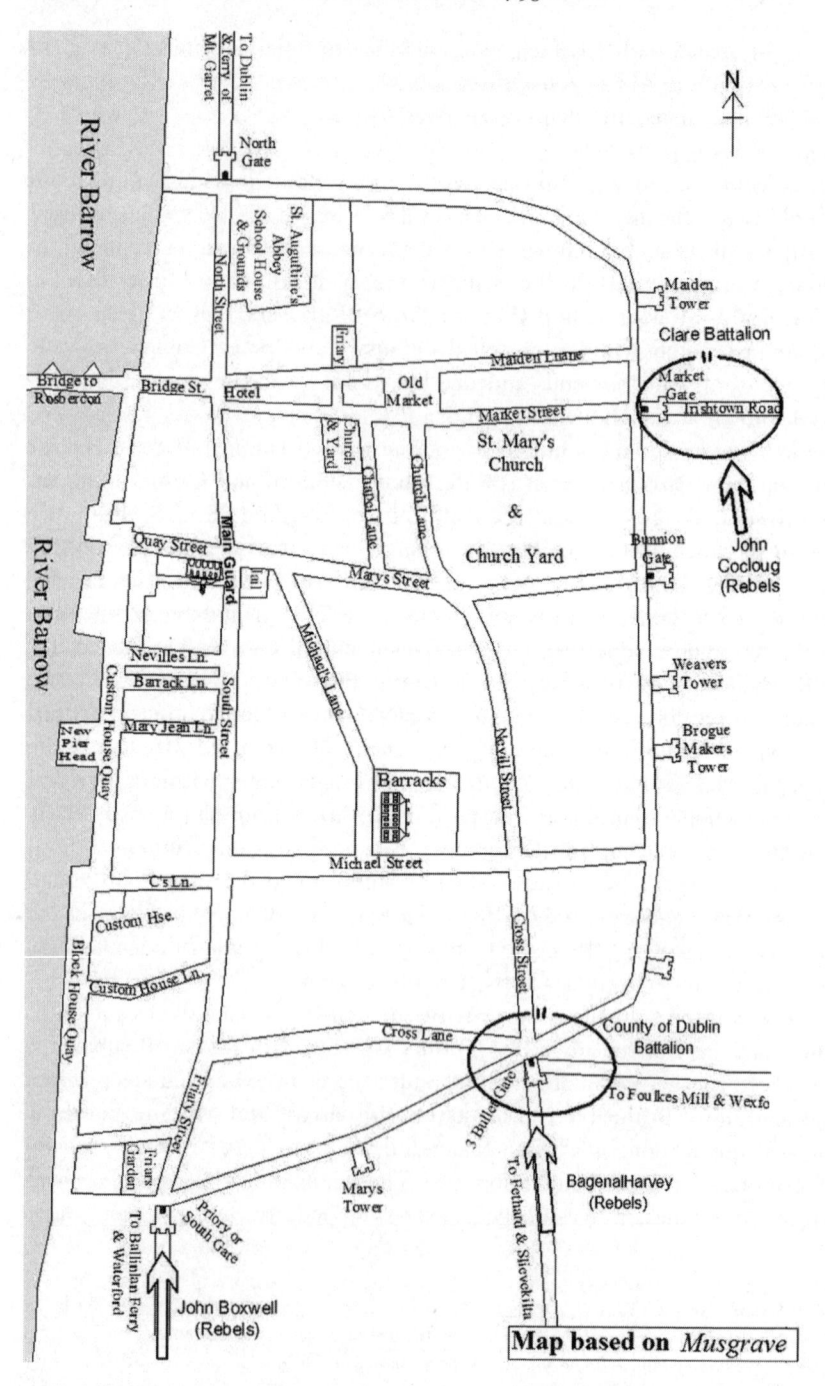

Map 5: New Ross town in 1798

to be correct, but what is incontrovertible is the fact that a force ten to fifteen times the size of their own opposed the militia.

New Ross is a battle that is difficult to describe because no one who participated has left an account giving the overall picture. We know the government forces engaged, but only know for certain the dispositions of the Clare Militia, the artillery and the Yeomanry. We can guess at the positions of the Dublin County, and we know that a detachment of sixteen men of the Donegal's under a sergeant were in the Main Guard (the market hall), but the actual positions of the rest of the Donegal's, the Meath, and the Light Infantry are unknown.

Harvey divided his force into three assault columns, one under John Coclough to attack the Market Gate and the other two under himself and John Boxwell to attack Three Bullet Gate and Priory Gate. Harvey himself took no further part in the battle; he was a landlord, not a soldier and had no taste for it. The rebels attacked in these three columns in the south and east of the town, from Priory gate near the river in the south, to Three Bullet Gate in the southeast, and Market Gate in the east. (They did not attack the North Gate.) Johnson had deployed his force in a quadrant from the river to the Market Gate, and back to the river, holding the bridge to Rosbercon. Other buildings in the town were defended including the barracks, and the Main Guard (the market house in the centre of the town). The Clare Battalion were in the Irishtown, the Dublin County Battalion at Three Bullet Gate, and possibly the Meath or the Donegal at the Priory Gate. Quite possibly the Light Infantry were supporting all these regiments. A study of the casualties shows that the light companies of the North Mayo, Antrim, Kilkenny, Queen's County, and Clare Militias, all part of the 4th Battalion Light Infantry, lost 65 men killed, wounded and missing so they were all engaged somewhere, and the Meath Battalion lost 35 killed, wounded and missing, the Clare 22, the Dublin County 34, and the Donegal 8. This suggests that apart from the detachment at the main guard, the Donegal's were not much engaged.

There is some doubt about the time the attack began, either three or five in the morning – possibly the latter, just after dawn. It was a ferocious battle with no quarter given or asked. The town was assaulted at Priory Gate, and at Three Bullet Gate, but the force detailed under John Colclough to assault Market Gate failed to do so. The troops at these gates stood firm but gradually the insurgents forced their way through Three Bullet Gate. This was another action where the assaulting rebels had the advantage of attacking downhill. Three Bullet Gate was some way before the summit of a hill, and although reinforced by trenches, there was no cannon. It is important to remember that the militia, artillery and cavalry arrived on 3 June. This action took place early on 5 June leaving only one day for defences to be prepared. Once the rebels had the momentum of their attack going the militia had to gradually give way as they were outnumbered. They are supposed to have retreated to Rosbercon, but whether this included the whole garrison or the County of Dublin Militia is unclear. However the attack was brought to a halt by the cannon of the Main Guard under Sergeant Hamilton of the Donegals, and at the churchyard by the artillery under Captain Bloomfield, which commanded Mary Street and a part of Neville Street respectively, as well as the counter-attack led by General Johnson himself. It is noteworthy that the successful defence of Market Gate – which also faces uphill – was partly because the Clare Militia were deployed in strength beyond it in the Irishtown.[58] There is considerable doubt about how far the rebels penetrated into the town. Because of the bend at the bottom of Nevill Street, the cannon in the Market Place and churchyard could not command the Three Bullet Gate. The cannon at the Main Guard commanded Mary Street and South Street. There are a number of lanes leading off South Street to the quays where Tottenham and his Yeomen were stationed. They were inactive all day so it is unlikely that the rebels got as far as South Street. Therefore it can be assumed that having penetrated Three Bullet Gate the rebels advanced down Nevill Street, Mary Street, Michaels Street, Michaels Lane and Cross Street. Accounts are confused about whether or not they captured Priory Gate, but if they did, they got no further.

At about 8 a.m., there was a lull in the fighting and General Johnson, recognizing the importance of the check at the Main Guard, went across the river, rallied the troops there, led them back to the battle and made a push against the rebels which they were unable to withstand. The loss by the rebels was considerable; they were reduced to 2–3,000 men. The militia lost Colonel Lord Mountjoy of the County of Dublin who was captured and killed with 86 other officers and men, one officer and 58 wounded, with five officers and 76 missing.[59] 'The carnage was shocking', said Major Vesey who had taken command of the Dublins, 'as no quarter was given and the soldiers were much too exasperated and could not be stopped'.[60] Vesey also said, 'Had the rebels been properly trained and seasoned, and were they to fight in a loyal cause, how valuable to their country they would be. The devil in hell and all his troops of fallen angels (provided they were mortal) could not withstand them. I shall think more of Irish courage than ever I did in my life.'[61] McCormick, the retired cavalryman, made two comments. He said of Major Vesey, 'there was a soldier for you', and 'next and equal to him I believe I may justly mention Major Vandeleur of the Clare Regiment. You know the whole garrison spoke of them with admiration.'[62]

58 Hamilton was commissioned for his bravery and devotion to duty. See Chapter 5. The Market Gate still exists although in ruinous condition. 59 *Faulkner's Journal*, 9 June 1798. 60 Camden to Portland, 8 June 1798 (NA, HO/100/7 7/8 0). 61 Alexander, p. 79. 62 Ibid.,

Plate 3: New Ross: Nevill Street from Three Bullet Gate. Unless the streetscape has changed significantly, the artillery in the churchyard could not have a clear field of fire because of the bend at the bottom of the street.

The importance of this victory cannot be over estimated. The militia wavered but were not defeated, they remained true to their salt, and the experience of facing huge numbers of enemy, which is terrifying in itself, would have given the soldiers great confidence in their ability. General Johnson commended General Eustace (who was there in a subordinate but undefined role), Lieutenant-Colonel Craufurd, Lieutenant-Colonels Stewart of the 89th Foot, commanding the Light Infantry, Maxwell of the Donegals, and Majors Vesey of the Dublin County and Vandeleur of the Clares. He commented also on five officers shown as missing who 'thought proper to make a precipitate retreat at an time I stood much in need of every persons assistance. They passed over the bridge and reached Waterford, representing our situation in so unfavourable a light as to prevent the Roscommon Regiment who were within four miles of us from proceeding'.[63] Lieutenant-Colonel Robert Craufurd, who had just arrived in Ireland to assume the appointment of Assistant Quartermaster General, said in a letter to General Lake, 'The militia behaved with spirit but are *quite ungovernable*'.[64] [*s i c*]. On the other hand, the rebels had suffered a traumatic defeat, with a loss of leaders – always in

p. 8 1. **63** Maj.-Gen. H. Johnson to Lt.-Gen. Lake, 7 June 1798 (NA, HO/1 0 0/7 7/1 o 8). **64** Craufurd to Lake, 6 June 1798 (NAI, RP/620/38/62).

short supply – weapons and men. There was no incentive for the Kilkenny United Irishmen to rise and they failed to do so. The defeat marked the end of attempts to extend the rebellion westwards.

There are two contemporary accounts of the action. One is by Thomas Cloney who was in the rebel column assaulting the town, and the other by James Alexander, a loyalist schoolmaster in New Ross.[65] Cloney has to be treated with a certain amount of caution – he was a rebel leader who managed to avoid the hangman and as a result was careful to minimize his actions and to present them in as favourable a light as possible. He described the attack of the rebels on 5 June at Three Bullet Gate, the brave soldier who stood his ground there, the charge of the 5th Dragoons, the death of Ensign Dodwell, and the retreat of the defenders into the county of Kilkenny:

> The main body of General Johnson's army, after a resistance not so formidable as might have been expected from beloved champions of the Irish ascendancy fled before us over the bridge into the County of Kilkenny, leaving a party of the Clare Militia at its extremity, in a part called the Irishtown; the main guard also remained at the market house, not far from the bridge.[66]

Cloney also says he led an abortive attack on the Clare Militia position. He claimed that the garrison comprised 2,000 men, the insurgents 3,000, and that there were 300 killed on either side, with about 500 wounded. This is not a satisfactory account of the major battle of the rebellion by one who was heavily engaged in it. The accurate comment has been made about Cloney, 'The difficulty in which he found himself when he came to write his book was that he was trapped by the image which had so successfully been created, so the web of pretence and subterfuge was carried into print'.[67]

Alexander's account is not perfect either, but he did make the pertinent point at the outset, that the people involved in the battle only saw their little corner of it. He says he got out of bed on 5 June at 8.30 a.m. (Since he lived in the town, this is hard to believe, for the assault started at 5 a.m., and the noise must have been horrendous.) Then he went 'exploring' from which he painted a picture of a hard fought contest. He had a hero in a retired cavalryman named McCormick, who fought gallantly whilst wearing a brass helmet, and was everywhere at once. McCormick told Alexander that not more than 600 soldiers had fought in the battle.[68] Alexander also asserted

---

[65] Thomas Cloney, *A personal narrative of those transactions in the County of Wexford in which the Author was engaged, during the awful period of 1798* (Dublin, 1832), and James Alexander, *Some account of the first apparent symptoms of the late rebellion in the County of Kildare, and an adjoining part of King's County*. [66] Ibid., p. 38. [67] John Joyce, *General Thomas Cloney, a Wexford rebel of 1798* (Dublin, 1988), p. 52. [68] Alexander, p. 128. This could well be true –

Plate 4: New Ross: The Tholsel or Main Guard defended by Sgt. Hamilton. In 1798 the ground floor was an open arcade

that the rebels were in possession of the upper part of the town for a very few minutes, and that it was the Dublin County Battalion which had retreated across the bridge to Rosbercon.

At the time of the assault on the town about 150 Protestants and some Catholics were imprisoned in a barn at a place called Scullabogue. When news of the defeat reached the gaolers of these innocent men, women and children, the barn was set on fire and they were burnt to death. Some modern historians have argued that this was in retaliation for the deliberate burning of a hospital in New Ross during the battle that contained about seventy wounded rebels. These men were supposedly in a four-storey slated building at the top of Main (or Mary) Street which would put it more or less in the front line. This seems unlikely, for one thing a 'hospital' in the front line of a battle is unheard of, collections of wounded maybe, but there was a real hospital in Priory Street (which lends credence to the assumption that the rebels did not penetrate that far). In fact what we have is an interpretation of Alexander's account. He said that the building was being used by the rebels to fire on the advancing soldiers, and that Michael McCormick and one Roger Unsworth, a trumpeter in the Ross Cavalry got into the bottom of the build-

but if troops were not attacked in their defensive positions, they could not leave them unless ordered to do so by the commander.

ing, and set it on fire with the result that the rebels within were burnt to death – all save one who escaped. Alexander does not mention the words 'hospital' or 'wounded'.[69]

The following day, 6 June, in the north of County Wicklow, General Lake ordered General Needham to advance on Arklow from Loughlinstown Camp. Arklow had been abandoned after the defeat at Tubberneering, and on arrival Needham set about constructing defences in the town. On 7 June rebellion broke out in Ulster with the unsuccessful attack by the United Irishmen on Antrim town. The militia units involved were the Monaghan Regiment, and the 2nd Battalion Light Infantry, which comprised the light companies of the Kerry, Dublin City, Tipperary, Armagh, and Monaghan Militias. They arrived towards the end of the battle and confirmed the rebels' defeat. The situation now was that there was rebellion in counties Antrim and Down that was totally uncoordinated with rebellion in Wicklow and Wexford, which it was supposed to be.

General Johnston held New Ross, Colonel L'Estrange held Newtownbarry, and General Needham had arrived in Arklow. The northern army of the rebels held north Wexford but were uncertain of what to do next. They moved to Gorey, and resolved to attack Arklow. If they were successful the route to Dublin would be opened. They could equally have moved to attack Rathdrum with the possibility of the same result. It is not known why they did not, but Lake had obviously recognized the threat when he ordered Major Hardy there, as well as a strengthened company of the City of Dublin Regiment under Captain Giffard who is reported to have said:

> From Baltinglass I was despatched with 220 infantry under my command, to steal a march in the night, through the mountains, and through the armies of rebels that occupied them. This is the proudest moment of my life. General Dundas and General Duff know that through good providence I succeeded, threw myself into Rathdrum which I fortified in a manner much approved of by every officer who saw it, and thus covered Dublin, and prevented the enemy from turning the left of our wing.[70]

Arklow is another town built on heights that lead down to a river, in this case the River Avoca. The Avoca flows from west to east. Needham's forces numbering 1,335 infantry and 500 cavalry were in a crescent from west to east. Colonel Maxwell Barry commanded the Antrim Regiment and the Grenadier Company of the Londonderry in the west, Colonel Skerrit com-

---

69 See Tom Dunne, *Rebellions* (Dublin, 2004), pp 214-64. 70 Quoted in R.R. Madden, *The United Irishmen, their life and times* (Dublin, 1858), p. 294.

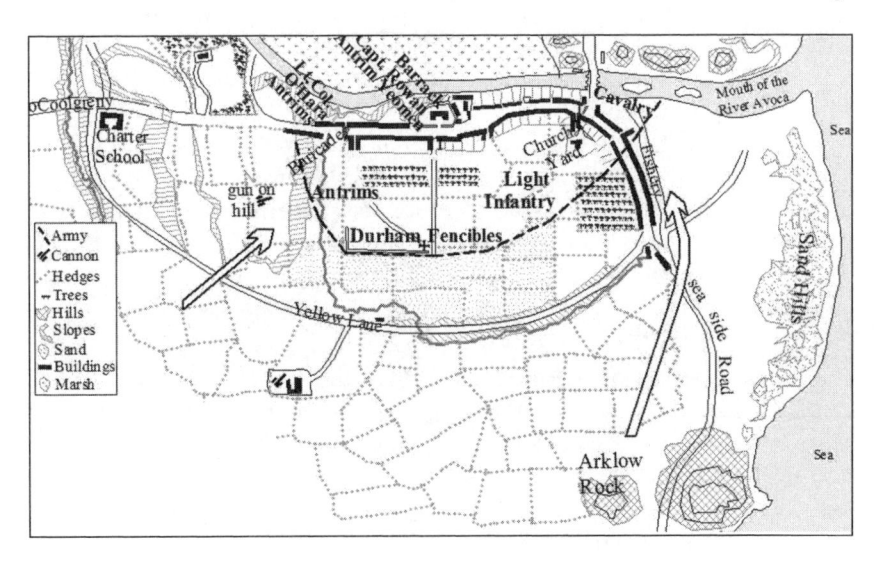

Map 6: Arklow town plan, 1798

manded the Durham and the Dunbarton Fencibles in the centre of the defences, and Lieutenant-Colonel Cope commanded the Armagh Regiment and Light Infantry in the east.

The rebels attacked on 9 June 1798, in two divisions. One division marched east and attacked the east of the town in an area known as the 'Fisheries', and the other attacked the western defences, defended by the Antrims. The fighting in the Fisheries was intense but eventually the rebels were forced to retire and were ridden down by the cavalry. The attacks in the west were defeated by the superior firepower of the garrison, and the defeated rebels retired to Gorey. This was the second serious defeat for the insurgent forces. They were now confined to the county of Wexford, and from this point on the rebellion began to collapse, with the result that actions involving the militia became smaller and more isolated.

Except, that is, in Ulster. When the Belfast stage was stopped at Santry, Co. Dublin on 23 May 1798, this signal for the start of the rising had no effect on the north of Ireland. Perhaps this is hardly surprising as Ulster had been virtually disarmed by General Lake in the preceding year. Many of the leaders of the United Irish movement had been seized by the military, and those that were left showed little enthusiasm for rebelling. Henry Joy McCracken became in effect the commander-in-chief. His plan was to launch simultaneous attacks on Randalstown and Antrim on 7 June to coincide with a meeting of magistrates in Antrim on that date. It was assumed that there would be similar activity in Co. Down with attacks on Ballynahinch, Saintfield, Newtownards, and Portaferry.

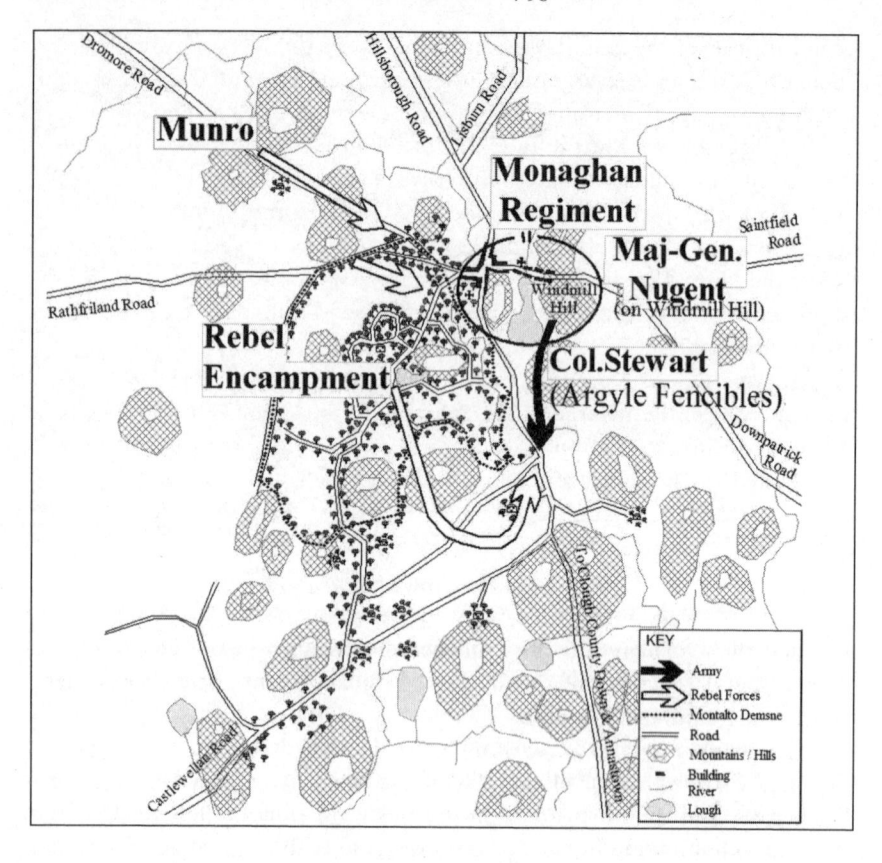

Map 7: Ballynahinch, 1798

    The attack on Antrim on 7 June was a failure. Suffice to say there was no militia involvement until the arrival of the Monaghan Regiment from Blaris in the latter stages of the battle when the rebels had been defeated. The town of Antrim was near the seat of Lord O'Neill at Shane's Castle. O'Neill was colonel of the Antrim Regiment and caught up in the fighting on his way home from Dublin, he was mortally wounded.

    The risings in Co Down were not coordinated with those in Antrim, any more than they were with those in the south of the country. On 9 June the insurgents inflicted a reverse on a mixed force of York Fencibles and local Yeomanry at Saintfield, some ten miles south of Belfast. Henry Munro, a linen draper from Lisburn, Co. Antrim, took command of the rebels. Like that of McCracken a few days earlier, this was a last minute appointment as those who had been in command refused to act. Munro moved his force of some 7,000 men from Saintfield to Ballynahinch. On 12 June, General Nugent, commanding in Ulster, marched from Belfast with the Monaghan regiment, part of the 22nd Dragoons, and artillery to Saintfield where he was joined by Colonel Stewart and 600 fencibles, making a total force of some 1,500 men. Nugent then marched his small army to Ballynahinch.

Ballynahinch is a town in the heart of the drumlin country of Co. Down. As a result it is built on small hills. It was and still is an important market town for mid Down. Munro camped his army in the Montalto demesne (home of Lord Moira), which adjoined the town. He was plagued with desertions, the United Irishmen from Killinchy went home, and the Defenders, supposedly allies of the United Irishmen, came to Ballynahinch but took no part in the fighting.

Munro attacked Nugent at dawn on 13 June. Despite losing many men to artillery fire, the insurgents pushed steadily into the centre of the town. Then, according to tradition, a bugle call made by the army to retreat was interpreted by the rebels as a signal to charge and they faltered. The army counter-attacked and pushed successfully against them. Nugent, however, described the action as follows:

> Accordingly about 3 o'clock in the morning having previously occupied two hills on the right and left of the town to prevent the rebels from having any other choice than the mountains in their rear for their retreat I sent Lt Coll Stewart to post himself with part of the Argyll Fencibles and some yeomanry, as well as a detachment of the 22nd Lt Dragoons, a situation where he could enfilade the rebel line; whilst Coll Leslie and part of the Monaghan Militia, some cavalry and Yeomen infantry should attack them on flank ... The rebels poured down with impetuosity upon Coll Leslie's detachment and even jumped into the road from the Earl of Moira's demesne to endeavour to take one of his guns but they were repulsed with slaughter. They attacked Lt Coll Stewart's detachment with the same activity but he repulsed them also and the fire from his howitzer obliged them to fly in all directions.[71]

Nugent thought that out of a total rebel force 4–5,000 men, they lost between three and four hundred killed. Nugent's force lost Captain Henry Evatt, adjutant of the Monaghan Militia, killed, Lieutenant Ellis of the same regiment badly wounded, as well as five others killed and 12 wounded, and several of the Yeoman infantry killed as well.[72] Munro was captured and executed, and the rising was effectively over in the north.

---

71 Gen. Nugent to Gen. Lake, 12 June 1798 (NAI, RP/620/33/129). 72 Ibid. The death of Capt. Evatt is the central theme of Thomas Robinson's famous painting, 'The battle of Ballynahinch 1798'.

The initiative now passed to General Lake. On 16 June he gave orders for the retaking of Co. Wexford. He knew that the rebellion in the north had been defeated, and the arrival of troops from Great Britain in Dublin protected his rear. The insurgents, defeated at Arklow, and now much depleted in numbers slipped away to cover their base at Vinegar Hill, beside Enniscorthy. Lake divided his army into three forces under the overall command of General Dundas. Generals Duff, Loftus, and Needham commanded these three forces, and they were to advance on Enniscorthy, supported by General Johnson from New Ross. Johnson was to advance to Old Ross and link up with Brigadier-General John Moore who was advancing with his Light Infantry to Foulkes Mills.

Moore reached Foulkes Mills on 20 June where he was attacked by a force of rebels sent from Wexford to oppose him. The battle that followed was critical, should Moore lose then the rebels could reinforce Vinegar Hill, but if Moore won, then the rebellion was doomed should Dundas's force take Vinegar Hill. Moore's force was 2nd Battalion Light Infantry, and the 5th Battalion 60th Regiment – the 'Yagers', a rifle regiment composed of Germans and other nationalities. The insurgents attacked Moore's force with their armed men in the centre, and their pikemen attempting to outflank Moore on the wings. What followed is a very good example of leadership in action. Moore said:

> The companies of light infantry, being unaccustomed to fire, hesitated a little. I was obliged to get off my horse to put myself at their head ... I met the light infantry ... all in the woods mixed and retreating. The enemy following close and firing. I succeeded in stopping some immediately, and got them to jump out of the road and make a front on each side of it. I then encouraged the rest first to halt, then to advance, and when I saw them ready for it, I took off my hat, put my horse into a trot, gave a huzza, and got them to make a push. The tide immediately turned.[73]

The insurgents' attack failed, and the commanders in Wexford realized that they would have to parlay for surrender.

Meanwhile Lake's force moved south to attack Vinegar Hill. His plan was to attack the hill in two columns under Generals Duff and Loftus, while at the same time General Johnson would assault Enniscorthy, and General Needham on the left of the assaulting force was to get around to the south of Vinegar hill in order to cut off any retreat. On 21 June the attacks went in. Johnson retook Enniscorthy but was held up by stiff resistance at the

---

73 Maurice, *Diary of Sir John Moore*, i, 297.

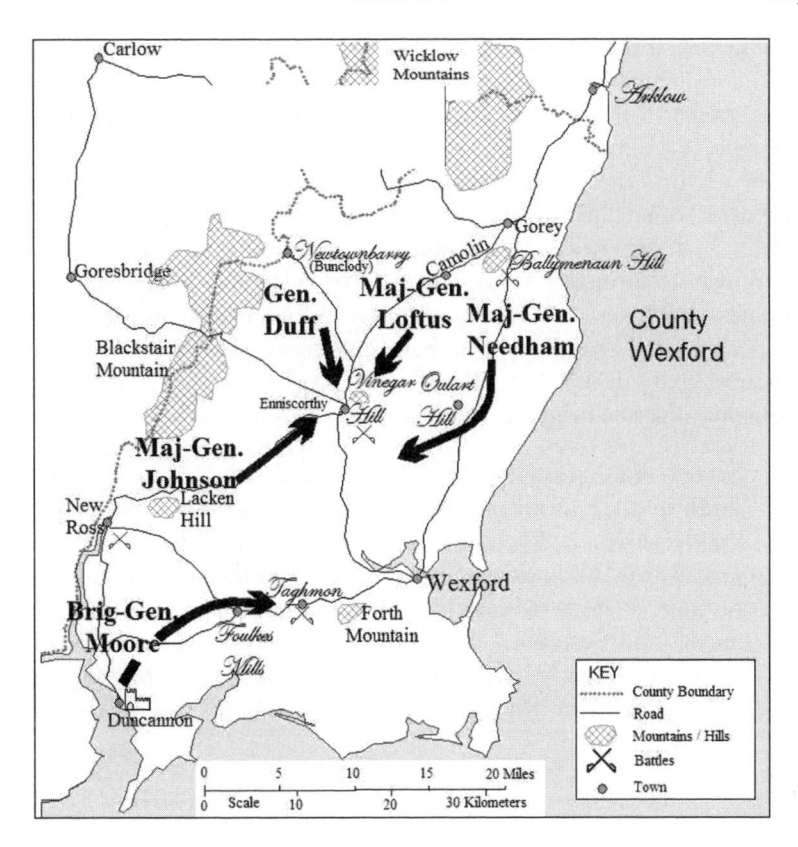

Map 8: Vinegar Hill, 21 July 1798. Army plan

bridge. However, the attacks on the hill itself were entirely successful and the position was captured in about an hour and a half. Needham failed to close the gap to the south (he was inconvenienced by contradictory orders, and the army's baggage), and it was through this gap that the surviving rebels escaped. The Irish militia provided the bulk of Lake's infantry, and also that of General Johnson. Lake had the 1st and 4th Light Battalions, the Armagh, Cavan, and Antrim Regiments as well as the Londonderry and Tyrone, and Johnston had the Donegal, Sligo, Meath, Roscommon, and Dublin County regiments. Vinegar Hill should have been very difficult to assault despite Lake's superiority in artillery because of the nature of the ground, but the rebels had made no attempt to fortify it during their occupation.

The insurgents who escaped divided into two groups. One group headed for the Wicklow Mountains, and the other, under Father John Murphy headed towards Kilkenny and the midlands in order to try to rekindle the seeds of rebellion there. The fortunes of the group led by Father Murphy have been well documented from the perspective of both the government and the insurgents. As a result it is possible to make an interesting comparison between them, not least because the Wexford rebels met the Wexford Regiment of Militia.

On 22 June the rebels had moved through the Scollogue Gap in the Blackstairs Mountains and had reached Goresbridge. There they surrounded a party of 25 men of the Wexford Regiment under Lieutenant Dixon, and forced them to surrender. Lieutenant Dixon was able to escape. The Wexford prisoners were taken to Hollymount Hill where six Protestant soldiers of the regiment and two cavalrymen were pointed out by a Private Brunton (or Bruslaun), and killed.[74] Miles Byrne, who many years later wrote his autobiography, described the incident:

> Several of the prisoners belonging to the Wexford Militia were put to death by their own comrades who, having met in our army many of their relatives, had been put at liberty ... One of the militia soldiers, named Bruslaun, was the prime instigator of this horrible and coward revenge. It appeared that he had been cruelly punished and flogged on the evidence sworn against him by these unfortunate men. He, of course, said in his defence, that they were all sworn Orangemen, and did everything in their power to have him and his fellow Catholic soldiers put to death.[75]

Byrne wrote his memoirs many years after the events he described. According to Musgrave, the soldiers of the Wexford Regiment were put to death on the express orders of Walter Devereux.[76] A year later a conspiracy was discovered in the Prince of Wales's Regiment in Guernsey. There are no details of what the conspiracy was, but information about one Private John Kelly was sought from Lieutenant-Colonel Abel Ram of the Wexford Regiment. Ram replied that,

> Kelly was one of the 25 men of the Regiment captured at Newbridge who pointed out the Protestants from the Roman Catholics to the Rebels on Hollymount Hill upon which eight Protestants and two dragoons were instantly murdered (as appeared at Devereux's trial). Alias Bruslaun, one of the greatest villains that ever disgraced a regiment.[77]

On 23 June Castlecomer was reinforced by a company of the Waterford Regiment, and another of the Downshire. This force met the rebels at

---

[74] Musgrave, *Rebellions*, p. 500.   [75] *Memoirs of Miles Byrne*, edited by his widow, 2 vols (Dublin, 1907) i, 158.   [76] Musgrave, *Rebellions*, pp 403 and 500.   [77] Memorial of Lt.-Col. Ram, n.d. (NA, HO/100/83/246).

Gurteen and was forced to retreat in a disorderly fashion back to Castlecomer where they occupied two houses beside the bridge and held off all attempts to dislodge them. There were negotiations for a surrender but the timely arrival of General Asgill from Kilkenny with the Wexford Regiment under Colonel Ram, and the Grenadier Company of the Wicklow brought relief. Asgill retreated back to Kilkenny. It was obvious to Father Murphy that the counties of Carlow and Kilkenny would not rebel, and he decided to retreat back to Wexford.

On the night of 25 June the rebels camped on Kilconnell or Kilcumney Hill, near Goresbridge. There was thick mist at dawn, when at 6am they were attacked by 1,200 men commanded by General Asgill, and 400 men of the Royal Downshire Regiment commanded by Major Matthews. The insurgents, about 5,000 strong were put to flight, they pushed through the Scollogue Gap, Father Murphy was captured, and his followers dispersed on the other side.

There are four contemporary accounts of the action that took place here in the early hours of the following morning. On the one hand there is that of Sir Charles Asgill, commander of the forces in Kilkenny,[78] and Major George Matthews, commanding officer of the Downshire Regiment,[79] and on the other hand, that of Miles Byrne, who was with the insurgents,[80] and Edward Hay, who was not there as far as is known, but who had undoubtedly been in Wexford, and was able to give a good description of what took place on that morning.[81] Asgill was interested in furthering his own reputation, Hay in deflecting accusations he had been a United Irishman who had been deeply involved in the rebellion, and Miles Byrne wrote his memoirs many years after the action. His is a very well known work, and is much used as an original contemporary source for the actions and intentions of the insurgents, but it must be treated with caution. Byrne wrote with the specific intention of restoring the fighting reputation of the rebels. As a result he was bombastic and boastful, his 'gunsmen' and pikemen were irresistible, never defeated, and never ran away, whilst all militia officers were cowards, their men savages, or just waiting to desert. Perhaps Major Matthews was the only one present that had nothing more than regimental pride and a determination to do his duty.

Asgill, in his account, considered the actions at Castlecomer and Kilcumney Hill to be the same battle. He claimed that the insurgents lost upwards of 1,000 men, ten cannon, arms, ammunition, and cattle.[82] Some

---

78 Sir Charles Asgill to Lord Castlereagh, 26 June 1798 (NAI, RP/620/3 80240). 79 George Matthews to Lord Downshire, 28 June 1798 (PRONI, D/607/F/281). 80 Byrne, *Memoirs*, p. 164. 81 Edward Hay, *History of the insurrection in the County of Wexford AD 1798* (Dublin, 1803), p. 257. 82 *Freeman's Journal*, 30 June 1798

soldiers of the Wexford Regiment, taken the previous day at Goresbridge were released (the survivors of Hollymount Hill). He lost only seven killed and wounded, and specifically mentions the assistance he received from Major Matthews. The Major, however, paints a somewhat different picture. He said that when he first saw the enemy, he sent a proposal to Asgill for a pincer attack on their flanks. Asgill refused. Matthews continued to follow the retreating insurgents for further twenty miles as they retreated through Queen's County, Kilkenny, and Carlow towards the Wicklow Mountains. (In fact Matthews and his men were on the march for 39 hours.) He then sent a second despatch to Asgill who agreed to a co-ordinated attack. The result was a defeat for the rebels. Matthews pointed out however, that he had acted contrary to orders, and that if he had done what Asgill had directed, he would never have brought the rebels to action. Matthews has a point, Asgill did behave timidly, but in his defence it must be borne in mind that he had only about 1,200 men and the rebels some 5,000. Asgill was showing a degree of prudence, well aware of what had happened to Major Lombard and the North Corks a few weeks previously.

Miles Byrne confirmed that the rebels were retreating back to Wexford, and were about 5,000 strong.[83] He said that there was thick fog on the morning of 26 June, but that he knew from his picquets that the army was almost upon them. He claimed that their pikemen dispersed Asgill's cavalry, and that the remainder of the force made an orderly retreat through the Scollogue Gap, on the other side of which they made a decision to disperse.[84] The trouble is that the fighting described by Byrne was that against a weak force guarding the pass, while he ignored the attacks made on Kilcumney Hill by Asgill and Matthews. It is five miles from Kilcumney Hill to Scollogue Gap, across rolling countryside, which lends credence to the account of the attack made by Matthews, and the assertion that the Yeoman cavalry were effective. It was Murphy's mounted men who effectively covered the retreat of their defeated force, and allowed those that survived to get away. Byrne also insisted that the rebels had no ordnance, or much in the way of supplies, but Asgill published his report that refutes this claim.[85] However, the list shows no powder for the cannon.

The account of Edward Hay has the ring of authenticity, Asgill's is self congratulatory, the major's straightforward, while Byrne's, written too long after the event, is evasive, and attempts to present everything as an orderly

---

[83] Byrne, *Memoirs*, p. 250.   [84] Byrne repeatedly made reference to the cowardice of cavalry in not attacking his pikemen. This is for the benefit of the non-military reader. Every soldier knew, or very quickly found out that horses cannot be made to attack a 'hedge' of pikes or bayonets, one reason why infantry 'formed square' against cavalry.   [85] *Freeman's Journal*, 30 June 1798.

retreat with a rational decision to disband after it. Evidently the 'fog of war' found on Kilcumney Hill on 26 June 1798 penetrated accounts of the action as well.

The northern group of rebels that headed towards the Wicklow Mountains believed there was a supply of arms and powder in Hacketstown, County Carlow. They were short of both and decided to make a diversion to capture them. On 25 June 1798, they assaulted the town and a vicious nine-hour battle ensued in which they were totally unsuccessful. Hacketstown was defended by Yeomen, and 50 men of the Antrim Regiment under the command of Lieutenant R.W. Gardner. After the action, Gardner realized that his men were exhausted, almost out of ammunition, and unable to withstand another assault so he retreated to Tullow.[86] After this defeat at Hacketstown, the heart went out of the rebellion. There were further actions, some successes, but desertions were increasing all the time, even though a small band under Miles Byrne joined the northern group, and they made their way as far north as County Louth, they could not raise the standard of rebellion and ended up in the mountains of Wicklow conducting a guerrilla campaign. The troops involved in this last stage of the rebellion included the Antrim, the King's County, and Louth Regiments, and the Limerick City and Leitrim Battalions.

The guerrilla campaign in the Wicklow Mountains conducted by Joseph Holt included a large number of deserters from the militia, and in particular from the Antrim and King's County Regiments. In the case of the former it is possible that the Antrim-born rebels who had migrated to west Wicklow (before the rebellion), had an influence on this. According to Holt himself, he had 28 deserters from the Antrims, and no less than 30 from the King's County.[87]

The pay lists and muster rolls of the Antrim Regiment show that in the four year period between 31 March 1794 and 31 March 1798, the regiment had 42 deserters. In the period 20 April to 30 September 1798, the regiment had no less than 49 deserters (the paymaster claimed 58 but the records do not support this figure). In the period immediately following 30 September 1798, they had one. The King's County record in the same period between 1794 and 1798 is not as good, they had 82 deserters, but in the period April to September 1798, they had at least 41.[88] This is prima facie evidence that the Wicklow rebels were allowing themselves to be recruited into these two regiments, receiving some training and arms, and then deserting with them. Militia regiments recruited where they were stationed, and it is known that the 49 deserters of the Antrim's were natives of Co. Wicklow.

---

86 Lt. R.W. Gardner to Lord Castlereagh, 26 June 1798 (NAI, RP/620/38/239). 87 Peter O'Shaughnessy (ed.), *Rebellion in Wicklow: General Joseph Holt's personal account of 1798* (Dublin, 1998), p. 161. 88 Pay lists and muster rolls, Antrim Militia (NA, WO/13/2574), King's County Militia (ibid., WO/13/2961).

It has been shown here that in almost all the principal actions of the rebellion the government was dependent on the militia as the major part of the infantry. In most of the modern accounts of the various actions the involvement of the militia has not been distinguished, indeed, it has frequently been ignored. The principal engagements and the degree of militia involvement can be summarized as follows:

	Action	Proportion of Militia in infantry engaged
24 May 1798	Naas	100 per cent
	Kilcullen	None
	Prosperous (defeat)	100 per cent
25 May 1798	Carlow	Not known–60 per cent?
27 May 1798	Oulart Hill (defeat)	100 per cent
28 May 1798	Enniscorthy	27 per cent
1 June 1798	Newtownbarry	61 per cent
4 June 1798	Tubberneering (defeat)	Almost all
5 June 1798	New Ross	100 per cent
7 June 1798	Antrim	100 per cent
9 June 1798	Arklow	64 per cent
12 June 1798	Ballynahinch	33 per cent (estimate)
21 June 1798	Vinegar Hill	65 per cent (estimate)
26 June 1798	Kilconnell Hill	100 per cent
5 July 1798	Whiteheaps	100 per cent (estimate)

Table 15: 1798 rebellion, militia involvement

Of numerous other engagements in which there was no militia involvement, perhaps the only one of note was Saintfield. The strategically important battles were those of 24 and 25 May 1798, which prevented the insurgents creating a ring around Dublin to stop government reinforcement of the city; New Ross which prevented the rebellion moving west, or north up the Barrow Valley, and dealt a severe blow to the morale and numbers of insurgents; and Antrim and Ballynahinch which prevented the north being lost; Arklow which stopped the northern advance of the insurgents, and Vinegar Hill which finally broke the rebellion in the south. We have seen that militia involvement in all of these actions was crucial to success, and thus Professor Hayes-McCoy made an appropriate comment, however inadvertently.

When the rebellion came the government was ill prepared. General Lake had taken over from Abercromby less than one month, and had had no opportunity to make his mark. He did not have the full confidence of the lord lieutenant in any case. The brunt of the fighting had to be borne by the militia; the government had no choice, since reinforcements from Great Britain did not arrive until July. In every action the militia were outnumbered, and the courage required of inexperienced troops to face what appeared to be overwhelming forces of insurgents was considerable, and has rarely been appreciated. It must be said that the discipline of the regiments held together. Once the militiamen had gained the experience of standing firm and dispersing mobs descending upon them, by volley fire, they became very difficult troops to defeat.

Rebel successes at Oulart Hill, Enniscorthy, and the first part of the battle of New Ross, were achieved by ferocious assaults made downhill, which were extremely difficult to stop without artillery because of the intensity of the charge and its speed. Although it was the artillery at New Ross that turned the tide, they were sited in the churchyard and at the Main Guard, some distance from Three Bullet Gate, while at Ballynahinch where the rebels made a similar ferocious charge, General Nugent had artillery to help disperse them. However, once this initial assault had been brought to a halt or had 'run out of steam', the rebels were vulnerable to counter-attack, as at Newtownbarry or New Ross. In both cases, the lack of junior officers and non-commissioned officers in the rebel army was most noticeable. It was not plunder, drink, or exhaustion which necessarily led to their defeat but a failure to consolidate gains, a task for which junior officers of whatever rank were essential, and the rebels had a fatal shortage of them. In a previous chapter it has been shown that the militia had a ratio of 1:5 or 1:7 private men to non-commissioned-officers, and two important actions, the defence of the Main Guard at New Ross, and the defence of Borris House, also in Co. Wexford, were made by men under the command of sergeants.

The militia were at their most confident when fighting behind walls or barricades as at Borris House, Hacketstown, Castlecomer, or at Arklow. But equally they could take on the rebels in the open when they were making the attacks as at Ballymenaun Hill, Newtownbarry, the counter-attack at New Ross, Ballynahinch, Vinegar Hill and Kilconnell Hill. The support of artillery must not be underestimated either. It prevented defeat at New Ross, it prevented the capture of Arklow, and played a crucial role in the capture of Vinegar Hill.

Finally, the quality of leadership must not be forgotten. This was the most crucial element in government success. The militia in this phase of the rebellion had good leadership – L'Estrange of the King's County, Cope of the Armagh, Matthews of the Royal Downshire, Maxwell of the Donegal, Hardy of the Antrim, and Vandeleur of the Clare were all good officers. Matthews in fact was mentioned in despatches twice for meritorious service, as Maxwell was for Wexford, Vesey and Vandeleur for New Ross, and Hardy for Ballinamuck where he was assistant quartermaster general of General Lake's division.

The rebellion was effectively over by July, although depredations continued for some time afterwards in isolated areas, particularly the Wicklow Mountains. Cornwallis had arrived in Ireland to take over as lord lieutenant and commander-in-chief. He turned his attentions to pacifying the country by a policy of firmness and leniency, and to the great object of a union of the British and Irish parliaments. Much of the destruction caused by the rebellion now had to be paid for, and this included the damage caused by the military in their journeys across Ireland. Calculations of this damage occupied the following three years. Some problems returned, attempts were still made to seduce militiamen from their allegiance, and there continued to be disaffection in some militia units. The proper role of the armed forces remained undecided, and the threat of an invasion from France was ever present.

CHAPTER EIGHT

A period of change: 1798–1802

The French invasion of Connacht being so well documented, I do not intend to consider all the details of the invasion, but only the involvement of the militia, which, of course, was considerable. There were three main actions – at Castlebar, Collooney, and Ballinamuck – and of these the first is by far and away the most controversial. It was another action in which the militia was defeated, one where much opprobrium was heaped upon them, and one in which this opprobrium has never been adequately countered, mainly because the lord lieutenant, Lord Cornwallis, never ordered an enquiry. As a result, the militia has been blamed for the defeat, and no alternative explanations for it have been explored.

Separating fact from the fiction surrounding the battle of Castlebar is difficult, but not entirely impossible. The problem is twofold. First, almost all contemporary British accounts of the action were written by people who were not there; maps were published which were inaccurate; and the actions and plans of the generals were glossed over. Second, many historians both at the time and since, have seized on the battle as the one thing in the 1798 rebellion which demonstrated how French military assistance would have been effective. There was also, probably a measure of political expediency in ascribing the defeat to the poor quality of the Irish militia soldiers and disaffection in the regiments, since this proved to contemporaries that the defence of Ireland was best handled by a Westminster government. French accounts of the action are equally unreliable, having been written for the benefit of the Directory in Paris, and for overstating what actually happened. However, in this battle a small homogeneous French force, accustomed to operating together and with active service experience, was commanded by a man who out thought his opponents and achieved surprise. This general was Jean Joseph Amable Humbert, who had suppressed the royalist rebellion in La Vendée. Humbert was somewhat impetuous. He had been ordered to land in Ireland and await reinforcements but had been unwilling to play a waiting game. He conducted a successful landing, but instead of doing as he had been ordered, marched to attack the crown forces. He was a capable commander as he proved at Castlebar where he was able to change his tactics during the battle, showing that he retained control of his men and their deployment. Nevertheless by marching south from Killala, Humbert left himself dangerously exposed, and unable to link with subsequent reinforcements from France.

The composition of his force of 1,025 men is given in table 16:

'Le 2e bataillon 70e ½ brig. d'inf. de ligne	843 h.
Une compagne de grenadiers France	51
Un detacht du 3e regt de chasseurs à cheval	43
Un detacht de la 11e Cie de cannoniers volent	42
Un general de brigade commandant en chef	1
Deux adjutants generaux	2
Officiers d'etat-major ou à la suite	39
Officiers de santé	4'

Table 16: French invasion force, August 1798

They brought with them 3,000 muskets, 400 pistols, three cannon, and four cannon with caissons.[1]

Major-General John Hely Hutchinson commanded the government forces in the western district. When the French arrived, he had been in command for two weeks.[2] He had some 4,000 odd troops in his district, but these men were spread out all around the province of Connacht, and were further subdivided into small detachments, serving where the need arose. Hutchinson himself was based in Galway. Cornwallis ordered that General Lake was to take command in Connacht, to assemble his forces in Galway, and he was not to risk action before a sufficient force had been assembled.[3] Meanwhile Hutchinson had advanced to Castlebar with the Kerry Militia and had ordered other forces within his command to join him there. Cornwallis was not happy with this. He thought, wisely, that it was much too near the enemy, and it exposed Hutchinson to surprise attack before the troops had gathered.[4] (Castlebar is 25 miles from Killala, and 18 from Ballina via Foxford.) Hutchinson ordered the Fraser Fencibles to join him from Tuam, 26 miles from Castlebar, the Kilkenny Regiment from Loughrea, 55 miles away, and the Longford Battalion from Ennis, 80 miles away. The troops marched rapidly (the Irish militia could march prodigious distances) – the Kerry and the Kilkenny arrived in two days, the Longford in three. Hutchinson arrived in Castlebar on 25 August 1798, and immediately despatched the Kerry Regiment and some regulars to Foxford, some ten miles towards Ballina on the road on the east side of Lough Conn, which separated Castlebar from Ballina. The reason for this is not known, but it weak-

---

[1] Nuala Costello (ed.), 'Two diaries of the French expedition, 1 7 9 8' in *Analecta Hibernica*, 11 July 1941, 12. [2] Marquis Cornwallis to Lt.-Gen. the earl of Clanricard, 1 3 Aug. 1798 (NLI, KP/1133/134). [3] Maurice, *Diary of Sir John Moore*, i, ch. xiii. [4] Ibid.

ened his force before it had assembled. Furthermore, we do not know what orders he gave to this force, or what reconnaissance he had carried out on the approaches to Castlebar from the north, all extremely important. On the face of it, there was inadequate reconnaissance, if any, and Hutchinson had divided his force in the face of the enemy without the two parts being mutually supporting, or in communication with each other. Such an action was to court military disaster, but in doing this Hutchinson was planning his moves to attack the French, rather than putting himself in the position of the French, and thinking about how they would attack him. This is an essential part of planning for battle, and his failure to appreciate possible French moves shows inexperience of active service command at general staff level, which was commented on later by Cornwallis, as we will see.

The size of Hutchinson's force has been a subject of controversy, confusion arising over the number of troops in his district, and the number available to him. Hutchinson himself added to this confusion, by claiming that he had 4,000 men available. Sir Henry McAnally, who as a retired civil servant was nothing if not meticulous, considered all the widely differing accounts of the size of the British force, and came to the conclusion that it amounted to no more than 1,100 infantry, and 500 cavalry.[5] McAnally's case was well argued, and may well be correct, though the Longford's four companies would have amounted to about 330 men, and the Kilkenny's six companies would have amounted to about 480 men, which gives a combined total rather more than the 750 estimate made by Sir Henry.[6] The Kerry Regiment, despatched to Foxford under General Taylor, comprised about 600 men.[7] About 800 French opposed Hutchinson, with a number of Irish auxiliaries of doubtful military value. Whether or not the British generals were aware of the size of this force is a moot point. Hutchinson had made contingency plans in case of attack, based on a French approach by Foxford, but it is quite possible that he did not believe that the French were likely to bother him just at that time. What lends credence to this idea is that when he handed over command to General Lake, who arrived at 11 p.m. on the evening of 26 August 1798, Lake retired to bed, which is hardly the act of a newly arrived commander who was likely to be attacked at any time. Their plans were based on the assumption that they would make an assault on the French, not that the French would attack. At the same time as Lake arrived in Castlebar, so too, did the Longford Militia, after three days on the road. They spent a disturbed night camped on the mall in Castlebar.

The French, who may have had better intelligence about the British than the British had about them, debouched from the hills above Castlebar before

---

5 Sir Henry McAnally, 'The government forces engaged at Castlebar', in *IHS*, 4:16 (1945).
6 Pay Lists and Muster Rolls, Longford and Kilkenny Militia (NA, WO/13/3059, and 2942).
7 Pay Lists and Muster Rolls, Kerry Militia (ibid., WO/13/2902).

five in the morning, having marched overnight down the west side of Lough Conn, a longer but not difficult route, except for the climb to the pass through the Barnagheera Gap. On the southern side of the gap, the ground fell in a series of ridges and depressions to Castlebar. It was rough, boggy country, with hedges, outcrops of rock, scrub and bogland. There were few trees. The government army formed up to oppose the French about a mile north of Castlebar, on a flattish depression between Rathbawn lake, and Tucker's lake, which were about 1,000 yards apart, west to east. It was very rough country, quite unsuitable for cavalry, which placed a premium on the skirmishing skills of light infantry.

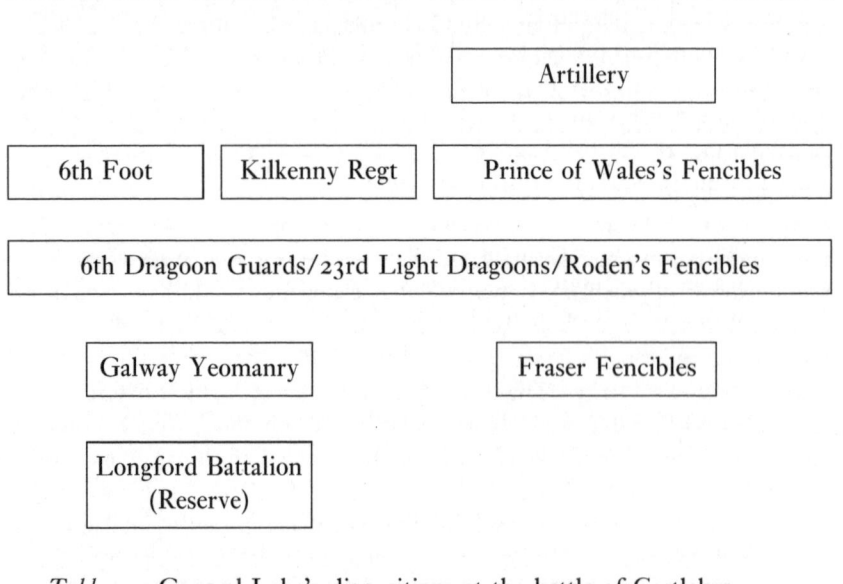

		Artillery
6th Foot	Kilkenny Regt	Prince of Wales's Fencibles
6th Dragoon Guards/23rd Light Dragoons/Roden's Fencibles		
Galway Yeomanry		Fraser Fencibles
Longford Battalion (Reserve)		

Table 17: General Lake's dispositions at the battle of Castlebar

When the French attacked in column, they were beaten off. The French then deployed into line, and attacked the whole of the British front line simultaneously while making left and right flanking movements using cover, and making a galling fire on the soldiers in the line, as was intended, for these were light infantry tactics, and volley fire did not have great effect.[8] It is at this point that histories of this battle say that the line broke, and that the Kilkenny, the Longford, and the others ran away. This story was repeated throughout the army with embellishments, not helped by the fact that some men of the Longford and the Kilkenny did indeed desert to the enemy. 'An

8 H.A. Richey, *A short history of the Royal Longford Militia, 1793–1893* (Dublin, 1894), ch. iii.

officer,' who in fact was not present at the battle, and in the map accompanying his account, showed that the French advanced by Foxford, published the principal account of the battle, which encouraged this view.[9] This account brought a little known, but important riposte, which, though obviously anonymous, was written by an officer of the Kilkenny Regiment who was present at the battle.[10] The writer corrects the mistake about the route of the French, and points out that in the battle itself the regiments were doing very well against the French, and gaining in confidence, when they were suddenly and without reason ordered to withdraw. This order was repeated twice, and the men did face about and retreat, but they had surrendered the commanding ground to the enemy, and fell into confusion when the enemy seized it. 'The enemy, instead of retreating, as they were preparing to do, instantly rushed forward, and gained the advantageous ground which our troops *by order* [*sic*] quitted; the whole were in motion, confusion ensued, and as there was no plan of retreat, it became extremely disorganized.'[11] This is a diplomatic way of saying that the British battle line became a shambles, an impression reinforced by another account of the Kilkennys:

> The Kilkenny Regiment formed a portion of the first line of the British force under the command of Lord Ormonde. The French advanced in close column ... Lord Ormonde ... but twice gave the very intelligible word of command, "Kilkennies, make ready, fire!" and two volleys were fired at the French ... whilst the Kilkenny Regiment was displaying great steadfastness before the enemy an ADC from the generals arrived with orders that they should retire. Lord Ormonde consulted Colonel Wemys ... madness of any retrograde movement ... declined to act, mistake of messenger. Major William Cunningham of the Aberdeenshire Fencibles received the same directions ... but consulting with Lord Ormonde and Colonel Wemys declined to act. A second ADC from the general rode up to Lord Ormonde with a pre-emptory order they should retire and a threat of punishment for disobedience of orders.[12]

---

9 *Impartial relation of the military operations which took place in Ireland in consequence of the landing of a body of French troops under General Humbert in August 1798,* by an officer who served in the corps under command of His Excellency Marquis Cornwallis (Dublin, 1799). The 'officer' was believed to be Captain Herbert Taylor, aide-de-camp to Cornwallis. The map, however, was repeated in Musgrave, *Rebellions,* and also in Bartlett & Jeffery (eds), *Military history of Ireland,* p. 252, despite its error. 10 Anonymous, *Observations on a pamphlet published by an officer entitled 'Impartial relation of the military operations which took place in Ireland'* (Dublin, 1799). 11 Ibid. 12 'Sketch of the history of the old Kilkenny Regiment of Militia', *Kilkenny Moderator,* 1859.

It is probable that the cavalry, stationed between the first and second lines of the infantry received the same order and this caused their precipitate and disastrous retreat in which they over-ran the Longford Battalion standing in reserve. In the ensuing confusion men were ready to advance or stand fast, but to retreat in an orderly fashion under fire was an extremely difficult operation for even well trained regular troops. Ormonde broke his sword attempting to rally his men, and Captain Murphy rescued the regimental colours.[13] In fact General Lake had no option but to retire as he was being outflanked.

The Longford, who subsequently held the bridge in Castlebar under Lords Granard and Ormond, had 28 killed, and 138 wounded and taken prisoner, and the Kilkenny lost 10 men killed, and 22 men wounded and taken prisoner.[14] Of the men who were captured, some five of the Kilkenny, and 50 of Longford are supposed to have joined the French subsequently. However, the point has to be made that there was no evidence of any disaffection in the troops during the action, all witnesses agreed that they obeyed orders, and did their duty.

The effect on the army of Castlebar was considerable, and immediately the Longford and the Kilkenny became the scapegoats. Hutchinson sent a report of the action to Cornwallis, with his resignation, as he had heard that his conduct had met with the lord lieutenant's 'disapprobation'.[15] He claimed that he had near 4,000 men, and, estimating the enemy to be not above 1,000, had advanced rapidly against them to prevent them either plundering property or organizing a civil war. He had arrived at Castlebar on Friday, 24 August, and General Lake arrived on the Sunday night. He described the action as that of a small French force fighting desperately against huge odds, whilst knowing that his cavalry, and the force at Foxford had cut off their retreat. 'There is too much reason to imagine that two of the regiments had been previously tampered with, the hope of which disaffection induced the French to make the attack, ... against a very superior body of troops, as their retreat on Killala and Ballina was cut off.' He also made the valid point that he did not place General Lake under the necessity of fighting, and, without blaming Lake for engaging the enemy, argued that he (Hutchinson), should not be blamed for the defeat. This was a shamelessly evasive letter, in which Hutchinson attempted to pass blame for the defeat on to subversion of the militia regiments, for which he had only the evidence of what had happened after the battle, rather than on the flawed dispositions and lack of command and control exhibited by Lake and himself. It availed him little.

13 Ibid. Murphy later became the step-father of the discoverer of the North-West Passage when he married Mrs McClure. 14 Pay Lists and Muster Rolls, Longford and Kilkenny Militia (NA, WO/13/3061 and 2942). The final figure for those killed is difficult to ascertain, but in the entire rebellion the Longford lost 48 men, and the Kilkenny 68. See the Army Medical Board Report, 31 Dec. 1800 (NAS, GD 364/1 129/2). 15 *Cornwallis Correspondence*, ii, 410 ff.

Cornwallis, who otherwise thought highly of Hutchinson, did not accept the substance of his report. He replied in a very direct manner, saying what he thought, and this reply probably shows why there was no official enquiry. He wrote that he thought Hutchinson guilty of an error of judgment, which an inexperienced general was liable to commit. He also contradicted Hutchinson, saying that he understood that he had no more than 1,000 infantry with him, when he 'exposed' himself to be attacked by the French, and, 'considering that your troops had never seen a regular enemy, I think it would not have been prudent or advisable to place that corps in such a situation as to be subject to receive an attack, or make a precipitate retreat.'[16]

Cornwallis was undoubtedly right, but there were other factors in the defeat that need to be taken into account. We have already seen that Cornwallis thought Hutchinson was forming up far too close to the enemy, so rendering himself liable to surprise, and that he divided his force into two parts, not mutually supporting, and not in communication with each other. To this must be added that Lake decided to fight a battle on ground not of his own choosing, with a force that was not homogeneous, and had never faced an enemy in open field. Moreover, the Galway Yeomanry were totally untrained for this type of action, while the Longford Battalion, who had only arrived in Castlebar at 11 p.m. the night before, were very tired after a three days forced march, and quite probably had not had a hot meal. There are doubts about reconnaissance created by a sight of the battlefield which gives the impression that the decision to fight on this ground was taken on the morning of the battle, before the French reached it. Lake reveals here an impetuosity that was not in his character. His decision to fight this battle has never been adequately examined. His actions in the north of Ireland in 1797, and subsequently in India against the Mahrattas, show that he was decisive and bold, but not impetuous. Perhaps he underestimated the French; perhaps the circumstances he found on arrival were controlling him rather than the other way round; perhaps he was too keen to impress after his success in disarming the north, and promotion to commander-in-chief which was followed immediately by demotion.

His force lacked unity. It was composed of regulars, yeomen, fencibles, and militia. The yeomen would have received almost no military training, fighting in the line was not part of their remit; none would have trained together, and the units themselves, because of the type of duties they had, would not have had the opportunity to train as a complete formation. The Longford marched from Ennis where they were divided into detachments at Clare Castle, Kilrush, Sixmilebridge, Newmarket, Bradford, Tuamgraney and Tullo.[17] Lake's force was very much an 'ad hoc' creation which lacked

16 Ibid. 17 Richey, *History*.

skill, manoeuvrability, and, on the day, good generalship. 'That we were surprised was known to every drummer boy, that the generals were unaware of the strength of the enemy, that they had no plans and that they did not know what they were doing was patent.'[18] Credence is lent to this statement by the fact that the ground Lake chose to fight on was no use for cavalry, which made his effective force not much greater than the French. It was a position that could easily be outflanked, as Lake did not have enough troops for an engagement in the open field: indeed, he had barely enough to defend Castlebar by fortifying the town.

There may well have been other lesser know reasons for the defeat. Lieutenant-Colonel William Westenra of the King's County Regiment confided in his diary:

> It appears that General Lake leaving Dublin on Saturday 2 5th and after travelling by Galway in search of the troops collecting under Generals Hutchinson and Trench he overtook them at Castlebar – making such dispositions as they said were befitting the occasion in order shortly to move against the enemy – according to their account not attempting to move from Killala 17 miles from Castlebar. But so false and ill founded was this report that if General Lake trusted to it and was surprised next morning on his post, the disgrace of the army, and the danger of encouraging insurrection will no doubt awaken the attention of the government and the nation to that destructive system so long carried on in the Western District by which insubordination has been encouraged and all zeal for the service almost stifled since the appointment of the present staff in those quarters.[19]

Westenra was repeating what was probably common gossip in military circles, that the Western District had been badly commanded, that ill discipline and insubordination were commonplace, that the staff were incompetent and that General Lake was foolish to believe any summation they had made of the enemy's intentions. He also makes the relevant point that Hutchinson had disobeyed Cornwallis's orders to remain in Galway and concentrate his forces there. This all points to muddle and confused thinking in the conduct of the battle which was a sure recipe for disaster.

An important factor in this defeat was the effect of the withdrawal of the light companies from the two militia regiments. When the French enveloped the front line using cover, the line had no answer to the galling fire that they had to endure. Volley fire was of limited use; light infantry were needed, but

---

18 Ibid.   19 Lt.-Col. Wm Westenra, *Notes and a General Memorandum of the Rebellion in Ireland 1798/99* (NAS GD/38/1/1253/27, Dalguise Muniments).

they were elsewhere with the light battalions. Lake obviously realized this, and in his next appointment, commanding the Southern District, in October 1798 he ordered that a certain number of men in every regiment in his district were to be trained to act as light infantry, and gave the details of what they were to be expected to do.

> It is General Lake's orders that a certain number of men in every regiment of the Southern District be immediately trained to act as light infantry, to practice firing at the target until they are perfect marksmen. In regiments whose light companies are with them, the whole of the light company and one man in twenty of the battalion companies are to be trained. Where the light company is detached one man in twelve is to be so trained.[20]

The light companies were always armed with muskets, not rifles, so accuracy with this weapon was possible given powder of good quality.

Regiments also had sought to find a solution to the loss of their light companies using their own initiative. In the final phase of the French incursion, the recapture of Ballina, Major-General Trench, the commander, praised all who helped him, especially the Kerry, Downshire, and Armagh Militia. 'I derived much advantage', he said, 'from 50 men of the Downshire Regiment, trained by Major Matthews as sharpshooters, and who under his command with a party of the Roxburgh Light Dragoons, formed my advance guard.'[21] This success was obviously noted in other regiments. The Louth Regiment, another that was regarded highly, was given authority to form sharpshooters in March 1799, comprising 64 rank-and-file, with 3 sergeants, and to be armed with 'short muskets' (the 1768 pattern musket, at this time being superseded in the regular army by the new 1793 land pattern),[22] but in the following month, a request by the North Cork for arms to form sharpshooters was refused.[23] Nevertheless the loss of the light company continued to be recognized as a problem until 1801, when all adopted General Lake's solution.

Castlebar was a disaster for the militia, redeemed to a large extent by two further actions in this French invasion. The first of these was at Collooney, near Sligo. After remaining some days at Castlebar, the French moved in the direction of Sligo. On 5 September 1798 Lieutenant-Colonel Charles Vereker, of the City of Limerick Battalion, commanding officer in Sligo, received news that the French and their Irish auxiliaries had reached Collooney, so he sent

---

20 General Order, Southern District, 9 Oct. 1798 (NA, WO/68/221). 21 Maj.-Gen. E.P. Trench to the Lord Lieutenant, 24 Sept. 1798 (ibid., HO/100/82/172). 22 E.B. Littlehales to Col. T. Foster, 29 Mar. 1799 (NLI, KP/1084/165). 23 E.B. Littlehales to Lt.-Col. Hodder, 11 Apr. 1799 (ibid., KP/1084/223).

out a patrol of the 24th Dragoons to find out what was happening. The officer who commanded the patrol, returned and told Vereker that there were no more than 300 rebel infantry in that place. Colonel Vereker immediately marched with 200 men of his regiment, arriving at Collooney at 3 p.m. He attacked the town, but found that instead of attacking the van, as he had thought, he had engaged the whole French force, which was more than twice the size of his own. He was outflanked, and had to retreat, losing his two curricle guns (but no ammunition), Lieutenant Rumley and six of his men were killed, 27 were wounded, and three officers and 65 rank-and-file captured. However, the French had lost 20 killed and 30 wounded.[24] It was a stiff, albeit brief contest.

The French marched off in the direction of Manorhamilton (though they turned south before it). Colonel Vereker, by his action, unsuccessful though it was, was credited with saving Sligo, and was rewarded by the City and Corporation of Limerick with an inscribed sword. The officers received £50 for plate for their mess, and each man received a silver medal.[25] Vereker had served in the 1st Foot (the Royals),[26] and undoubtedly thought he was attacking the van of the French force. Cornwallis thought their 'mistaken confidence' unfortunate,[27] while Bartholomew Teeling, captured at Ballinamuck, told Edward Cooke that the Limerick Militia behaved gallantly at Collooney, but were 'ill posted and ill conducted'.[28] The point is, however, that the regiment had confidence in its colonel, and, despite Teeling's strictures, was greatly outnumbered. None of the men deserted to the French, and this was a regiment much suspected of being subverted in 1797. Their behaviour stands in stark contrast to that of the Longford and Kilkenny, and tends to reinforce the claim that Castlebar degenerated into confusion over the order to 'retreat'.

The French were finally brought to bay at Ballinamuck, which was a most confused, if brief action. The force commanded by Cornwallis, which never ceased to cover Dublin since he believed the city to be always the prime objective of the French, comprised four divisions, commanded by Major-Generals Campbell, Hutchinson, Hunter, and Moore, with 7,824 men. Lake was shadowing the French. Campbell commanded fencibles, Hutchinson commanded the Antrim, Downshire, and Armagh Regiments of Militia, Hunter commanded two of the three battalions of regulars, and the Louth Militia, and Moore the third battalion of regulars, two battalions of Irish light infantry, and two companies of English militia.[29] Most of this force was not

---

24 Lake to the Adjutant General, 6 Sept. 1798 (PRONI, MIC 67/133. Lake-Hewitt correspondence).   25 Records of the Limerick Artillery Militia (NA, WO/6 8/59). The National Museum of Ireland possesses one of the medals.   26 The Royal Scots.   27 *Cornwallis correspondence*, p. 401.   28 Edward Cooke to William Wickham, 11 Sept. 1798, quoted in *Cornwallis correspondence*, p. 404.   29 An officer, *Impartial relation*.

involved in the battle, except the light company of the Armagh, who charged the French and captured the regimental colour of the 2nd battalion of the 70th Demi-Brigade of the French Army.[30] 'The 3rd Light Infantry, and part of the Armagh Militia, the only infantry that were engaged, behaved most gallantly and deserve my warmest praise', said General Lake, no doubt much relieved.[31] Ironically, all the units engaged in the action were Irish militia.

From the perspective of the crown forces, one of the reasons for the defeat at Castlebar was the confusion created by the orders to withdraw. The Longford and the Kilkenny, and no doubt the fencibles as well, were asked to perform a manoeuvre for which they had obviously had little or no training. An order to 'retreat' without clear detailed instructions, which is what appears to have happened, was a manoeuvre that was extremely difficult for troops to perform under fire and in the face of the enemy, which needed much practice, experience, and confidence. For the inadequately trained soldiers of the Irish militia it was an impossibility that was exacerbated by a lack of calm, clear command and control by the generals. Lake and Hutchinson could have foreseen this, but, as Cornwallis said, there was inexperience in the practice of generalship on that day.

Collooney was also a failure, strictly speaking. However, at this action the men were led with some vigour, and were 'going forward', when outflanked. It was not a defensive battle like Castlebar. Ballinamuck was similar to Collooney, except that it was crowned with success. The difference between them was that Vereker was greatly outnumbered by the French at Collooney, whereas Lake greatly outnumbered the French at Ballinamuck. It is impossible to be definitive about the quality of all the regiments and battalions of militia, but at this stage conclusions can be drawn about some of them. Lords Granard and Ormond, who were both with their regiments, took their duties seriously, and were keen that their men should do well. The City of Limerick Battalion, however, had been one of those believed to be disaffected in 1796-7, both in Belfast and Derry. In the event, they behaved well at Collooney, and none joined the French. The Armagh and the Downshire were in a different situation. For a start, both regiments had seen action earlier in the year, some of it extremely hard fought. Lord Gosford, of the Armagh, paid a great deal of attention to his regiment, and in Lieutenant-Colonel Robert Camden Cope he had a very good soldier indeed. Although Lord Downshire himself neglected his regiment, he had in Major George Matthews one of the best officers in the entire militia. As Captain Taylor, ADC to Lord Cornwallis said, 'The Downshire appear to be a good regi-

---

30 Now conserved, framed, and in Armagh Public Library, the only enemy colour ever captured in action by British or Irish militia.   31 Lake to Cornwallis, 8 Sept. 1798 (NA, HO/100/82/56).

ment as well as the Louth, in better order and more attentive to their officers than the generality.'[32] Both the Armagh and the Downshire as well as the Louth, must be considered as among the best of the militia regiments.

POST REBELLION PROBLEMS

Whilst the French were loose in Connacht, and earlier, in May and June during the rebellion, the civil government continued in most of Ireland, not always 'as normal', but at least did not break down. When 'peace' was restored a great number of claims for damages were made to the government as a direct result of military actions. Much is made of the 'licentiousness' of the Irish soldiery, but, in many cases, they were brought to book for their behaviour in the months immediately after the rebellion. Claims made by 'suffering loyalists' amounted to £1,023,337 6s. 4d.[33] for the depredations caused by the rebels, and some of this represents claims made against the army for damages and livestock taken during the insurrection, and admitted by the government. (A 'suffering loyalist' could be anyone not involved in the rebellion.) In many other cases, where damage could be directly attributed, regiments were ordered to make retribution. Most claims, however, were made as a result of actions by the militia.

Date	Place	Claimant	Amount	Remarks
15 Dec. 1798	Punchestown	Jos. Brunton	£76 8s. 0d.	8 cattle taken by 1st Light Infantry
	—	Hugh O'Neale	£ —	Horse taken by Major Hardy
16 July 1799	—	Jas. Flanagan	£12 12s. 0d.	Horse taken by the King's County
18 June 1800	Castleruddery	Mr Collins	£7 7s. 0d.	Horse taken by Wicklow Regt.
4 Dec. 1800	Mayvore	B. Loughlin	£ —	Houses burnt by Wicklow Regt.
29 Dec. 1800	Sligo	Fra. McCann	Billet money	Not paid by Limerick City Militia[34]

Table 18: Claims against the militia after the rebellion

32 Taylor to Castlereagh, 21 Aug. 1798 (ibid., HO/100/82/3). 33 Musgrave, *Rebellions* p. 594. 34 Sources. All refer to incidents in 1798, although the claim may have been made much

Earlier it was claimed that the Armagh Regiment was one of the best of the militia regiments. When it came to fighting, this was so, but their internal administration left something to be desired, especially in the actions of their paymaster, Lieutenant Walpole. He was extremely dilatory about settling the regiment's bills, and we have a record of what remained outstanding. All of these amounts refer to the crisis of 1798:

Date	Claimant	Amount	Remarks
3 Nov. 1798	Bridget Foley of Blessington	£150 0s. 0d.	Damage to property
5 Nov. 1798	Wm Russell of Limerick	£15 13s. 9d.	Two baskets of English Figs
Late 1798	Mr Patrickson of Blessington	—	For cattle taken by Lieutenant Walpole
20 Jan. 1799	Mr Cassidy	—	For bullock taken by Lieutenant Lucas
1 Nov. 1799	Mr Yeates	£30 0s. 0d.	For 10 fat sheep taken by Ensign Thompson
13 June 1800	Lord Kilwarden	£24 0s. 0d.	For 12 sheep taken by Lieutenant Lucas[35]

Table 19: Claims against the Armagh Regiment

It took a considerable time for these claims to be met. For example, Mr Cassidy's claim for his bullock went to the Castle in January 1799; in July Major Acheson said that arrangements had been made to pay compensation;[36] but at the end of October the matter still had not been settled.[37] Eventually Lieutenant Walpole, the paymaster, was summoned to Dublin to answer for the claims against the regiment, and after illness and prevarication, he obeyed.[38] We know that there were ten matters which he had to answer for,

later: Brunton – H. Taylor to Maj.-Gen. Moore, 15 Dec. 1798 (NLI, KP/1 134/3 2 7); O'Neale – H. Taylor the Lt.-Gen. Lake, 11 July 1799 (ibid., KP/1 136/1 99); (Maj. Hardy of the Antrim Regiment was garrison commander for County Wicklow); Memorial of James Flanagan, 16 July 1799 (ibid., KP/1 136/2 2 2); Collins and Loughlin – E.B. Littlehales to Brig.-Gen. Barnett, 18 June 1800 (ibid., KP/1140/129 and 3 1 9); McCann – E.B. Littlehales to Maj.-Gen. Trench, 29 Dec. 1800 (ibid., KP/1142/9 0). **35** Sources: Foley and Russell – Taylor to Maj.-Gen. Dundas, 3 Nov. 1798 (NLI, KP/ 1134/145 and 1 5 7); Patrickson to Edward Cooke, n.d. (NAI, RP/620/54/32); Cassidy – E.B. Littlehales to O.C. Armagh Militia, 26 June 1799 (NLI, KP/1085/235); Yeates – E.B. Littlehales to O.C. Armagh Regiment, 1 Nov. 1799 (ibid., KP/1086/380); E.B. Littlehales to Lord Gosford, 13 June 1800 (ibid., KP/1089/6 8). **36** Maj. the Hon. A. Acheson to E.B. Littlehales, 10 July 1799 (ibid., KP/1085/285). **37** E.B. Littlehales to O.C. Armagh Militia, 30 Oct. 1799 (ibid., KP/1086/366). **38** E.B. Littlehales

but, unfortunately, not all the details. Of those that are known, he had to answer a claim from Catherine Martin for £24 8s. 4d. for beer consumed at Naas. Other claims were for Lord Kilwarden's sheep, Mr Patrickson's cattle, and claims from a Mr Hayden and a Mr Griffiths, the details of which are lost.[39] The outcome is not known but the only claim they escaped was that of Mr Yeates, whose sheep had been consumed at a time of 'free quarters', and no compensation was paid.[40] The Armagh Regiment was notable throughout the period 1798 to 1802 for its reluctance to settle accounts, and while it may be one of the most glaring examples, almost every other regiment in the militia earned the displeasure of the lord lieutenant in failing to meet obligations to pay for depredations committed in 1798. It is perhaps worth noting that in 1802, Lieutenant Walpole deserted from the Armagh Regiment, having embezzled regimental funds.[41] He was never caught.

Whilst the regiments of militia were being called to account for some of their actions in 1798, at the same time men of the Longford and Kilkenny Regiments had to account for their actions after Castlebar. Tradition has it that all the men who deserted to the French were either killed in action or by summary justice immediately afterwards. This does not appear to be the case. The records of the Longford Battalion are incomplete, and it is impossible to get a definitive list of all the men who were missing after Castlebar. Lord Granard reported in September 1798 that there had been 28 killed, and 138 wounded and taken prisoner.[42] Of this number, some 50 or so are reputed to have deserted to the French, and some of these men were killed in the remainder of the incursion, or summarily executed if captured by the Crown forces in action. Most of those taken prisoner by the crown forces were sentenced to death: eight of the Longford, and one of the Kilkenny on 11 September 1798.[43] On the Longford returns, only two of these men are shown as missing, and two others were shown as killed. On 20 September 1798 Corporal Hoey was sentenced to death for desertion at Castlebar (he was not shown as missing on the returns), but in November his sentence was commuted to service abroad for life.[44] In October 1798 a further six men had their sentences of death confirmed, but two sergeants and five privates had death sentences commuted to service abroad for life, as they had joined the French to escape, and one, Private Bartry Leonard, was acquitted. In total,

---

to Maj.-Gen. Cradock and Col. Handfield, 28 Sept. 1799 (ibid., KP/1137/156). (Cradock was Quartermaster General, and Handfield his assistant.)   39 E.B. Littlehales to Lord Gosford, 26 Jan. 1799 (ibid., KP/1083/235 and 177). Hayden lived at Naas, but there are no other details.   40 E.B. Littlehales to Mr Yeates, 14 Nov. 1799 (ibid., KP/1208/200).   41 T.G.F. Patterson (ed.), 'Armagh Militia extracts from the diaries of Lt. Col. William Blacker', iii, 256. Blacker lost £400 of his company funds, which his father made good.   42 Memorial of Lord Granard, 28 Sept. 1799 (NAI, M₃475/39. Royal Longford Militia Letter Book).   43 H. Taylor to Lt.-Gen. Lake, 11 Sept. 1798 (NA, HO/100/85/63).

these figures account for barely half of the men reported to have joined the French, and, of these, almost half had their sentences commuted. The number who joined the French will probably never be known for certain. All that can be said is that the lord lieutenant recognized that some joined the French to escape, that there may have been an element of compulsion in other cases, and he acted accordingly in commuting sentences. It is important to note that all sentences of courts martial had to be submitted to the lord lieutenant for confirmation. Although Cornwallis exercised clemency in the case of civilians it is extremely unlikely that he would have done so in the case of soldiers without good cause. All sentences of the Longford men appear in the Kilmainham Papers. Half of the men who were supposed to have deserted to the French were court martialled, and half killed in action, or summarily on capture (or maybe not as many as fifty deserted). Of those court martialled, half had death sentences commuted or were sentenced to serve abroad.

In the aftermath of the rebellion, attempts to subvert soldiers continued and both the Antrim and the Meath suffered a spate of desertions, quite out of proportion to their rates of desertion for the previous five years. The Antrim Regiment was stationed in Wicklow, and had seen hard fighting. There had been no problems with their discipline or their loyalty – which had been epitomized by Drummer Hunter who reputedly put his foot through his drum rather than play it for rebels.[45] It is believed that the regiment recruited men in Wicklow, who, when they had received arms and accoutrements, promptly deserted.[46] It was known also, that men of the regiment had been subverted by 'General' Joseph Holt, a United Irish leader, who at one stage had no less than 28 Antrim militiamen in his gang in the Wicklow Mountains.[47] Gradually most were captured. In October 1798 four men were confined in Galway for court martial, and 17 in Wicklow, the latter being offered the option of service abroad for life or a court martial.[48] In December 1798 a sergeant and a private were sentenced to death, and another private was transported for life.[49] Finally, Private John Moore, a deserter who murdered William Hume, the only member of parliament to be killed in the rebellion, was executed for his crime in June 1799.[50] Moore, incidentally, was a Wicklowman.[51] It is worth noting that the Antrim Regiment had a total of 42 deserters in the period 31 March 1794 to 31 March 1798, but no less than 49 between 20 April and 30 September 1798, losing 19 on 24 July. Four of these were noted on the return as 'enlisted and deserted'.[52] It looks suspi-

---

44 H. Taylor to Brig.-Gen. Barnett, 20 Sept. 1798 (ibid., HO/100/71 and 8 7). 45 *Faulkner's Journal*, 16 June 1798. 46 Ibid., 10 Feb. 1799. 47 P. O'Shaughnessy (ed.), *Rebellion in Wicklow*, p. 162. 48 E.B. Littlehales to Maj.-Gen. Eustace, 2 Nov. 1798 (NLI, KP/1092/141). 49 E.B. Littlehales to Maj.-Gen. Johnston, 7 Dec. 1798 (ibid., KP/1134/287). 50 *Freeman's Journal*, 15 June 1799. 51 Ibid. 52 Pay lists and muster roll, Antrim Militia (NA, WO/13/2574).

ciously as if the Antrims were being targeted by the disaffected as a means of obtaining arms.

Details of what happened in the Meath Regiment are sparse. What is known is that sixteen men liberated two prisoners from the guardhouse, and made off. They were not recaptured.[53] The regiment was at Mallow, which Lake considered a badly disaffected town, and he removed the regiment to Cork, but 'never in his life saw men so miserable as Lord Bective and Lieutenant Colonel Cleghorne.'[54]

Looking at the picture as a whole, this incident in the Meath Regiment was not all that unusual. In the period 31 March 1794 and 31 March 1798 they had a total of 116 deserters. A comparison with other eight company regiments in the same period given in table 20:

Dublin City	186	Monaghan	40
Kilkenny	140	King's County	82
Antrim	42	Kerry	32
North Cork	4	Armagh	95

Table 20: Desertion figures, regiments with eight companies, 1794–8

There is no regular army return to compare these figures with as the regulars had standard ten company battalions. Some conclusions can be drawn though; first, most desertions occurred in the enlistment period when the 'shock' of military service hit home. Second, the regiments themselves had their own characteristics, even idiosyncrasies. The Dublin City was not a particularly well-disciplined regiment, the North Cork was very homogeneous, not only did they have few desertions, but they also gave least men to the regulars when volunteering to the line began in 1800. Undoubtedly Lord Kingsborough's method of recruitment played a part in this. The figures for the Antrim, Monaghan, and Kerry must be considered good for a four-year period considering that desertion was endemic in the army at this time. Between July 1798, and December of that year, nineteen militiamen were sentenced to death for this crime, six to service abroad, and two to one year's imprisonment, from regiments other than the Antrim, Longford, or Kilkenny.[55]

Many of the attempts at subversion in this period were in the Wicklow and Wexford areas. The Antrim deserters were mostly in Wicklow at first, and it

53 Lt.-Col. George Cleghorne to Lt.-Gen. Lake, 7 May 1799 (ibid., WO/100/87/302). 54 Lake to Littlehales, 8 May 1799 (ibid., WO/100/87/318). 55 Detail extracted from the Kilmainham papers.

is interesting that the only court martial of an officer for showing United Irish sympathies was that of Captain Alcock of the Wexford Regiment, who, as was discussed earlier, was accused of having drunk treasonable toasts with Patrick Twomey of the Cloyne Yeomanry, declaring he would support the French when they should land, aiding and abetting the swearing of United Irishmen, concealing a conspiracy to murder, adhering to the United Irishmen, and attempting to seduce Twomey from his allegiance. He was found guilty of the first two and the last charge, and acquitted of the rest. He was sentenced to be transported to Botany Bay for life[56] On 24 August 1799, he left Cork on the transport *Minerva*. One of his fellow passengers was Joseph Holt, the rebel leader from Wicklow, who had surrendered and been pardoned.[57]

An example of the dangers of troops being sent on detachment without adequate supervision after the rebellion had ended was to be found when the North Cork Regiment returned to their duties on the canal, and one of their detachments near the 12th lock provided evidence that it was dangerous to allow people to be at the 'sole disposal of military officers.'[58] On arrival at their post the detachment robbed the local people of bedding, furniture and food, and their officer, Lieutenant Maxwell, insulted the local women. He attacked the pilot of the luggage boat, and eventually had to be removed before the local people took violent action against him.[59] He was required to resign as a result of a court of enquiry into his conduct.[60]

Another problem which started in 1799 and continued until 1801 was famine. A study of the corn returns (the price per barrel of corn at the various markets in Ireland), which were printed weekly in the press, showed that in Belfast and Dublin, between 1796 and February 1799, the average price of wheat was between 2 5s. and 3 0s. per barrel. In February 1799 in Dublin, and in May 1799 in Belfast, the price started to climb, and by July 1800, had reached 7 9s.. It reached 8 0s. in March 1801, before declining later in the year to less than 40s. This reflected famine in the countryside, and it affected the militia because it was dependent on local markets for supplies of food, which they became unable to supply. This shortage of food resulted in soldiers stopping farmers who were going to market, and stealing their potatoes.

On 12 November 1799 a circular from the adjutant general authorized militiamen to assist farmers with potato gathering since the corn harvest had failed.[61] A few days later soldiers were ordered to stop using powder on their hair.[62] By the end of the month, Dublin market was beginning to face a shortage

---

56 General Order, 25 Nov. 1798 (NA, WO/6 8/221. Donegal Militia Order Book). 57 David Miller, *The wreck of the Isabella* (London, 1995), p. 14. 58 G.M. Warner to Sir John McCartney Bt., 27 Feb. 1799 (NAI, RP/620/46/62). 59 Ibid. 60 Col. R.U. Fitzgerald to (Gen. Peter Craig), 6 Mar. 1799 (ibid., RP/620/46/64). 61 Adjutant-General, Circular, 9 Nov. 1799 (PRONI, D/3574/D/1, Armagh Militia Letter Book). 62 Ibid.

of potatoes because regular soldiers, not just militia, were stopping carriers at Tullow, and were taking potatoes from them, saying they would pay on the carriers' return.[63] In December 1799 there was a complaint that soldiers of the Leitrim were doing the same thing, and General Dundas was told to enforce the lord lieutenant's order in 'the most pre-emptory manner.'[64] A general order was issued and printed in the press on 23 February 1800, holding officers responsible if their men continued to steal potatoes.[65] This did not have the required effect, and in March 1800 another order was issued which authorized quartermasters to go to more distant markets to purchase supplies.[66] The problem continued until the harvest of 1801. Indeed, in July 1801 four officers of the militia, Lieutenants Toole of the Kilkenny, Allen of the Waterford, Ensigns Grame of the Galway, and Brown of the Kildare, were brought to court martial for allowing their men to forage for food. No evidence was offered against them, and they were acquitted, so this was evidently a warning.[67]

CONDUCT OF CHANGE

The period 1798 to 1802 saw the beginnings of change in attitudes to the militia within the army. The commanders had already come to accept the idea of Roman Catholics being armed in the defence of the kingdom. They had difficulty in widening their concept of what the militia should be, mainly because they regarded the officer structure as being inefficient and inadequate. However the demands of the war for manpower were forcing the pace of change. The war against France was proving to be like no other that had gone before. The campaigns in France and Flanders, and in the West Indies had created a critical need for manpower which normal recruiting efforts were unable to fulfil. This is reflected in the keenness of militia regiments to serve outside Ireland, which can be contrasted with the reluctance of Horse Guards to allow them to serve within Great Britain. Cornwallis could see the advantage in service outside Ireland as a lever to persuade the upper classes to support the union bill. He was initially very reluctant to go further, but he was being pressed by Dundas to allow militiamen to volunteer to the line.

In early 1799, Cornwallis thought that the Union bill was safe, and was thus very conscious of the need to do something which would, 'very much flatter the vanity of this country, which is one of its most powerful passions.'[68]

---

63 E.B. Littlehales to Lt.-Gen. Dundas, 27 Nov. 1799 (NLI, KP/1138/10). 64 Ibid., 7 Dec. 1799 (ibid., KP/1138/55). 65 Circular, 23 Feb. 1800 (ibid., KP/1330). 66 Circular to general officers commanding districts, 10 Mar. 1800 (ibid., KP/1330). 67 General Order, 15 Oct. 1801 (ibid., KP/1331). 68 Cornwallis to Dundas, 14 Mar. 1799 quoted in *Cornwallis correspondence*, iii, 76.

A period of change: 1798–1802

Service outside Ireland by a militia regiment could do this. Many of the militia regiments were publicly offering themselves to serve out of Ireland, in Great Britain, Europe or wherever the king would send them. Undoubtedly, some of this was done by the colonels alone with no reference to the men, but others came from the ranks, and usually were published in the press, for example, that made by Sergeant-Major Edward Stewart, on behalf of the non-commissioned officers and privates of the Roscommon Militia to his colonel, Robert King, who forwarded it to the Castle.[69] On 21 January 1799 the King's County Regiment volunteered to serve in any part of Europe,[70] and on 3 February 1799 Lord Loftus, having heard that the idea of the Irish militia serving in England was contemplated, volunteered the Wexford Regiment to serve wherever the king should wish.[71] These letters, and the replies from the Castle were published in the press, and may be counted as demonstrable declarations of loyalty to the crown and constitution. Cornwallis could not ignore these requests forever, and was especially conscious of the shortage of trained soldiers for the regular army. The regulars had been drained by the fruitless campaigns of the 1790s, and in 1799 another campaign in Holland was being contemplated. Militia could be used to perform routine functions at home, which would release regulars for offensive service. However, Dundas, the secretary at war, was trying to assist Cornwallis by providing him with more Scots fencibles, in order to render him less dependent on English and Irish militia.[72] (Dundas, of course, may have had the intention of creating the situation where men from both the English and Irish militia could volunteer to the line.) He suggested that if Cornwallis really wanted militia to serve outside Ireland, then it could be possible to send them to Canada, or Minorca, or the Channel Islands, or even Great Britain, but pointed out that the shortage was for regular and offensive troops, and not troops for home defence.[73] The king intervened, and said that regiments of Irish militia coming to Great Britain would offend the English militia, but that the Channel Islands or North America were possibilities. The English militia were serving in Ireland because of operational necessity, but to send the Irish regiments to England without a crisis requiring their presence there would certainly have offended the powerful English militia colonels, who were even more sensitive about their status than their Irish counterparts. Service outside Ireland by the Irish militia, should thus be seen as a political gesture to the Irish magnates, and not simply the removal of troublesome, ill disciplined militiamen, most of whom were Roman Catholics. For one thing, they were to go for only one year, and there would be a constant traffic of men between the home county and the regiment. Another rea-

69 *Freeman's Journal*, 9 Feb. 1799. 70 Ibid. 71 Ibid. 72 *Cornwallis correspondence*, iii, 78.
73 Ibid.

son an exchange of militia was regarded as desirable was because of the influence that better disciplined soldiers in a more peaceful environment would have on the Irish, and, in fact, exchange of militias started in 1811.

It should be noted that in the correspondence between Cornwallis and Dundas on this subject, there is a suggestion by the latter that the Irish parliament should be asked to allow volunteers from the militia to join the regulars.[74] Cornwallis thought that this was an impossibility, but that he could send two 'tolerably good' militia regiments to Jersey and Guernsey.[75] On 14 April 1799 he reported that the King's County Regiment under Colonel L'Estrange, 600 strong, and stationed in Dublin, had volunteered to go to Jersey or Guernsey for a year. They were to be ready 'in about three weeks.'[76]

In July Cornwallis said he would ask the commanding officer of the Wexford, whether they would volunteer to serve in the Channel Islands, and, if not, then he would approach the Louth, 'which is the best disciplined of the whole, and commanded by the Speaker's son, who is a better soldier than a politician.'[77] In the event, the Wexford Regiment did volunteer. On 10 July 1799 the King's County Regiment embarked for Guernsey, from Dublin, with 32 officers, 38 sergeants, 38 corporals, 18 drummers, and 588 private men, accompanied by 285 women, and 254 children. They left behind five officers, four sergeants, two corporals, and 90 private men, basically this was the light company, which was serving in the light brigade.[78]

The King's County and the Wexford served for a year in the Channel Islands. Judging from reports, their conduct was good, and they did well. The experiment must be adjudged a success, but it was not repeated until 1811, when there were exchanges of the English and Irish militias made possible by the Act of Union, which abolished separate armies. On 13 May 1800 the King's County returned from Guernsey with 32 officers, 37 sergeants, 17 drummers, and 611 corporals and private men, 271 women, and 222 children.[79] On 4 July 1800 the Wexford Regiment returned from Jersey with 25 officers, 37 sergeants, 18 drummers, 600 corporals and private men, 232 women, and 236 children.[80] The sending of these regiments to serve outside Ireland did, however, make the point that the militia could be used in a more flexible way, and the idea that volunteers could be obtained for the regulars from the militia, continued to gain ground despite the misgivings of Lord Cornwallis. The argument was that men were needed for the line, and the militia had a pool of suitable manpower that could be tapped, against the counter-argument that these men were needed for the defence of the coun-

---

74 Cornwallis to Dundas, 14 Mar. 1799 quoted in *Cornwallis correspondence*, iii, 76.   75 Ibid., p. 86.   76 Ibid., p. 88.   77 Ibid., p. 110.   78 Cornwallis to Portland, 14 July 1799 (NA, HO/100/8 4/ 173).   79 Disembarkation return of the King's County Regiment, 13 May 1800 (ibid., HO/ 100/92/60).   80 Disembarkation return of the Wexford Regiment, 4 July 1800 (ibid., HO/100/91/134).

A period of change: 1798–1802

try. A possible solution to this dilemma would be to divide responsibility for the defence of the country between the militia and the yeomanry, recruit more militiamen, and then allow volunteering to the line.

In May 1799 there had been yet another French invasion scare. Cornwallis had perpetual problems over the defence of Ireland being dependent on non-regular forces. He was finding the English militia an even bigger problem than the Irish. They did not want to serve in Ireland a moment longer than they had to, and no amount of cajoling could persuade them otherwise. In fact, this was a very good example of what the generals hated about any militia, that is, the power of the colonels, which could frustrate any military plan. Cornwallis' problems with the English militia can be laid at the door of Lord Buckingham, commander of the Royal Buckinghamshire Militia, and a former lord lieutenant of Ireland, 1787-90. When Cornwallis took the Royal Buckinghamshire flank company to join his army to counter the French, and did not take Buckingham, it was regarded as a personal slight. Relations between the two men became impossible,[81] and Buckingham did everything he could to ruin Cornwallis' plans for the English militia.[82] When this is seen in conjunction with the imperfect control the commander-in-chief had over the militia regiments, it is obvious why the militia generally were regarded as less than perfect troops.

There can be no question that Cornwallis did not like non-regular soldiers, and did not trust them. His correspondence shows that he realized the problems in obtaining regulars, but wanted fencibles in lieu. At the same time he was under pressure to get the Union bill through the Irish parliament, and from Dundas to get agreement from the Irish parliament to allow 10,000 militiamen to volunteer to the line (55 per cent of the Irish militia's strength). He did not want to recall parliament to deal with the militia question, but for it to meet as planned. Its principal business was to be the union, but it could also, of course, authorize volunteering to the line. Since 10,000 men constituted such a substantial part of the militia's strength, Cornwallis decided to augment the militia before getting the agreement of parliament to the volunteers. He certainly had the authority to do this.[83] In October 1799, he augmented the militia to 100 rank-and-file per company before parliament assembled. All the men were volunteers, there were no balloted men or substitutes, and the bounty was four guineas. In July 1799 the strength of the army was 41,108 men, of which 16,765 were Irish militiamen (41 per cent), a year later, after the volunteering period, the strength of the army was

---

81 *Cornwallis correspondence*, ii, 450. 82 'The new Lord Lieutenant was one of those men who in all the relations of life seldom fail to create friction and irritation': W.E.H. Lecky, *History of Ireland in the eighteenth century* (London, 1892), ii, p. 463. An apt description of Buckingham.
83 *Cornwallis correspondence*, ii, p. 135.

43,775, of which 16,765, exactly the same number, were Irish militia (38 per cent, the lowest proportion reached before 1802).[84]

By January 1800, Cornwallis had become enthusiastic about the proposal for volunteers to the line. He recognized the quality of the men, whatever he may have said about their discipline. He called a meeting of the colonels, 'and met on the whole as good humoured an acquiescence in the wishes of government as could reasonably be expected in the present situation of things.' Lord Downshire was the only one who disagreed.[85] Cornwallis also proposed to get as many volunteers for general service as he could by offering more bounty, and an ensigncy for every forty volunteers.[86]

The instructions for volunteering were given in a series of circulars to general officers, between 22 and 25 January 1800. The important one, on 23 January, gave the details. There were to be two classes of volunteers, those for the duration of the war, and those for life. Nine regiments, all serving in Ireland, were designated to receive men for war service only, and thirteen regiments, not all of which had arrived in Ireland, were designated to receive volunteers for life. Minimum heights and ages were designated, as were the numbers of men permitted to volunteer from each regiment. The volunteering period was to be from 27 January to 28 February, 1800.[87] Two more circulars gave the bounties, eight guineas for service in Europe, and twelve guineas for service for life.[88] The ceiling was to be 10,000 men, and there was to be one ensigncy for each sixty men volunteering for Europe only, and one ensigncy for each forty men volunteering for life.[89] It is an interesting comment on eighteenth-century administration, that instead of one consolidated circular, each department issued its own; the adjutant general for the men, the muster-master general for the bounty, the quartermaster-general dealt with equipment, and the military secretary, officers. There were other separate orders – the light battalions were temporarily disbanded, and sergeants, drill sergeants, armourers, and bandsmen were prohibited from volunteering.[90] Officers given ensigncies could not sell them later, but could purchase further steps that they could sell,[91] and deserters from the militia who had already enlisted were to be pardoned, and allowed to remain. Six deserters from the Longford who had enlisted in the 54th Foot were pardoned, two of them at least, Hopkins and McCone, were men who had gone missing at Castlebar.[92]

---

84 Ferguson, 'Army in Ireland', p. 149.   85 *Cornwallis correspondence*, iii, p. 165.   86 Ibid.
87 Circular to general officers, 23 Jan. 1800 (NA, HO/100/90/37).   88 Circular to general officers, 22 Jan. 1800 (ibid., HO/100/90/41).   89 Ibid.   90 Circular to general officers, 7 Feb. 1800 (PRONI, D/3574/D/1. Armagh Regiment Letter Book).   91 E.B. Littlehales to Col. King, Sligo Regiment, 1 Feb. 1800 (NLI, KP/1087/304).   92 Maj.-Gen. Sir James Duff to Maj. Thompson, 10 Feb. 1800 (NAI, M3475, Longford Militia Letter Book).

A period of change: 1798–1802

The total number of volunteers achieved was 8,138,[93] but the total number of men received by the designated regiments is not known. The total number of officers who accepted ensigncies is uncertain – many refused, but a consolidated return, as accurate as possible, drawn from general orders to 12 July 1800, is given in table 21:

Limited Service (Officers)		General Service (Officers)	
Regiment	Volunteers	Regiment	Volunteers
9th Foot	1	1st Foot	14
15 "	3	13 "	13
17 "	1	54 "	14
35 "	3	64 "	17
16 "	3	68 "	35
20 "	1	23 "	2
56 "	2	25 "	2
		27 "	17
		49 "	2
		55 "	1
		69 "	1
		85 "	14

Table 21: Officer volunteers to the Line, 1800

It is worth noting how popular general service was compared to service for the war only, and how popular the 68th Foot was compared to all the others. This is also reflected in the numbers of men who also volunteered for this regiment.[94] Table 22 shows the quota for the different regiments, and the numbers that volunteered.

Some regiments did not achieve their quotas, in particular the Kerry at 93, and the North Cork at 38. The reasons for this are now obscure, but in the case of the latter this low figure should be connected with the low desertion rate described earlier, and Lord Kingsborough's offer of a small farm to Protestant volunteers in 1793. No final return for the numbers received by each regiment of the line can be found, but there is one for the situation at 19 February 1800, which accounts for 5,733 of the 8,138 who volunteered.[95]

---

93 Wakefield, *Account of Ireland*, i, p. 833. 94 Which eventually became the Durham Light Infantry. 95 Return of volunteers to the line, 19 Feb. 1800 (ibid., HO/100/90/89).

Regiment	Quota	Volunteers	Regiment	Quota	Volunteers
Antrim	344	345	Limerick County	232	140
Armagh	232	238	Limerick City	174	70
Carlow	215	215	Londonderry	290	290
Cavan	174	99	Longford	258	131
Clare	174	154	Louth	387	293
Cork North	232	38	Mayo North	301	301
Cork South	232	137	Mayo South	301	221
Cork City	232	232	Meath	344	344
Donegal	290	207	Monaghan	344	296
Downshire	348	348	Queen's County	258	223
Dublin County	258	258	Roscommon	312	249
Dublin City	232	223	Sligo	258	232
Fermanagh	258	141	Tipperary	430	418
Galway	290	290	Tyrone	430	398
Kerry	232	93	Waterford	232	168
Kildare	215	215	Westmeath	234	232
King's County	344	213	Wexford	290	101
Leitrim	258	246	Wicklow	174	107
Kilkenny	232	232	Drogheda	Part of the Louth Regt.[96]	

Limited Service		General Service	
Regiment	Volunteers	Regiment	Volunteers
9th Foot	19	1st Foot	411
9 "	8	13 "	535
35 "	151	54 "	800
40 "	6	64 "	592
62 "	4	68 "	1777
20 "	71	23 "	68
56 "	1	25 "	17
82 "	2	27 "	410
49 "	23	55 "	48
69 "	9	85 "	771[97]

Table 23: Volunteers at 19 February 1800

[96] Circular to general officers, 23 Jan. 1800 (NA, HO/100/90/37), and Wakefield, *Account of Ireland*, i, 833.   [97] Ibid.

We know the original strengths of some of these regiments, and how they benefited from this injection of trained men, the Royals for example, doubled their strength to 882, but the 13th and the 68th more than doubled theirs. Reasons for the popularity of some of the regiments can only be surmised. It is likely that militiamen had served alongside some of the regiments, and knew all about them. Moreover, it may well have been the case that men went with their friends, and there is some evidence that this was what happened. The Tyrone's sent 298 men out of 398 to the Royals, the North Mayo, 206 out of 301 to the 13th Foot, the Roscommon 183 out of 249 to the 5 4th Foot, the Meath 213 out of 344 to the 68th Foot, and the Louth sent 175 out of 293 to the 27th Inniskillings. There is no question that the addition of men who had received training, and, in many cases, had seen hard fighting, was welcome to the regular army. Sir Ralph Abercromby, commanding many former militiamen in Egypt, said that the militiaman who volunteered for the army were a decidedly superior class of recruit, and Fortescue commented that the army depended on militiamen for its recruits until the signature of the preliminaries of peace at Amiens in October 1801.[98]

A study of the regimental returns shows that the militia regained its strength fairly quickly, and never had any real problems recruiting once the inefficient ballot had been relegated to a lowly place in the methods of obtaining men. In January 1800, the militia stood at 18,183 men, in July it was 16,765 men, and in January 1801, it had 16,473 men, but by July 1801, it stood at 25,337 men.[99]

At same time as volunteering to the line was taking place, the Union drama was being played out on the political front, and in the person of Lord Downshire military and political aims collided. Downshire was colonel of the Royal Downshire Militia, a privy councillor, and governor of Co. Down. He was also sponsor of the original Militia Bill in 1793. However, he was a leading opponent of the Union. He felt that although it was possibly desirable, the middle of a difficult war was not the correct time to do it. This put him in an awkward position. In the days before political parties, members of parliament were 'friends of the government,' be generally opposed to it, or be of genuinely independent mind, but there was no officially formed opposition, and those who were opposed were looked at somewhat askance, if not as suspected potential trouble makers. The opponents of the Irish administration were the Irish Whigs, and one has only to look at the suspicions entertained of Henry Grattan that he was a United Irishman at the time of the rebellion that led to his removal from the privy council.[1] Downshire's refusal

---

[98] Hon. J.W. Fortescue, *The county lieutenancies and the army* (London, 1909), 5–6. [99] Ferguson, 'Army in Ireland', p. 149. [1] *Cornwallis correspondence*, ii, 417. This deposit contains an original copy of the notice.

to support the administration placed him on the same side as the Whigs, and his signature on a notice urging that county petitions be sent to parliament against the union, alongside those of Lord Charlemont, and W.B. Ponsonby (both noted Whigs), caused great concern to Cornwallis.[2] Although Downshire was not the only militia colonel to oppose the union (Lord Enniskillen of the Fermanagh, and Lord Clements of the Donegal were two others), he was the most important, and he was actively involved in politics. At this stage, in early 1800, Cornwallis was by no means certain that the Union would be carried, and he did fear a serious division in the propertied classes of the country on the precedent of the Volunteers, with the possibility that this might descend to violence. Opposition, which became violent, and which was led by members of the upper classes, would have had very serious consequences.

Then Downshire committed what has always been considered as a serious error of judgment. He sent down to his regiment in Carlow a petition against the Union to be signed by members of the regiment, officers and men, whether freeholders or not. The regiment was being commanded by Major George Matthews, who allowed the petition to be displayed and signed. This incident has been considered as a major tactical error on the part of Downshire and his behaviour afterwards did little to dispel confusion about his motives or his reasoning. It can be argued that Downshire was within his rights; the militia was a constitutional army, its soldiers were subjects who had submitted to military discipline for the duration of an emergency, but who had not given up their civil rights and responsibilities. There was a very fine dividing line here between the militia soldier and the regular, but the latter on enlistment had given up many of his civil rights which the former had not. For example, militia officers were appointed to positions such as high sheriff of a county, or members of the grand jury, or as magistrates. The regular officer was exempt from these duties, and to involve a regular regiment in anything which could be regarded as 'political' was regarded as very serious, since the regular army still had the stigma of being an 'instrument of oppression' which the militia did not. Downshire may have been acting within his rights, but whether or not his actions were sensible is a moot point, especially as the regiment had internal tensions and political differences among the officers.

Lord Castlereagh, who was leading the fight for the Union in the Irish parliament, received two letters, both dated 2 February 1800, one from Captain D.H. Boyd of the Downshire Regiment in Carlow, and one from 'Jefrey Foresight'.[3] Boyd's letter reported the petition, and said that if there

---

[2] Cornwallis to Portland, 14 Feb. 1800 (NA, HO/100/93/105).   [3] D.H. Boyd to Lord Castlereagh, 2 Feb. 1800, and 'Jefrey Foresight' to Lord Castlereagh, 2 Feb. 1800 (NA, HO/100/93/70 and 72).

were to be a counter petition from the county, he would like to support it. 'Foresight' reported the petition in a well written and argued letter, in which it was obvious that he had access to the Royal Downshire barracks or 'lines'. He gave details of who was to sign, and mentioned the dangers of involving the army in a political matter. It could well be that both letters were written by Boyd, from the way the subject matters were arranged in each, the understanding of the differences between a militiaman and a professional soldier, and the intimate knowledge of the regiment displayed by 'Foresight'. If this deduction is correct, they epitomize the civil and military problems faced by the militia officer. The letter to Castlereagh represented the civil rights of the militiaman, Jefrey Foresight the dangers of involving the soldier in political matters. There had been considerable friction between Boyd and Matthews some six months earlier. Command of the Grenadier Company had become vacant, Lord Annesley had promised it to Boyd, but Matthews appointed another officer to the position. Downshire was out of the country, Annesley, who was at Mount Panther, considered he had the right to nominate an officer to it, but Matthews, actually in command of the regiment, considered he had the authority to appoint. This matter has been considered earlier, but although Matthews was proved correct, the incident left bad blood between Boyd and Matthews. Furthermore, Boyd's estate at Summerhill, Kircubbin in Co.Down, was close to Castlereagh's at Mount Stewart, and Matthews at Springvale (Ballywalter). Castlereagh, Boyd, and Matthews would have known each other in civil life, and Boyd was a supporter of the Stewarts in county politics, whereas Matthews supported Downshire.

Castlereagh gave both letters to Cornwallis, who immediately ordered his friend, Major-General Sir Charles Ross, to go to Carlow to investigate the matter.[4] Ross found the report to be true, that anyone could sign the petition, freeholder or not. Major Matthews confirmed all that he found, but refused to put anything into writing, because he believed the matter to be a civil one not impinging on his military status, despite Ross's explanations of the differences between military and civil duty.[5] Cornwallis put the matter before the king, recommending that Downshire be dismissed as colonel of his regiment.[6] He explained his actions later to Portland. He wrote that he was concerned about the security of the country, the involvement of the yeomanry and the militia in a political matter, and regarded Downshire's 'petition' as poisoning the minds of people against the union. He was concerned that the Downshire Regiment would not raise its quota of volunteers for the

---

4 *Cornwallis correspondence*, iii, 178.   5 Sir Charles Ross to E.B. Littlehales, 5 Feb. 1800 (NA, HO/100/93/78).   6 Cornwallis to Portland, 7 Feb. 1800 (ibid., HO/100/93/82). Cornwallis had only recommended dismissal from his regiment. Removal from the privy council, and governorship of the county came from the machinations of the duke of Portland.

line and could resist the union itself. Downshire's action had compromised the security of the country and the authority of government. Cornwallis said he had sought the opinion of the lord chancellor, the chancellor of the exchequer, and other members of the privy council (Lords Waterford, and Shannon, and the archbishop of Cashel). All had supported him. Finally he did not want to court martial Downshire because the composition of the court would have been pro or anti union and impartiality would have been impossible.[7] On 12 February, Cornwallis was informed that Downshire was to be dismissed from his regiment, his governorship, and from the privy council. In addition, Matthews was also to be dismissed. This was promulgated to the army on 3 April 1800.[8]

The refusal of Major Matthews to put anything in writing confirms that militia officers did not consider that they had given up their civil responsibilities, and that signing a petition against the Union bill was perfectly within their remit. The attitude of the military command, which at this time was also the political command, was exactly the opposite. There is no doubt that the personality and activities of Downshire had a bearing on the way in which the matter was dealt with, but from the military point of view it is obvious that the Castle was determined to treat the militia in exactly the same way as the regular army. This incident is important evidence of a change in the perceptions about the militia. Its members may have retained their civil rights but when on military duty, they were to be treated on the same basis as the rest of the army. This was one of the first real steps in increasing professionalism within the militia, which went on steadily, especially after 1803.

The removal of Lord Downshire created an opportunity to divide the Downshire Regiment into two smaller battalions, the Royal South Down Militia, and the Royal North Down Militia.[9] The old regiment had really been too big for easy management, billeting for example, and it also solved some of the problems of officer manning. No doubt, also, it helped to remove any lingering doubts about the loyalty of the men. Downshire, however, although he still had a position and a public voice as a member of the house of lords, never recovered from the blow to his honour and prestige, and died later in the year from 'gout of the stomach'.[10] Sir Josiah Blackwood became colonel of the Royal North Downs, and Lord Annesley became colonel of the Royal South Downs, with D.H. Boyd as his major.

---

[7] Cornwallis to Portland, 14 Feb. 1800 (ibid., HO/100/93/105). [8] E.B. Littlehales to William Elliott, 3 Apr. 1800 (NLI, KP/1015/34). It has to be said that the dismissal of Matthews was hard on a man mentioned twice in despatches for meritorious service. [9] Sir Josiah Blackwood to E.B. Littlehales, 8 Apr. 1800 (ibid., KP/1015/141). Note the tacit dropping of 'shire' in the titles, the county was never known as 'Downshire.' [10] *Faulkner's Journal*, 10 Sept. 1800. Almost certainly a heart attack, he had pains in his arms before the 'gout' attacked him.

Shortly afterwards, Cornwallis produced a viable plan for the defence of Ireland. His problem was the old one of not having enough soldiers to be able to divide his force into two parts, one to counter local insurrection which involved subdivision into small detachments serving in dispersed locations, and the other, to have an army to counter invasion. No one ever defined the role of the militia and it continued in this period to suffer from dispersed service with all the problems of discipline and supervision that this brought. Cornwallis decided to divide his army into two parts, the first, a movable force to counter invasion, and the second, a stationary force to counter insurrection, troops in both being interchangeable when they completed tours of duty.

The plan was implemented in April 1800.[11] Initially, the movable force was to consist of the regulars, cavalry, fencibles, and the light battalions, and the stationary force the militia and fencibles, supported by the yeomanry. The movable force consisted of 20,007 men, and the stationary, 15,129. The order also gave the numbers of men who could assemble at Athlone, Belturbet, the Blackwater, and the Shannon west of Limerick, in no more than five days. It was comprehensive, but suffered, as Cornwallis was well aware, from a shortage of troops. It was updated every six months, since the units involved were continually changing. In the very first order, the only militia in the movable force were the light battalions. This changed at the first update, when the movable force had four light battalions, and the Antrim, Roscommon, Fermanagh, and Londonderry Regiments in it, stationed at Cork, Tarbert, Athlone, Londonderry, and Belfast.[12] By May 1801, the movable force had even more militia in it, the light brigade (as it now was), and the Leitrim, Antrim, Cavan, Louth, Roscommon, Fermanagh, Londonderry, and the Tyrone, the remainder being in the stationary force.[13] There is unlikely to be any reason for selection of these regiments other than their proximity to the bases of the movable force, although it must be noted that there was a huge increase in the size of the militia in the returns of July 1801, when it had increased from 16,473 in January, to 25,337.[14] The plain truth is that the commander-in-chief could not do without the militia as there were never enough troops to provide for the defence of Ireland, the defence of Great Britain, and to provide a field army. It is perhaps worth noting in this context, that for the campaign in Egypt in 1801, the expeditionary force under Abercromby was to be joined by a large contingent from the army of the East India Company, this was the first, but not the last, time this was planned. The period, however, marks the beginning of a more determined approach to the defence of Ireland, with responsibilities more clearly defined,

---

11 General Order, 5 Apr. 1800 (NLI, KP/1 3 3 0/2 7). 12 General Order, 24 Oct. 1800 (ibid., KP/1330/34). 13 General Order, 8 May 1801 (ibid., KP/330/37). 14 Ferguson, 'Army in Ireland', p. 149.

although the effect was not consistent throughout the country. The yeomanry could be used more as a 'police force' for which it was well suited, allowing the militia to become part of the army to counter invasion, but this could not happen everywhere as the yeomanry were not strong enough in numbers in the south and west of the country. Cornwallis' plan could take account of this by increasing or decreasing the size of the stationary force as necessary. However, attitudes were changing, and the militia was becoming to be considered as more a part of the regular army, and to lose its 'constitutional' ethos. There is further evidence for this contention

In 1801 Colonel the Hon. Alexander Hope became assistant quartermaster general of the army in Ireland. One of the first things he did, was to go on a tour of the southern part of the country, of which he has left a short account.[15] He set out on 17 August 1801, and visited the Westmeath Militia at Naas. They had 'stout men', but 'some old officers, clothing and equipment good', but the Durham Fencibles had 'stout men', but 'indifferent officers'. By 24 August, he had reached Fethard, where he found the Lancashire Fencibles, 'not to be surpassed in any service'. At Fermoy, on 27 August, he found the detachment of the Leitrim in good order. He reached Cork on 31 August, and commented on the Galway and the Kilkenny as being 'tolerable', but that the Wexford was a 'stout regiment'. 'Stout' seems to have been used in the old sense of well trained and dependable.

This is another of the few contemporary reports on regiments, and possibly the shortest. The army as a whole, including the militia was becoming more efficient, as it faced up to the disasters of the 1790s. In 1800, the Army Medical Board had reported on the militia.[16] They were weeding out the chronically disabled and the incurably diseased, and in 1801 issued a report on the state of the barracks in Ireland.[17] In May 1801 a corps of Pioneers was formed comprising three field officers, six captains, 30 subalterns, and 660 rank-and-file. It was never embodied, but organized to support the moveable force should it have to go into action. The officers and men were to come from the Irish militia.[18] In June 1801 General Medows became commander-of-the-forces.[19] In October 1801 drill books were issued down to the level of sergeant.[20]

---

15 Hope's memorandum book, Ireland 1801 (NAS, GD364/1/1118 Hope of Luffness). Written using 'Hall and Co.'s much improved velvet paper memorandum books and metallic pencils.' Two hundred years later, the pencil still writes, if lightly.   16 Chapter 5.   17 Report on the state of barracks in Ireland (NAS, GD364/1.1125).   18 General Order, 9 May 1801 (NAI, M₃ 480. General and standing orders, Royal Longford Militia).   19 General Order, 10 June 1801 (PRONI, D/3574/D/2. Armagh Militia general orders). Medows (1738-1813), was a 'soldiers' soldier' in a way that Cornwallis never was. He distinguished himself at Brandywine in 1776, commanding light infantry. After Seringapatam, he gave his prize money, £15,000, to be distributed among the troops.   20 Ibid.

However before any further reforms could be considered the possibility of peace arose after the British expulsion of the French from Egypt. The preliminaries were concluded in October 1801, but the peace treaty was not announced until 2 April 1802.[21] Immediately, arrangements were set in train to disband the militia, which would return to being a part-time force. General Medows issued his farewell message on 3 May 1802, in which he thanked the militia, and, in particular, their light companies, for their services in fulsome prose.[22] On 5 May 1802 a circular was sent to all the colonels of the Irish militia enclosing a warrant for the disembodiment of each regiment or battalion.[23] A small cadre was not to be disembodied, which included the adjutant, surgeon, and quartermaster, and a number of sergeants, corporals, and private men, which varied in number from regiment to regiment. All the others were to go: each subaltern and the captain lieutenant received two months' pay, the paymaster received two months' full allowances, and his regimental pay, each non-commissioned officer and private man received a bounty of fourteen days' pay, and were allowed to retain their clothing.[24]

The retained men, who were to form the nucleus of the remustered regiments less than one year later, were stationed where the arms of the regiment were stored. Between 9 and 25 May 1802, the regiments marched back to their counties to be disbanded. They may have thought that this was the end of their service, but it was not to be. The peace was a device to gain time to regroup and rearm, and did not last, so that in 1803, the men were back on duty, in the militia, not in fencibles or the yeomanry. The government did have an opportunity in 1803 to make a new beginning, but they chose to reform the militia regiments. At this remove it is difficult to know if there was some form of 'mental straitjacket' in governmental thinking, or if they considered that Ireland had to be same as Great Britain where the militia was retained. It must be assumed that that a militia was deemed to be satisfactory for the defence of Ireland together with the regular army, the fencibles, and the yeomanry.

---

21 General Order, 2 Apr. 1802 (PRONI, D/3574/D/2. Armagh Militia Letter Book). 22 General Order, 3 May 1802 (NLI, KP/1331). 23 Circular to the colonels of Irish Militia, 5 May 1802 (NA, WO/43/400). 24 Ibid.

CHAPTER NINE

Conclusion

The importance of the militia to the Castle must not be under-estimated. Throughout this work, reference has been made to the numbers in the militia. At one time it represented 75 per cent of the Irish army. A consolidated return for the period 1793–1802 shows that on average throughout the period, the militia furnished 53 per cent of the army.[1]

Date of return		Militia	Fencibles	Regulars	Other	Total	Percentage Militia
1793	July	5,150		11,094		16,244	32
1794	Jan.	9,495		8,514		18,009	53
	July	11,967		4,134		16,101	74
1795	Jan.	13,366		6,708		20,074	67
	July	15,959		13,335		29,294	54
1796	Jan.	17,437	10,068	1,676		29,181	60
	July	18,093	8,612	1,936		28,641	63
1797	Jan.	18,132	9,141	1,906		29,179	62
	July	20,753	11,874	1,821		34,448	60
1798	Jan.	22,728	10,751	1,830		35,309	64
	July	22,930	13,247	2,380	2,516	41,073	56
1799	Jan.	22,383	12,490	2,335	14,339	51,547	43
	July	16,765	14,661	2,839	6,843	41,108	41
1800	Jan.	18,183	16,934	2,338	2,108	39,589	46
	July	16,765	15,965	8,258	2,787	43,775	38
1801	Jan.	16,473	16,368		8,259	41,100	40
	July	25,337	16,368	8,259		49,964	51
1802	Jan.	25,245	14,827	10,407		50,479	50

Table 24: Militia, fencible, and regular army strengths, 1793–1802

1 Sources: NLI, Kilmainham Papers; NAI, Rebellion Papers; and Ferguson, 'Army in Ireland', 149. 'Other' refers to the English militia. Percentage figure is Irish militia only.

It can quite clearly be seen from this table how small the regular component of the forces really was, and these figures for the regulars include both cavalry and infantry. The figures for the fencibles include a small component of cavalry. Inadequate as the militia may have been, the Castle simply could not afford to do without it.

The officers and men of the Irish militia have been held responsible for its performance and its reputation. It is almost as if the militia was a complete self-contained entity, separate from the other parts of the army in Ireland, and not perhaps wholly respectable. In one respect of course, it was very different from the rest of the army, but to see the militia in this light is to ignore the state of administration and discipline of the whole army that I outlined at the beginning. The Irish militia was essentially the creation of the Militia Act that set it up, and the application of the act by the generals set in command of the force.

It is obvious that there were failures in both. But to take an overview, the act had two structural weaknesses. In taking the English Militia Act of 1757 as a model, Lord Hillsborough and the Irish parliament did not think that an English act, then 36 years old, having well known and well publicized weaknesses, and noting in particular the ferocity of the rioting with which it had been greeted, should be modernized and adapted to the conditions of Ireland. Yet Ireland had a different system of landholding that would make the compulsory removal of young men from the land to serve in a militia a very serious matter, likely to be resisted. Of course, parts of the country already had a considerable problem with the agrarian violence being created by the Defenders. The act established a constitutional militia that was to be a part-time force. When it was called out for full-time service, the inadequacies of the act were revealed, and it became necessary to pass a new militia act almost every year, each one amending parts of the original. One of the problems was that there was a sort of 'mental straitjacket' in political thought. Politicians and the landowners in general believed that the Williamite settlement of 1691 had produced the best possible constitution. It was the product of a struggle that had seen the beginning of the transfer of executive power from the crown to parliament. This was reflected in the army and its reserves. The latter was the militia, which had long historical antecedents, and was perceived as the army of the people.[2] It was voluntary and part-time, but in time of emergency could be raised by ballot, and officered by the landed classes. It was the constitutional balance against the regular army that was perceived as a potential instrument of tyranny. This was because the regular army owed its allegiance to the monarch, not to parliament, and its

---

[2] The antecedents of the militia went back to the assize of arms in 1181, and the Statute of Westminster, 1285, which defined its responsibilities under the sheriff.

officers held the 'king's commission', whereas the militia, whilst being loyal to the monarch, had its officers appointed by the lord lieutenant or governor of the county, and they held his commission. It can be argued that by the end of the eighteenth century these perceptions were long out of date, but the trauma of the wars that produced the Williamite settlement lasted throughout the eighteenth century, and well into the nineteenth. These principles were regarded as being immutable. Once the Irish militia was called out for full-time service and the inadequacies of the act stood revealed, little was done to make a thorough reform, and as a result military efficiency was never high.

The first inadequacy was the ballot. It may have been adequate to raise a part-time force as it was originally envisaged, but it was totally unable to produce sufficient men for a full-time one. A regiment on permanent duty continually 'leaked' men, whether in peace or in war. Men died, deserted, or were discharged, and a constant stream of new recruits was needed to replace them. A ballot held once a year could not do this. Furthermore, the cost to the parish cess, and later the county cess, was too much, quite apart from the difficulties in collecting it, or of getting deputy governors to do their duty. These must be the prime reasons for the decline of the ballot.

The second inadequacy was of greater importance, and this was the method of selection of officers. The governor of the county selected them, which may have been adequate in militia arrays of the sixteenth and seventeenth centuries. But by the late eighteenth century, when militia officers were working alongside regulars on a full-time basis, there could be considerable friction. Irrespective of the quality of regular or militia officers, the command structure was weak. The regular officer made the army his profession, he gave up many of his civil rights and responsibilities, and was appointed by a central authority. Furthermore, about two-thirds of regular officers purchased their commissions, which gave them a financial interest in their profession.[3] The governor of the county, or the colonel of the regiment appointed the militia officer. Confirmation of his commission by the lord lieutenant was automatic. The militia officer did not give up his civil rights and responsibilities, nor did he have to purchase his commission. Not being allowed to give up the former made his life extremely complicated; it created difficulties in the command and control of the regiments, and in the command and control of the militia. If officers could circumvent the wishes of the generals through parliamentary and other pressures, these incidents would have an effect on regimental discipline down to the lowliest private. The commander-in-chief could not order militia regiments or battalions to provide men for the artillery, or to garrison the Cork forts, give their light

3 J.A. Houlding, *Fit for service*, p. 100.

companies to a light battalion, or allow men to volunteer to the line, without calling the militia colonels together to get them to agree to these courses of action. Usually they did, but it was not a satisfactory system.

Matters were not helped by the fact that the regular army retained a monopoly of appointments to the staff. With the exception of Major Sandys of the Longford who served as a brigade major in Dublin for the whole of the period, and Major Hardy of the Antrim, who did likewise as garrison commander in Wicklow, militia officers were forbidden to serve on the staff in any capacity. No doubt the reason for this was to keep the militia units up to strength in officers, but it prevented them also from obtaining a broad general experience of the army, and contributing their local knowledge to commanders who were not necessarily Irish. Nor was there any promotion to higher army rank than brevet colonel. No militia officer became a brigadier-general, and no militia (or regular), officer was appointed to command the militia, which would have helped to centralize command and control, as well as giving more incentive to militia officers to concentrate on their temporary profession, and to ease the burden on the regular officer commanders. There is no question that the militia could have provided officers to fill staff appointments, as many were ex-regulars, such as Lord Granard of the Longford, Charles Vereker of the City of Limerick, or Joseph Hardy of the Antrim. In fact the actions of the latter in Wicklow were excellent examples of what could be achieved demonstrating that he was not afraid to take firm action when necessary but always retaining flexibility of command and movement. Hardy also seems to have been the only commander who mixed regulars and yeomen together to provide power and local knowledge. There is no doubt that such opportunities would have been welcomed, as there were many keen officers in the militia. Indeed, Lord Granard, who had served as a junior officer in the regular army, did not wish to be a brevet colonel, and was allowed to purchase his way through the ranks to substantive lieutenant-colonel.[4]

There is very little evidence to show that regular officers had any appreciation of the problems faced by militia officers, particularly over the matter of civic rights and responsibilities. The Downshire affair shows that the Castle expected militia officers, when the militia was embodied, to serve on the same terms as the regulars. This was an impossibility, and it can be argued that Downshire was not behaving improperly when he sent his petition down to the regiment in Carlow, whilst his dismissal, and that of Matthews, was in fact an instance of executive 'tyranny'.

---

[4] Memorial of George, earl of Granard, [–] Aug. 1794 (NA, HO 1 0 0/4 9/1 7 0). Granard had been a captain in the 68th Foot. (His great-great grandfather raised the 18th Royal Irish Regiment.)

In setting up the militia in 1793 the regular army was not consulted, as far as can be ascertained. Perhaps this was a part of the 'straitjacket' in thought discussed earlier, that if there was to be a reserve army, it could only be a militia. However, before long it became obvious that regular commanders would have preferred fencibles. These soldiers were enlisted for the duration of the war to serve in Great Britain and Ireland only, otherwise they were enlisted on the same terms and conditions as regulars, except that officers did not have to purchase their commissions. They had a very poor military reputation, but if they had been raised in Ireland instead of the militia no doubt this could have been changed.[5] It is difficult to know why fencibles would have been preferred, but almost certainly it was because of the perceived weaknesses in the militia act, and the greater control that the Castle would have had over fencible officers. This always supposes that the fencibles would have attracted officers of suitable ability, which is debatable. There is no doubt, however, that the commanders of the army had little sympathy with the civic responsibilities of militia officers. There was constant pressure to perform their military duties to the exclusion of all else, and a reluctance to grant extra leave other than for attendance at parliament. The result of this was absence without leave, leave extended without permission, and the leave rules being deliberately 'fudged'. None of this was satisfactory from any point of view.

Things did change slowly, particularly after 1798, and after the re-embodiment of the militia in 1803. However, the generals themselves were not of a high quality. The exception was Cornwallis but he arrived when the rebellion was almost over, and his prime task became the passage of the Union bill. His predecessors and subordinates had not inspired confidence. The marquess of Buckingham, before he fell out with Cornwallis, believed that the breakdown of law and order in the countryside, and the violence of the disaffected, caused the forces of the Crown to be violent and firm in suppressing them. He also believed that weak generals did not keep the troops under firm control, they had allowed too much detached service, and this had led to the outrages committed by the soldiery. He thought that the militia had fought well in the rebellion, but that the generals had not brought them back under control subsequently. 'His generals (I believe the worst in Europe)', he wrote of the lord lieutenant, 'do not seem to have an idea of enforcing any one of the first principles necessary for a soldier.'[6]

Whatever one may think of Buckingham as a person, it is difficult not to agree with him on this point. Lord Castlereagh, serving with the London-

---

5 The reputation of the fencibles would be a suitable subject for further investigation. Lord Roden's Fencible Dragoons, the 'foxhunters', were highly regarded by Robert Craufurd, and some of the Fraser Fencibles fought to the last man at Castlebar. 6 Marquess of Buckingham to Lord Grenville, 23 July 1798 (HMC, *Fortescue MSS*, iv, 245).

derry Regiment in December 1796, wrote to his wife to say that he thought the French had left Bantry, 'but all that I can collect in the confusion of General Stewart's orderly room – the general and his aides-de-camp being complete fools – is that they are gone'.[7] The previous year Camden had complained to Portland about the wisdom of sending General Fawcett to Ireland. His father had a 'high character' but the general had spent the past 'two or three' years in the Fleet Prison, he had no military knowledge, and his manners corresponded with the company he kept. On top of this, when asked, General Rowley was unable to name a regiment in the camp he commanded.[8] There is much other evidence of poor generalship. Carhampton did not have the confidence of the lord lieutenant, Lord Camden, nor of his subordinates, Lake and Knox. His actions in the west were violent, illegal, and precipitate. Lake himself did not have the complete confidence of Camden either. His performance in Ulster may have produced results but this did not change Camden's opinion of him, and it remains a mystery why Lake offered battle to the French at Castlebar on 27 August 1798. There were other problems: General Goldie had lost money at 'play' in Belfast for example, and General Dalrymple was too fat to mount a horse. General Duff in Limerick marched his men off towards Dublin when the rebellion broke out, before he received any orders, and left his rear unprotected, and General Hutchinson not only disobeyed orders but sought to explain away the defeat at Castlebar by blaming prior seduction of the militia. What is described here is but the tip of an iceberg, but what is certain is that the competence of the generals would be reflected in the behaviour of the troops, regular, fencible, or militia.

One of the most difficult things about the army in this period is trying to find out what plan there was to defend Ireland from internal subversion and an invasion. Before the arrival of the French at Bantry in 1796 the army was expected to be able to perform both tasks. There were never enough troops for a coherent plan, and they were dispersed in 'penny packets' around the countryside. The arrival of General Abercromby started a process of change. He may have been very tactless in his description of the army as 'formidable to everyone but the enemy', but he was determined to alter the 'loose' character of the Irish infantry, bring it under proper command, and prevent it acting in aid of the civil power without the presence of a magistrate. He may have been circumvented by the influence of the Irish parliament and the weakness of Lord Camden, but a change did come after the rebellion, which broke out less than a month after his departure. When Cornwallis introduced his plan for the stationary and moveable forces in 1799, there were sufficient troops to put it into practice, and this period marks the

---

7 Castlereagh to Lady Castlereagh, 29 Dec. 1796 (PRONI, D/3030/T/MC/3/290).   8 Camden to Portland, 24 Sept. 1795 (NA, HO/100/58/330).

start of a change in the military affairs of Ireland. There were reforms in administration, the establishment of much needed departments, and a curtailment of the civic rights and responsibilities of militia officers by the Downshire affair. There was also the start of a massive increase in the size of the yeomanry, and after 1803, it can be argued that the forces of the crown in Ireland became much better organized.

If the main weaknesses in the militia were caused by the Militia Act itself, and the higher command of the army, there were other problems that exacerbated them. The ballot was one. It was not effective enough to sustain a full-time force, but when it was introduced there were riots across a broad swathe of Ireland. These riots occurred in the period between the proclamation to raise a county militia, and complaisance with it. The raising of the regiments was another cause for the disaffected to show their displeasure, but the riots they fomented were transitory, they did not stop the raising of any regiment, and can be seen as a part of the disturbances in Ireland which had existed before the militia was proposed, and continued after it had been embodied. McAnally probably summed up the position correctly when he wrote:[9]

> That there was playboyism, ferment and unrest, disturbance and violence and even more threat of violence seems established, but that in May 1793 there was in Ireland a sort of carnival of bloodshed cannot be substantiated. One proof of this is that, however much some elements were infuriated, either on principle or sheer ignorance, by the militia measure, and however much their opposition may have been manipulated, there is no evidence that the events of that month left in the popular soul any such bitter memories as remained after other episodes in Irish history.

The question of religion is a different matter. There are two aspects to this: first, religion in the army itself; and second, the attitude of the landed classes to the defence of the kingdom being entrusted to armed Catholics. With regard to the first, the army was a pragmatic organization, and once all barriers to Catholics being enlisted had been removed, the Castle regarded its task to be the provision of facilities, and opportunity for all soldiers to worship in their own particular faith. The Bellew affair shows that the Castle was sensitive to any interference with this provision, but otherwise the men were left alone. No regiment was recruited on strict sectarian lines, and no regiment was divided on sectarian lines. This does not mean that there was no discrimination, undoubtedly there was, particularly on the question of promotion from the ranks to non-commissioned officer, but it does not seem

[9] McAnally, *Irish Militia*, p. 36.

to have been an issue, and there are no reports anywhere of sectarian trouble in a regiment or battalion. Pope Pius VI had appointed Thomas Hussey, Catholic bishop of Waterford and Lismore, chaplain-general. He raised the issue of Catholic soldiers attending Protestant services, even though there were no bars to attendance at mass. He caused much deliberation in the Castle although that was not his intention. No action seems to have been taken, and it does not seem to have been an issue.[10] The nearest thing was Lord Annesley's declaration that he did not want to serve in a 'papist regiment', which, of course, he did.[11]

Evidence of the second aspect of the religion of the soldiers is much more difficult to find. Professor Cookson has asserted that 'Catholic' regiments were 'overlooked' by Protestant ones, and that the defence of the country after the rebellion shifted from the militia to the (Protestant) yeomanry. Professor Bartlett makes a similar assertion, that the yeomanry assumed the position of the militia in the defence of the country, and that the militia became a 'nursery' for the regulars. Finding contemporary evidence for these statements in the period before 1802 is well nigh impossible. The evidence, indeed, points in a rather different direction, that the proportion of Protestants in the regiments and battalions was higher than the proportion in the counties. Furthermore, for historians to place the yeomanry in the situation of an army (which the militia was), is to ignore the rudimentary training of the yeomanry and their unequal distribution throughout the country.

The absence of evidence for sectarian tensions within the militia units is also a pointer towards their loyalty. This helps to explain the 'Wexford question', which can be expressed by asking why if Wexford rebelled so dramatically in 1798, did the Wexford Regiment not do likewise? Whatever the number of militiamen executed for treason, the larger number sent overseas to serve abroad for life, and the even larger number who were 'forgiven', the loyalty of the militia never faltered. It was of course doubted by many: Abercromby thought they would 'dissolve' in the face of an enemy,[12] and Robert Craufurd thought there was no fund of 'steady determined loyalty'.[13] In the event both were to be proved wrong, but doubts about the loyalty of the militia were expressed from time to time by both Camden and Cornwallis, and have been endorsed by many modern historians. Yet there was one official in the heart of government who had a militia appointment, and who had actually served full-time with his regiment 1796–7, and that was Lord Castlereagh. He was not at all blind to the faults of the militia, but never

---

10 Dáire Keogh, *'The French disease'* (Dublin, 1993), p. 105.   11 Matthews to Downshire, 3 July 1794 (PRONI, D/607/C/42).   12 Craufurd to Wickham, 30 Apr. 1798 (NA, HO/100/66/98). Craufurd was reporting Abercromby's opinion.   13 Craufurd to Wickham, 30 Apr. 1798 (ibid.).

ceased to support the institution, believed in its loyalty, and never wavered from that belief. As he said:

> The conduct of the militia and yeomanry has in point of fidelity exceeded our most sanguine expectations. Some few corps of the latter and but very few in that vast military establishment have been corrupted, but in no instance has the militia failed to show the most determined spirit – in this point of view the insurrection if suppressed with energy will have proved an invaluable test of our national force, on the disaffection of which our enemies either actually did or professed very extensively to rely.[14]

If the ballot, the riots, doubts about loyalty, and the potential for sectarian strife were problems which exacerbated the shortcomings of the militia act itself, there was one area controlled by commanders which was the most important of all. That was training. There can be no question that the training of the men, both individual and collective, left a great deal to be desired. The regiments were marched out of their counties to be given operational tasks before they had been properly disciplined, as Major Matthews graphically described. They were divided into small detachments, often under a junior non-commissioned-officer, before basic training was completed, they were given very little opportunity to train as formations, and still less to train in larger formations than the regiment or battalion. The newspapers report only two accounts of large-scale exercises throughout the entire period from 1793 to 1802. No doubt others took place that went unreported, but the conduct of the militia in action depended on the quality of its training, and this can only be regarded as inadequate. The collapse of the Longford and Kilkenny at Castlebar is a good example of this. They were called on to perform a manoeuvre that in theory they had practised but clearly had not. There were mitigating circumstances, but the conclusion has to be that when faced with action, the performance of the militia was inconsistent, and this had a great deal to do with the quality of the training their officers and men had received.

The best trained battalion in the world, however, will not perform well if its officers do not lead by example. The militia had disasters at Oulart Hill, Taghmon, and Tuberneering, but there were successes as well. They fought well at Newtownbarry, Ballymenaun Hill, Ballynahinch, Hacketstown, Borris House, or at Arklow, both when under some sort of cover, and in the open. They also 'snatched victory from the jaws of defeat' at New Ross. This is a classic example of an action where the powers of leadership displayed by the commanding general decided the outcome of a ferocious battle. Yet, General

---

14 Castlereagh to 'sir', 12 June 1798 (ibid., HO/100/77/143).

Johnston, who won the battle, was regarded as a 'blockhead'. The militia also fought well at Vinegar Hill, and it can be argued that officers and men learnt quickly how to overcome many of the deficiencies in their training with the experience of active service.

It is of course on their performance that the militia must be judged. From 1793 to 1795 they operated as a 'police force'. This may have allowed the units to settle down, but it did little to further their training. In 1796 and 1797 they had to sustain a very determined effort to subvert them from their loyalty. This failed, though not before the militia had been 'purged'. At the same time their duties were changing. Small detachments continued, but there were many more operations against Defenderism, and searching for arms. They were involved in 'free-quarters' in 1797-8 in proscribed areas, which was ruinous of discipline. The soldiers became harder to handle, and very difficult to control after any kind of action, as they tended to regard any civilian they found as disaffected. This was the malaise found throughout the Irish army by General Abercromby, when he arrived in the country in December 1797. Ultimately responsibility lay with his predecessor and his subordinate generals.

At the end of 1798, Lieutenant-Colonel Robert Craufurd wrote a long letter to William Wickham outlining his ideas on the union, on permanent defences, and on the militia.[15] On the latter he was very critical, if at times sweeping in his comments. Without question, he did not like a 'militia army', particularly when he regarded the regulars in Ireland as officers without men, and the militia as plenty of men without proper officers. He was very critical of the officers, but ignored the fact that they were 'civilians in uniform'. He wanted to draft the militia into the fencibles and regulars, and considered that the men would become well disciplined, brave and efficient if this happened. He thought the soldiers of a high quality, 'I am convinced that with good officers, discipline and a little experience it would be as fine an army and as loyal a one as the King ever had'.[16]

Craufurd's advice was not followed up, although his ideas of an interchange of the English and Irish militias occurred in the following decade. The questions he raises are interesting, and were indeed raised by others. If the officer corps had been as bad as he depicted (he excused the field officers from his strictures for some unknown reason), it would appear to be difficult to understand why the government did not amend the Militia Act, or amalgamate the militia with the fencibles and regulars. Although the men were allowed to vol-

15 Craufurd to Wickham, 19 Nov. 1798 (NA, HO/100/79/116). 16 Ibid. Craufurd got his wish. He commanded many former Irish militiamen in the Peninsula War. One of them, Edward Costello of the 95th Rifles, who had served in the City of Dublin Militia, 1805-08, wrote his memoirs, *Adventures of a soldier* in 1841. See Eileen Hathaway, *Costello* (Swanage, 1997).

unteer into the line in 1800, the answer must be that to remove the right of appointing officers from the governor of the county would have been to destroy one of the principles of a militia, which was regarded as sacrosanct. To amalgamate them with the fencibles or regulars would have been contrary to the terms under which the men had been enlisted, as substitutes, volunteers, or balloted men. They were not liable for service outside Ireland unless they volunteered. To make the sort of changes advocated by Craufurd and other officers, would have been tantamount to disbanding the force in the middle of a war, and with large parts of the country disaffected. The government could not afford to take this risk. In many ways Craufurd's criticisms show a woeful ignorance of the causes of the symptoms that he described.

I have treated the Irish militia from an Irish point of view and also as a national force. I have not considered it in the context of the struggle in Europe or the parliamentary struggle for the union of Great Britain and Ireland. It was not a 'political' force in the way the old Volunteers had been and in this the government succeeded in its aim to keep it subordinate to the civil power. Undoubtedly not allowing regiments to serve in their home or an adjacent county or an adjacent county helped with this aim. The militia has had many detractors, but despite the well publicized disasters such as Oulart, Taghmon, or Tubberneering, they had many successes. They were the force that defeated the '98 rebellion, in almost all successful actions, 'hundreds facing thousands' as Major Hardy said. As contemporaries would have expected of Irishmen, they showed ferocity and spirit in attack. They had difficulties in maintaining their discipline in 'police' work, but when action became hot, they remained subordinate to their officers, who in turn could hold the men steady. This in itself shows that the force, imperfect as it may have been, retained its cohesion and discipline. As McAnally said:

> There was never any question ... of the instrument, admittedly not of the highest tempered steel, bending or breaking in the hand – as the United Irishmen on the one hand hoped and as their English commanders and their political superiors on the other dreaded.[17]

The militia, disbanded in 1802, was reformed in 1803 on the resumption of the war. It served full-time until 1816 when it went into suspended animation. This lasted until 1854 when the regiments were reformed on the outbreak of the Crimean War. They were reorganized in 1881 along with the rest of the British militia, and continued until 1908 when the militia was abolished, becoming the 'special reserve' of the new Territorial Army. But this is another story.

17 McAnally, *Irish Militia*, p. 288.

Bibliography

PRIMARY SOURCES – MANUSCRIPT

Belfast, Public Record Office of Northern Ireland
D/162 Dobbs papers
D/183 Armagh Militia – Muster roll 1793–1801
D/272 McCance papers
D/374 Downshire Militia papers, including the court martial book, 1793–96
D/607 Downshire papers
D/1503 Lord Annesley and Sophie Connor papers
D/1606 Gosford papers
D/2620 Letters of James Nugent of Clonbost, Co. Westmeath, major in the Westmeath Militia, before and during the 1798 rebellion
D/2672 Will of David Hamilton Boyd of Summerhill, Kircubbin, Co. Down, 1825
D/3030 Castlereagh papers
D/3574 Armagh Militia, letter books and general orders
T/755 Pelham transcripts
T/808 Militia ballot book, Inch parish, Co. Down
T/877 Will of George Matthews of Springvale. Co. Down 1839
T/3048 McPeake papers
T/3465 Additional Sheffield papers
T/3502 Lord Ancram's diary of Vinegar Hill
MIC 67 Lake–Hewitt correspondence
ENV/5/HP/8/1 History of the Irish Parliament project, working papers, constituency files (Co. Down)

Dublin, National Archives of Ireland
R.P. 620/23–60. Rebellion papers
M 999 A collection of military states compiled by Mr. Handcock, Deputy Mustermaster General in Ireland, 1772–1822
M 3474–3483 Letter, order, and court martial books of the Longford Militia
S.O.C/1015/18 State of the Country papers

Dublin, National Library of Ireland
MS 55/217 Memorial of Joseph Hardy to Charles Lennox, duke of Richmond.
MS 809 Transcripts of documents relating to the French Invasion of Ireland, 1796
MS 1002–1331 Kilmainham papers
MS 5006 The trials of Francis Arthur and other matters
MS 5785 Notes for a history of the Irish militia before 1793
MS 8029 Fingall papers, Royal Meath Regiment 1793–1810
MS 8124 State of the militia, May 1795, and July 1796.

MS 8124 cont'd Example of a militia commission, Fermanagh Battalion
MS 8351 Statement of the numbers of troops in Ireland, In 1798–99–1800
MS 9889 Order book of a regiment stationed in Birr, 1794. (Donegal Militia)
MS 10,120 Pakenham-Mahon military papers
MS 10,873 Account of property destroyed by the military at Connorville, Aug.–Sept. 1798
P.C. 630, 633, 930, 933, 934, 945 Clements papers (uncatalogued)
p.5641 Major Joseph Hardy. *Journal of the principal occurrences in Ireland and principally in the county Wicklow between September 1797 and September 1798 when the French surrendered at Ballinamuck in which Major Hardy was engaged.*

Edinburgh, National Archives of Scotland
GD 26/9/527 Leven and Melville papers
GD 38/1/1253 Dalguise papers
GD 40/10/24 Ancram papers
GD 307/16 Heron of Heron and Killoughtree papers
GD 364/1/1082–1125 Hope of Luffness papers
GD 51/1/327–334 Melville papers

Kew, Public Record Office
HO/100/35–102 Home Office correspondence. Ireland, 1792–1802
WO/13 Pay lists and muster rolls, Irish militia regiments and battalions
WO/ 27/83 Half-yearly inspection report, King's County Militia, 5 Mar. 1800
WO/28/23 Clare Militia, digest of services
WO/43/400 Instructions for disbandment, Irish militia, 1802
WO/69/59 Limerick City Militia, digest of services
WO/68/76 Sligo Militia, digest of services
WO/68/88 Tipperary Militia, digest of services
WO/68/118 Wicklow Militia, digest of services
WO/68/221–2 Donegal Militia, letter book and general orders.
WO/68/296 & 302 Carlow Militia, enrolment book, and general order book
WO/68/319 & 325 North Mayo Militia, digest of services, and enrolment book.
WO/68/329 Longford and Westmeath Militia, digest of services
WO/68/385 Armagh Militia, monthly returns, 1 Oct. 1801–1 May 1802
WO/68/402–3 Cavan Militia, letter book
WO/68/411 Kerry Militia, order book
WO/79/45 Roscommon Militia, standing orders
WO/118/36 Royal Hospital, Kilmainham, admissions book

PRIMARY SOURCES – PRINTED

Army List, 1803.
Alexander, James, *Some account of the first apparent symptoms of the late rebellion in the county of Kildare and in an adjoining part of King's County* (Dublin, 1800).
Bartlett, Thomas, 'Select documents xxxviii: Defenders and Defenderism in 1795' in *IHS*, 24:95 (May 1985), 373–94.
Belfast Newsletter, 1793–1802.

Barrington, Sir Jonah, *Personal sketches and recollections of his own time* (Dublin, 1997).
Bunbury, Lt.-Gen. Sir Henry, *Narratives of some passages in the great war with France from 1799 to 1810* (London, 1854).
Cloney, Thomas, *A personal narrative of those transactions in the county of Wexford in which the Author was engaged in the awful period of 1798* (Dublin, 1832).
Drennan–McTier letters, 1794–1801, ed., Jean Agnew, 2 vols (Dublin, 1999).
Faulkner's Dublin Journal, 1793–1801.
Freeman's Journal, 1793–1801.
Hay, Edward, *History of the insurrection in the county of Wexford AD1798* (Dublin, 1803).
H.M.C., *Fortescue MSS*, iii (1899).
Journals of the House of Commons of the Kingdom of Ireland, 18 vols (Dublin, 1793–1800).
List of officers of the several regiments and battalions of militia and of the several regiments of fencible cavalry and infantry (Dublin, 1793–1801).
Miller, Rowley, 'An officer's experience of '98' in *Ulster Journal of Archaeology*, 4 (1898), pp 228–31.
Musgrave, Sir Richard, *Memoirs of the different rebellions in Ireland* (4th ed., Fort Wayne, Indiana, 1995).
Observations on a pamphlet lately published by an officer entitled 'Impartial relation of the military operations which took place in Ireland (Dublin, 1799).
Officer, An, *Impartial relation of the military operations which took place in Ireland in consequence of the landing of a body of French troops under General Humbert in August 1798* (Dublin, 1799).
Officer, An, *Military observations regarding Ireland* (1804).
Officer, An, *On the defence of Ireland* (1797).
Rules and regulations for the formation, field exercise, and movement of H.M. Forces (1793).
Sentimental and Masonic Magazine, January–June 1794.
Standing orders and regulations for the army in Ireland (1794).
Statutes: Ireland, 5 vols (Dublin, 1793–1800).

SECONDARY SOURCES

Bartlett, Thomas, and Keith Jeffery (eds), *A military history of Ireland* (Cambridge, 1996).
Bartlett, Thomas, and D.W. Hayton, *Penal era and golden age* (Belfast, 1979).
Bartlett, Thomas, 'Indiscipline and disaffection in the armed forces of Ireland in the 1790s' in P.J. Corish (ed.), *Radicals, rebels, and establishments* (Belfast, 1985), pp 115–34.
—— 'An end to moral economy: the Irish militia disturbances of 1793' in *Past and Present*, 99 (May 1983), pp 41–64.
Barry, J.M., *Pitchcap and triangle. The North Cork Militia in the Wexford rising* (Cork, 1998).
Beckett, I.F.W., *The amateur military tradition* (Manchester, 1991).

Bence-Jones, Mark, *Burke's guide to country houses, volume 1: Ireland* (London, 1978).
Blackstock, Allan, *An ascendancy army. The Irish Yeomanry, 1796–1834* (Dublin, 1998).
Bolton, G.C., *The passing of the Irish Act of Union* (Oxford, 1996).
Bredin, Brig. A.E.C., *A history of the Irish soldier* (Belfast, 1987).
Brett-James, Antony, *Escape from the French* (London, 1981).
Brock, F. van, 'Dilemma at Killala' in *Irish Sword*, 8 (1968), 261–73.
— 'Morress's memorial' in *Irish Sword*, 15 (1982), 36–44.
Bruce, Anthony, *The purchase system in the British Army, 1660–1871* (London, 1988).
Cullen, L.M., 'The 1798 rebellion in its eighteenth-century context' in P.J. Corish (ed.), *Radicals, rebels, and establishments* (Belfast, 1985), pp 91–113.
Connolly, S.J. (ed.), *Oxford companion to Irish history* (Oxford, 1998).
Cookson, J.E., *The British armed nation 1793–1815* (Oxford, 1997).
Costello, Nuala (ed.), 'Two diaries of the French expedition 1798', in *Analecta Hibernica*, 11 July 1941.
Courtney-Moore, Revd, 'Some account of the North Cork Regiment of Militia, especially with reference to its services in the year 1798' in *Journal of the Cork Historical and Archaeological Society*, ser. 2, iv (1898).
Cox, L., 'Westmeath in the 1798 period' in *Irish Sword*, 9 (1969), 1–15.
Curtin, N.J., *The United Irishmen* (Oxford, 1994).
— 'The transformation of the Society of United Irishmen into a mass based revolutionary organization' in *IHS*, 24:96 (Nov. 1985), pp 463–92.
Day, R., 'A short sketch of the North Cork Regiment of Militia, 9th Battalion, King's Royal Rifle Corps' in *Journal of the Cork Historical and Archaeological Society*, ser. 2, 14 (1908).
de Latocnaye, le chevalier, *A Frenchman's walk through Ireland 1796* (Belfast, 1984).
Denman, Terence, 'Hibernia officina militum: Irish recruitment to the British regular army 1660–1815' in *Irish Sword*, 20 (1996), 148–66.
Dickson, Charles, *The Wexford Rising in 1798* (London, 1997).
Dickson, David, Dáire Keogh and Kevin Whelan (eds), *The United Irishmen: republicanism, radicalism, and rebellion* (Dublin, 1993).
Dunne, Tom, *Rebellions* (Dublin, 2004).
Duffy, Michael, *The younger Pitt* (London, 2000).
Dunfermline, Lord, *Lieutenant-General Sir Ralph Abercromby, 1793–1801* (Edinburgh, 1861).
Durey, Michael (ed.), *Andrew Bryson's ordeal* (Cork, 1998).
Ehrman, John, *The younger Pitt*, 3 vols (London, 1996).
Elliott, Marianne, *Partners in revolution: the United Irishmen and France* (Yale, 1982).
Fortescue, Hon. J.W., *The county lieutenancies and the army* (London, 1909).
Gahan, Daniel, *The people's rising* (Dublin, 1995).
Geoghegan, P.M., *The Irish act of union* (Dublin, 1999).
Gilbert, J.T. (ed.), *Documents relating to Ireland, 1795–1804* (Dublin, 1893).
Guy, A.J. (ed.), *The road to Waterloo* (London, 1990).
Hathaway, Eileen, *Costello* (Swanage, 1997).
Hayes, Richard, 'The battle of Castlebar 1798' in *Irish Sword*, 3 (1957), 107–14.
Hayes, R.J. (ed.), *Manuscript sources for the history of Irish civilization*, 11 vols (Boston, 1965).

Bibliography

Hayes-McCoy, G.A., *Irish battles* (Belfast, 1970).
Hewitt, Esther (ed.), *Lord Shannon's letters to his son* (Belfast, 1982).
Hill, Myrtle, Brian Turner, and Kenneth Dickson (eds), *1798 rebellion in County Down* (Newtownards, 1998).
Houlding, J.A., *Fit for service. The training of the British Army, 1715-95* (Oxford, 1981).
Inglis, Brian, *The freedom of the press in Ireland, 1784-1841* (London, 1954).
Joyce, John, *General Thomas Cloney, a Wexford rebel of 1798* (Dublin, 1988).
Jupp, P.J., 'County Down elections, 1783-1831' in *IHS*, 18 (Sept. 1972), 201-2.
Keogh, Dáire, *'The French disease': the Catholic Church and Irish Radicalism, 1790-1800* (Dublin, 1993).
Keogh, Dáire, and Nicholas Furlong (eds), *The mighty wave* (Dublin, 1996).
Kilkenny Moderator 'Sketch of the old Kilkenny Regiment of Militia' (1859).
Kilpatrick, C. (ed.), *The formation of the Orange Order, 1795-98* (Belfast, 1994).
Kinsella, Mick, Edward N. Moran, and Conor Murphy, *Kilcumney '98* (Kilkenny, 1998).
Lecky, W.E.H., *History of Ireland in the eighteenth century*, 5 vols (London, 1892).
McAnally, Sir Henry, *The Irish militia, 1793-1816* (Dublin, 1949).
— 'Government forces engaged at Castlebar in 1798' in *IHS*, 4 (Sept., 1945), 316-31.
— 'David McAnally and the Armagh militia' in *Armagh Guardian*, May-June 1934.
— 'The Kilmainham Papers' in *Journal of the Society for Army Historical Research*, 14 (1937).
McCormack, W.J., *From Burke to Beckett: ascendancy tradition and betrayal in literary history* (Cork, 1994).
— *Ascendancy and tradition in Anglo-Irish history from 1789 to 1939* (Oxford, 1985).
McDowell, R.B., 'Ireland in the eighteenth century British Empire' in *Historical Studies*, 9 (1974), p. 58.
— 'The Fitzwilliam episode' in *IHS*, 16 (Sept. 1966), pp 115-30.
— *Ireland in the age of imperialism and revolution, 1760-1801* (Oxford, 1979).
Madden, R.R., *The United Irishmen, their life and times* (Dublin, 1858).
— *Irish periodical literature*, 2 vols (London, 1867).
Malcomson, A.P.W., *John Foster. The politics of the Anglo-Irish ascendancy* (Oxford, 1978).
— 'The gentle Leviathan: Arthur Hill, 2nd Marquis of Downshire' in Peter Roebuck (ed.), *Plantation to partition: essays in honour of J.L. McCracken* (Belfast, 1981), pp 102-18.
Maurice, Maj.-Gen. Sir J.F. (ed.), *The diary of Sir John Moore* (London, 1904).
Memoirs of Miles Byrne edited by his widow (Dublin, 1907).
Miller, David, *The wreck of the 'Isabella'* (London, 1995).
Miller, D.W. (ed.), *Peep o'Day boys and Defenders* (Belfast, 1990).
Money-Barnes, Maj. R., *A history of the regiments and uniforms of the British Army* (4th ed., London, 1957).
Murphy, J.A. (ed.), *The French are in the bay* (Cork, 1997).
O'Donnell, Ruan, *Wicklow, 1799-1803* (Dublin, 2000)
O'Grada, Cormac, *Ireland: a new economic history* (Oxford, 1994).
O'Shaughnessy, Peter (ed.), *Rebellion in Wicklow: General Joseph Holt's account of 1798* (Dublin, 1998).

O'Loingsigh, Seamus, 'The burning of Ballinaugh' in *Breifne, journal of Cumman Seanchas Bhreifne* 2:7 (1964).
Parkinson, R.E., *History of the grand Lodge of free and accepted masons of Ireland* (Dublin, 1957).
Porteir, Cathal (ed.), *The great Irish rebellion of 1798* (Cork, 1998).
Richey, H.A., *A short history of the Royal Longford Militia, 1793-1893* (Dublin, 1894).
Ross, Charles (ed.), *Correspondence of Charles, first Marquis Cornwallis*, 3 vols (London, 1859).
Senior, Hereward, *Orangeism in Ireland and Britain, 1794-1836* (London, 1996).
Sheppard, Maj. E.W., *A short history of the British Army* (4th ed., London, 1950).
Smith, E.A., *Whig principles and party politics. Earl Fitzwilliam and the Whig party, 1748-1833* (Manchester, 1975).
Smyth, Jim, *The men of no property* (London 1992).
Snoddy, Oliver, 'Two military medals by William Mossop (1751-1805)' in *Irish Sword*, 6 (1964), 252-6.
Steppler, G.A., 'British military law and the conduct of regimental courts martial in the later eighteenth-century' in *English Historical Review*, 102 (1987), 859-85.
Stephen, Leslie (ed.), *Dictionary of National Biography* (London, 1885).
T.A.L., 'Ferat qui mercuit, palman. Some account of the North Cork Regiment of Militia especially with reference to its services in 1798' in *Journal of the Cork Historical and Archaeological Society*, ser. 2, iv (1898).
Tillyard, Stella, *Citizen Lord* (London, 1997).
Townend, Peter (ed.), *Burke's peerage, baronetage, and knightage* (105th ed., London, 1970).
Wall, Maureen, 'The rise of a Catholic middle class in eighteenth-century Ireland' in *IHS*, 9 (Sept. 1958), 91-115.
Western, J.R., *The English militia in the eighteenth-century* (London, 1965).
Whelan, Kevin, *The tree of liberty* (Cork, 1996).
Whitten, J.R., *Murder without sin* (Belfast, 1996).
Wylie, J.C.W., *Irish land law* (3rd ed., Dublin, 1997).
Wheeler, H.B., and A.M. Broadley, 'Mrs. Brownrigg's journal at Wexford 20 May-21 June 1798' in *The war in Wexford* (London, 1910), pp 162-99.

THESES

Blackstock, Allan, 'Origin and development of the Irish Yeomanry 1796-1807', PhD, Queen's University of Belfast, 1995.
Ferguson, K.P., 'The army in Ireland from the restoration to the act of Union', PhD, Trinity College, Dublin, 1980.
Smyth, P.D.H., 'The Volunteer movement in Ulster: background and development 1745-85', PhD, Queen's University of Belfast, 1974.
Stoddart, P.C., 'Counter-insurgency and defence in Ireland, 1790-1805', DPhil, Oxford University, 1972.

Index

Abercromby, Lt.-Gen. Sir Ralph, commissariat, 34; concentration of army, 81; initial barrack inspection, 86; appointment, 137–8; on Camden, 169; order of 26 Feb. 1798, 175–9; resignation, 179; militiamen, 241; plans, 253
Adams, Capt., 188
adjutant, 51
age (and height) of militiamen, 127
agistment, 39
Ahmuty, Lt.-Col. Samuel, 111
Alcock, Capt. William, 106, 233
Alexander, James, 202–3
allowances, family, 51, 61, 128, 144; revenue, 145; escort duty, 145; postage, 145; lying-in hospital, 145; Hibernian Military Institute, 145
American revolution, 32, 37, 41, 166, 180, 197
Ancram, Lord, 95, 102
Annesley, Lord, problem of command, 52, 243; opposition to ballot, 64; house of lords, 97; Montgomery and Bradford, 103
Antrim Regiment, Lord O'Neill, 44; subscriptions to avoid ballot, 67; loss of Maj. Hardy, 98; murder of Edward Birch, 113; loyalty, 151; Carrigrew Hill, 194; Arklow, 204–5; Hacketstown, 213; deserters, 213, 231; Drummer Hunter, 231
approbations to regiments, 149
Ardfinnan camp, 81, 126, 157
Arklow, 204–5
Armagh county, 39–40
Armagh Regiment, embodiment, 70; officer appointments, 92; officer ages and experience, 96; public office holders 98; standing orders, 92, 102;

Ballybay affair, 115–16; Capt. Kay, 116; promotion of Sgt Collins, 148; at Naas, 183; Clane, 184; Tubberneering, 195; Ballinamuck, 226–7; claims against, 229; Lt. Walpole desertion, 230
Armstrong, Capt. J.W., 106, 149
Army, establishment, 1793, 13; organization after 1767, 30; condition in late 18th century, 31; staff ratio, 34; Cork forts, 34; military districts, 34; reforms, 1797, 35; Roman Catholics in, 36–7; Handcock's comments, 37; Army Medical Board, 94, 130, augmentation, 1795, 154; strength 1793–1802, 248
artillery, 167
Asgill, Gen., 211–13
attendance of officers, Donegal, Downshire, Kilkenny Regiments, 108

background of soldiers, 36
Bagwell, Col. John, 161
Bailieborough, Co. Cavan, 56
Ballot, Militia Act, 23; rules, 49; exemptions, 49; Co. Down, 63–4; Meath, 65; Dublin, 65–66; insurance against, 64–6; difficulties, Donegal, Tyrone, Co. Dublin, Carlow, Leitrim, Wicklow, Tipperary, 67; beat of drum and subscriptions, 67; riots, 57–60; efficiency, 68; order of precedence, 72; Waterford, 73–4; conclusion, 250, 254
Ballybay, Co. Monaghan, 113, 167
Ballinamuck, 226–7
Ballymenaun Hill, 194
Ballynahinch, 206–7
Bantry, 162

barracks, importance, 24; Killough, 71; locations, 83; poor coals, 84; Monaghan Regiment, 84; accommodation for Royal Downshire Regiment, 85; Clare Battalion, 85; Lough Glynn house, 86; New Geneva, 87; report of Army Medical Board, 88
barrack damages, 142
barrackmasters, 84, 88
Bartlett, Thomas, 20–1, 40, 42
Belfast, 38, 84, 88
Bellew, Capt. Sir Edward, 126
Beresford, John, 29
Birch, Edward, 113
Blacker, Col. William, 119, 148, 166
Blaris, 81–2, 157
Bloomfield, Capt., 200
Bodkin, Capt. Hyacinth, 114
Borris House, 215
Boyd, Capt. D.H., 242–3
Burke, Cpl., 159–60
Boxwell, John, 199
Brawls, inter-regimental, 138–9
Break o'Day men, 120
brigading of the army, 166
Brennan, Bridget, 125
Browne, Denis, MP, 62
Browne, Capt. John, 110
Bruff, Co. Limerick, 57, 60
Buckingham, Lord, 237, 252
Bunbury, Sir Henry, 32
Byrne, Miles, 210–212

Camden, Lord, establishment of camps, 81; on Carhampton, 155–6; doubts about militia, 160; Defenders, 156; defence of Ireland, 157–8; on generals, 164; Abercromby, 138, 178; Walpole, 196–7
camps of instruction, 78, 81–3, 157–8, 180
Carhampton, Lord: powerlessness over barracks, 84, 86; Sir Edward O'Brien, 110; Lt.-Col. Robert Ward, 112; pacification of Connacht, 136–7, 155–6, 164; reorganization of army, 165, 170, 253
Carlow Battalion, 74, 77, 122–3

Carrickfergus, 108
Carrigrew Hill, 194
Castlebar, 217–24, 230
Castlecomer, 211
Castlereagh, Lord, deputy governor, 46; Londonderry Regiment, 92; restoration of discipline, 139; Downshire affair, 242–3; Bantry, 252–3; on militia, 256
casualties, 69
Catholic Committee, 55–6
Catholic Relief Acts, 36, 42, 56
Cavan Battalion, 94, 135, 146
cess, 61, 67, 69, 128
chaplains, 51
charity, 147
Church of Ireland, 38–9
civilian employ, 144
claims against militia, 228
Clane, Co. Kildare, 184
Clare Battalion, 85, 135–6, 199–200
Clare, earl of, 29, 38
Clements, Lord, 17, 67, 91, 242
Cloney, Thomas, 202
Coclough, John, 199
Cole-Bowen, Lt. Nicholas, 104
Collooney, nr Sligo, 225–6
Colours, 72, 149
command, rules of, 52
commissions, officers, 90–1; dual, 93; purchase of, 94; militia, 97; civic duties, 97; from ranks, 147–9
conacre, 39–40
concentration time, 24, 77
Conolly, Lady Louisa, 170
Cooke, Edward, 118, 160, 194
Cookson, Professor, J.E., 21–2
Cope, Lt.-Col. Robert Camden, 116, 195, 205, 227
Cork, 162
Cork Regiment, City of, attempt to become 'Royal', 54; family appointments, 92; Newbridge, Co. Kildare, 138; Prosperous, Co. Kildare, 183, 184
corn returns, 142, 233–4
Cornwallis, Marquess, state of the army, 33; inspections, 35; Lord

Downshire, 33; on barrack board, 86–7; Sgt. Power, 135; Castlebar, 222–3; problems with English militia, 237; volunteering to line, 236–8; Downshire affair, 242–4; dismissal of Downshire, 244; plan for defence of Ireland, 244–5
Corry, Isaac, MP, 87
Courtney, Lt., 100
Courts martial, 132, 135–6
Crofton, Sir Edward, 63
Crosby, Gen., 77, 82
Craufurd, Lt.-Col. Robert, military career, 91; comment on education, 95; on duty, 101; on loyalty, 140; on Abercromby, 178; New Ross, 201; on militia, 257
Cunninghame, Gen. Robert, 42–3, 153

Dalyrmple, Sir Huw, 102, 114, 141
Dalyrmple, Gen. William, 118, 253
defence of Ireland, 157–8, 244–5
Defenders, violence pre and post Militia Act, 28; origin, 39; attacks in Louth, 56; Bailieborough, Co. Cavan, 56; Edward Brown, 62; the Diamond, 119; Ballynahinch, 207
Deputy governors, 46–7, 69
desertion, 73, 213, 220, 232
Diamond, battle of, 119
Dillon, Charles Drake, 57
Dingle, 60
dissenters, 37–8
districts, 34
Donegal, 67
Donegal Regiment, royal patronage, 54; ballot, 67; embodiment, 70; concentration time, 77; locations in 1794, 79; Lough Glynn House, 86; half yearly inspection, 1799, 89; Lt. Colhoun, 95; officers to be superceded, 103; locations, 1796, 108; adjutant's notebook, 116; Sgt. Hamilton, 147–8; Wexford, 189; New Ross, 199–200
Down, county, 60
Downshire, marquess of, character, 26; presenting colours, 73; on officers, 90; political alliances of officers, 93; slowness to fill officer vacancies, 96; civic duty, 97; opinion of Union, 241; petition 2 4 2; dismissal, 2 4 4; death, 2 4 4
Downshire Regiment, companies, 45; Royal, 52; ballot, 63–4; embodiment, 71; presentation of colours, 73; desertion, 73; concentration time, 77; Youghal, 78; accommodation on march to Youghal, 85; inter-relationships, officers, 92; officer appointments, 93; political alliances, 93; purchase of commission, 94; slowness to fill officer vacancies, 96; civic duties of officers, 97–8; Courtney affair, 100; Dublin, 108; Lt.-Col. Robert Ward, 112; court martial book, 132–4; Orange clubs, 139; Goresbridge, 211; sharpshooters, 225; division of regiment, 244
drill, 75
Drogheda, 72, 115–16
Drogheda Battalion, 72, 144
dual call, 97
dual commissions, 52
Dublin, 65–6
Dublin Garrison, 82
Dublin Battalion, County of, 125, 199–200, 200
Dublin Regiment, City of, desertion, 73; nepotism, 95; discipline, 102; Giffard-Sankey dispute, 104–6; dismissal of Lt.-Col. Edward Sankey, 106; Portadown, 119; Antient Britons, 138; recruiting, 144; Sgt. Kirkus, 144; Ballinaugh, 155; Gibbet Rath, 184
duelling, 98–100
Duff, Maj.-Gen. Sir James, 178, 184, 253
Duncannon, 190
Dundas, David, 75
duty, perceptions, 101

Edenderry, Co. Kildare, 186
Education, officers, 95
Elliott, Lt., 194
Elwin and Hawker court martial, 135

Embodiment of militia regiments, 55
encampment, 180
English militia, 22
Enniscorthy, 188–9
Enniskillen, Lord, 45, 125, 242
enrolment, 122
ensigns, 95
establishments, 1661, 13; headquarters, 30; regular army, 1796, 31; Irishmen in army, 1793–6, 36; army establishment in Ireland, 42; Sept. 1793, 68; camping, 81; detachments, 152; militia, 1796, 154; militia, 1795, 158; militia, 1798, 180; militia, 1800, 241
Evatt, Capt. Henry, 207
executions, militiamen, 150, 174
exercise of troops, 82

families, 128–9, 130
Famine, 1799, 233–4
Faulkner's Journal, 60, 100, 104, 157
Fawcett, Gen., 160, 253
Fermanagh Battalion, 45, 156
field officers, 49, 97
Fingal, Lord, 65
Finn, Catherine, 104, 177
Fitzgerald, Lord Edward, 34, 182
flogging, 134
Foster's family bill, 1793, 61
Foster, John, 29, 38
Foster, Col. Thomas, 72
Foulkes Mills, 208
France, outbreak of war, 42
Freeman's Journal, 62, 83, 157
free quarters, 152, 179
French forces, 19, 28, 162–4, 218, 226–7

Galway Regiment, 114, 157, 246
Gardner, Lt. R.W., 213
Gibbet Rath, 186
Giffard, Ambrose Harding, 120
Giffard, John, duel with John Sankey, 99; Sankey dispute, 104–6; Orangeman, 117, formation of Orange order, 118–20; 'Switcher' Donnelly, 162; capture of arms, 168, 184; Wicklow, 193, 204

Giffard, Lt. William, 184
Goldie, Gen., 253
Goresbridge, 210–11
Gosford, Lord, quartering his regiment, 71; officers' ages, 96; civil appointments, 98; Capt. Kay, 116; attention to regiment, 227
Gough, Lt.-Col. George, 186
Gough, Ens. Hugh, 48
governors of counties, 46
Granard, Lord, 52, 227, 251
grand division, 76
Grattan, Henry, 43, 244
Guernsey, 115

Hacketstown, 149, 213
Hamilton, Sgt. John, 147–8, 200
Handcock, Edward, 37
Hardy, Maj. Joseph, 98, 192–6, 251
Harvey, B.B., 192, 197, 199
Hay, Edward, 212–13
Hayes, Sir Harry, 103
Hayes-McCoy, G.A., 180, 182, 214
Health, 130–1
Hely-Hutchinson, Maj.-Gen. John, 218, 222, 253
heights and ages of militiamen, 127
Hepenstall, Lt. Edward, 168
Herbert, Lt.-Col Henry, 107–8
Hill, Sir George Fitzgerald, 126, 158, 161
Hillsborough, Lord, 43, 46, 249
Hobart, Maj., 98
Hogg, Lt. Edward, 113, 135, 193
Hollymount Hill, 210
Holt, Joseph, 213, 231, 233
Hope, Col. Hon. Alexander, 246
Humbert, Gen. J.J.A., 217
Hunter, Drummer, 231
Hurst, Lt. Peter, 116
Hussey, Revd. Thomas, 255

Inniskillings, 36, 77
inspections, 74, 77–8, 90
insurance against ballot, 64

Jephson, Lt., 116, 184
'Jefrey Foresight', 242

Index

Johnson, Maj.-Gen. Henry, Stony Point, 197; New Ross, 200, 204; Enniscorthy, 208; opinion of Cornwallis, 257

Kay, Capt. Arthur, 115–16, 168
Kerr, Maj., 113
Kerry, county, 60
Kerry Regiment, volunteers, 49; barrack accommodation, 84; Annesley Strain affair, 107–8; Stewartstown riot, 139; sedition, 162; Foxford, 218
Kilconnel or Kilcumney Hill, 211–13
Kilcullen, 184
Kilkenny Regiment, Castlebar, 220; battle of Castlebar, 221; scapegoats, 222; aftermath, 230; Col. Hon. Alexander Hope, 246
Killough, 71
Kilmainham Hospital, 51, 61
Kingsborough, Lord, 68, 104, 125
King's County Regiment, refused royal patronage, 54; Guernsey, 102, 236; Capt. J.W. Armstrong, 106; Lt. Palmer affair, 114; families, 129, 141; Philipstown, 168; Newtownbarry, 194; deserters, 213; serve overseas, 235; Guernsey, 236; Lt.-Col. Westenra, 224
Knox, Brig.-Gen., 170

Lake, Gen. Gerard, disarming north, 137, 170; plan against insurgents, 194; advice to Maj. Hardy, 196; retaking Wexford, 204, 208–9; Galway, 218; Castlebar, 220–3; light infantry, 224; aftermath of Castlebar, 253
landholding, system, 38–9
leave, 108–11, 252
Leinster, duke of, 92
Lagan canal, 150
Lane, Thomas, 64, 82
Leitrim Battalion, 77, 246
L'Estrange, Col. Henry, 194
light infantry, Pelham, 35; 'flank' company, 50; light battalions, 165–6; New Ross, 199; Antrim town, 204; absence at Castlebar, 220; light infantry reserves, 224–5
Limerick Battalion, City of, 77, 138, 142, 225–7
Limerick, county, 60–1
Limerick, County of, Battalion, 60–1, 125, 158, 160
Littlehales, Lt.-Col. E.B., 52, 94
Llandaff, Lord, 98
Loftus, Gen., 194–5
Londonderry Regiment, 47, 92, 95, 155
Longford Battalion, Prince of Wales's, 52–4; concentration time, 77; movements 1796–7, 79–80; Maj. Sandys, 98; Lt.-Col. Samuel Ahmuty, 111; routes, 1796, 164; Castlebar, 218–20; casualties, 222; stations in Co. Clare, 223; accounting for Castlebar deserters, 230
Loughlinstown (or Leehaunstown), 81, 82, 157
Louth Regiment, 45, 72, 126, 225–6
loyalty, 26

McAnally, David, 93
McAnally, Sir Henry, 18, 19, 219, 254, 258
McCracken, Henry Joy, 41, 205–6
magistrate, 137
manual exercise, 76
marriage, 128–9
Massy, Gen., 77
Matthews, Maj. George, Lord Annesley, 52; comments on initial deployment, Royal Downshire, 78; accommodation on march, 85; duties of an officer, 90; member, Grand Jury, 98; leave delayed, 109–10; on Orangemen, 118; on officers, 120; Kilconnel Hill, 211–12; sharpshooters, 225–7; petition against Union, 242; dispute with Capt. Boyd, 243; dismissal, 244
Maxwell, Lt.-Col. Richard, 189–92
Mayo, South, Battalion, 110, 177
Mayo, North, Battalion, 109, 123, 142, 241
McCormick, Michael, 200

Meath Regiment, 'Royal' regiment, 54; insurance against ballot, 64–5; tenant drawn, 69; desertion, 73; defenders, 155; desertion at Mallow, 231–2
Medical Board, Army, 130, 246
Medows, Gen., 246
militia, antecedents, 13–14; discipline, 25; 'constitutional', 28, 249; Cork forts, 34; riots, 55–60; camps of instruction, 1795–7, 83; Castlereagh on discipline, 139; duties, 154–6; French incursion 1796, 163–4; purge, 171–3; degree of involvement in rebellion, 1798, 214–16; Ballinamuck, 225–6; aftermath, 227–8; claims against, 1799, 228; successes and failures, 256–7
Militia Act, size of regiments, 46; deputy governors, 46; property qualifications, 48; Vereker and Gough, 48; ballot, 49; ratio, NCOs to men, 50; provisions 51; flaws in Act, 51–2; explanatory acts, 61–2; criticism, 62–3
Militia bill, 42, 44, 45
militia, English, 23
militiamen, ages and height, 127; marriage rules 128; health, 130; comparison with regulars, health, 131; loyalty, 140; numbers, 154, 158, 182
Minerva, 233
Monaghan, county, 85
Monaghan Regiment, draw for precedence, 72; barracks, 84–5; Ballybay affair, 113; *Northern Star*, 149–50, 174; destruction of smithy, 168; execution of militiamen, 171; Antrim, 204; Ballynahinch, 206–7
Moore, Brig.-Gen. John, militia officers, 89; Orangemen, 117; on government, 169; free quarters, 137, 179; Foulkes Mills, 208
Montgomery, Lt. Robert, 103
Mountjoy, Lord (Luke Gardiner), 197, 200
movable and stationary forces, 245
Munro, Henry, 206

murder, 135
Murphy, Fr John, 209–12
mutiny, 31, 156, 142
Mutiny Act, 131

Naas, 183
National Archives, Kew, 17
necessaries, 142
Needham, Maj.-Gen., 204–5
nepotism, 92
Newbridge, Co. Kildare, 138
New Geneva, 87
New Ross, 103, 147–9, 197–203
Newtownbarry (Bunclody), 194
North Cork Regiment, officers, 50; farms for volunteers, 68; officer inter-relationships, 92, 188; field officer absence, 98; courts martial, Lord Kingsborough and Lt. Nicholas Cole-Bowen, 188, 192; Oulart Hill, 186–8; Enniscorthy, 188–9; Wexford, 190; refusal of sharpshooters, 225; disturbance on canal, 233
North Mayo Battalion, *see* Mayo, North
Nugent, Gen. George, 150, 159–60; 206–7
Nugent, Maj. James, 179

Oakboys, 38, 40
obedience of men, 102
O'Brien, Sir Edward, MP, 110
officers, duty, 25
officer selection, 251
officers, regimental, 51
O'Neill, Lord, 44, 206
Orangeism, 117–20
Ormonde, Lord, 227
Oxford Militia, 23
Oulart Hill, 186–8

Palmer, Lt., 114
parliament, Irish, powers, 29
patronage, 54–55
pay, 51–2, 142–3
Peep o'Day boys, 40
Pelham, Thomas, advice on army, 35; Irish recruiting, 1793–6, 36; landholders and 'mechanics', 62,

122–3; executions, 150; Tipperary Regiment, 161; Defender outrages,168–9
penal laws, 29, 38
pensioners, 51, 146–7
petition against Union, 242
Pioneers, corps of, 246
Pitt, William, 19, 30–2, 56
Portarlington, Lord, 45
Portland, duke of, 30, 178, 194
Power, Sgt., 135
precedence, order of, 72
Price, Nicholas, 63
proclamation, 17 May 1797: 137, 169
promotions to officer rank, 147–9
property qualifications, 44, 47–8
Prosperous, Co. Kildare, 183
Protestants, 23, 39–40, 68, 124
proportions, Catholics to Protestants, 124–5
Public Record Office of Northern Ireland, 17
purge of militia, 171–3

Queen's County Regiment, 45, 118
quota for embodiment of regiments, 55

rape, 135
Rathangan, Co. Kildare:184
ratio, NCOs to private men, 141
rebellion of 1798: 182, 183
regiments, precedence, 72
religion, 124–6, 254–5
reviews, 82
Rights of man, 21, 62
riots, 55–60
Roche, Edward, 192
Roman Catholics, serving in armed forces, 15; suspicion, 23; policy towards, 29; penal laws, 38–9; in militia, 43; religion in militia, 124–6, chaplain-general, 255
Ross, Maj.-Gen. Sir Robert, 90
Ross, Maj.-Gen. Sir Charles, 243–4
Roscommon Regiment, balloting, 63; recruiting instructions, 127; New Ross, 201; serve outside Ireland, 235; volunteers to line, 241

Royal Barracks, 130
Royal Commission on Militia and Volunteers (1903), 19
Royal Hibernian Military School, 30, 145
Royal Hospital, Kilmainham, 30
Royal North Down Battalion, 244
Royal South Down Battalion, 244
Rowan Hamilton, 41
Rowley, Gen., 253
Ryan, Capt., 137n, 184

Sandys, Maj., 98, 192
Sankey, Col. H.G., 102, 105
Sankey, Maj. John, 99, 104–6
Sankey, Capt., later Lt.-Col. Edward, 105–6
Savage, Francis, MP, 98
schools, 145–6
Scullabogue, 203
Sentimental and Masonic Magazine, 68
service on staff, 251
service overseas, 235
sharpshooters, 225
Sheares brothers, 41
Sirr, Maj., 34
Sligo Battalion, 95
Snowe, Capt., 87, 188–9
South Cork Regiment, 156, 184
Standing Orders, 101, 102
Steelboys, 38, 40
Stewart, Gen., 253
stoppages of pay, 42
strength of army in Ireland, 1793–1802: 248
subscriptions, military charity, 147
substitutes, 67, 69
subversion, 159–60, 171–3
suffering loyalists, 228
supercession, absence, 110
Swayne, Capt. John, 183

Taghmon, Co. Wexford, 189
Tandy, James Napper, 41
Tipperary Regiment, 51, 73, 146, 161
tithes, 39
Tone, Wolfe, 41
Tottenham, Charles, 197, 200

training, 24, 75–83, 256
Tralee, 60
Trench, Maj. Gen., 225
Tyrawley, Lord, 84, 88
Tyrone Regiment, 54, 72, 241
Tubberneering, 195

Uniake, Jasper, 104, 177
United Irishmen, 28, 39, 41, 135, 150–1, 183

Valloton, Maj., 60
Vandeleur, Maj., 200
Vennel-Lawler affair, 104, 135, 177–8
Vereker, Lt.-Col. Charles, 48, 225–6, 251
Vesey, Maj., 200
Vinegar Hill, 208–9
Volunteers, 14, 40, 42, 258
volunteering to line, 234–5, 238, 239, 240

Wakefield, Edward, 22, 124–5
Wallace, Col. R.H., 119
Walpole, Col. L.T., 194–5
Walpole, Lt., 117, 230, 229
war, declaration of, 42

Ward, Lt.-Col. Hon. Robert, 93, 98, 112
Waterford Regiment, 67, 73
Westmeath Battalion, 139, 180, 246
Wellesley, Arthur, duke of Wellington, 37
Westenra, Lt.-Col. William, 224
Wexford town, 189–92
Wexford Regiment, precedence, 72; desertion in 1793, 73; concentration time, 77; Capt. Alcock, 106, 233; families, 129; loyalty, 151; poison, 157; Hollymount Hill, 210; Pte Kelly, 210; Jersey 236; Col. Hope, 246; 'Wexford question', 255
Whigs, Irish, 241
Whiteboys, 38, 40
Whyte, Gen. Richard, 20
Wickham, William, 67
Wicklow, county, 192
Wicklow Regiment, 78, 168
Wilford, Gen., 184
Williamite settlement, 38, 249–50
Williams, Lt. Daniel, 52, 93
wives, 128
Woodward, Maj. B.B., 94

yeomanry, 114